BEYOND BELIEFS

To Chris

I hope you enjoy the story

Best wishes

Sohail

16.12.2023

BEYOND BELIEFS

The incredible true story of a German refugee,
an Indian migrant and the families left behind

Sohail Husain

Daisa
PUBLISHING

Beyond Beliefs
First published in Great Britain in 2023 by
DAISA PUBLISHING
An imprint of PARTNERSHIP PUBLISHING

Written by Sohail Husain
Copyright © Sohail Husain

All material used for this book is from external sources, the Author's memory and personal history. This book is a work of non-fiction based on the true life, research, recollections, and experiences of the author. The editors have ensured a true reflection of the author's tone and voice has remained present throughout. Pictures are reproduced by permission of the author unless otherwise stated. Every effort has been made to trace copyright holders. The publishers would be pleased to rectify any unintentional omission in subsequent printings.

A CIP catalogue record for this book is available from the British Library.
ISBN 978-1-915200-49-5

Book cover design by: Partnership Publishing
Book Cover Images ©Shutterstock 1868907139 ©Shutterstock 28742545
©https://www.theguardian.com/world/2017/aug/14/everything-changed-readers-stories-of-india-partition

Book typeset by:
PARTNERSHIP PUBLISHING
North Lincolnshire, United Kingdom
www.partnershippublishing.co.uk

Printed in England

Partnership Publishing is committed to a sustainable future for our business, our readers, and our planet. This book is made from paper certified by the Forestry Stewardship Council (FSC) an organisation dedicated to promoting responsible management of forest resources.

We operate a distinctive and ethical publishing philosophy in all areas of our business, from our global network of Authors to production and worldwide distribution.

For my amazing daughters, Nicola and Michelle, and wonderful grandchildren, Imogen, Lyla, Elodie, Amelie and Ralphie. Now you can get to know the family you never got to meet.

About the Author

Sohail Husain was born in 1951 to mixed-race immigrant parents, who scraped a living working London's famous street markets. After leaving school, he studied geography at the University of Nottingham and was awarded a PhD there in 1976. Subsequently, he enjoyed a varied career that included 13 years as a university lecturer, 15 years with an NGO dedicated to creating safer communities and 12 years as an adviser to the UN on programmes to prevent violence against women and girls. Following retirement, and using his professional skills as a social scientist, he embarked on research into his family's history that led to many amazing discoveries and ultimately to the publication of this memoir. Sohail has two daughters and five grandchildren, and has lived with his wife, Caroline, in south Hampshire for more than 45 years.

Connect with Sohail on Facebook @sohail.husain.92
or by Email to beyond_beliefs@outlook.com

Contents

Abbreviations

CBF   Central British Fund for German Jewry
FR80   *Füsilier Regiment 80*
GJAC   German Jewish Aid Committee
IR87   *Infanterie Regiment 87*
SA   *Sturmabteilung* (Assault Division)
SS   *Schutzstaffel* (Protection Squad)
WJR   World Jewish Relief
WW1   First World War
WW2   Second World War

The following account includes many extracts from correspondence and other documents. Although most were written in English, a significant proportion were in German or Urdu and quotes from these have been translated into English. Those translations are indicated with a (T). Many of them contain grammatical errors or simply do not read well. This applies particularly to letters sent by my maternal grandfather from the German trenches during WW1 and letters written by my parents, neither of whom spoke English as their first language. All quotes have been cited verbatim and to avoid the repeated use of [sic] it should be assumed that any solecisms and misspellings were present in the original text.

Curiosity

My mother died on 1 June 1979 in West Middlesex Hospital, Isleworth, London. It was a Friday and I was at work in the Geography Department at Southampton University when the sad news came through. Throughout my younger days, she had been the rock in our family: strong, stable and resilient, but always loving, supportive and incredibly hard-working. Now, at just 58 years old, she was gone. Her death was a shock, but not a surprise. She had been diagnosed with breast cancer two years earlier, no doubt caused by heavy smoking, and her health had steadily deteriorated ever since. I don't know how many cigarettes she got through each day, but she would only buy WD & HO Wills' Gold Flake, a brand that was firmly categorised as 'high tar' when the UK Government introduced cigarette classification in the 1970s. However, when she had started smoking, it was marketed as a brand associated with sophistication, luxury, passion and independence, with adverts specifically targeted at women.[1] My sister and I encouraged her to break the habit, but she never showed any inclination to do so, explaining that traumatic experiences in her younger days had led her into smoking and that it was too late for her to change.

---

[1] Rosemary Elizabeth Eliot, '"Destructive but Sweet": Cigarette Smoking Among Women 1890–1990' (PhD, University of Glasgow, 2001), https://theses.gla.ac.uk/1091/; Penny Tinkler, '"Red Tips for Hot Lips": Advertising Cigarettes for Young Women in Britain, 1920–70', *Women's History Review* 10, no. 2 (June 2001): 249–72, https://doi.org/10.1080/09612020100200289.

It was only in the subsequent years that I came to realise how little I knew about my mother's earlier life, growing up in Germany, going on to live in the UK and for a short period residing in Pakistan. In fact, to tell the truth, I knew almost nothing. One reason for this was that she rarely spoke about her past, probably because it was too painful. It was very different with my father. He was loquacious and a natural raconteur, who loved to talk about his childhood and later adventures, which took him from Punjab (India) to South America and eventually Europe. But I showed only limited interest in either side's stories and regrettably rarely asked them the questions that now seem so important. Consequently, there were big gaps in my awareness of their life histories and their wider families.

This may seem surprising but, as well as my mother's reticence to speak, there were several other reasons for my lack of curiosity. I had never met or spoken to any of my grandparents. Only one - my paternal grandmother - was definitely alive when I was born, and she was in Pakistan. My paternal grandfather was last known to be living in Montevideo (Uruguay), but that was in 1948 and nothing had been heard of him since. I had seen a couple of photographs, but that was all. So, none of them really existed in my consciousness and I had no innate inquisitiveness about them. Perhaps subconsciously I even pushed them to the back of my mind. At my grammar school, I was acutely aware of being different. No other pupil past or present had such a mixed heritage, a parent with a different skin colour, or been brought up in a Muslim home. Not wanting to feel or appear apart from my peers, I did nothing to highlight or explore my own cultural identity.

Much later, I gradually came to recognise that both my parents and grandparents had extraordinary and tragic life stories, having been directly and deeply affected by four of the most turbulent and violent events of the 20th century: First World War (WW1), the Great Depression, the Holocaust and the Partition of India. At the same time, I began to see my heritage as an advantage and became more curious about my background. However, by then it was too late. My father died suddenly on Thursday 4 March 1976 (the day after my 25th birthday) and my mother just three years later.

Now I am conscious of history repeating itself. My daughters, Nicola and Michelle, never met their paternal grandparents and they similarly have shown little curiosity about them. So what follows began as a project to fill my own knowledge gap and to bring alive to them and their cousins the grandparents they never knew. However, the search to uncover their life stories led on to astonishing discoveries about our multicultural family's earlier history. I wrote up some of the findings and shared them with family members and a few friends. It was never my intention for this to be published, but their unanimous reaction was that this incredible tale deserved a much wider audience. And that is how this book came about.

The story draws on many different information sources, but the most important are documents in various languages, some of which were written more than one hundred years ago, that had been stored in an old suitcase, untouched and unread for decades. On my mother's side, many are personal letters sent to her by family members and friends from Europe, South America, Asia and Africa between 1940 and 1961. Most are in German, which I was able to read and translate without too much difficulty. However, a few are in *Sütterlinschrift*, an old form of handwriting that is indecipherable even to most Germans today. Fortunately, my great friends Gabriele Klüter and Gabi Kretschmer-Schurer (with the help of an elderly neighbour) were able to make sense of them for me. Frustratingly, as all these letters are 'incoming', they provide details about the lives of the authors, but my mother's outgoing mail, which would have told me much more about her own life, is lost. Nevertheless, their replies provided many interesting insights.

The old suitcase containing the documents
on which much of this story is based

Another large group of documents comprises official papers, forms and correspondence from German lawyers purportedly acting on behalf of my mother in her long struggle to get compensation for losses suffered under the Nazis. Inevitably, these include horrific accounts of what happened to her and her family before, during and after the Second World War (WW2). Beyond this I have been able to draw on the considerable knowledge and records gathered by Christiane Kühn in her genealogical research into the Grünebaum family.[2]

I was also greatly helped by four other people who deserve special mention. Richard and David Oldcorn are two brothers who

---

[2] Christiane Kühn is my second cousin once removed. Her great-great-grandparents were my great-grandparents.

my mother looked after as a childminder when she first came to the UK in 1939. I traced Richard to Sydney (Australia) and, although too young to remember much about her, he put me in touch with his older sibling. In his 80s and still living in England, David generously shared memories that provided a unique perspective on that period of my mother's life. The third person was Herta Stiefel, with whom I was able to have a wonderful conversation soon after she celebrated her 100th birthday. Unfortunately, this had to be done virtually because of the COVID-19 pandemic, but she told me about her own remarkable life and how she and my mother had become very close after they had both escaped from Germany. Her memory was lucid and very warm, but what she told me about their time in London was both surprising and disturbing. And finally, I had the privilege of getting to know Wilma Feick. She and my mother were childhood friends and, at the age of 95 and more than 80 years after they had last seen each other, she was still so concerned about my mother's fate that it led to her granddaughter searching for an answer and finding me. Wilma's astonishingly vivid memories of her Jewish friend, her parents and their home have enriched this account with details that could only have come through personal acquaintance. As far as I know, these were the only four people alive at the time I embarked on my research who knew my mother as a teenager.

Invaluable contributions to her story have also been made by archivists, librarians, military historians, genealogists, other researchers and volunteers in institutions and organisations visited or contacted during the research. They include:

- Arolsen Archives - International Center on Nazi Persecution (Bad Arolsen, Germany), previously the International Tracing Service
- *Bibliothèque nationale de France* - French National Library (France)

- *Centro de Estudios Migratorios Latinoamericanos* - Centre for Latin American Migration Studies (Buenos Aires, Argentina)
- *Das Bundesarchiv* - The Federal Archives (Germany)
- *Das Haus der Stadtgeschichte* – The House of City History (Offenbach am Main, Germany)[3]
- *Hessisches Landesarchiv* – The Hessian State Archives (Marburg and Wiesbaden, Germany)
- International Committee of the Red Cross Archives (Geneva, Switzerland)
- Leo Baeck Institute (New York, USA)
- *Militärhistorisches Museum der Bundeswehr* - Armed Forces Military History Museum, (Dresden, Germany)
- Parkes Institute for the Study of Jewish/non-Jewish Relations (Southampton, UK)
- *Projektu holocaust.cz* - Czech Holocaust Archive (Czech Republic)
- *Stadtarchiv Mainz* - Mainz City Archive (Mainz, Germany)
- *Terezínská iniciativa* - the Terezín Initiative (Czech Republic)
- The National Archives (London, UK)
- United States Holocaust Memorial Museum (Washington DC, USA)
- Wiener Holocaust Library (London, UK)
- World Jewish Relief (London, UK)
- *Yad Vashem* - The World Holocaust Remembrance Center (Jerusalem, Israel)
- *Zentrum für Militärgeschichte und Sozialwissenschaften der Bundeswehr* - Centre for Military History and Social Sciences of the Armed Forces (Potsdam, Germany)

---

[3] Subsequently referred to as the Offenbach City Archive.

Specific mention is due to several individuals who tirelessly answered my questions, shared their knowledge and provided guidance. They are Gabriele Hauschke-Wicklaus and Barbara Leissing from the *Geschichtswerkstatt Offenbach* (Offenbach History Workshop), and Michael Beseler and Dominik Mangelmann who individually have also been undertaking historical research into the community of Bürgel.

Little 'official' information has been found for my father's side of the family, whose origins are in Kashmir and Punjab. However, this is more than balanced by the fascinating correspondence sent by my paternal grandfather from South America to my father and other family members in India between 1911 and 1948. There are around 20 letters, some of them extremely long, as well as a range of other documents. While most are in English, a few are in Urdu and Dr Farzana Hasan kindly translated these for me. Further help was given by individuals in Argentina, Uruguay and the USA, including archivists, genealogists and volunteers with whom I made contact through online forums, and who generously travelled to government offices and libraries in Buenos Aires, Montevideo and New York to search through historical records on my behalf. The information gathered from the correspondence and other sources not only provides an insight into my grandfather's life and character, but also portrays the countries and societies in which he was living. However, they also pose many intriguing questions about his mysterious departure from India and what happened to him in later life; questions that have proved difficult to answer.

Through my grandfather's letters it is also possible to trace my own father's ill-fated attempts to join his father in Uruguay. It was his lack of success in achieving this, combined with ambition, a free spirit and a strong streak of filial disobedience, that eventually brought him to London, where he met my mother. Just like his father before him, he left behind a wife, who would not see him again for a very long time. The subsequent intense and complicated relationship that developed between my parents is revealed by more than 30 letters from my father to my mother, mostly sent in the first three months of 1948 just before she became his second wife, when he was in Pakistan and she in London. The letters not only disclose a great deal about him, their love for each other and his extended family, but also about life on the sub-continent during the historic and extraordinarily turbulent months following the creation of this new country. That correspondence has been supplemented by many other personal documents connected to my father from diverse sources, as well as papers relating to the pursuit of compensation for the losses his family incurred in India prior to Partition.

In addition to all of the above, I have also been able to draw on the personal memories of other members of the Husain family—most notably my sister, Marium Riedel, in Germany; my half-sister, Nusrat Mazhar, in Pakistan; and my half-brother, Asif Hussain, in Canada—and of course, the vast amount of material now accessible online in genealogical databases and other knowledge websites.

This is, therefore, a narrative largely based on documentary research, enriched with my own and others' anecdotes and personal recollections. In a few places, I have drawn inferences from the sources, but the narrative is essentially based on fact. It is impossible, though, to make sense of the family's story without an awareness of what was going on in the world around them. So I have set their actions and experiences within the contemporary socio-economic, political and technological context. In addition to the cataclysmic events already mentioned, this includes connections to the pioneering transatlantic flights of the Zeppelin airship, the assassination of Mahatma Gandhi and a meeting with the incomparable Muhammad Ali in a London mosque.

Piecing this all together has been an incredible journey of discovery. When I started what I envisaged would take a few weeks, I never imagined that I could uncover so much and that the work would still be ongoing six years later. At times it has been a slow process. Days and sometimes weeks have been spent interpreting old letters, trawling though official records, poring over historical maps and interrogating online resources. It has taken me physically and virtually to numerous countries. And it has been a journey that is a story in itself, full of wonderful surprises, disturbing revelations, unsolved mysteries, frustrating disappointments and astonishing coincidences. Alongside the family history, I have therefore also described my own quest to find the invaluable fragments of information that enabled me to construct it. And although there are undoubtedly gaps that others may be able to fill, and perhaps errors that others can correct, it is now a surprisingly detailed account.

What follows has at its heart an extraordinary tale about two people, my parents. And at first it might seem difficult to imagine a couple with less in common. They were born in different countries on different continents, one country highly developed, the other one of the least developed. They spoke different languages, had different faiths and came from very different cultures. There was a considerable difference in their ages. Yet in many respects their lives ran in parallel. Both had left their country of birth, both lost their homes and property as a consequence of violent extremism, both struggled for years to get compensation and both ended up penniless in London: one a refugee, the other an immigrant. Here their paths eventually crossed and here they fell in love. Their lives before and after their marriage were shaped by heartbreak, adversity and mystery, but their love and support for each other enabled them to survive and eventually succeed.

Jewish Roots in Germany

Bürgel and Jewish Emancipation

My mother was born into the Grünebaum family in her parents' home at 10:30am on Thursday 12 May 1921 and given the name Karola. They lived at 69 Luisenstrasse, Offenbach am Main, in what is now the state of Hessen (Germany). Her father, Friedrich, and her mother, Sophie (*née* Reiss), came from Jewish families that had deep roots in the nearby community of Bürgel.[4]

---

[4] The family's surname is spelt 'Reis' in various documents, and her given name is sometimes recorded as 'Sofie'. But for simplicity and consistency, 'Reiss' and 'Sophie' are used throughout this narrative.

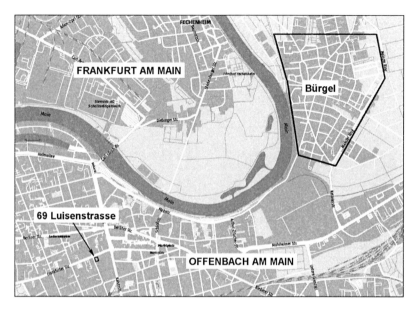

Location of Bürgel and 69 Luisenstrasse in Offenbach am Main[5]

Situated north-east of the city centre and on the banks of the river Main, Bürgel today is administratively part of Offenbach. However, before 1908 it was an independent parish, where there had long been a small Jewish presence, certainly since the end of the sixteenth century and possibly much earlier.[6] The community grew steadily through the eighteenth century and by 1828 the 233 Jewish residents accounted for more than a quarter of all inhabitants. By then the prayer room in the *Falltorturm* (gate tower) had been superseded by a purpose-built synagogue, and by 1842 the unfenced burial ground in a field outside the village had become a walled cemetery.

---

[5] Image © mapz.com – Map Data: OpenStreetMap ODbL.
[6] Kaspar Lammert, *Die Israelitische Gemeinde Bürgel am Main* (Offenbach am Main: Rothschild, 1924), https://sammlungen.ub.uni-frankfurt.de/freimann/content/titleinfo/426758.

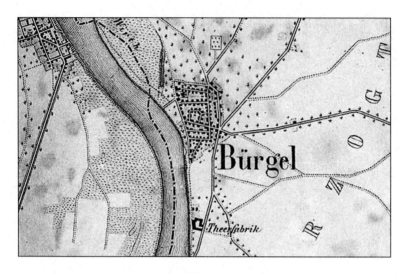

Extent of Bürgel in 1865[7]

The evolution of the Jewish community in Bürgel mirrored that of Jewish communities across Europe. Prior to their 'emancipation', Jews were socially, culturally, economically and to some extent geographically isolated.[8] In Germanic states they were marginalised and penalised through denial of citizenship rights, prohibition from owning land and exclusion from craft industries and agriculture; but they were required to pay a range of punitive taxes. Running a small retail business was one of the few occupations left open to them, although some were able to earn an income by trading in commodities or livestock. The Jewish families in Bürgel were overwhelmingly poor; an estimated three-quarters were living in poverty, many dependent on alms from more affluent fellow believers to survive.[9]

---

[7] 'Karte der Umgegend von Frankfurt, Darmstadt', ca 1865, https://www.lag-is-hessen.de/de/subjects/gsrec/current/1/sn/hkw?q=offenbach.

[8] Unlike in parts of Europe, Jews in what was then-called Hessen-Darmstadt were not forced to live in ghettos, but were to be found concentrated in certain areas, such as Bürgel, where they lived amongst Christian neighbours.

[9] Lammert, *Die Israelitische Gemeinde Bürgel am Main*. In Bürgel, it was not

European emancipation took place between the late eighteenth and early twentieth centuries, and brought about significant change. Most importantly, much discriminatory legislation was repealed and Jews were granted equal citizenship rights. In Germanic states, restrictions were gradually eased from the early nineteenth century onwards but legal equality was not guaranteed everywhere until 1871 when the Constitution of the newly created Deutsches Reich (German Empire) was adopted. These societal changes were accompanied by the so-called 'Jewish Enlightenment', an internal movement that advocated theological reform, increased secularisation and greater open-mindedness. Gradually, Jewish participation in wider society increased. More Jews entered professions such as medicine and law, became prominent in the arts and academic life, and were increasingly involved in banking and commerce. As a result, there was some improvement in their economic fortunes as they took advantage of opportunities to use and develop their skills and expertise. They also began to disperse from residential areas where they had lived, often highly concentrated, to other nearby areas within non-Jewish populations.

The occupational aspirations of the Jewish families in Bürgel were generally more modest. Most wanted to ensure that their young men took the opportunity now open to them to learn a craft or trade. With financial support from Jewish and non-Jewish organisations, to buy tools and work clothes, for example, they trained to become carpenters, locksmiths, tailors and shoemakers. However, perhaps surprisingly, during this period of momentous change, the size of the Jewish community declined sharply

only Jews who were poor. Meyer cites an 1834 report which stated that 90 per cent of the population were suffering financial hardship. But Jews were subjected to additional taxation. See Rudolf Meyer, 'Geschichte der Jüdischen Gemeinde in Bürgel', *Bürgel. Geschichte und Geschichten. Blätter des Vereins Pro Bürgel* 15 (2019): 5–15.

while the population of Bürgel continued to grow. From 304 in 1861, the number of Jews fell to just 131 in 1905, just 3% of the total population.[10] This dramatic fall was partly attributable to the exceedingly high infant mortality rate - around half the 200 children born between 1835 and 1875 died within their first 10 years - but a major cause was outmigration of young people, especially to Offenbach, which had developed rapidly as a major industrial town with many employment and business opportunities.

Karola's grandparents suffered for decades under the oppressive and discriminatory restrictions on Jews and then lived through the most significant and transformative changes that followed. Their children, all born in the last quarter of the nineteenth century, were citizens of the Deutsches Reich from birth and were able to take full advantage of the opportunities that had opened up. And that meant Karola entered a very different world from that of her parents' childhood. Not only was she born outside Bürgel, but into a society where Jews were becoming more integrated; where religion was no longer synonymous with culture and education; where girls had a right to schooling; where young women were no longer confined to traditional (usually domestic) work; and where there were real possibilities for economic advancement.

The Grünebaum Family

Friedrich Grünebaum, Karola's father, was born in Bürgel, as were his parents, Heinrich and Jeanette (known as Käthchen, *née* Oppenheim); his paternal grandparents, Lazarus and Lottchen (known as Betty, *née* Trier); his great-grandfather, Elias, and many other family members. In fact, 'Grünebaum' seems to have been one of the most common names in the village and they

---

[10] Lammert, *Die Israelitische Gemeinde Bürgel am Main*; Meyer, 'Geschichte der Jüdischen Gemeinde in Bürgel'.

played an important role in the community, holding positions of responsibility in the parish. In the Old Jewish Cemetery, one-third of the gravestones with legible inscriptions bear their name,[11] and in a paper on the village history, Rudolf Meyer wrote:

> At the beginning of the twentieth century, the Jewish families in Bürgel included three branches of Grünebaums, the Grünewald, Reiss, Katz, Lind, Haas, Wenig, Schlesinger, Reinwald, Hess, Steigerwald, Nachmann, Wolf, Blumenstein, Bodenheimer families, to name just the most well known. (T)[12]

Curiously, Heinrich and his five siblings - Emil, Fannie, Regina, Mathilde and Hedwig - were born in at least four different houses, which were simply identified in the birth register by their numbers, as streets were not named until the latter part of the nineteenth century.[13]

---

[11] The graves are listed in Heinz-Peter Tilly and Klaus Werner, 'Der Jüdische Friedhof in Offenbach am Main – Bürgel', in *Zur Geschichte der Juden in Offenbach am Main*, ed. Klaus Werner, vol. 3 (Offenbach: Der Magistrat, 1994), 79–102.

[12] Meyer, 'Geschichte der Jüdischen Gemeinde in Bürgel'.

[13] Houses were renumbered when streets were named and no map showing the old numbering has been found. So it has not been possible to establish the locations of these houses.

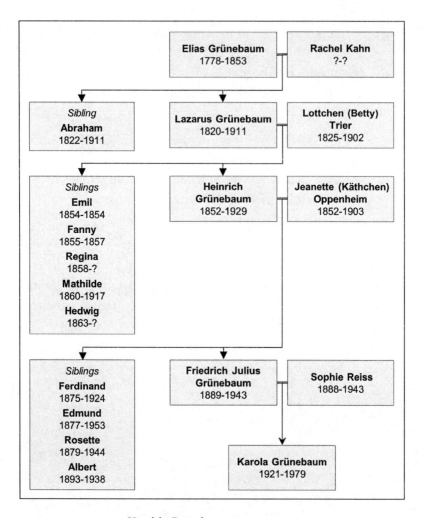

Karola's Grünebaum ancestry tree

Heinrich and Käthchen married in 1875, just a few years after the ending of the Franco-Prussian War (1870-71) and the creation of the Deutsches Reich. They lived together at 22 Offenbacherstrasse in the centre of the village until her death in

1903, when she was 50 and Friedrich was just 14 years old.[14] By profession, Heinrich was a *Metzgermeister* (master butcher), renowned for the quality of his beef and sausages, and he had his own small shop at the same address, from where he supplied several local restaurants. But in 1911, he sold that property and bought 14 Offenbacherstrasse just a few doors along the road, from where he continued his business until March 1927.[15] Heinrich died two years later, aged 77, and was buried alongside his wife in Bürgel Old Jewish Cemetery. He was fondly remembered by the Bürgel poet, Ludo Bopp. In 1924, when Bopp was just four years old, his parents moved in with Heinrich and looked after him through his final years. The young boy came to look upon the older man almost as his grandfather and recalled how he was a great raconteur who loved talking about the history of their parish and the families that lived there.[16] He also remembered that Heinrich could read and write Hebrew and was very active in the community, being a leader of the choir and often reading prayers in the synagogue.

---

[14] Property ownership and occupancy details are to be found in the official address books of the period.

[15] Index cards in the Offenbach *Gewerberegister* (business directory) show that the business closed on 9 March 1927.

[16] Ludo Bopp, 'Die Jüdische Gemeinde Bürgel/Main' (unpublished, undated).

Käthchen and Heinrich Grünebaum, parents of Friedrich

Käthchen gave birth to her fourth child, my grandfather, on Wednesday 10 April 1889. The Registry Office birth record shows his given names as Julius Friedrich, but in various later documents he appears as Friedrich Julius Grünebaum. His three older siblings were two brothers (Ferdinand and Edmund) and a sister (Rosette). They were all born within a four-year period in the decade after the Franco-Prussian War. But there was then a 10-year gap before Friedrich arrived and a further four years before the youngest brother (Albert) was born. This significant difference in age undoubtedly accounts for Ferdinand, Edmund and Rosette all marrying and having children before WW1, while for Friedrich and Albert the course of family life was very different.

Nr. _41_ _____ Bürgel am 11 April _____ 1889. Vor dem unterzeichneten Standesbeamten erschien heute, der Persönlichkeit nach _____ _____ bn kannt, Der Metzger Heinrich Grünebaum _____ wohnhaft zu Bürgel _____ israelitischer ____ Religion, und zeigte an, daß von der Katharina Grünebaum geborene Oppenheim, seiner Ehefrau, _____ _____ israelitischer Religion, wohnhaft bei ihm _____ zu Bürgel in seiner Wohnung ___ am _____ zehn im April _____ des Jahres tausend acht hundert achtzig und neunzig vormittags um _____ acht Uhr ein Kind männlichen Geschlechts geboren worden sei, welches _____ Die Vornamen Julius Friedrich _____ erhalten habe. _____ Vorgelesen, genehmigt und untaschrieben Heinrich Grünebaum _____	No. 41 Bürgel, 11th April 1889 The person known as the butcher Heinrich Grünebaum, resident of Bürgel and of the Jewish faith, appeared today before the undersigned Registrar and reported that his wife Katharina, née Oppenheim, of the Jewish faith, resident with him at his apartment in Bürgel, gave birth at 8am on 10th April 1889 to a male child, who has been given the forenames Julius Friedrich. Read out, approved and signed by Heinrich Grünebaum

Registry Office record of the birth of Julius Friedrich Grünebaum
(with translation)

Friedrich's occupational destiny was probably never in doubt. As well as his father, his brother (Edmund), his grandfather (Lazarus), his great-grandfather (Elias) and other relatives were all butchers.[17] Friedrich continued that family tradition, eventually also qualifying as a *Metzgermeister* and opening his own shop. That, though, was well into the future. Before then he had to complete his national service in the German Imperial Army and survive WW1.

---

[17] Occupational data has been taken from business directories, address books and other sources.

Grünebaum Abraham, Rentier, Schönborn-
straße 2
--- Edmund, Metzgermeister, Langstraße 50
— Edmund, Reisender, Strackgasse 29
— Eduard, Kfm., Offenbacherstraße 32
— Elias, Schreiner, Offenbacherstraße 18
— Emanuel, Metzgermstr., Strackgasse 29
--- Emil I, Metzgermeister, Kreuzstraße 15
— Emil II, Ww., Minna, geb. Fleischmann
(Fa.: Grünebaum & Co.), Schönborn-
straße 3
— Ferdin., Schlosser, Ernst-Ludwigstr. 94
— Hrch., Metzgermstr., Offenbacherstr. 22

Extract from the 1911 Address Book showing *Metzgermeister* Heinrich
and Edmund Grünebaum, as well as two other Grünebaum
master butchers in Bürgel

The Reiss Family

Less is known about the Reiss family. Sophie, my maternal
grandmother, was born on Wednesday 21 March 1888, so she
was a year older than her future husband. Like him, she was part
of a large family and grew up in Bürgel, but her father's roots were
elsewhere. Markus was born in 1856 in the village of Ulrichstein,
about 65 kilometres to the north-east. He was a skilled *Portefeuiller*,
a maker of fine leather goods such as wallets and briefcases, and a
foreman, so he would have held a supervisory position in a leather
workshop or factory.[18] Two years older than his wife Rebecka (*née*
Meier), Markus died aged 67, in April 1923, while she survived
him by 18 months, passing away in October 1924, shortly before

---

[18] On two of his children's birth certificates, Markus's profession is shown as
Portefeuiller. However, in an article about his son, Salomon, on the Offenbach
city website, he is described as a *Werkführer* (foreman). See 'Stolperstein für Lilli
Reiss, geb. Löwenstein, Salomon Reiss, Selma, Hertha, Irene und Gertrude
Reiss', Stadt Offenbach, https://www.offenbach.de/verzeichnisse/yellowpages/
common/stolpersteine/wegweiser_81097.php.

her 66th birthday. They too are buried together in Bürgel Old Jewish Cemetery.[19]

Gravestone of Markus and Rebecka Reiss in Bürgel Old Jewish Cemetery

Sophie had six siblings, five brothers and one sister. So her family structure was very similar to Friedrich's and at the beginning of the twentieth century their homes were just a few doors apart, with the Reiss household at 7 Offenbacherstrasse, which they owned, and the Grünebaums at 22.[20] The similarities between

---

[19] Her name is spelt Rebecka on the gravestone and on her children's birth certificates, but appears as Rebekka in other documents.

[20] The Reiss family address is listed in the Bürgel section of the 1912 *Alphabetisch Verzeichnis der Einwohner und Kaufmännische Firmen* (Alphabetical Directory

the families did not end there. Sophie's eldest brother, Salomon, also became a butcher and in 1906 opened his own shop.[21] Known to everyone as 'Sally', he became a prominent member of the Jewish community. Together with Leo Grünebaum and Emil Grünebaum, he was a member of the parish council in 1933, and in 1937, when there were just 27 Jewish residents remaining, he and Leo were their representatives.[22]

---

of Inhabitants and Commercial Firms), a copy of which is in the Offenbach City Archive.

[21] 'Stolperstein für Lilli Reiss, geb. Löwenstein, Salomon Reiss, Selma, Hertha, Irene und Gertrude Reiss'. Confusingly, this article states that Salomon was born at 8 Offenbacherstrasse, but his parental home was House No 8, which today is Bürgerplatz 15.

[22] Leo and Emil were both second cousins of Friedrich.

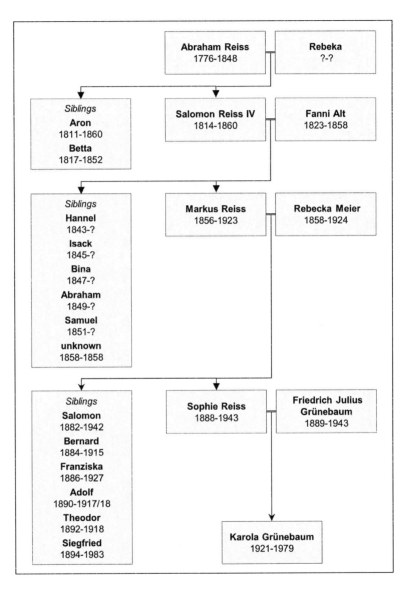

Karola's Reiss ancestry tree

In 1906 Salomon married Lilli Löwenstein. He was remembered as having a 'good figure' and his wife as being 'a strong woman with black hair.' (T)[23] By 1914, the couple had four daughters, Selma Marta, Hertha, Irene and Gertrude. They all survived WW1 although, as will become evident, none of them was able to escape the Holocaust. Two more of Sophie's siblings, Franziska and Siegfried, also survived, but the war took a very heavy toll on this side of Karola's family. Sophie's brothers, Bernhard, Adolph and Theodor, all perished in the conflict.[24]

---

[23] 'Stolpersteine Bürgel – Aktion am 14. Februar 2009', Pro Bürgel e.V, http://www.pro-buergel.de/stolpersteine-buergel-aktion-am-14-februar-2009/.
[24] 'Die Synagoge in Bürgel (Stadt Offenbach)', Alemannia Judaica, https://www.alemannia-judaica.de/buergel_synagoge.htm.

A Soldier in the Great War

National Service in the German Army

Universal conscription in Prussia began in the early nineteenth century and it continued after the creation of the German state in 1871. By the early twentieth century, the German Army was the strongest and most highly organised force in Europe. Men were usually called up at the age of 20 and, if they joined the infantry, were required to serve for two years.[25] After this they became Reservists for four or five years, ready to quickly bring the standing army to war strength and be deployed to the front line if needed.[26] This is what happened to Friedrich.

At the start of my research, the only evidence I had of his involvement with the armed forces were three photographs in my mother's album. To learn as much as possible from them, I sent them to two German military historians for analysis and what they were able to tell me provided the initial pieces of a jigsaw that over subsequent years gradually came closer and closer to completion. The first photo is of a group of soldiers in uniform posing for the camera.

---

[25] Men were liable to be called up to serve in the reserve militia at age 17 but this rarely happened. It was more usually at the age of 20 or 21.

[26] This was not the end of a German man's military obligations, however. At the age of 27, he transferred to the *Landwehr*, a second-line support force, liable to be called up until the age of 38. He then moved into the *Landsturm*, envisaged principally as a home defence force, until finally discharged aged 45.

Julius Friedrich Grünebaum (kneeling far left) in military uniform

Dr Gerhard Bauer, Head of the Department of Uniforms and Military Insignia at the *Militärhistorisches Museum der Bundeswehr* (Armed Forces Military History Museum) in Dresden, provided this assessment of the photo:

> Your grandfather seems to have been a proud soldier. As a matter of fact, he did belong to a crack unit, Leibgarde-Infanterie-Regiment (1. Grossherzoglich Hessisches) Nr. 115,[27] the oldest regiment of the German armed forces ... It belonged to the forces of the Grand Duchy of Hesse. It had been formed in 1621 and existed until 1919. In 1806 the regiment had been elevated to the rank of a guard regiment, then receiving the title 'Leibgarde Regiment'. Looking at the uniforms you can easily see the white, so-called guard lace, displayed on the collars and cuff patches of

[27] Lifeguard Infantry Regiment (1st Grand Ducal Hessian). No 115.

the soldiers' tunics. The spiked helmets are decorated with the emblem of the Grand Duchy of Hesse, a sword wielding, crowned lion in a laurel wreath.

The photograph was most certainly taken before the Great War because the soldiers are wearing well-fitting, colourful peacetime uniforms. Your grandfather as well as his comrades are common soldiers, so the picture was possibly taken during your grandfather's national service. He would have been called up at the age of 21 to serve for two years. Then he would have been allotted to the 'Reserve'.[28]

The image is printed on a 'real photo postcard' that was sent by Friedrich to his father, and the message on the reverse provides an interesting insight to his circumstances.[29] He told his father that he urgently needed money to get his uniform cleaned and buy a new pair of boots ahead of an imminent inspection. The address included his father's name and Bürgel, but no house number. The community was probably small enough to make that detail unnecessary.

---

[28] Personal communication, 5 September 2017.
[29] In 1903 Kodak began marketing a small pocket camera with postcard format film and in 1907 introduced the 'real photo postcard service'. Together these developments enabled the general public to take photos and easily have them made into postcards, such as this one.

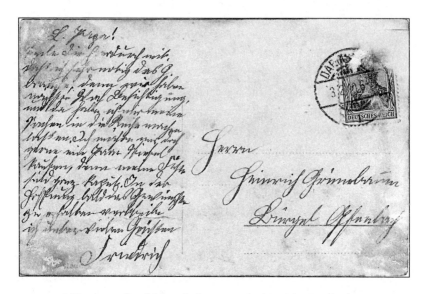

Reverse side of the real photo postcard sent by Friedrich
to his father requesting money

Having considered the reverse and its postal frank, Dr Stefan
Maximilian Brenner of the *Zentrum für Militärgeschichte und
Sozialwissenschaften der Bundeswehr* (Centre for Military History
and Social Sciences of the Armed Forces) in Potsdam noted:

> The additional information on the back of your
> grandfather's postcard locates the garrison in
> Darmstadt. Since there is no postmark or clear date, I
> can only speculate that your grandfather was a recruit
> in one of the following regiments:
>
> - Leibgarde-Infanterie-Regiment
>   (1 Grossherzoglich Hessisches) Nr.115
> - Garde-Dragoner-Regiment
>   (1 Grossherzoglich Hessisches) Nr. 23
> - Leib-Dragoner-Regiment
>   (2 Grossherzoglich Hessisches) Nr. 24

I was able to assign these regiments to the Darmstadt area around 1900. (T)[30]

A second photo, taken in a military kitchen, shows that Friedrich worked as a butcher in the army, possibly in the officers' mess.

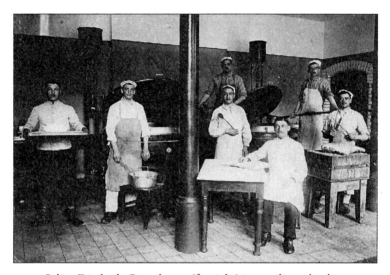

Julius Friedrich Grünebaum (far right) in a military kitchen

Dr Bauer offered the following comment on this image:

Based on this, I assume that your grandfather was employed as a regimental member of the garrison's butchery. The soldiers in the photograph are wearing military clothing, but in variations that would be used to work in a kitchen. I'm pretty sure your grandfather did not cook for the whole regiment … but, because of his qualifications, was put to work in the kitchen of the regimental officers' mess. I came to this conclusion because the soldier on the far left, with the tray in his

---

[30] Personal communication, 19 September 2017.

hand, is dressed as an orderly. (T)[31]

The experts therefore concluded that these two photos were taken prior to the outbreak of WW1, probably during Friedrich's national service, and that he was attached to *Leibgarde-Infanterie-Regiment (1 Grossherzoglich Hessisches) Nr.115* based in Darmstadt, where he worked in the garrison's kitchen.

The third photograph is very different. It appears to have been taken at the family home in Bürgel and suggests that Friedrich did eventually enter active service. He is again wearing army uniform and, according to Dr Bauer, this particular tunic was in use from 1914. The shoulder straps are not visible, making it impossible to identify his regiment, but the absence of any collar insignia indicates that Friedrich was still a 'common soldier'.[32] Dr Bauer surmised that the photo may have been taken just before he was sent into action or in the early days of the conflict, which would explain his smart, well-fed, fit and healthy appearance, something that would not have persisted for long once combat started.

---

[31] Personal communication, 28 September 2017.
[32] Personal communication, 4 October 2018.

Friedrich in army uniform, probably at his father's house

Information confirming some of the above can be found on the Grünebaum household's index card in the *Jüdische Meldekartei* (register of Jewish residents).[33]   It shows that on Thursday 14 October 1909, when he was 20 years old and living with his

---

[33] From the late nineteenth century, all citizens in Germany were required to register with the local police or other authority, who documented each individual's address, date of birth, marriage and periods spent away from home, as well as their occupation and details of their children and parents. The information was usually recorded on index cards, with wives included on their husbands' cards. In Offenbach, as in many locations, details of Jewish citizens were held in a separate register, the *Jüdische Meldekartei*, which is preserved in the City Archive.

father at 22 Offenbacherstrasse, Friedrich went to Darmstadt and was indeed enlisted in *Infanterie-Regiment 115*. After an absence of almost two years, the normal duration of national service, he returned on Friday 22 September 1911, by which time his father had moved to his new address. The card incorrectly shows this as the address of his parents, although his mother, Käthchen, had actually died several years earlier.

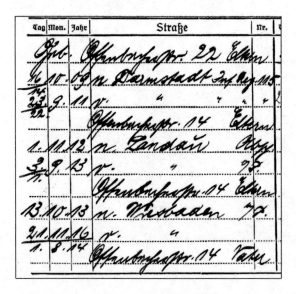

Extract from the Grünebaum household's index card in the *Jüdische Meldekartei* showing Friedrich's movements to and from the home address[34]

A Fusilier on the Western Front

After his national service, Friedrich became a Reservist and was able to go home and resume civilian life. However, the index card

---

[34] For most periods that Friedrich spent away from home, two return dates are given, one below the other. The first is later than the second and, in all but one instance, the difference is just a few days. It is thought that these pairs of dates indicate respectively the date on which the register was updated and the date on which the event actually occurred.

indicates that a year after returning to Bürgel, on Friday 1 November 1912, he departed for Landau and was away for ten months, not coming back until Monday 1 September 1913. Then after just six weeks, on Monday 13 October 1913, he relocated once more, this time to Wiesbaden, and did not re-register until Tuesday 21 November 1916, midway through WW1. As a Reservist, he would have had to take part in annual refresher training, but his pre-war absences were much longer than required and the gap between them was extremely short. It seems more likely that he went away to complete his training to become a master butcher or possibly to find work. Whatever the reason, once the conflict started, he was liable to be called up.[35]

The photos and fragments of information on the index card made me want to find out more. Had my grandfather actually been drafted back into the army? Had he been sent to the Eastern or Western Front? Did he become directly involved in the fighting or did he continue to work in the field kitchens? And did his involvement in the war end in November 1916, as suggested by the index card, at the end of one of the bloodiest battles in human history, the Somme Offensive? It felt important to resolve these questions, but I knew that getting answers from military personnel files was almost impossible. Records of German soldiers who served in WW1 were stored in the Potsdam Reichsarchiv (Potsdam Imperial Archive), which was bombed in February 1945. Virtually the whole collection was destroyed, so it was no surprise to learn that there were no documents relating to Friedrich in the small number that did survive.

---

[35] The final entry on the index card, 1 August 1914, is perplexing. It appears out of sequence and is a highly significant date: the day that Germany declared war on Russia and the Kaiser ordered full mobilisation of the German forces. Friedrich was apparently already living away from home at the time and no relocation is recorded, just the Offenbacherstrasse address and '*Vater*' (father). This could simply have been a correction of the error noted above to show that his father was actually living there alone.

I had, though, identified one other potential source to explore and this led to an intriguing find. Amongst the eight million names published throughout the war in the *Deutsche Verlustlisten* (German casualty lists), three entries stood out. Each related to a Friedrich Grünebaum from Offenbach, who had served in two different regiments.

List date	Name	Rank	Address	Regiment	Battalion/ Company	Desc.
6 Nov 1914	Friedrich Jul. Grünebaum	Fusilier	Bürgel, Offenbach	Fusilier 80	I / 2	Seriously wounded
15 May 1915	Friedr. Grünebaum	Reservist	Offenbach am Main	Infanterie 87	- / 6	Lightly wounded
17 Mar 1916	Friedrich Grünebaum	-	Offenbach am Main	Infanterie 87	- / 6	Lightly wounded

Extracts from German WW1 casualty lists

Could one of these wounded soldiers be my grandfather? Disappointingly, the detail in the listings was insufficient to enable me to draw a conclusion. As already noted, there were many Grünebaums in Bürgel at this time, many more in Offenbach, several Friedrichs amongst them and at least one also named Friedrich Julius.

Extract from the *Deutsche Verlustliste* issued on 6 November 1914, which includes a Fusilier Friedrich Jul. Grünebaum from Bürgel

A further fortuitous discovery provided the answer. I learned that, although most military personnel records had been destroyed, 50,000 files containing medical registers of Prussian soldiers treated in military hospitals had survived and were now in the *Bundesarchiv* (Federal Archive) in Berlin. Those files are not online and access to their content is strictly controlled. Detailed written enquiries were submitted and led to confirmation that some unspecified information was held about one of the Friedrich Grünebaums in the casualty lists. It was more than a year later that I eventually received a copy of the relevant document, but the wait was worthwhile. The 1914 register of *Reserve-Lazarett I Wiesbaden* (military rehabilitation hospital) included an entry for a Friedrich Julius Grünebaum from Bürgel who was born on 10 April 1889, my grandfather's date of birth. Moreover, this soldier had entered the army on Thursday 14 October 1909, the date on which, according to the *Jüdische Meldekartei*, my grandfather left his home address and went to Darmstadt to begin his national service. This soldier had been wounded at Roye (France) and admitted to the hospital on 6 October, a month before the same name was published in the casualty list. And when admitted, he was a Reservist in 2 Company of *Fusilier Regiment 80* (FR80). This proved beyond doubt that the patient with the hospital record and the wounded soldier listed in November 1914 were one and the same person, and that person was my grandfather, Friedrich Julius Grünebaum.

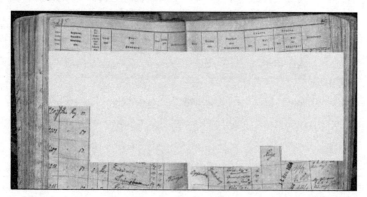

Extract from the Wiesbaden military hospital register (redacted)[36]

---

[36] Source: Bundesarchiv, B578/32947, Seite 205.

According to the medical record, Friedrich had been shot in his left hand on Friday 2 October and the *Verlustliste* shows that the men in 2 Company wounded on that date had been involved in fighting around Roye and St Mard (communes in the Somme department, about 50 kilometres south-east of Amiens). Friedrich was initially treated in a field hospital, before being transferred to Wiesbaden four days later.

So Friedrich was serving in an infantry battalion on the Western Front just a few weeks after war broke out. Although a Reservist, he may have been drafted into FR80 on mobilisation but, alternatively, could have been sent to the front as an early replacement for men who had been wounded or killed. Either way, the events following the declaration of war would have been largely the same. The order to mobilise was followed by five days of intense garrison activity, during which detailed plans were put into practice. For the ranks this involved medical examinations, kitting out, sharpening bayonets, being issued with cartridges, loading vehicles, equipping horses and marching practice. Once completed, the men paraded through Wiesbaden with the local population waving flags, showering them with flowers and cheering loudly. Then on Friday 7 August, accompanied by large crowds, FR80 boarded a train that took them west across the Rhine and up the Nahe valley. The first replacements followed just a couple of weeks later and, as will become clear, if Friedrich was not in the initial deployment, he would certainly have been amongst the men in that second contingent.

FR80 was assigned to the 21st Infantry Division in XVIII Army Corps, which formed part of the German Fourth Army. This was to take up a central position in the line of six armies expected by military command to sweep rapidly and victoriously in an arc through Luxembourg and Belgium and then down into France. There is no information from Friedrich himself about his involvement during the first few weeks of the conflict, but in 1925 a remarkable account of FR80's role was published.[37] Written by Bernhard von Fumetti, a regimental adjutant, it documents in immense detail the soldiers' movements and engagements, their victories and defeats, and the conditions they had to endure.

According to Fumetti, FR80 left the train at Beurig-Saarburg, about 15 kilometres from the Luxembourg border, and set off on foot. Pausing only for firing practice, they crossed the Mosel and marched on into Luxembourg City. In scorching summer weather, they continued north-westwards into the Ardennes uplands, marching up to 40 kilometres a day. Singing patriotic songs and eager to engage the enemy, they met no resistance until well inside Belgium. But on Friday 21 August they had their first experience of the bloody conflict that was to come. At Neufchateau, having initially routed the French infantry, they came under heavy artillery fire and suffered their first casualties. When the fighting died down, French and German corpses, dead horses, shattered helmets, abandoned weapons and broken lances scattered the battlefield, suddenly and vividly bringing home to them the horrific realities of the war.

Fierce fighting continued for the next ten days with both sides experiencing heavy losses. Infantry with rifle bayonets, armed bicycle companies and cavalry with lances fought hand-to-hand, whilst coming under fire from cannons, howitzers and machine guns. The ranks had to bivouac overnight in open countryside, enduring searing heat during the day and bitterly cold nights. Gradually, though, the French were pushed back and FR80, together with other units, advanced south. By the end

---

[37] Bernhard von Fumetti, *Das Königlich Preußische Füsilier-Regt. Von Gersdorff (Kurhessisches) 80 im Weltkriege 1914-18. I. Teil*, Erinnerungsblätter Deutscher Regimenter, Band 130 (Oldenburg iO/Berlin: Stalling, 1925), https://digital.wlb-stuttgart.de/index.php?id=6&tx_dlf%5Bid%5D=7639&tx_dlf%5Bpage%5D=1.

of the month, they had fought their way over the border into France and across the river Maas, but the relentless marching over difficult terrain, ferocious combat and extreme weather had taken their toll. The men were exhausted and the regiment was depleted; one-fifth of its strength, 558 men, had been killed.

The first regimental replacements arrived on Tuesday 1 September. They immediately joined the push southwards, fighting their way across the river Aisne and Rhein-Marne Canal to Étrepy, inflicting and suffering grievous losses. The French had been forced back again, but this was as far south as FR80 would reach. On other sections of the front, in what came to be known as the First Battle of the Marne, French and British forces were prevailing and on Friday 11 September the regiment was ordered to retreat.

Over subsequent days, pursued by the enemy, the men retraced the route along which they had so recently advanced, and then continued to the defensible higher ground north of the Aisne. It was here that German military command decided to make a stand. Having experienced the devastating power of artillery and machine guns, both sides resorted to digging trenches for greater protection and with neither able to succeed through frontal attack, each tried to outflank the other. Trench warfare unfolded and the 'Race to the Sea' developed as lines were extended ever further towards to the coast. Having retreated 75 kilometres northwards, FR80 was now sent a further 150 kilometres north-westwards. By Saturday 26 September, I Battalion in which Friedrich was serving was embroiled in a bloody battle for Champien (five kilometres to the east of Roye). After days of ferocious fighting, culminating in house-to-house and hand-to-hand combat during which both sides suffered terrible losses, the French withdrew. On Wednesday 30 September, Champien was finally in German hands and FR80, together with other units of the 21st Infantry Division, was able to move forward into Roye. But there was no respite from the fighting. Early on Thursday 1 October, French artillery began shelling Roye from nearby St Mard, while sharpshooters fired from the trees. The Germans were unable to advance and suffered further heavy casualties. The following day, on the outskirts of the town, Friedrich was shot in his left hand.[38]

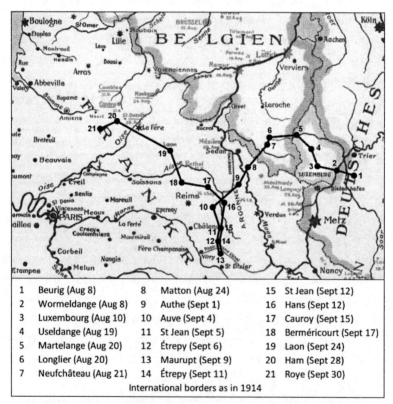

1	Beurig (Aug 8)	8	Matton (Aug 24)	15	St Jean (Sept 12)
2	Wormeldange (Aug 8)	9	Authe (Sept 1)	16	Hans (Sept 12)
3	Luxembourg (Aug 10)	10	Auve (Sept 4)	17	Cauroy (Sept 15)
4	Useldange (Aug 19)	11	St Jean (Sept 5)	18	Berméricourt (Sept 17)
5	Martelange (Aug 20)	12	Étrepy (Sept 6)	19	Laon (Sept 24)
6	Longlier (Aug 20)	13	Maurupt (Sept 9)	20	Ham (Sept 28)
7	Neufchâteau (Aug 21)	14	Étrepy (Sept 11)	21	Roye (Sept 30)

International borders as in 1914

Movement of 2 Company of FR80, in which Friedrich served from deployment in August 1914 until his wounding in September 1914, based on Fumetti (1925)[39]

---

[38] In another source, detailed in the following pages, Friedrich revealed that the location was between Roye and Gruny.

[39] Base map extracted from 'World War I Map (German), Nr. 1. Military Events … to September 1914', David Rumsey Historical Map Collection, https://

40

Life in the Trenches of Picardy

The medical record shows that Friedrich was declared fit for duty and discharged on Wednesday 11 November, when he returned to an *Ersatz-Bataillon* (replacement battalion), one of the units used to fill gaps in the front line. But what happened to him from then until his recorded return to Bürgel in 1916? The answer to this question comes from Friedrich himself. Around the same time that I received the medical record, I also received copies of 28 letters and postcards that he had written to his sister, Rosette, and which were found by her great-granddaughter. His individualistic handwriting was almost unintelligible to anyone other than his sister, so they had probably not been read for over a hundred years. However, with help from German friends, they were painstakingly deciphered and their content provided a remarkable insight into the next phase of his involvement in the war.

The correspondence was penned over the 15 months between February 1915 and May 1916 and it confirms that, after a few months in barracks, Friedrich was sent back to the front line in March 1915. Almost all the letters and cards were *Feldpost* (post sent via the army's postal service) and written in the trenches. Although there were strict rules about not disclosing in mail details that could benefit the enemy, Friedrich seems initially to have taken little notice of these restrictions. And while Fumetti's account of FR80 was full of patriotic fervour, the tone of Friedrich's writing was very different. In his first few letters he openly gave away his location, wrote freely about the terrible ordeal he and his fellow soldiers were experiencing, and made no secret of his increasing disenchantment and cynicism about the conflict.

Friedrich's deployment took him back close to Roye, where he had been shot. And he was still there a year later. He moved between Fresnoy-lès-Roye, Parvillers-le-Quesnoy and Amy,

---

www.davidrumsey.com/rumsey/download.pl?image=/D5005/7821004.sid.

all within ten kilometres of the town, and for short periods to places slightly further away. For many months the front line barely shifted, although there was constant and bloody fighting, and little respite. When Friedrich was withdrawn from the front for a few days, the time was used for military exercises, not just recuperation, and only on one or two occasions in that year was he able to make a short return trip to Germany. In the trenches, he and his compatriots faced the French across a narrow tract of no-mans-land and he matter-of-factly told his sister about the risks and horrific consequences of them being in such close proximity:

> *20 April 1915* All of this wouldn't be so bad if the artillery wasn't shooting from such close range. When they start, there will be 15–20 shots one after the other. The night before we were relieved, we dug a flanking trench towards the non-commissioned officer post. When ... 10 Company relieved us, they straightaway had several fatalities and woundings. (T)

> *1 May 1915* Last week in Fresnoy three men from 7 Company also got hit by grenades. It was a completely stray shot which went a long way. The whole upper body was blown off one of them. (T)

> *18 May 1915* The place where we'll now be going to will be quite dangerous because it's an advanced position ... Hopefully we'll be lucky and again get out of there alive, because the aim of the French artillery was very good, so every shot was on target. (T)

> *7 June 1915* On the 4th we were resting again in Fresnoy but this time it was different from before. Yesterday, for example, the French fired more than 300 grenades into the village, which had not been fired on before. I found a huge detonator and a shell

fragment that was about 2cm thick. You can't imagine how the shrapnel flies around. (T)

But it was not just the enemy that posed a risk or caused the loss of life. Sometimes, the danger came from his compatriots' inexperience or lack of care:

> *27 April 1915* Last night I and a guy called Brückmann from Frankfurt were on patrol and two recruits shot at us without calling out. When they realised who we were, we went to them and gave them each a firm slap on the cheek. (T)

> *1 May 1915* Last night a very good friend of mine was on patrol. He tripped over the barbed wire and a hand grenade that he was carrying exploded. He was blown to pieces. (T)

Contact between the enemy troops was not limited to firing. They were within hearing distance of each other and in quieter periods each side hurled insults at their foe:

> *20 April 1915* Last week the [French] guys were drunk again. You can hear something going on there in the morning. They scream 'cock-a-doodle-do' … We yell back that they should lick our arses. We are not more than 150m from each other. (T)

> *6 August 1915* The news came yesterday evening that Warsaw and Ivangorod had fallen. A nice [thing] happened in 7 [Company]. Two men made a large sign and wrote on it in French. The same guys filled their pockets with hand grenades and dragged this sign up to the French barbed wire. We'll hear something from there again early tomorrow morning. They're screaming all the time 'Germany is done for'. I just want to see whether this victory actually has an effect

on things. I don't have much hope. (T)[40]

Friedrich seemingly realised that it was impossible for anyone not actually there to imagine what it was like on the front line and tried to paint a verbal picture for Rosette, describing the layout of the defences and the men's daily routine:

> *27 April 1915* We've been back in the trenches since 25 April and right at the furthest point, which is the most forward position in France. It is near Roye, between the village of Gruny, where I was wounded before … At the position there is an embrasure to the other side. These are holes in which the rifles are laid at night. At night you are on duty for two hours, then two hours' rest. There is barbed wire in front of our position. Because we are only 150m apart, it is even electrified. The electricity is only switched on when it is quite dark or when the French are planning an attack. (T)
>
> *1 May 1915* You have to imagine that from our position there is a trench which you have to walk along for an hour to reach Parvillers. If you could walk direct, you'd be there in 20 minutes. The trenches are all dug zig-zag simply because of the artillery fire, which is very heavy every day. (T)
>
> *7 June 1915* With all this firing going on, we had to go out into the light night and excavate a new trench. That's what they call rest. Exercises during the day and digging trenches at night, and nothing decent to eat. (T)

---

[40] Ivangorod is today known as Dęblin, which is located 100 kilometres southeast of Warsaw. Although in Poland, it had been under Russian rule for many decades until it was taken by German troops in August 1914.

29 July 1915 We are always busy together digging tunnels. At the moment we are again making a new gallery. When I write to you about a gallery, you won't be able to imagine what that actually is. This thing is about 7m below ground, is 15m long and has 2 exits with a staircase with 12 steps. It would take a good grenade to penetrate it. (T)

He could see, though, that some aspects of his situation compared favourably with the bloody man-to-man fighting, gruelling marching and food shortages he had experienced in FR80 a few months earlier. And he realised that conditions in other parts of the front were much worse:

20 April 1915 The one good thing is that one no longer has to keep running for 3–4 days and then be in a battle for 5 days with nothing to eat. At Étrepy … we fed on mangolds for five days. (T)

27 April 1915 The food here is brilliant. For example, today there was soup from canned beans. (T)

29 July 1915 … I met Aloys Müller at the station in Nessle. He had come back from Arras three weeks earlier. He told me how terrible it is there. There are practically no trenches – one can't dig there because you're immediately in water. Each infantry soldier takes two sacks filled with sand and lays them down in front of him. They don't need rifles either, they each take two sacks of hand grenades. They lie there often only 30–40m apart. The battery where Aloys is has already lost 35 men. When one hears that there is a cannon every 20m, you have to wonder. It's a human slaughterhouse right there. We have to thank God that we are here. (T)

Nevertheless, he became more and more miserable as conditions became utterly intolerable. Infestation from lice, waterlogged trenches, hunger, winter weather and lack of shelter made personal hygiene and staying healthy virtually impossible:

27 April 1915 Sleeping here in these conditions is out of the question. Because here it's like Otto Reutter sang: 'Lice oh lice are here in this room, dancing the polka and the waltz dream'. (T)[41]

1 May 1915 If I really look at life here, one is worse off than in prison. You go from your louse container here to the embrasure and back again. That's all you've got. (T)

6 August 1915 You must excuse me for writing so little in the last 8 days. We've now come to a position where we have never been before. The section was always occupied by the 116 [Regiment]. There's a lot of confusion. We had to put the dugouts in order ourselves. The first night we were inside, we were completely under water. The shelter we are in is bombproof but not rainproof. (T)

30 October 1915 Now I will tell you some things that will not give you any pleasure. I have never written that I'm not doing well, but today I have to. It was my turn to fetch dinner today. You have to pick it up in Roye, which is a good 1½ hours' walk. It is the same distance as from Frankfurt Central Station to Bürgel. By the time you get back into position with it, it's ice cold and [we] don't have a stove to warm it up. This is the first thing. Second, we are only getting a third of a loaf, which you can eat in one go. In addition to all

---

[41] Otto Reutter (1870–1931) was a German comedian and singer.

of this, on the march you are still called an arsehole, while in Germany they speak of our brave men in grey.

As long as we were behind the front, we felt a lot better. Every now and then we were able to cook potatoes and buy something to smoke in the canteen. But you just don't have anything anymore. Don't believe that I'm the only one who is writing things like that. We're just sitting together in the trench and all complaining in correspondence about our wretched situation. (T)

3 December 1915 It's also been very cold here for two days, but now there's continuous rain ... Soaked by rain, and still no opportunity to dry our rags. (T)

10 January 1916 The village we're going to is called Amy, it's very close to Roye. There the damned life starts again. There we'll go into the cellar, which will be shot at like at Parvillers. There the lice will be eating us again. (T)

Throwing caution to the wind, he wrote ever more indiscreetly about his disillusion with the war, which he described as a gigantic fraud, and the need to seek peace. He contemptuously derided advocates of the conflict who had never been near the front and admiringly commented on men who had evaded conscription or deserted. He even pondered how he might escape from the military himself:

1 May 1915 That's why it's time [to] talk a little about peace. According to the newspaper, that's not happening. I can't understand why the French aren't doing that. (T)

30 October 1915 So you can't blame someone if they

desert, because half fed and on their feet day and night, no one can hold us.

You wrote that Albert has also received the Hessen Ribbon. For all of us these are club badges which I can do without. (T)

3 December 1915 I've so often said that I would like to get a minor gunshot in my hand again, then I would be thankful. Because if we continue through the winter as we have so far, in spring everything will be screwed up.

A Reservist, who has always been with me, was smart. He was on leave and called in sick from home, and he is not coming back. [Brother] Albert will have come to Offenbach by now. He'll know what to do. If I were in his place, they wouldn't get me here again. I think the whole thing is a big fraud. But one can't really say that too loudly. Should I ever have the opportunity to go on leave, I know what I have to do. (T)

10 January 1916 I would like to be at home and not have to bring anyone else into this squalor and misery. If it were up to me, those who have dodged [military service] would get the Iron Cross First Class.[42]

[When in the military hospital] I said to medical officer Meyer at the time: a shell would have to explode over Wiesbaden for people to get an idea of exactly what was going on out there in the field. There could be no greater miracle than if the whole fraud

---

[42] The Iron Cross was awarded for outstanding bravery or service in the battlefield without regard to rank. A 1st class award was not higher than a 2nd Class; they were progressive. A first act of gallantry was recognised with a 2nd Class award and a subsequent act with a 1st Class award.

finally came to an end. (T)

Staying in touch with family and friends was incredibly important. Friedrich sent up to ten letters and cards daily. Occasionally he heard from his elder brothers, both of whom were too old to be sent to frontline positions immediately. Ferdinand, 39 years old when war broke out, served in a *Landwehr* (reserve) unit attached to *Infanterie Regiment 116*, while, Edmund, two years younger, was a *Matrose* (Able Seaman) in the *Ersatz Depot des Marine Korps* (base for marine reserves) ready to be called into action. But Friedrich was more frequently in contact with his younger siblings, his sister Rosette and his brother Albert, who was also enlisted. Little is known about his involvement in the fighting, but Bopp noted that he was awarded the Iron Cross 1st Class.

Left: Photo postcard sent by Edmund to Ferdinand in October 1917
Right: Albert (seated) wearing the ribbon of the Iron Cross

The purpose of their exchanges was not just to share news; they were also a vital sign of life, and when several days passed without contact, Friedrich became increasingly anxious about his younger brother's safety:

> *1 May 1915* ... Albert has not written for such a long time. Please write to me right away when you get something from him. (T)

> *2 June 1915* In vain I looked in [the packet] for a letter, since I would really still like to know if Albert has written, because I have still not received anything from him, and he was recently in pursuit. (T)

There was also correspondence with his father, although they evidently did not always see eye to eye, especially in matters relating to the war:

> *10 January 1916* ... our dear father is just not himself any more. It just seems to me as though he wanted one of us to die a heroic death for the fatherland. Frankly, I attribute it to his stupidity. I mean, young people our age have to know what to do and what not to do.
>
> A friend of mine who served with me, Hannes Brinkmann, was on vacation over the New Year and also paid a visit home. He told us a lot about Frankfurt and about home. Among other things, he told us of people my age who had served in the military still walking around in civilian clothes. When asked why they weren't soldiers, they answered him that the war had nothing to do with them. Looking at life and the guys in Frankfurt, you wouldn't think there was a war on. And then Papa wants his own son to volunteer for the field again. It's disgusting even to have such thoughts.

It's noticeable too that Friedrich wrote of plans to visit family members in Mittelsinn (Bavaria) and he went to Mainz during a period of leave, but there is no mention of visiting Offenbach to see his father. Undoubtedly, though, it was with his sister – to whom he wrote every other day – that he had the closest connection. He looked forward not only to the delivery of her letters, but also her frequent parcels that provided food and other items vital for his sustenance and survival:

> *27 April 1915* Please be so good as to send me something for the teeth. Above all a small brush and something for the lice. (T)

> *7 May 1915* Yesterday morning received a card of 1.5.1915 from you, in which you asked if I had got your 3 packets. So far I have received two, one with sausage and one with cigarettes, and your card from Würzburg. (T)

> *18 May 1915* I received the parcel of oranges and toothpaste, but nothing else yet. (T)

> *2 June 1915* I've just got your dear packet with sausage and cigarettes … (T)

> *7 June 1915* I got your letter of 2/6, card of 3/6 as well as Else's parcel of sausage, for which many thanks. (T)

> *14 July 1915* I received your dear letter with writing paper today, and was very pleased about that. The eggs that Else sent to me arrived safely, many thanks for them. (T)

> *29 July 1915* In your last letter you asked if you should send me some jelly. I don't need jelly for now, but you can send me some raspberry juice. We just get jelly by the bucket load. (T)

3 December 1915 I got your lovely little parcel and letter today and I would like to thank you very much for it. I also received the stationery. (T)

11 December 1915 I also received the socks and gloves. Once again, many thanks for them.

Generally, the military mail system worked well. It took only a few days for post to reach Friedrich from Mittelsinn, but there were occasional glitches:

29 July 1915 I learned from Else's card that you haven't received my last letter. That's quite possible because I threw it into the mail box when I was out of the trenches fetching meals, and found out afterwards that someone had poured into it a whole mess-tin of food. So the dirty letters were not delivered. (T)

There was often a strange juxtaposition in the correspondence of gory descriptions of the slaughter going on at the front with mundane gossip about 'normal' events; but perhaps they had both become normal to Friedrich by then. He passed on news from other contacts and told his sister about friends from Offenbach who were with him in the trenches:

14 April 1915 We've just had visitors in the trench. Jesse Kopp and Erhard Belle, schoolmates of mine, were here with us. The latter even photographed us in our position. When the pictures are ready, I'll send you them. We also always meet Kurt Menge when we get out of the trench. (T)

20 April 1915 I want to close now, because we want to go looking for Karl. Last week he had a baby boy, which we also have to celebrate. (T)

Friedrich's letters also included some further very significant details. He not only gave his location, he also disclosed his rank (Reservist) and the unit in which he was serving. And from this it is clear that on returning to the front line after being shot, he did not go back to FR80. Although still in the 4th Army and 21st Infantry Division, he was assigned to *Infanterie Regiment 87* (IR87), and more specifically, to 6 Company in II Battalion of that Regiment.[43] This is the very same unit in which, as shown in the *Verlustlisten* extracts above, a Reservist Friedrich Grünebaum from Offenbach was twice lightly wounded, once in May 1915 and then again in March 1916. Evidently, all three entries in the *Verlustlisten* relate to my grandfather and he was wounded not just once, but at least three times.

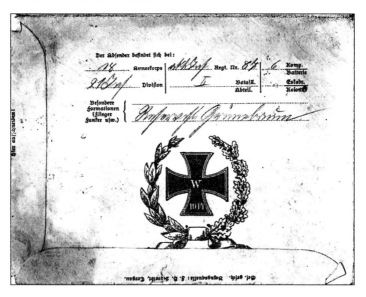

Envelope of letter Friedrich sent in April 1915 showing his rank (Reservist) and army unit (6 Company, II Battalion, IR87, 21 Infantry Division)

---

[43] According to Fumetti (1925, 128), after six months of uninterrupted combat, FR80 was withdrawn from the front line during the night of 25–26 February 1915 for 10 days of rest and recuperation, and its positions were taken over by IR87.

In fact, in the letter that he wrote to his sister on 7 May 1915, Friedrich confided that he had been wounded again and described how it had happened, but he beseeched her not to share that information with other family members, whom he had told all was well:

> *7 May 1915* I have something to tell you on condition that you don't write home [about it]. Yesterday Peter Kämmerer was again discharged from the infirmary and I was admitted. This is what happened to me. On the 5th to 6th I was on night patrol with my friend Brinkmann. It was 10 minutes before 12 and we were standing in the ditch behind the sergeant's post and waiting for our relief. At that moment a mine came flying over and exploded very close to us. We were both hurled about 10 metres. I got a small splinter in my left upper arm, which isn't that bad. We were both covered in mud up to our necks … We went in the night to the doctor, who immediately vaccinated us against blood poisoning. One doesn't hear such a mine coming like a shell – it's not fired but thrown. Here the Frenchmen also have stink bombs, which stink of sulphur. If they don't stop with those things, they'll get something from us. We have some that are 180–200 pounds … I think that in a few days I will be going back to the company … Hopefully, I can depend on you not to write home. I have just written to everyone that all is well. (T)

Friedrich's last known communication was a picture postcard with a view of the river Rhine, sent on 22 May 1916 from Mainz. Perhaps he was there recovering from his third wounding and subsequently returned to his regiment. Perhaps he was on leave or perhaps his regiment had been pulled back from the front line.

So what happened to Friedrich between his wounding in early 1916 and his return to Offenbach in November of that year? In February his regiment was transferred eastwards, where it became heavily involved in the Battle of Verdun. Then in September it was moved back to bolster German forces in the Battle of the Somme.[44] If Friedrich was embroiled in those bloodiest of battles, in which more than 80 of the 250 men in 6 Company lost their lives, it would be unsurprising if he had again been wounded.[45] And given the carnage and chaos that prevailed, his name may not have made it to the casualty lists. Remarkably, not only did Friedrich survive the conflict, but so did all the Grünebaum brothers and their sister.

---

[44] '21. Division (Alte Armee)', GenWiki, https://wiki.genealogy.net/21._Division_(Alte_Armee).

[45] 'Königlich Preußisches Infanterie-Regiment (1. Nassauisches, Offiziere) Nr. 87, Mainz', Onlineprojekt Gefallenendenkmäler, http://www.denkmalprojekt.org/2013/buch_ir-87-offiziere_wk1.html.

Monument to *Infanterie Regiment 87* in Mainz

Married Life
in the Weimar Republic

A Wedding, a New Home and a Baby

By early November 1918, German leaders were facing military defeat and an internal socialist uprising, triggered by wartime suffering and opposition to the aristocratic elite. On the 9 November, Kaiser Wilhelm II announced his abdication and the country morphed from a constitutional monarchy into a democratic republic. Two days later, the Armistice was signed and fighting came to an end. In June the following year, the Treaty of Versailles was adopted. It ended the state of war between Germany and the Allied Powers and required Germany to make onerous reparation payments. Then in August 1919, at a meeting in Weimar, a new constitution was adopted and the government began the task of both rebuilding the country and meeting its Treaty obligations.

Ten months later, on Thursday 17 June 1920, Friedrich Grünebaum and Sophie Reiss were married in Bürgel.[46] He was 31 and she 32 years old. Her parents, Markus and Rebecka, and his father, Heinrich, were probably all present, but his mother, Käthchen, had passed away in 1903. On the same day as their wedding, they moved into their own rented accommodation in Offenbach, the address of which was officially and rather oddly recorded in the *Jüdische Meldekartei* not just with a street name and number, but as 'Luisenstrasse 69 Blameser'[sic].

---

[46] Recorded on the couple's index card in the *Jüdische Meldekartei*.

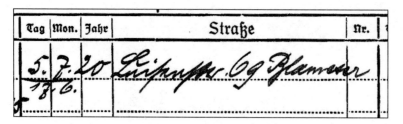

Tag	Mon.	Jahr	Straße	Nr.
5.	7.	20	*Luisenstr. 69 Blammeser*	
13.	6.			

Extract from Friedrich and Sophie Grünebaum's index card in the
Jüdische Meldekartei showing their address from June 1920

The name 'Blammeser' is of significance to this narrative.
Philipp Blammeser was an Offenbach businessman who owned
the multi-storey building at 69 Luisenstrasse, which is why it bore
his name. In the early 1900s he opened three butcher's shops,
including one at that address in 1903. Blammeser had four
children, two of whom died in childhood, while a third, who
was also a butcher, died in WW1. The surviving daughter did
not take over the business, meaning he had no familial successor.
Consequently, by early 1920 all three shops had closed and the
Luisenstrasse building was sold to Löwenberger & Scheuer, a
leather wholesaling company.[47] It was perhaps the opportunity
that Friedrich had been waiting for. He took over the retail
premises and on Wednesday 14 April 1920, two months before
his marriage, opened his own butcher's shop.

---

[47] Gabriele Hauschke-Wicklaus and Geschichtswerkstatt Offenbach, eds.,
Jüdische Bürgerinnen und Bürger Erinnern Sich, Erste Auflage (Offenbach: OE
Offenbacher Editionen, 2017), 186.

Record card for Friedrich Grünebaum's butcher's shop
from the Offenbach *Gewerberegister* (buisness register)[48]

The Blammeser building stood at the junction of Luisenstrasse and Frankfurterstrasse, the town's main shopping street. In 1920 it had commercial premises at ground level, which were accessed from Frankfurterstrasse, and residential apartments on the upper floors accessed from Luisenstrasse, resulting in the building having two quite different addresses.[49] Confusingly, these were used

---

[48] As well as having names, streets were allocated a number, which did not change, even if the street was renamed. The address of Friedrich's shop was recorded as '49/69', which was No 69 in Luisenstrasse.

[49] According to Georg Hellwig, (son of Georg Hellwig, a future owner of the building), its design and layout changed considerably over time. When first constructed, the entrance off Luisenstrasse did not exist, the ground floor windows on Luisenstrasse were doorways into small rooms for travellers, and the first floor was a large hall for banquets and other events. Floors above this were used for residential accommodation and the first floor was converted to the same use at a later date. It was only after an extension was built at the back to provide additional storage, that an entrance to the upper floors from Luisenstrasse was created. Initially there was one flat per floor, but each was subsequently divided into two, one slightly larger than the other. There was

interchangeably. And despite Friedrich's business address being officially recorded as 69 Luisenstrasse, it was not on that road or in the main building. It was actually in an adjoining construction infilling the space between 68 and 70 Frankfurterstrasse.

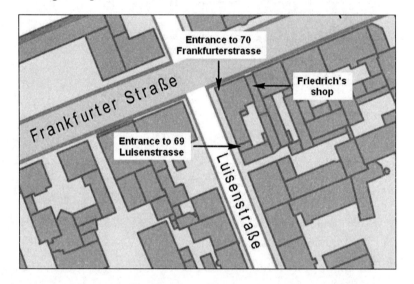

Entrances to the former Blammeser building and the location of
Friedrich's butcher's shop (based on a 1927 street plan)

More than a century later, the butcher's shop had become the Soupreme soup café and looked very different, but some elements of the original building that Friedrich took over are still visible.

little difference between the residential accommodation on the two lower levels. However, the top floor was smaller, being built into the roof space. There are no surviving records of individual tenancies.

The building at the corner of Luisenstrasse
and Frankfurterstrasse (photo taken about 1938)[50]

Friedrich outside his shop with his niece Greta in 1921
and the Soupreme soup café occupying the premises in 2022

[50] Photo courtesy of Georg Hellwig.

As well as the newlyweds, the upper floors of the main building accommodated a diverse range of tenants. The 1925 *Einwohnerverzeichnis* (directory of residents) listed their occupations as a locomotive driver, quarryman, labourer, greengrocer and factory worker.[51] They probably all considered themselves very fortunate because Germany was in the midst of a housing crisis. There was simply not enough to meet demand. For Sophie and Friedrich, the apartment would be their home for more than two decades and the only one the couple would ever know.

Extracts from the 1925 Offenbach address book showing the entry for 70 Frankfurterstrasse (above), referring readers to 69 Louisenstrasse (below), where occupants and their occupations are listed.[52]

---

[51] Einwohnerverzeichnis (Adressbuch) der Stadt und Landkreis Offenbach a.M. 1925, (Offenbach am Main: Seiboldsche Buchdruckerei Dohany, n.d., 1925).

[52] Under the Nazis, street names were changed to 'Germanic' spelling. What

The Grünebaums' apartment was reached by a winding staircase at the back of the building. They had two bedrooms, a living room, a salon and a kitchen with windows overlooking both roads. Around the time of their wedding, they bought period oak furniture for their bedroom and the living room from *Möbel-Herbst* in Salmünster, a town 55 kilometres away, for about Reichsmark RM800. The second bedroom was furnished later at an estimated cost of RM600.[53] Kitchen appliances and fittings costing RM300–400 were probably bought from *Möbel-Wilzbacher* in the same town and they also acquired a considerable amount of bed and table linen.

Whilst not conspicuously wealthy, there can be no doubt that at the time of their wedding the young couple and their parents were comfortably off. Sophie's father, Markus Reiss, was a skilled craftsman and a foreman working in the booming leather industry, so would have received a decent wage. Friedrich's father, Heinrich Grünebaum, was a master butcher with his own shop, so he too could earn a good living. According to the *Einwohnerverzeichnis*, both owned their own homes in Offenbacherstrasse in Bürgel. Moreover, Friedrich's qualification as a master butcher required a substantial investment of time and money. It involved at least two years of theoretical and practical learning before passing an exam, and a further three years' work experience, before he could trade independently. Having done all this, he then set up his own business and rented a sizeable apartment close to the town centre, furnished it to a high standard and got married. All this necessitated considerable expenditure, which they evidently could afford. For Sophie and Friedrich, the future must have looked bright. They had comfortable well-furnished accommodation,

---

had been Louisenstrasse became Luisenstrasse. Women occupants were only listed in the address book if they were the sole occupier.
[53] Statement from Friedrich Kühn, 4 September 1952.

a business that could provide a good income and, within a few weeks, Sophie knew she was expecting her first baby. They could never have imagined how dramatically their happiness would be shattered within a few years.

It was in their apartment 11 months after the wedding that Karola Grünebaum was born. At the same time, Sophie and Friedrich's niece, Margareta ('Greta'), moved in to help the new parents. She was the daughter of his sister, Rosette, and her husband, Friedrich Kühn, who lived in the small Bavarian village of Mittelsinn, and with whom he was very close. Greta was 19 years old and stayed for several months, working in the butcher's shop and assisting with household chores.[54] The photograph of Friedrich with Greta at the entrance to his shop is thought to have been taken on the day of the birth. Curiously, the space for recording religion is left blank on the birth registration.

---

[54] Greta received no remuneration for the help she gave, something which irked her and finally surfaced in a furious tirade against Karola nearly 40 years later.

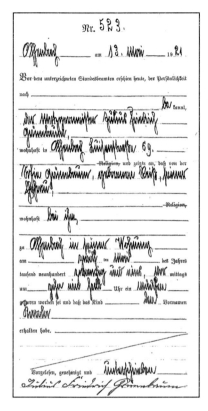

Nr 523

Offenbach, 13th May 1921

The person known as the master butcher Julius Friedrich Grünebaum, resident at Offenbach 69 Luisenstrasse, appeared today before the undersigned Registrar and announced that his wife Sofie Grünebaum, née Reiss, resident with him at his apartment in Offenbach, gave birth at 10.30am on 12th May 1921 to a girl and that the child has been given the forename Karola.

Read out, approved and signed
Julius Friedrich Grünebaum

Registry Office record of the birth of Karola Grünebaum
(with translation)

The Impact of Economic Crisis on People and Politics

By 1921 the Weimar government was struggling to overcome severe social and economic challenges. Food shortages, hyperinflation, a stagnant economy and high unemployment prompted civil unrest and gave succour to extremist political groups, including the *Nationalsozialistische Deutsche Arbeiterpartei* (National Socialist German Workers' or Nazi Party). Less than three months after Karola's birth, Adolf Hitler became chairman of that party and before the end of the year was given the title of *Führer*. He was 32 years old, 10 days younger than Karola's father, Friedrich. Support for the Nazis remained at a low level for the next few years as the new Chancellor, Gustav Stresemann, restored order, stabilised the currency, improved social conditions and oversaw economic revival. All that changed, however, with the fallout from the Wall Street Crash in October 1929 and the subsequent Great Depression in the USA. American banks withdrew the massive loans they had made to German companies, resulting in deflation and recession. By 1930, unemployment had grown to 3–4 million and, disillusioned with the government, the population turned to more extreme political parties. In that year's Reichstag election, the Nazis won 19% of the vote and 107 seats, a huge increase on their previous standing.

Offenbach was severely impacted by the recession and a record card in the *Gewerberegister* shows that Friedrich's butcher's shop closed on Monday 6 January 1930. Curiously, a second card indicates that another butcher's business opened on the same day at the same address, only for that to close permanently seven months later on Monday 18 August. The only difference between them is that both Friedrich and Sophie, who were not married when the first business was registered, were both included as proprietors at the later date, so the change of registration may have been made for administrative or accounting purposes. Whatever the reason, after the second closure, Friedrich never again found regular employment and consequently had no regular income. Although the family had some savings, they became increasingly dependent on state benefits and the generosity of friends.

Perversely, it was because of the housing crisis that they were able to stay in their apartment. To prevent the shortage of accommodation leading to price inflation, controls had been introduced in 1922 by the *Reichsmietengesetz* (Imperial Rent

Law).[55] These linked the rent of property built before 1918 to the July 1914 level, the so-called *Friedensmiete* (Peace Rent), and it limited subsequent increases. The restrictions remained in force to a greater or lesser extent throughout most of the inter-war period.[56] The young couple were undoubtedly beneficiaries of these controls and other governmental support mechanisms, as a result of which they actually paid very little. Their rent book, which each month was stamped by their landlord 'Löwenberger & Scheuer', shows that the *Friedensmiete* was RM35 and by January 1931 the chargeable rent had increased 24% to RM43.40. However, they received a tax allowance of RM16.80 and housing benefit of RM26.00, meaning that they just had to pay RM0.60. The figures varied over the subsequent years, but a significant subsidy continued throughout their tenure and in many months they appear to have paid nothing at all.

---

[55] 'Reichsmietengesetz vom 22 März 1922', *Reichsgesetzblatt*, no. 23 (1922): 273–74, https://alex.onb.ac.at/cgi-content/alex?aid=dra&datum=1922&page =371&size=45.

[56] Dan P. Silverman, 'A Pledge Unredeemed: The Housing Crisis in Weimar Germany', *Central European History* 3, no. 1–2 (March 1970): 112–39, https://doi.org/10.1017/S0008938900015168; A Kholodilin and Mark G Meerovich, *Similar Challenges - Different Responses: Housing Policy in Germany and Russia between the Two World Wars*, Discussion papers of DIW Berlin 1391 (DIW Berlin, German Institute for Economic Research, 2014), https://ideas. repec.org/p/diw/diwwpp/dp1391.html.

Pages from the Grünebaums' rent book for their apartment at
69 Luisenstrasse for the period June 1934 to April 1935

In the following years, the economic situation continued to worsen. By 1932 unemployment had reached 32%, with more than five million out of work. Support for extreme political groups on the left and right rose further and the Nazis became the largest party in the Reichstag. In January 1933, Hitler was sworn in as Chancellor. Many of his party members already had long-held anti-Semitic views, blaming the Jews for the country's problems and perpetrating violence against them. Now anti-Semitism became official government policy and the persecution of Jews was not only condoned but advocated by its leaders.[57]

---

[57] Richard J. Evans, *The Third Reich in Power, 1933–1939* (London: Penguin, 2006).

Growing Up
in Turbulent Times

Children and Childhood

Karola was her parents' first child and would be their only one. Before the war, that would have been unusual. However, for several reasons, the birth rate in Germany declined from the late nineteenth century onwards, and it declined earlier in the Jewish population.[58] By 1923 Jewish women in Prussia had just 1.3 children on average and roughly a quarter of married Jewish women did not have any. This change was reflected in both the Grünebaum and Reiss families. The older siblings of Friedrich and Sophie who married and started families before the war had significantly more children than their younger brothers and sister.

---

[58] Franz Rothenbacher and Georg Fertig, 'Population, Households and Families – Deutschland in Daten', http://www.deutschland-in-daten.de/en/population/; Miriam Rürup, 'Demographics and Social Structure in Key Documents of German-Jewish History', 2016, https://dx.doi.org/10.23691/jgo:article-224.en.v1.

Sibling	Birth year	Children pre-1914	Children post-1918
Ferdinand Grünebaum	1875	4	0
Edmund Grünebaum	1877	2	0
Rosette Grünebaum	1879	3	0
Salomon Reiss	1882	4	0
Franziska Reiss	1886	0	0
Sophie Reiss & Friedrich Grünebaum	1888/1889	0	1
Albert Grünebaum	1893	0	1
Siegfried Reiss	1894	0	1

Number of children born to Friedrich Grünebaum and Sophie Reiss
and their married siblings (none were born 1914 - 18)

So Karola had a considerable number of older cousins, most of whom were living nearby, but few of a similar age. Not all of them were brought up as Jews. Of Friedrich's four siblings, only his older brother, Edmund, married a partner of the same faith. His other brothers, Ferdinand and Albert, took Protestant wives, while his sister, Rosette, married a Catholic. The children from each of these relationships were raised according to the religion of the non-Jewish parent. Perhaps this was because of concern about anti-Semitism, which had been steadily increasing; however, not adhering to Judaism did not mean that they escaped Nazi persecution.

Rosette Kühn (*née* Grünebaum), with her children, Else,
Greta and Wilhelm taken between 1910 and 1914[59]

Not much is known for sure about Karola's early years. A
photograph in the only album she kept is believed to show her as
a baby, distinguished by her dark curly hair.

---

[59] Photo courtesy of Christiane Kühn.

Undated photo thought to be of Karola as a baby with her parents,
Friedrich and Sophie, standing behind (centre) and other family members

In October 1927, when six years old, she started her formal
education at the girls' primary school located at 38 Bahnhofstrasse,
very close to her home.[60] There are no surviving images of this
school, which opened in 1873, but its location is marked on a city
plan dated 1900.

---

[60] The school originally opened as a *Mittelschule* (middle school) but became a
Volksschule (primary school) in 1925. 'Vor 65 Jahren Entstand die Bürgerschule',
Offenbacher Nachrichten, 21 November 1938.

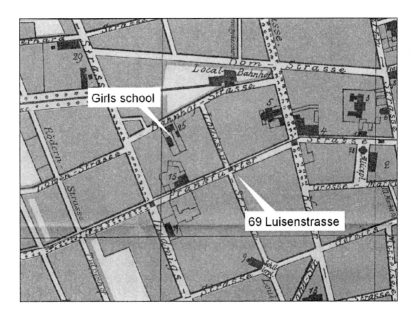

Location of Karola's first school in Bahnhofstrasse [61]

A studio photo shows her dressed for the occasion with a satchel on her back and ribbon in her hair.[62]

---

[61] 'Offenbacher Schulen Bis 1918 - Wikimedia Commons', https://commons.wikimedia.org/wiki/Offenbacher_Schulen_bis_1918.
[62] The start date of her formal education is included in a register for the *Jüdische Bezirksschule* (Jewish District School) which is archived in Yad Vashem, Jerusalem.

Karola ready for her first day at school, 1927

Another album photograph shows her in her class of 38 children, together with their teacher, Fräulein Klara Kuhl. She stands out as the only girl with very wavy hair and wears a worried expression as she holds hands with a friend to her left. It is inscribed on the reverse, in a child's handwriting, *'Mein erstes Schulbild 1930'* (My first school photo 1930).

Karola (second row, third from left) with her class in 1930

Remarkably, this same photograph appeared in the *Offenbach-Post* newspaper 60 years later. In May 1990 it was reprinted, together with two letters from former pupils recalling their time in the school, their classmates and what became of them.[63] Most of the girls in the photo are named and the information shared about them makes it clear that the school was multi-denominational. The largest number of pupils came from Protestant families, but the group also included several from Catholic and Jewish homes.

---

[63] 'Hoffnung auf Kontaktaufnahme der Mitschülerinnen', *Offenbach-Post*, 12 May 1990.

Irmgard Immel, evangelisch; Dora Sonn, evangelisch; Gretel Witzel, evangelisch; **die in der zweiten:** Lotti Lochmann, evangelisch, Lieselotte Forster, evangelisch, Carola Grünebaum (es sollte wohl Karola geschrieben sein) sie war **die einzige Jüdin in der Klasse, die von armer Familie kam.** Die Familie

Extract from correspondence in the *Offenbach-Post* about Karola's 1930 school class, May 1990

Of all the details shared, the comment about Karola is quite different from the other remarks:

> ... in the second [row]: Lotti Loschmann, Protestant, Lieselotte Forster, Protestant, Carola Grünebaum (it should probably be written Karola) she was the only Jewish girl in the class who came from a poor family.
> (T)

This relative poverty must have been quite evident, as well as unusual, for it to be the one thing about Karola that the writer mentioned after all that time. And it is quite perplexing. There were very wealthy Jewish families in the town and the contrast with Karola's family would certainly have been noticeable. The assessment also fits with the family receiving a considerable rent subsidy and the fact that, in the year the photo was taken, Friedrich closed his butcher's shop, after which the family had no regular income. However, there were many other Jewish families facing a similar predicament, so it's somewhat surprising that Karola was singled out in this way.

The extent to which financial constraints impacted on the

family's standard of living and social life can only be guessed, but there is one thing that they definitely did do together: go swimming. From the late nineteenth century onwards, and especially after the 1896 Athens Olympics, more and more Germans took to recreational swimming. In Offenbach, an indoor pool and outdoor lidos were constructed along the river Main and, although initially for swimming club members only, by the 1920s they had been opened up to the wider public and became extremely popular. In 1921, one of these lidos, owned by Andreas Leicher, was the first to allow mixed bathing.[64] The 'Leicher', as it was known, had several different pools, a flume, sunbathing lawns, a playground and a restaurant overlooking the Main.[65] It became a trendy destination for family excursions and, located just a short distance from their home, it is here that Karola went with her parents.

---

[64] Angelika Amborn-Morgenstern, 'Die Neuen Badegebiete: die Hafeninsel und das Fechenheimer Ufer', in *Bäder in Offenbach 1781–1994, Offenbacher Geschichtsblätter* 41 (Offenbacher Geschichtsverein, n.d.): 37–41.

[65] Angelika Amborn-Morgenstern, 'Badesaison am Offenbacher Mainufer bis Oktober', *Wir im Quartier. Stadtteilzeitung Östliche Innenstadt*, September 2005, Ausgabe 4.

Karola with her parents, Sophie and Friedrich (right) at the 'Leicher', 1929

Her social life also included participation in more organised youth activities. She was a member of the Girl Guides for a while, but that would have ended by 1934, after which Hitler Youth was the only permitted youth organisation.

Karola (back row, fifth from left) in her Girl Guide group, 1934

Sport also had a place in her recreational time, as shown by a photo of a girls' hockey team. It appears to have been taken after a match on a very wet day and, judging by the kit she is wearing, her position was that of goalkeeper.

Karola (back row, third from left) and her sports team

Expulsion of Jews from Public Schools

The seemingly normal routine of going to school, enjoying family outings and participating in youth activities was, however, taking place against an ominous backdrop of growing support for the Nazis and their anti-Semitic rhetoric. Within months of Hitler becoming Chancellor in January 1933, there was a series of portentous developments that affected the lives of all Jews, but especially those of Jewish children.

In April the Nazi Party passed the *Gesetz gegen die Überfüllung deutscher Schulen und Hochschulen* (Law Against the Overcrowding of German Schools), limiting the places in state schools that could be filled by Jewish children to a tiny percentage. Karola did not get one of those places. In the same month, the *Gesetz zur Wiederherstellung des Berufsbeamtentums* (Law for the Restoration of the Professional

Civil Service) gave the party power to remove Jewish teachers from their posts and, two years later, all Jewish teachers still in post were summarily dismissed under a further decree. Moreover, education became a crucial instrument for the promotion of Nazi ideology. Teachers who supported the party started wearing its uniform to work and giving the Nazi salute. Lessons about democracy and equality were replaced with compulsory lessons on race, opening the door to the promulgation of the notion of Aryan superiority and the inferiority of Jews.

The impact on Jewish children was immediate and devastating. Many experienced humiliation, social isolation and abuse from teachers and fellow pupils both inside and outside the classroom. Over time, they were excluded from school because of the restrictions or left because of their alienation. However, the Nazi actions only applied to state schools. In response, Jewish communities began establishing more of their own private schools and this is what happened in Offenbach, where the *Jüdische Bezirksschule* (Jewish District School) was established inside the synagogue in Goethestrasse.[66] Completed in 1916, the synagogue had been built to meet the needs of the growing Jewish population, which by then was around 2000.[67] With its grand Doric-columned entrance, its 30-metre-high glass-topped dome, ornate open courtyard and capacity for 700 worshippers, it was not only one of the largest in Hessen, but also a statement of Jewish confidence and achievement. The classrooms were located on the upper floor at the corner of the building overlooking the junction with Kaiserstrasse. It was less than a kilometre from Karola's home and she was amongst its first pupils.

---

[66] 'Geschichte des Capitols', Stadt Offenbach, https://www.offenbach.de/stadtwerke/microsite/capitol/das-capitol/historie/historie.php.

[67] Much of the growth in the Jewish population has been attributed to immigration from areas further east because the regime in Hessen was seen to be more liberal. Klaus Werner, 'Zur Wirtschafts- und Sozialstruktur der Juden in Offenbach', in *Zur Geschichte der Juden in Offenbach am Main. Unter der Herrschaft des Nationalsozialismus*, vol. 1 (Offenbach am Main: Der Magistrat der Stadt Offenbach, 1988), 31–46.

The synagogue where the *Jüdische Bezirksschule* was established
in rooms at the corner of the building on the upper floor[68]

The columned courtyard and portico of the former synagogue,
transformed into a cultural and exhibition centre, 2019

---

[68] Image: 'Synagogue in Offenbach at Goethestrasse 5' © Leo Baeck Institute,
https://www.lbi.org/griffinger/record/226635.

Dr Herbert Strauss was appointed headmaster; his teaching staff had all been made redundant in public schools. The opening was marked with a celebratory event in the hall of the Jewish community centre. An initial intake of 75 pupils was divided into three classes and on their first day, Tuesday 17 April 1934, they gathered to have their photo taken in the school grounds.

Karola (back row, left) with her class on the opening of the
Jüdische Bezirksschule, April 1934

As the photo makes clear, this was a coeducational school. The register shows that most of the children lived close by and that, being less than 13 years old, Karola was one of the younger pupils, so started in Class I. She was not the only Karola, nor the only Grünebaum. As well as each pupil's date of birth, the register also recorded their father's name and occupation. The listing gives an interesting insight into the economic profile of the Jewish community at that time. Fifteen of the 26 were described as businessmen, four were tailors, two worked in the leather industry, and there was one each of doctor, manufacturer, wine merchant and government official. Finally, there was one butcher, Friedrich.

Ordn.-Nr.	Name des Kindes	Der Eltern			Des Kindes				Erste Aufnahme		Eintritt in Offenbach
		Name	Wohnung	Beruf	Geburtsort	Geburtszeit	Religion	Schulklasse	Ort	Zeit	

The 1934 *Jüdische Bezirksschule* register, listing each pupil
(including Karola Günebaum), their address and a parent's occupation

Irmgard Lorch was also a pupil at the school.[69] She was a couple of years younger than Karola and enrolled a year later. In the first volume of her memoir, she wrote about her impressions and experiences:

> For the first time, I went to school with boys. They seemed silly to us eleven-year-old girls and we took little notice of them. Also for the first time I was immersed in a totally Jewish community. We greeted

[69] Irmgard Lorch came from a wealthy Jewish family that lived in August-Bebel Ring, Offenbach. In 1938 they emigrated to the UK, where she took the name Joan and later married Peter Staple. Dr I J Staple became an eminent biologist, eventually settling in the USA, where she died in 2022, aged 99 years.

each other with 'Shalom' instead of 'Heil Hitler' and
sang the *Hatikvah* (Jewish National Anthem) instead
of 'Die Fahne hoch'. We had interesting classes about
Judaism, given by our rabbi, Herr Dr Max Dienemann,
a well-known scholar and pioneer of Liberal Judaism.
While 13-year-old boys had their Bar Mizvah, we girls
had nothing to recognize our coming of age. (Bat
Mizvahs did not exist yet.) But Dr Dienemann gave
classes just for us girls and made us feel less excluded.[70]

The school curriculum included the usual range of academic
subjects: languages, mathematics, science and religion, but what
distinguished it from the state schools was its educational objective.
Its primary aim was to prepare pupils for life in another country,
in other words to make them *'auswanderungsreif'* (emigration
ready) and, more specifically, ready to live in Palestine or the
USA.[71] With that in mind, lessons included Hebrew, shorthand,
typewriting, bookkeeping and training for manual trades and
craft professions, and even agriculture, for which the school had
both workshops and a large garden.[72] Karola would have started
to learn English here too.

Being a Jewish school meant that the school community
celebrated Jewish festivals. One of these is Purim, commemorating
the salvation of the Jewish people in ancient Persia from a plot
to annihilate them in a single day.[73] In 1935 it fell on Sunday
17 February and, being a joyous event, the pupils and teachers

---

[70] Joan Lorch Staple, *Chance and Choice: My First Thirty Years* (United States:
Lulu.com, 2007).
[71] Klaus Werner, 'Juden in Offenbach am Main 1933-45. Gemeinderleben –
Sozialstruktur – Verfolgung und Vernichtung' (Abschlussarbeit zur Erlangung
des Magister Artium im Fachbereich Geschichtswissenschaften, Frankfurt-am-
Main, Johann Wolfgang Goethe-Universität, 1986).
[72] Staple, *Chance and Choice*.
[73] 'What Is Purim?', Chabad.org, https://www.chabad.org/holidays/purim/
article_cdo/aid/645309/jewish/What-Is-Purim.htm.

dressed up accordingly. Karola wore baggy checked trousers and a beret, and took central place in the group photograph.

Karola and other pupils in fancy dress to celebrate Purim
at the Jewish District School, February 1935

The initial plan was to expand the school, adding classes for older children, and the school roll did indeed increase to over 100 in its second year. However, as more and more families and the staff themselves emigrated, numbers declined and by December 1938 only 30 names remained on the register. In fact, Karola was herself a pupil there for less than a year, but not because of emigration. She left school before her 14th birthday and on Monday 15 April 1935 started a three-year business apprenticeship with a leather goods company. The owner was Jewish and someone in a senior position was a family friend, which probably helped her to get her first job.[74]

---

[74] Letters from Karola to Otto Stein, 3 March and 25 October 1960.

A Career in Leather

Work in the leather industry has now been mentioned several times in this narrative. Sophie's father was a *Portefeuiller*, as was the father of a school pupil, while another was a shoemaker. In addition, Friedrich's great-uncle, Abraham, owned a leather business; his brother, Albert, was a shoe sales representative; and Sophie's younger brother, Siegfried, was also a maker of fine leather goods. The building in which the Grünebaum family lived was owned by a leather wholesaler, and Karola found employment in a leather goods company. The reason for the concentration on this one activity was that leather working had become the largest industry in Offenbach.

It started to expand there at the beginning of the nineteenth century. The ruling nobility created conditions that made the city attractive for industrial development, in contrast to the restrictive practices across the river in Frankfurt, where the emphasis was on banking and other financial services. As a result, there was substantial commercial investment and the leather sector experienced major growth, although it continued to be characterised by many small and medium-sized enterprises, rather than large concerns, and many still operated with 'home working'.[75] With this expansion, the range of products also widened to include purses, wallets, handbags, briefcases, photo albums, cigar cases, shoes, saddlery, equestrian clothing, bookbinding and other fancy goods. Specialist expertise developed to combine leather with wood and to decorate items with saffian (coloured goatskin) or silk. Although initially

---

[75] '1776 - Geburtsstunde Des Offenbacher Leder-Gewerbes', Stadt Offenbach, https://www.offenbach.de/gaeste/stadtgeschichte/geschichte-offenbach/18-jahrhundert/geburt-offenbacher-leder.php; 'Die Entwicklung der Offenbacher Lederwarenindustrie', in Wolfgang Jäger, *Vom Handwerk zur Industrie: Entstehung und Entwicklung des Ledergewerbes in Offenbach am Main: Festschrift zum 75 Jährigen Bestehen des Deutschen Ledermuseums mit dem Angeschlossenen Deutschen Schuhmuseum, am 13. März 1992* (Offenbach am Main: Deutsches Ledermuseum/Deutsches Schuhmuseum, 1992).

distinguished by an emphasis on creative, fashionable, luxury items, the industry diversified to meet the growing market for more affordable consumer goods. By the end of the nineteenth century, Offenbach was the largest centre for leather working across the German states and had a global reputation. Of the 236 factories in the city in 1871, a quarter were making leather goods and by the early twentieth century an estimated 10,000 workers depended on the leather industry. In 1914 three-quarters of its production was exported and, as early as 1917, a Leather Museum opened, which also supported the training of young designers and craftsmen.[76]

The possibilities for Jewish involvement in the leather industry opened up with emancipation, as restrictions on Jewish business activities were reduced. Jews engaged in producing and trading in finished goods, rather than tanning, since their technical and commercial skills, well developed through experience in textiles and clothing, could be adapted and applied to leather. Many companies were set up and owned by Jews, who provided work for thousands of others, mainly immigrants from eastern Europe.[77] They were credited with playing a major and pioneering role in advancing the industry, but in turn many members of the Jewish community became dependent on its success. In fact, it has been suggested that the main source of income for families in Bürgel in the 1920s was the production of leather goods.[78]

The growth of the leather industry also stimulated businesses producing metal accessories, such as clasps, locks and zips for wallets, briefcases, bags, camera cases and cigar boxes. One such

[76] More than a century later, the museum is still open, although much less remains of the leather industry, https://www.ledermuseum.de/.
[77] 'Leather Industry & Trade', Jewish Virtual Library, https://www.jewishvirtuallibrary.org/leather-industry-trade.
[78] 'Jüdische Gemeinde - Bürgel (Hessen)', Aus der Geschichte der Jüdischen Gemeinden im Deutschen Sprachraum, https://www.xn--jdische-gemeinden-22b.de/index.php/gemeinden/a-b/499-buergel-hessen.

company was owned by Adolph Merzbach, a Jewish entrepreneur, whose factory was at 110 Kaiserstrasse, just a few steps away from the synagogue. However, there was insufficient space here to expand and, as demand increased, he bought a more spacious seventeenth century water-powered grain mill and converted it to work metal. That mill was about 70 kilometres to the east of Offenbach in the small Bavarian village of Obersinn, employing members of the long-established and significant Jewish community in the adjoining village of Mittelsinn.[79] In 1898 Merzbach decided to sell his business and it was jointly bought by Karola's (Catholic) uncle, Friedrich Kühn (husband of Rosette), his brother and Herr Neeb, who previously worked for Merzbach. As Merzbach was a highly regarded brand, the company name was initially retained, while the mill was converted to electrical power. However, once the Nazis took control of government, all business connections with Jews needed to be removed, so in 1941 Merzbach became Neeb und Kühn. Friedrich's son, Wilhelm, and then his grandson, Roland, succeeded Friedrich in running the business, which thrived both before and after WW2. At one time the company owned 47 patents and sold its prestigious products across the world. During the war, however, it was required to produce components for armaments, a vital function that gave its Jewish workers some protection from deportation.[80]

---

[79] 'Jüdische Gemeinde - Mittelsinn (Unterfranken/Bayern)', Aus der Geschichte der Jüdischen Gemeinden im Deutschen Sprachraum, https://www.xn--jdische-gemeinden-22b.de/index.php/gemeinden/m-o/1327-mittelsinn-unterfranken-bayern.

[80] In more recent times, the company experienced financial difficulties and was finally dissolved in 2013.

The Neeb und Kühn factory building and former Kühn family home in
Obersinn (Bavaria), photographed in 2012 after its closure

Examples of fasteners for leather goods produced at the
Neeb und Kühn factory (post 1945)

Also amongst the Jewish entrepreneurs in Offenbach were two brothers, Adolf and Nathan Schmidt, who founded their company A N Schmidt & Co before WW1. It produced handbags and travel goods and became a well-known name in the trade. After the war, they opened six retail stores in major cities, including one in Offenbach, under the name Alligator. It was here that Karola embarked on her apprenticeship. The business was located at 63–65 Frankfurterstrasse, almost opposite the Grünebaums' apartment, so they could probably see her workplace from its window. Exactly three years later, a few weeks before her 17th birthday, she successfully completed her training and on Friday 15 April 1938 took up a permanent position in the Despatch and Costing Department on a salary of RM458 per month.

Family Life under Nazi Terror

Nazi Control over Everyday Life

After the Nazis gained power, and through the years of Karola's apprenticeship, Germany was transformed into a totalitarian state and the party leaders set about realising their ideological goals of rearmament, military expansion and racial purification.[81] Jews and other groups considered to be racially, biologically or socially unfit were subjected to hundreds of laws, decrees and regulations that restricted every aspect of their public and private lives. As early as March 1933, Dachau Concentration Camp opened and was used to incarcerate anyone considered to be an enemy of the Reich. In the same year, legislation was passed mandating the forced sterilisation or castration of individuals of mixed race or with health conditions thought to be hereditary, such as deafness, epilepsy or alcoholism. Jews were banned from posts in the civil service, the judiciary, universities and other state-funded institutions; professions such as medicine, dentistry and journalism; and from entering cultural and entertainment venues, such as theatres, cinemas and libraries. The paramilitary 'brownshirts' and the equally violent SS made it increasingly difficult for Jewish businesses to continue trading.[82] Excluded

---

[81] For a summary of the laws and decrees that transformed Germany from a democracy to a dictatorship, see 'Law, Justice and the Holocaust', Holocaust Encyclopedia, https://encyclopedia.ushmm.org/content/en/article/law-justice-and-the-holocaust.

[82] The 'brownshirts' were members of the *Sturmabteilung* (the SA or Assault

from public contracts, they were subjected to boycott campaigns; their customers were threatened, intimidated and physically attacked; and their premises were ransacked and looted.

Public notice calling for a boycott of Jewish businesses on 1 April 1933

In 1935, the Nuremberg Laws stripped non-Aryans of their citizenship and the rights that went with it, and banned intermarriages and sexual relations between Jews and people of 'German blood'.[83] Then, under a law passed in January 1938,

Division), a paramilitary wing of the Nazi Party. Its activities included providing protection at Nazi rallies; fighting paramilitary units of opposing parties; and intimidating groups perceived as enemies of the state. The SS was the *Schutzstaffel* (Protection Squad), also a Nazi paramilitary organisation, which had been established by Hitler and was fiercely loyal to him. Its role after 1933 included enforcing racial policy and general policing, and it developed into the state's primary agency of security, surveillance and terror. In 1934, under Hitler's orders, the SS carried out a murderous purge of the SA because it was perceived to have become a threat to the Führer.

[83] The Nuremberg Laws were two laws enacted in September 1935. They were the *Reichsbürgergesetz* (Reich Citizenship Law) and the *Gesetz zum Schutze des*

the government required Jews to identify themselves in ways that distinguished them from the rest of the population.[84] Not only were they obliged to carry identity cards stamped with a red 'J', but a subsequent order forced men and women to add 'Israel' and 'Sara' respectively to their given names. These additions were entered on each individual's birth record in local Registry Offices. Friedrich's and Karola's registrations (and presumably Sophie's, which has not been found) were amended accordingly. All the measures increased the ability of the Nazis to discriminate against Jews and control their destiny.

Deutschen Blutes und der Deutschen Ehre (Law for the Protection of German Blood and German Honour). 'The Nuremberg Race Laws', Holocaust Encyclopedia, https://encyclopedia.ushmm.org/content/en/article/the-nuremberg-race-laws.
[84] Gesetz über die Änderung von Familiennamen und Vornamen (Namensänderungsgesetz). See 'Law on Alteration of Family and Personal Names', Holocaust Encyclopedia, https://encyclopedia.ushmm.org/content/en/timeline-event/holocaust/1933-1938/law-on-alteration-of-family-and-personal-names.

Offenbach, 19th December 1938.

According to §2 of the regulation of 17th August 1938, Karola Grünebaum has the additional forename "Sara" with effect from 1 January 1939.

The Registrar
Müller

Note added to Karola's birth registration imposing a name change
(with translation)

The November Pogroms and Detention in Buchenwald

Daily life for Jews became ever more difficult and hazardous. Driven by fascist propaganda and orders from party leaders, attacks were carried out on more and more Jewish families and properties under the banner of *Judenaktion* (Jewish Action). The Grünebaum family was one of many in Offenbach that fell victim. On the night of 9 November 1938, their apartment was ransacked. Around the same time, the *Jüdische Bezirksschule* was trashed and the synagogue building set on fire.[85] However, as it was one of the largest and most impressive buildings in the town, it was seen by some in authority as a useful future asset. For this reason, the fire brigade was called to extinguish the flames and it suffered only limited damage. Much more worryingly, two days later, on Friday 11 November, Friedrich was detained and transported to Buchenwald concentration camp, where he became prisoner number 23305.[86] Located 280 kilometres northeast of Offenbach, near Weimar, Buchenwald had opened the previous year. He was just one of the many thousands who were incarcerated at this time.

Germany has a legendary tradition of bureaucracy and

[85] In the past, the attacks on Jews and Jewish property that took place across Germany were labelled 'Kristallnacht' (Night of Broken Glass). This term is now widely rejected because it falsely implies that violence only affected property, only took place at night and only occurred on one day. Instead, the term 'November pogroms' is considered more appropriate.

[86] In 1951 the International Tracing Service (ITS) certified that Friedrich had been incarcerated in Buchenwald Camp from 11 to 30 November 1938. Document 6.3.3.2/89590144/ITS Digital Archive, Arolsen Archives. There is, however, no definitive evidence of his date of arrival. The ITS drew inferences from a document listing the release of a Julius Friedrich Grünebaum on 30 November 1938, which gives his prisoner number as 23305. Document 1.1.5.1/5278175/ITS Digital Archive, Arolsen Archives. Another document shows that this number was in the range of those allocated to new prisoners on 11 November 1938. Document 1.1.5.1/5278097/ITS Digital Archive, Arolsen Archives.

meticulous record keeping that can be traced back to the Middle Ages, and this continued through the Third Reich.[87] The Nazis kept detailed reports of movements into and out of camps and these provide an insight into the scale and speed of the detentions. After Buchenwald opened, the number of internees rose rapidly with the arrest of so-called 'asocial elements' and by July 1938 its population was already around 7,700.[88] The rate of expansion accelerated in the wake of the November pogroms and on the evening of 11 November the headcount was already 10,735. However, 18 prisoners were then released, a few of them listed as Jewish, but most categorised as *Arbeitsscheu* (work-shy), *Schutzhäftling* (in protective custody) or *Polizeihäftling* (police prisoner).[89,90] In their place came 3,275 prisoners, all Jewish men, 27 of them from Offenbach, including Friedrich. By midnight the recorded camp population had risen to 13,992. It has been estimated that in the days after the pogrom, a total of 9,815 Jews were taken to Buchenwald, 82 of whom came from Offenbach.[91]

A Gestapo officer recorded his memory of accompanying those Jewish men on that journey.[92] He recalled there were two

---

[87] Thea Miller, 'The German Registry: The Evolution of a Recordkeeping Model', *Archival Science* 3, no. 1 (March 2003): 43–63, https://doi. org/10.1007/BF02438928.

[88] 'Buchenwald', Yad Vashem, n.d., https://www.yadvashem.org/odot_pdf/ Microsoft Word - 6088.pdf.

[89] Document 1.1.5.1./5278101/ITS Digital Archive, Arolsen Archives.

[90] These are just a few of the categories used by the Nazis to classify prisoners, who were forced to wear badges or uniforms that identified the reason for their incarceration. For example, those considered work-shy had to wear an inverted black triangle. Those in 'protective custody' were supposedly imprisoned for their own safety, but this was just an excuse to detain those identified as asocial or regime opponents, and other targeted groups. 'Police prisoners' were prisoners awaiting trial.

[91] Eugen Kogon, *Der SS-Staat: Das System der Deutschen Konzentrationslager*, genehmigte Lizenzausgabe (Hamburg: Nikol, 2009).

[92] Renate Hess, Lisette Nichtweiss, and Ingrid Zahedi, *Juden-Deportation aus Darmstadt 1942/43*. (Darmstadt: Magistrat der Stadt Darmstadt, 1992), 21–22.

busloads, each with about 40 prisoners, and they set off at about 8am. He was in the second vehicle, together with another Gestapo officer and three members of the SS. It was his role to protect the Jews from violence, presumably from the SS officers, since he also wrote that they behaved properly throughout the journey. On the way they made a stop and he not only bought food for the men, but also postcards for them to send news to their families. He heard later that his colleagues on the other bus, which arrived at Buchenwald one hour earlier, wanted to warn him about what would happen on arrival and the treatment the Jews would receive, but they were unable to do this. When the bus stopped, 20 SS men with sticks were waiting and, as soon as the men got out, they were herded into the camp and beaten. He was shocked and reported it to his superiors the next day and said that he was close to a nervous breakdown, not knowing what would become of those men.

Newly arrived prisoners, with shaven heads, stand at attention
during a roll call in Buchenwald concentration camp, November 1938[93]

The Jewish detainees were held in a *Sonderlager* (Special Camp),
a separate area enclosed by barbed wire within the main camp,
where they were subjected to exceptionally cruel treatment and
terrible living conditions.[94] Their accommodation, adjacent to the
parade ground, was in five barn-like structures about 100m long
and 12m wide. without windows, heating or even a floor.[95] One

[93] Image © United States Holocaust Memorial Museum, courtesy of Robert
A. Schmuhl.
[94] Megargee G P (2009). Encyclopedia of Camps and Ghettos, 1933-1945.
Volume I Early Camps, Youth Camps, and Concentration Camps and Sub-
Camps under the SS-Business Administration Main Office, Part A. United
States Holocaust Memorial Museum. Indiana University Press, Bloomington.
https://www.ushmm.org/research/publications/encyclopedia-camps-ghettos;
'Buchenwald Concentration Camp', Holocaust Research Project, http://www.
holocaustresearchproject.org/othercamps/buchenwald.html.
[95] Harry Stein and Gedenkstätte Buchenwald, eds, *Buchenwald Concentration*

side was lined with sleeping shelves, divided into compartments 135cm wide and 50cms high, within which four men would have to sleep. There were no blankets and sanitary facilities comprised two open latrines and a small washroom. Some of the men were forced to work up to 15 hours a day in the infamous quarry within the camp boundary:

> The Nazis' object at this point was to exert pressure on the Jews and their families to emigrate from Germany within the shortest possible time. Thus in the winter of 1938–1939, 9,370 Jews were released after their families, as well as Jewish and international organisations, had made arrangements for their emigration. Of the Kristallnacht detainees, in the short time that these prisoners were held in Buchenwald, 600 were killed, committed suicide, or died from other causes.[96]

Certainly, the release of a number of Offenbach detainees was conditional on them leaving the country.[97] Whether Friedrich was amongst those forced to agree to emigrate is unclear but, on Wednesday 30 November, after nearly three weeks' incarceration, he was released and able to return home.

Camp, 1937-1945: a Guide to the Permanent Historical Exhibition (Göttingen: Wallstein, 2004).
[96] 'Buchenwald Concentration Camp'.
[97] Klaus Werner, 'Die "Reichskristallnacht" in Offenbach', in *Zur Geschichte der Juden in Offenbach am Main. Unter der Herrschaft des Nationalsozialismus*, vol. 1 (Offenbach am Main: Magistrat der Stadt Offenbach, 1988), 98–113.

```
Anlage zur Veränderungs-          K.L.Buchenwald, den 30.November 1938
meldung vom 30.Nov.1938.

              Namentliche Liste der am 30.November 1938 entlassenen
                              Aktions-Juden.

Lfd.Nr. 1 Hftl.Nr.26137 Aaron, Ludwig
        2          29333 Abraham, Nathan
        3          26559 Abraham, Nathan
        4          21426 Adler, Josef
        5          21411 Adler, Joachim
        6          26808 Adler, Julius
        7          26247 Altmaier, Hermann
        8          26846 Appel, Hermann
        9                Abon, Artur, geb. 21.11.92 Hadamar
       10          26022 Aumann, Hugo
       11          29348 Bacharach, Ludwig
       12          21128 Bachrach, Jessias
       13          27269 Badrian, Wilhelm
       14          29974 Baer, Berthold
       15          26172 Bamberger, Julius

       80          26978 Goldschmitt, David
       81          22687 Golombek, Jock, Mordka
       82          24342 Gottschalk, Sali
       83          24559 Gottschalk, Siegfried
       84          23243 Grün, Alfred
       85          29880 Grünbaum, Heinrich
       86          25008 Grünebaum, Arthur
       87          23305 Grünebaum, Friedrich, Julius  ←
       88          24686 Grünebaum, Julius
       89          25303 Grünebaum, Leo
       90          24970 Grünewald, Henry
       91          24516 Gümprich, Max
       92          21615 Gunzenhäuser, Aron
       93          21469 Gutenstein, Alfred
       94          21798 Gutheim, Walter
       95          21449 Haas, Willi
```

Extracts from Buchenwald concentration camp record of
prisoner releases on 30 November 1938[98]

Despite being 'freed' from captivity, it was now impossible
for Friedrich to earn a living. Non-Jewish employers refused to
take on any new Jewish workers and the aggressive boycotting of
Jewish businesses meant they were already overstaffed. His only
income came from a Georg Hellwig, who gave him occasional
jobs. However, Hellwig later confirmed that this was not really

[98] Reports Detailing Changes Concerning Prisoners in Concentration Camp
Buchenwald (men), 1938. Document 1.1.5.1./5278175/ ITS Digital Archive,
Arolsen Archives.

employment, it was more a case of doing someone a favour and the payment was 'more at the level of a tip than a wage'. (T)[99] So from the time that she started her apprenticeship, Karola was the family's main breadwinner.[100] Her parents depended on her financially but, as controls over Jewish businesses and workers were progressively tightened, her appointment came to an abrupt end.

In 1938, the Nazi leaders issued a series of decrees that first required compilation of a register of Jewish-owned enterprises, then made it illegal for Jews to conduct certain types of trade, before requiring the 'Aryanisation' of those businesses. Finally, they decreed that all Jewish-owned concerns had to close before 1 January 1939. Branches of the Alligator chain were duly categorised as Jewish-owned businesses. Like many Jewish proprietors, the Schmidt brothers were coerced into selling well below their firm's true value, reportedly to their business manageress.[101] However, some years previously they had set up a subsidiary company in London and in 1938 were able to emigrate with their families. Later that same year, the reincarnated Alligator Leather Goods Company Ltd began manufacturing leather goods again, but this time in County Durham, England.[102]

---

[99] Letter from Otto Stein (solicitor) to Karola, 19 June 1959.
[100] Statement by Karola, 14 March 1960.
[101] Benno Nietzel, *Handeln und Überleben: Jüdische Unternehmer aus Frankfurt am Main 1924–1964*, Kritische Studien zur Geschichtswissenschaft, Band 204 (Göttingen: Vandenhoeck & Ruprecht, 2012).
[102] Herbert Loebl, 'Government-Financed Factories and the Establishment of Industries by Refugees in the Special Area of the North of England 1937–1961' (Masters Thesis, Durham, 1978), http://etheses.dur.ac.uk/10025/.

den Herrn Oberbürgermeister der
Reichshauptstadt Berlin,
Stadtsteueramt Abteilung C,

        B e r l i n   C 2 ,
    Stadthaus.

                                26.9.1938.

            22.9.1938.

Betr. Fa. Alligator Lederwaren Kom.Ges. Adolf
      Schmidt & Co., Zweigniederlassung Offen-
      bach a.M.

        Auf Ihre Anfrage vom 22.9.1938 teilen
    wir Ihnen mit, dass die obengenannte Firm
    bei uns in das Verzeichnis der jüdischen
    Gewerbebetriebe aufgenommen wurde, da der
    Gesellschaft Adolf Schmidt, Frankfurt a.M
    Jude ist. Nach dem Handelsregistereintrag
    ist der Hauptsitz der Firma in Berlin.

To The Lord Mayor of the Imperial Capital Berlin
City Tax Office Department C

Berlin C2, City Hall
26th September 1938, 22nd September 1938

Re: The Alligator Leather Goods Limited Partnership. Adolf Schmidt & Co.
Offenbach am Main branch

In response to your inquiry of 22nd September 1938, I can inform you that the above-named firm is in our directory of Jewish businesses because the Adolf Schmidt company is Jewish. According to the commercial register, its head office is in Berlin.

Letter sent by authorities in Offenbach to Berlin confirming that Alligator
Lederwaren was a Jewish business (with translation)[103]

---

[103] © Offenbach City Archive.

On Saturday 31 December 1938, the day before all Jewish businesses had to shut, Karola was made redundant. She had been in post for less than nine months and, although she received a glowing testimonial, there was no possibility of finding any comparable alternative job. Her employer obliquely explained that she had left 'in view of the general changes' (T).

```
ALLIGATOR ZENTRALE OFFENBACH a.M.
              Frankfurter Straße 63 - 65


          Z e u g n i s
          ============


                    Tag  12. Dezember 1938.


Fräulein Karola G r ü n e b a u m, geboren am 12. Mai 1921 ist
am 15. April 1935 als kfm. Lehrling in unser Haus eingetreten.
Ihre Lehrzeit beendigte sie am 15. April 1938.

Fräulein Grünebaum hatte in ihrer Lehre bei uns bestens Gelegen-
heit, sich mit den Arbeiten aller Abteilungen gut vertraut zu
machen, und sie hat es verstanden, mit Hilfe ihrer guten Auffas-
sungsgabe alle an sie herangetretenen Arbeiten zu unserer Zu-
friedenheit zu erledigen. Nach Beendigung ihrer Lehrzeit wurde
sie vorzugsweise in der Expedition- und Kalkulationsabteilung
verwandt, wo sie sich auch bestens bewährt hat.
Ihre Führung war stets einwandfrei.

In Anbetracht der allgemeinen Umstellung verlässt Fräulein
Grünebaum mit dem 31. Dezember 1938 unser Haus.


                    Alligator Lederwaren
                 Kommanditgesellschaft
                    Adolf Schmidt & Co.
                          gez.Unterschrift
```

Karola's reference from her employer, Alligator

ALLIGATOR HEADQUARTERS OFFENBACH AM MAIN
Frankfurter Strasse 63-65

Testimonial

Date 12 December 1938

Miss Karola Grünebaum, born 12 May 1921, joined our company on 15 April 1935 as a commercial apprentice. Her apprenticeship ended on 15 April 1938.

During her apprenticeship, Miss Grünebaum had great opportunities to familiarise herself with the work of all the departments and, with her good intelligence, she learned how to do all the work and it was done to our satisfaction. After her apprenticeship ended, she was mainly employed in the Despatch and Costing Department, where she also performed very well. Her conduct was always impeccable.

In view of the general changes, Miss Grünebaum left our company on 31 December 1938.

Alligator Leather Goods Limited Partnership, Adolf Schmidt & Co.

[signed]

Karola's reference from her employer, Alligator (translation)

The Aryanisation process explains why in November 1938 the stamp in the Grünebaums' rent book changed from 'Löwenberger & Scheuer' to 'Georg Hellwig'. Löwenberger and Scheuer were also Jewish and, in that month, under duress, they sold their business and properties to Georg Hellwig, also a leather trader. The transfer included the main building at 70 Frankfurter Strasse, as well as the adjacent premises where Friedrich had opened his butcher's shop 18 years earlier. So Hellwig became the Grünebaums' landlord, but he was also

Friedrich's benefactor, occasionally giving him money for doing odd jobs.[104]

Meanwhile, Karola was taken on temporarily as a house help by Leonie Löwenberger, the wife of Wilhelm, the former business co-owner, whose family home was nearby at 18 Körnerstrasse.[105] But when Leonie's regular maidservant returned from a lengthy stay in hospital, that job also came to an end. In her testimonial, Karola was described by her new employer as diligent and willing, executing all that was required to her employer's complete satisfaction.

An Unexpected Contact from a Special Nonagenarian

Although I have written at some length about my grandparents' married life, their family home and my mother's childhood, my words are largely based on documents, photographs and other archival sources. Very little is based on personal testimony from Karola or anyone else and I had no expectation of ever being able to add to this. After all, my mother would have been 100 years old in 2021 and it seemed highly unlikely that I would find anyone who knew her who had not only survived the Holocaust but also reached a similar age. So when I received a message from a local historian in Offenbach saying that she had been contacted by someone whose 94-year-old grandmother claimed to have been a friend of Karola, I was rather taken aback and sceptical. Not only because this person was so much younger, but also because

---

[104] Georg Hellwig died in 1977 and ownership of the property passed to his son, also Georg. It was finally sold in 2018 when in need of extensive refurbishment.

[105] Wilhelm Löwenberger was a decorated soldier, having been awarded the Iron Cross in WW1. He died in August 1938. Leonie escaped via Portugal to Cuba in 1941, and to New York in 1944, where she died in 1969. Hauschke-Wicklaus and Geschichtswerkstatt Offenbach, *Jüdische Bürgerinnen und Bürger erinnern sich*, 186.

there was no mention of this person's name in any of my mother's papers or in the pupil register of the *Jüdische Bezirksschule* that my mother had attended. Several days passed and I heard nothing more, so assumed my scepticism had been justified. Then I received an email that proved me totally wrong:

> *18 December 2020* My name is Bettina Mehner. I am 43 years old and I live with my husband and my two children in Gross-Zimmern near Darmstadt.
>
> Every day I telephone my grandmother, Wilma Feick, who lives in Darmstadt-Eberstadt. In January she will be 95 years old, but despite her great age she is still in such good health that she can live alone in her apartment. A few weeks ago, she told me about a newspaper article in which somebody suggested setting up a kindergarten just for Jewish children. I was astonished how concerned she was about this article. She told me that in her view it was wrong to separate children on the basis of their faith because they would not then build friendships with each other. In connection with this, she told me for the first time of a girlfriend from her childhood days. Karola was a Jewish girl, but that didn't make any difference to her. She often visited the family and ate with them. However, Karola was never allowed to come to her house because my grandmother's grandmother was pro Hitler. I don't know why she had been allowed to visit Karola.
>
> She was very preoccupied with this issue and she spoke to me about it repeatedly. She told me that at some point Karola said to her that she would soon 'flutter' away. My grandmother didn't really understand what she meant, but didn't ask her any

more about it. She was just 13 years old and probably still too young to understand what was going on in Germany. Some time after, Karola was gone and she never heard from her again.

The newspaper article brought back many memories to my grandmother and she kept on talking about Karola. Not knowing whether her friend's escape had been successful seemed to torment her. When she mentioned to me for the first time that Karola's surname was Grünebaum, I began to search the internet. However, I wrongly assumed that Karola lived in Eberstadt, where my grandmother grew up. That's why, at first, I couldn't find any information. It was only a few days ago that I found out that Karola met my grandmother when she was visiting her grandparents in Offenbach.

That was a decisive bit of information. Even as we were speaking to each other on the telephone, I found an article online about the laying of the Stolpersteine (stumbling stones) in Offenbach in 2019. My grandmother confirmed that Karola's parents had a butcher's shop and even knew the street name and house number. So I was able to tell my grandmother that her friend's escape had been successful. She was completely speechless – after 81 years she finally had certainty! (T)[106]

It is impossible to convey the excitement and emotions that I felt when reading this message for the first time, realising that, not only did it connect me to someone who knew both my mother as a young person and my maternal grandparents, but also someone

---

[106] Karola's escape and the laying of *Stolpersteine* (stumbling stones) are described later in this story.

who felt so passionately about the injustice Karola had endured that she was still concerned about my mother's fate more than 80 years later. To that excitement was added incredulity when I discovered that Oma Wilma (Grandma Wilma) also had the most phenomenal childhood memory and was able to tell me more about the Grünebaums and their home than I could ever have imagined. Of course, I immediately wanted to go to Germany and meet this person, but the COVID-19 pandemic made such travel frustratingly impossible. So over the next 18 months we exchanged messages, and she answered questions and spontaneously shared details that brought the family to life in a way that could only have come from having been there with them.[107]

Karola and Wilma first met in about 1931 when Wilma went to stay with her grandparents during the school holidays. They also lived at 69 Luisenstrasse, but in an apartment separate from the main building above their greengrocery business. Wilma was then just five years old, while Karola was ten and still a pupil at the girls' state school. Despite the age difference they became good friends, playing together and with other children who lived nearby, and on a few occasions they ate together in the Grünebaums' kitchen. Her memory of Karola was of a happy girl who laughed a lot and she recalled in particular the fun they had surreptitiously sliding down the banister in the stairwell.

Of course, Wilma also got to know Karola's parents and became very fond of Sophie, who looked after her during visits. She remembered her as a warm and kindly woman with slightly wavy hair that hung loosely down her neck. Friedrich was very different and she had much less contact with him. He was not unfriendly, but was a little distant, did not speak much and at times seemed quite strict. She remembered that he was a butcher

---

[107] Oma Wilma did not use the internet, so communication was through her granddaughter, Bettina Mehner.

by trade and that downstairs was a butcher's shop, which she was able to describe in some detail. Customers had to climb two steps to get to the entrance and once inside they queued on the right to be served from behind the long counter that ran down the left-hand side, while behind the shop was a smokehouse.[108]

Generally, Wilma's account fitted neatly with the narrative I had already compiled with information from other sources and her description of the butcher's shop closely matched the photograph of Friedrich and Greta in the shop entrance taken on the day Karola was born. But there was one point from my narrative with which she vehemently disagreed. In contrast to the comment in the *Offenbach-Post*, she was adamant that the Grünebaum family did not seem poor. She recalled that the apartment was the larger of two on the first floor and that it was very spacious. Karola had her own bedroom overlooking Frankfurterstrasse and, in addition to a living room, there was also a large salon. Although the children were not allowed to play there, what she saw through the open door left a lasting impression. No one else she knew had such a large, well-furnished and elegantly decorated room and she remembered in particular the upholstered armchairs. How can these two conflicting perceptions be reconciled? To some extent they probably reflected the benchmarks against which the assessments were made. As already suggested, in comparison with the grand mansions occupied by some Jewish families in the early 1930s, the apartment would have seemed quite modest. However, it was large and the Grünebaums had been able to furnish it well when they married and had an income from their business, so it may well have appeared almost opulent to Wilma. And they

---

[108] Oma Wilma was unsure whether Friedrich was still working as a butcher in the shop downstairs when she first met him. However, according to the *Gewerberegister*, his business had already closed by 1931. If he was still working, she may have been mistaken about the date of her first visit. Alternatively, it may have reopened with a new proprietor.

were able to retain it, even when Friedrich had no regular income, because of the rent subsidies. So the quality of the accommodation and its furnishing would not have been a true reflection of their financial circumstances.

Wilma's grandmother and her daughter Wilhelmine (Wilma's 'Aunt Mim'), who lived with her, were both supporters of Hitler. However, they never said anything critical about the Grünebaum family, nor did they stop Wilma visiting them. Nevertheless, Wilma became aware of growing anti-Jewish sentiment. 'The Jews are our misfortune' (T) was a refrain she overheard many times, but as a very young girl never thought to question. She also witnessed the treatment meted out to Jews and one particular incident was burned into her memory. It happened while she was standing with her grandparents in Frankfurterstrasse watching the *Fastnacht* (Shrove Tuesday) parade. Cardboard figures could be seen on the floats and on one of them a Jew's head poked out from inside a box, while next to it stood an SA officer with his boot on the lid, pushing the Jew back in. Wilma remembered the crowd at the roadside laughing, but at that moment she looked up to Karola's bedroom window, where her friend was standing with her parents. They stopped watching immediately and closed the window. When the parade ended, her grandparents went for a coffee, but Wilma told them that she wanted to go and play with her friend. This she did and pretended that nothing untoward had happened. It was only much later that Wilma began to realise the enormity of the terror that had been perpetrated on the Jews and how abhorrent the parade scene had been. It made her wonder how she could have possibly let it pass without comment and not knowing what happened to Karola and her other Jewish friends had tormented her ever since. The recent newspaper article evoked vivid images in her mind, led her to voice her anxieties to her granddaughter and ultimately also brought us together, enabling me to provide answers to some of her questions and for my family story to be enriched by her memories.

As the years passed, Wilma and Karola had less and less contact, perhaps because of the age difference or because Karola had started work, and by 1939 they rarely saw each other. However, it did happen on one more notable occasion that Wilma remembers clearly and, moreover, her family was involved in one further remarkable encounter with Friedrich. I will write about both these incidents shortly, but in May 2022 I was finally able to visit Oma Wilma and her granddaughter, Bettina, in Darmstadt-Eberstadt. It was an exciting and emotional meeting for us both and another opportunity for me to hear at first hand the incredible recollections of this amazing lady.

Censored by the Census

The widespread discrimination and persecution of Jews that occurred throughout the 1930s may suggest that both the authorities and local communities knew which members of the population were Jewish. However, under the 1935 Nuremberg Laws, the Nazis had defined Jews not by religious affiliation but according to race. A person with three or four Jewish grandparents was legally considered to be a Jew, irrespective of whether or not they practised Judaism. If only two grandparents were Jewish, but that person was a member of the Jewish religious community or married to a Jew, they too were included. Otherwise, they were labelled a *Mischling ersten Grades* (mixed race of the first degree), while someone with only one Jewish grandparent was a *Mischling zweiten Grades* (mixed race of the second degree).

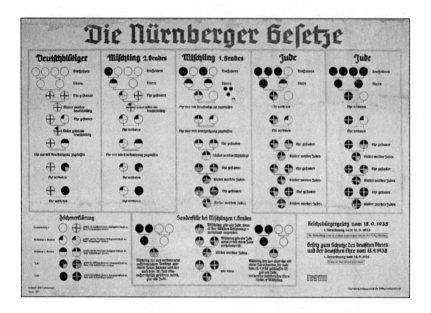

Categorisation of Jews under the Nuremberg Laws

On this basis, many Germans legally defined as Jews were not easy to recognise.[109] A considerable number had given up traditional practices and appearances and integrated into mainstream society. Some no longer practised Judaism and others had converted to Christianity. So, on 17 May 1939, the national population census was used to identify, label and count all those individuals who the Nazis considered to be Jews or *Mischlinge*. The head of the household was required to record on a supplementary card whether or not each resident's four grandparents were Jewish, resulting in every member of the household being racially defined by a four-letter code, ranging from NNNN, when none of the grandparents were Jews to JJJJ, when all of them were. Completion of the supplementary cards

---

[109] 'What Were the Nuremberg Laws?', My Jewish Learning, https://www.myjewishlearning.com/article/what-were-the-nuremberg-laws/.

would have seemed a further ominous development for Karola's extended family. Those defined as Jews must have expected the information to be used against them, while those so-called *Mischlinge* and non-Jews in *Mischehe* (mixed marriages) knew that they could no longer escape notice and would also be subjected to restrictions and discrimination.

Despite the repugnant purpose of what is now called the German Minority Census, the data in the returns provides an interesting snapshot of the family at a single point in time. For instance, it highlights the prevalence of interfaith relationships. Only eight of 30 family members had four Jewish grandparents. It also offers an insight into the location and composition of individual households, raising questions about how and why these changed over time.[110]

---

[110] Changes have been identified by comparing addresses in the census data with official annual address books and telephone directories for preceding years, which are available in the Offenbach City Archive and at https://www.ancestry.de/.

Address	Members of the household	Relationship to Karola	'Racial Status'
69 Luisenstr. Offenbach	Friedrich Grünebaum	Father	J J J J
	Sophie Grünebaum	Mother	J J J J
	Karola Grünebaum	-	J J J J
	Käthchen Ottenheimer	Cousin	J J J J
30 Bahnhofstr. Offenbach	Edmund Grünebaum	Uncle	J J J J
38 Hermannstr. Offenbach	Ernst Grünebaum	Cousin	J J J N N
	Katharina Grünebaum	Cousin	N N N N
7 Offenbacherstr. Bürgel	Salomon Reiss	Uncle	J J J J
	Lilli Reiss	Aunt	J J N N
	Gertrude Reiss	Cousin	J J J N
	Hertha Reiss	Cousin	J J J N
	Irene Reiss	Cousin	J J J N
	Martha Reiss	Cousin	J J J N
	Rosette Kaufmann	First cousin once removed	J J J J
18 Faltorstr. Bürgel	Maria Grünebaum	Aunt	N N N N
	Friedericke Grünebaum	Cousin	J J N N
	Rina Grünebaum	Cousin	J J N N
89D Mittelsinn Bavaria	Michel Reusch	Cousin	N N N N
	Greta Reusch	Cousin	N N J J
	Edgar Reusch	Nephew	N N N J
	Ludwig Reusch	Nephew	N N N J
89E Mittelsinn Bavaria	Wilhelm Kühn	Cousin	N N J J
	Anna Kühn	Cousin	N N N N
	Helmut Kühn	Nephew	N J N N
	Roland Kühn	Nephew	N J N N
141 Obersinn Bavaria	Friedrich Kühn	Uncle	N N N N
	Rosette Kühn	Aunt	J J J J
7 Wilhelm-Busch Str. Wiesbaden	Ewald Ortloff	Cousin	N N N N
	Else Ortloff	Cousin	N N J J
	Kurt Ortloff	Nephew	N N N J

The letters used for 'racial status' represent 'Ja' (J) or 'Nein' (N), indicating whether or not a grandparent was Jewish. They are ordered as follows: paternal grandfather, paternal grandmother, maternal grandfather, and maternal grandmother.

Nazi classification of Karola's close family members after the 1939 German Minority Census[111]

---

[111] The composition of households recorded in the German Minority Census

Although Karola had, as far as is known, grown up with just her parents in the 69 Luisenstrasse apartment, the census shows that by May 1939 her cousin, Käthchen Ottenheimer (*née* Grünebaum), who worked as a domestic servant, had moved in with them. Moreover, in the months before the census, Käthchen's father, Edmund Grünebaum (Friedrich's brother), moved to 30 Bahnhofstrasse, just 200 metres away. These two relocations were almost certainly connected. Until then, Edmund had spent his whole life in Bürgel and from about 1930 was living at 14 Faltorstrasse with his wife Rosa, his daughter Käthchen and his son-in-law Jakob Ottenheimer.[112] Both Edmund and Jakob were butchers and had a shop at that address. However, they then suffered a series of tragedies. Rosa and Jakob died within six weeks of each other in late 1934 and Käthchen's older brother, Hugo, died a few months later. One can only speculate, but perhaps Edmund was no longer able to continue the business on his own or, like Friedrich, was forced to close it for economic reasons, and the widowed Käthchen moved in with her aunt and uncle.

Faltorstrasse did remain the home of other family members. Friedrich's eldest brother, Ferdinand, had occupied a rented apartment at number 18 since the early 1920s, well before Edmund moved in two doors away.[113] A locksmith by trade, he had died in 1924, but the census shows that his widow,

is available on the MyHeritage website, https://www.myheritage.de/. Addresses and the 'racial status' of grandparents have been made available through Mapping the Lives, a project of Tracing the Past, a non-profit organisation in Berlin. https://www.mappingthelives.org/.

[112] The official address books and telephone directories show that in 1906 Edmund was living at 50 Langstrasse, but by no later than 1922 had moved down the road to 3 Langstrasse, before relocating just 200 metres to 14 Faltorstrasse.

[113] *Einwohnerverzeichnis der Industrie- und Handelsstadt Offenbach am Main Einschließlich Bürgel und Umgegend, 1922-23.* (Offenbach am Main: Seiboldsche Buchdruckerei Dohany, n.d.).

Maria (*née* Jobst) and their two unmarried daughters, Friederike ('Friedel') and Regina ('Rina'), continued to live there. In fact, they stayed there for the rest of their lives. However, by May 1939 their son, Ernst, had moved into the city centre with his wife, Katharina (*née* Englert). Also in Bürgel, just a short walk from Faltorstrasse, lived Sophie's eldest brother Salomon, with his wife and four daughters. They shared their accommodation at 7 Offenbacherstrasse with Rosette Kaufmann, whose marriage had ended in divorce. The daughter of Leopold Nachmann and Friedrich's cousin, Mathilde, she was a close friend to both sides of Karola's family and, as I will describe later, she would have a lot of contact with Karola over the following years.[114]

Another of Friedrich's siblings, Rosette, was then living with her husband, Friedrich Kühn, in Obersinn (Bavaria), the location of his metalworking factory. However, by May 1939 their children had married and dispersed. Eldest daughter Elisabeth ('Else') was with her husband Ewald Ortloff and son Kurt in Wiesbaden. The other two children did not move so far. They were neighbours in the village of Mittelsinn, just a couple of kilometres away. Greta was married to Michel Reusch with two sons, Edgar and Ludwig ('Ludo'), while Wilhelm Kühn had married Anna (*née* Stein) and also had two sons, Helmut and Roland.

Despite the threatening nature of the census questions, it seems that the data was never actually used to target individuals. The supplementary cards were delivered to the *Reichssippenamt* (Reich Genealogy Office), where they remained until after WW2.

---

[114] Mathilde was a younger sister of Heinrich Grünebaum, Karola's paternal grandfather.

Escape to Foreign Lands

Family Departures to Africa and the Americas

The relentlessly increasing subjugation and persecution of Jews across Germany was reflected in the flow of people leaving the country, although the numbers were also affected by the willingness of other countries to accept them. There were two periods of exceptionally high emigration.[115] The first followed soon after the Nazis came to power in 1933, when almost 40,000 Jews fled abroad. But it was the pogroms in November 1938 and the annexation of Austria earlier that year that prompted the largest movements. In the ten months after November 1938, an estimated 115,000 left the two countries, taking the total to around 400,000.[116] Initially, most travelled to neighbouring European states in the expectation that they would be able to return. Over time, however, more and more settled overseas, notably in Palestine, the USA, South America and the UK. The high taxation of those with any capital and the difficulty of converting assets into another currency meant that most had to leave with very little.

Amongst the early 'leavers' were members of both sides of

---

[115] Evans, *The Third Reich in Power, 1933–1939*, 555–602; 'German Jewish Refugees, 1933–1939', Holocaust Encyclopedia, https://encyclopedia.ushmm.org/content/en/article/german-jewish-refugees-1933-1939.

[116] Yad Vashem, the World Holocaust Remembrance Centre, estimates that previously there were 566,000 Jews in Germany and 185,000 in Austria, https://www.yadvashem.org/holocaust/faqs.html.

Karola's family and the outflow of her relatives and friends gathered pace as conditions worsened. Within a few years, strong social networks that had been focused on a small geographical area were torn apart as those fleeing Nazism dispersed across the globe. Nuclear families became divided because it was not possible or affordable for them all to escape. On her mother's side, the first to go was her uncle, Abraham Lipson, the widowed husband of Sophie's sister, Franziska. Abraham had been living with Salomon Reiss and his family at 7 Offenbacherstrasse (Bürgel), but he was born in Poland and returned there in May 1933.[117] Three years later, another of Sophie's siblings, her youngest brother, Siegfried, together with his wife Elizabeth (Betty, *née* Stern), departed for South Africa, where he set up a property development business in Cape Town. Rosette Kaufmann, who had also been living at 7 Offenbacherstrasse, fled to London, arriving there on Wednesday 30 August 1939, just four days before war was declared.[118]

On her father's side, three of her cousins also took the decision to move to another continent. Rosette Katzenstein (*née* Grünebaum), the daughter of Friedrich's eldest brother, Ferdinand, left Germany with her nine-year-old daughter, Marion, in February 1938. They travelled to Hamburg, where they boarded the SS *Hamburg* and steamed to New York. The passenger manifest shows that they had been living in the family home at 18 Faltorstrasse (Bürgel) with Rosette's mother and sisters.[119] The same document suggests that lengthy planning preceded their journey and illustrates the screening of would-be immigrants by the American authorities. Their visa to enter the USA was obtained more than a year before

---

[117] 'Listen der von 1933 bis 31.03.1941 aus Hessen Ausgewanderten Juden (Auswanderungsliste)', Stadtarchiv Mainz: Nachlass Oppenheim, File NL Oppenheim / 49, 6.
[118] 'Rosette Kaufmann née Nachmann', Mapping the Lives, https://mappingthelives.org/bio/35decffa-45a4-4d29-80c8-e295b77a2787?language=en.; GJAC file on Rosette Kaufmann.
119 Rosette's father, Ferdinand, had died in 1924.

their departure and the manifest confirms that they were not polygamists, anarchists, advocates for the violent overthrow of the government, or deformed or crippled! Rosette had divorced her husband, Solomon, before leaving for the USA, but the manifest indicates that she was going to join her widowed brother-in-law, Hermann Katzenstein. Curiously, five days after landing in New York, they were married.

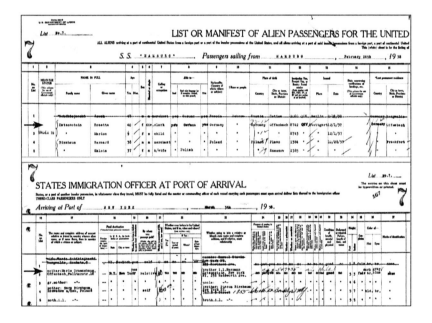

Extracts from the passenger manifest of the SS *Hamburg*
that carried Rosette Katzenstein to New York in 1938[120]

Karola's cousin, Albert, the son of Friedrich's younger brother (also called Albert) went to Argentina, a country that had close links with Germany. Confirmation of his journey is in the CEMLA

---

[120] *Passenger Lists of Vessels Arriving at New York, 1820–1897.* www.ancestry.de.

database of immigrant arrivals in Buenos Aires.[121] Just 18 years old, he travelled on the French ship, SS *Jamaique*, from Hamburg or Antwerp to South America, reaching Buenos Aires on 2 March 1938.[122] His occupation was recorded as 'student'. Yet another cousin to leave was Käthchen Ottenheimer, who in May 1939 was living with Karola and her parents at 69 Luisenstrasse. She had remarried and also travelled to Buenos Aires with her new husband, Albert Buxbaum. The same database shows that her father, Edmund Grünebaum, joined them there in May 1941. He was one of the last to escape, for although the Nazis had initially encouraged Jews to leave the country, those wanting to go were subjected to progressively more punitive conditions. At the same time, entry restrictions imposed by some destination countries, notably the USA, became ever tighter. Then, in October 1941 a decree issued by the *Reichssicherheitshauptamt* (Reich Security Main Office) that the emigration of Jews was to be prevented effectively brought all legal departures to an end.[123]

Reluctantly separated from almost everything and everyone close to them, these emigrants must have been in mental turmoil and disoriented, unsure about the way forward. For many, their initial destination was probably determined more by expediency than careful selection. So it is unsurprising that many came to the conclusion that it was not where they would spend the rest of their lives. Several of Karola's friends found sanctuary in London and did stay there, but for others it became just a stop on a much

---

[121] CEMLA is the *Centro de Estudios Migratorios Latinoamericanos* (Centre for Latin American Migration Studies). Based in Buenos Aires, its online database is compiled from immigrant landing lists, https://cemla.com/.

[122] 'Compagnie Maritime Des Chargeurs Réunis - Compagnie de Navigation Sud-Atlantique', Maritime Timetable Images, http://www.timetableimages.com/maritime/images/cr.htm.

[123] 'Order Banning the Emigration of Jews from the Reich', Jewish Virtual Library, https://www.jewishvirtuallibrary.org/order-banning-the-emigration-of-jews-from-the-reich.

longer journey, albeit a stop that may have lasted several years. Rosette Kaufmann remained there for ten years. However, in July 1949 she emigrated to New York on the SS *Ile de France* and in 1955 became an American citizen.[124] Similarly, having arrived in London in April 1939, Herta Sichel, about whom I will write more shortly, left in January 1947 to join her fiancé, who had emigrated from Germany to Southern Rhodesia.

A Teenager's Flight to London

With the level of racial intolerance and violence rising, and without any source of income or economic opportunity, Karola's parents decided that she too should leave Germany and travel to England. She went alone because they could not afford all to go and, moreover, a young adult was more likely to be allowed to enter the UK. It must have been a desperately hard decision in some respects and, even once taken, leaving the country was not without difficulty. First, she had to obtain permission from the German authorities. This required notifying them of her intended move and submitting for approval an inventory of everything she wanted to take out of the country.

So on Saturday 22 July 1939, Karola prepared a four-page list of all the things she planned to take with her, separating those that were to be packed away in two suitcases and a large trunk, those to be carried as hand baggage and those that she would be wearing or carrying on her person. In keeping with German bureaucracy and Nazi control, each item had to be named, numbered, valued and dated, and its origin stated. For example, suitcase item number 27 comprised two pairs of slippers (summer and winter) bought in 1936 and 1937 at a cost of RM10.50. Item 54 was a German-

---

[124] Her German Jewish Aid Committee (GJAC) file shows that the fare of £63 10s to the USA was paid for by GJAC. She died on 24 April 1983 and is buried in New Jersey.
https://www.findagrave.com/memorial/227024330/rosette-kaufmann.

English dictionary bought in 1935 at a cost of RM3.60. The hand baggage included many smaller items, such as a three-piece cutlery set (knife, fork and spoon) described as a family possession, as well as a watch, a ring and a prayer book.

			Koffer & Kofferkiste	Karola,Sara Grünebaum, 22.Juli 1939		
16	II	4	Wintergarnituren(Hemd&Hosen)	12.--1936 - 38	Ersatzstücke
17	"	3	Strickhosen	10.501935 - 37	"
18	"	6	Unterziehhöschen	3.-- 1937-38	"
19	"	9	Büstenhalter	10.801934- 38	"
20	"	7	Sommergarnituren(Hemd&Hosen)	12.- 35- 37	
21	"	2	Hemdhosen	3:- 1935	"
22	"	5	Unterröcke	15.- 33- 38	"
23	"	3	Schlafanzüge	25.- 35-38	"
24	"	2	Nachthemden	25.20 ,34-37	"
25	"	6	Paar Schuhe	60.- 34-38	"
26	"	1	Paar Ueberschuhe	8.50 1935	"
27	"	2	Paar Hausschuhe(Sommer&Winter)	10.50 34&36	"
28	"	2	Dtzd.Paar Strümpfe(Sommer&Winter	30.- 34-38	"
29	"	1	Moltondecke	1.25 1937	"
30	I	1	Kolter	Altbesitz	
31	II	6	bunte Arbeitskittel	"	
32	II	3	weisse Kittel	13.50 35-37	
33	I	1	Uebergangsmantel	Altbesitz	
34	II	2	Wintermantel	"	
35	II	1	Regenmantel	18.- 1937	
36	"	2	Jackenkleider	38.- 1936	
37	"	1	Lodenmantel	14.- 1937	
38	"	2	Sommerpullover (Wolle)	3.- 36-37	selbstgearbe
39	"	3	Winterpullover (Wolle)	5.- 1937	"
40	I	2	Sportröcke	Altbesitz	
41	II	3	Blusen	18.- 36-38	Ersatzstü
42	I	2	Winterstrickkleid(Wolle)	8.- 1938	selbstgearb
43	"	2	Sommerstrickkleid (Garn)	7.- 1938	"
44	"	3	Winterkleider	45.- 34-37	
45	"	3	Hauskleider	6.- 34-38	"

A page from the inventory of items in Karola's baggage

There was also a very considerable amount of bedding, table linen and towels, including 12 sheets, 6 quilt covers, 14 pillowcases, 12 tablecloths, 12 damask hand towels and 12 tea towels. All were described as family possessions without a purchase date or value. In total, there were over 60 items of packed luggage and a further 17 in the hand baggage. A number of items, including a swimming costume, pullovers and dresses, were described as *'selbstgemacht'* (self-made). Remarkably, next to me as I write is that same aged German-English dictionary, albeit now rather battered.

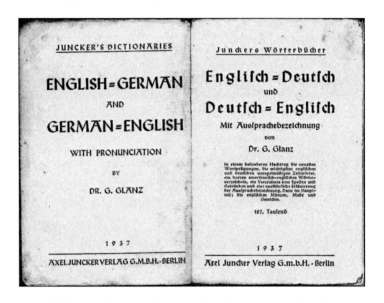

Title page from the dictionary Karola brought to London

Some of the bedding and table linen also survives, having been stored for decades in a suitcase in my attic. Each item is embroidered with the initials 'SR' or 'KG', for Sophie Reiss and Karola Grünebaum. Given the use of their maiden names, and their description in the inventory as family possessions, it seems certain that these were part of mother's and daughter's trousseaux.

Embroidered initials on the linen Karola brought to England

A week after compiling her inventory, on Monday 31 July 1939, Karola notified the Offenbach police of her intention to relocate to England. On the relevant form, she had to include her imposed forename (Sara), her work status (unemployed), her religion (Jew) and marital status (single). The form was signed by 'Hellwig', her landlord and the man who was providing Friedrich with occasional work. Finally, it was stamped by the police and the Darmstadt *Devisenstelle* (exchange office), giving her permission to leave.

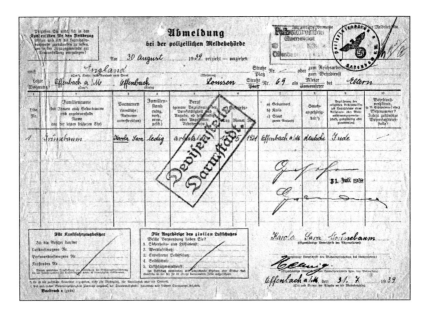

Karola's change of address form, effectively a permit to leave Germany

This was not the end of the formalities, however. Her emigration to the UK did not just have to be sanctioned by the Nazis, she also had to hold a permit issued by the British authorities. As there was considerable resistance to letting in Jewish refugees and workers throughout the inter-war period, obtaining that document was also not straightforward. Nevertheless, on Monday 14 August 1939 she was ready to leave. More than 80 years later, Wilma Feick recalled seeing her childhood friend on that day for the last time. She had looked out of the window of her grandparents' apartment to the courtyard below and saw a young woman very elegantly dressed. She did not recognise who it was until her Aunt Mim told her, at which point Wilma opened the window and called out. That's when Karola told her that she would soon 'flutter away', but Wilma could say no more. Her aunt was standing behind her. Karola boarded a train in Frankfurt with a one-way 2nd class ticket to leave her country of birth and emigrate to England alone. She was 18 years and 3 months old. Her departure for England was duly recorded on her index card in the *Jüdische Meldekartei*.

Tag	Mon.	Jahr	Straße	Nr.
14.	8.	39.	*Verlant Luisenstr. 69 Uhren n England*	

Extract from Karola's index card in the *Jüdische Meldekartei* recording her move to England

The journey was not without further trauma. At Aachen, she was taken off the train by German border guards, her cases were forced open and various personal possessions stolen before she was able to continue via Brussels to Ostend. There she boarded a ferry to Dover and then a train to London, arriving in the capital on Tuesday 15 August 1939. Within 48 hours she had started her first job as a domestic servant with a family in Buckinghamshire.

Eighteen days after her arrival, Germany invaded Poland, and 21 days later Britain and France declared war on Germany.

Reminders of Family and Friends

Noticeably missing from the inventory of items that Karola brought with her was any photo album or even photographs. Yet in later years she certainly had an album containing pictures taken before she left Germany, so it is probable that she brought these with her, but concealed them from the authorities, fearing that they might be confiscated. Her most cherished photos must have been those of her parents. Judging by how old they look, the pictures were taken shortly before her departure, when Sophie was 51 and Friedrich 50. Both were smartly, almost formally, dressed, Sophie in a black dress with a large white bow, and Friedrich wearing a collar and tie with a dark suit and two lapel badges, perhaps related to his wartime service. Their facial expressions are striking. There are no smiles. They appear serious, perhaps sad. Karola's photo collection also included a few group pictures of the extended family taken in happier times, but these are the only known portraits of her parents.

Sophie and Friedrich Grünebaum, photos probably taken
shortly before Karola left Germany

She also brought with her several photos of friends. Some of these are dated July and August 1939, indicating not only that they were given to her shortly before she left, but also that her plans had been made and made known a few weeks in advance. Most were inscribed on the reverse. Those from her female friends bore messages of affection and expressions of hope for a reunion at some later date. The wording chosen by her male friends was rather more prosaic.

A selection of photos and their inscriptions from Karola's girlfriends (Irmgard, Ilse and Thea) and boyfriends (Paul, Ziggi and Löb)

Building a New Life in England

Jewish Refugees in Domestic Service

How did Karola manage to escape from Germany, obtain a permit to enter Britain and start a new job so soon after arriving there? After all, the Grünebaums had little money to pay for her journey and no strong connections with England. Moreover, for various reasons, it was difficult for Jews to enter Britain through much of the 1930s. There is nothing to answer these questions in Karola's papers, but answers have been found. They were discovered in a very different source, one that also shed light on subsequent highly unusual developments that had a huge impact on Karola's life.

However, before revealing this source, it is first necessary to highlight a major social concern that emerged in Britain during the inter-war years. That was a severe shortage of domestic workers, which had arisen because many women, having tasted alternative employment during WW1, chose not to go back into 'service'. Today it is difficult to conceive that this could be a particularly serious issue, but in the 1930s it became a focus for considerable political debate. To fill this gap, 'alien' workers began to be recruited. Initially, most were not Jewish or refugees. In fact, the entry of Jews was tightly restricted, partly because of anti-Semitism, partly because of concern that jobs would be taken away from British workers at a time of high unemployment. As a result, the government refused to provide any financial help to refugees or refugee organisations and stipulated that those accepted should not make any call on the public purse.[125] However, as Nazi persecution intensified, pressure on the government to adopt a more liberal policy increased, and recruitment of Jews into domestic service was seen as a response that would relieve such pressure, whilst at the same time addressing a serious social problem. Consequently, domestic service became one of the main channels through which Jewish refugees were allowed to enter Britain.

Crucial to making this possible was the work of Jewish and non-Jewish refugee organisations, amongst which the Central British Fund for German Jewry (CBF) played a central role. Founded in 1933 by Otto Schiff, it guaranteed to the government that refugees from Nazi oppression would not become a burden on public finances, and it raised substantial amounts of money to meet all their costs and housing needs. Some of these funds were used to sponsor another organisation established in the same year, the Jewish Refugees Committee (renamed in 1938 the German Jewish Aid Committee, GJAC), which at a practical level arranged for the rescue of refugees, and their admission, maintenance and

---

[125] This section is based on interviews with Dr Jennifer Craig-Norton, Honorary Fellow at the Parkes Institute for the Study of Jewish/non-Jewish Relations (University of Southampton), as well as representatives of WJR and multiple references, including the following:

Tony Kushner, *Journeys from the Abyss: The Holocaust and Forced Migration from the 1880s to the Present*: Liverpool University Press, 2017); Anthony Grenville, 'Anglo-Jewry and the Jewish Refugees from Nazism', *AJR Journal*, December 2012, https://ajr.org.uk/wp-content/uploads/2018/02/2012_December.pdf; Werner Eugen Mosse, ed., *Second Chance: Two Centuries of German-Speaking Jews in the United Kingdom*, Schriftenreihe Wissenschaftlicher Abhandlungen des Leo Baeck Instituts 48 (Tübingen: J.C.B. Mohr, 1991); Pamela Shatzkes, 'Anglo-Jewish Rescue and Relief Efforts, 1938–1944' (PhD thesis, London, LSE, 1999), http://etheses.lse.ac.uk/1585/1/U144585.pdf.

employment in Britain.[126] Essentially, it was responsible for much of the individual casework. The extent to which the CBF and GJAC actually accelerated the movement of Jews into Britain before 1939 is a matter of debate. Some arrangements were put in place specifically to assist their recruitment into domestic service, arrangements that were separate from the more general recruitment of aliens. However, the CBF was also concerned about the potential increase in anti-Semitism and the drain on its finances if numbers escalated and new arrivals could not be found employment. It therefore maintained a 'pre-selection' process to ensure that only those considered suitably qualified and well motivated were admitted.

As the situation of Jews abroad worsened and demand for asylum increased further, especially following the Nazi annexation of Austria and the November 1938 pogroms, the British Government took steps to process applications more expeditiously and reduce the workload on the Home Office and passport control officers. More and more responsibility was devolved to Jewish and non-Jewish aid organisations, who in 1938 were brought together in the Central Office for Refugees and accommodated in Bloomsbury House, the former Palace Hotel opposite the British Museum. With the GJAC playing a lead role, it became the operations centre for handling the influx of Jewish refugees. In fact, all refugees were required to go there and register immediately on arrival. Inside, GJAC set up a Domestic Bureau, which took over from the Home Office certain responsibilities relating to applications for domestic work. For the huge numbers of mainly German and Austrian Jews that passed through, it was not a particularly pleasant experience.

---

[126] It was renamed so as not perpetuate labelling as 'refugees' the individuals it was helping who had settled in the UK.

> ... the refugees called it 'Das Bloomsburyhaus' - on
> the corner of Gower Street and Bedford Avenue,
> vast and decaying but big enough for many separate
> departments and with a huge reception hall where
> refugees sat all day waiting in line to discuss their
> case:[127]
>
> The task of administering the admission and
> allocation of refugee domestic servants passed to
> Bloomsbury House, where the Domestic Bureau
> coped as best it could; it is not fondly remembered by
> its former clients.[128]

The Domestic Bureau established links with organisations in countries where Jews were being subjected to Nazi persecution. In Germany, the main partner was the *Hilfsverein der deutschen Juden* (Aid Organisation of German Jews), which through its network of local branches was active in distributing information, providing advice and assisting with permit applications.[129] Initially, final decisions on applications for entry to undertake domestic work were made in London by central government officials. However, in early 1939 the Domestic Bureau was given authority to issue work permits ('Green Cards') and subsequently to give a block grant of permits to the *Hilfsverein* for issue in Germany.[130] At its peak the Bureau was issuing about 500 permits each week.

Prospective Jewish refugees found their domestic work in

---

[127] 'My Bloomsbury House Days', The Spectator Archive, 6 January 1990, http://archive.spectator.co.uk/article/6th-january-1990/14/my-bloomsbury-house-days.

[128] Anthony Grenville, 'Underpaid, Underfed and Overworked: Refugees in Domestic Service', *AJR Journal* 8, no. 12 (12 December 2008), https://ajr.org.uk/wp-content/uploads/2018/02/2008_december.pdf.

[129] 'Hilfsverein Der Deutschen Juden', Yad Vashem, n.d., http://www.yadvashem.org/odot_pdf/Microsoft%20Word%20-%206371.pdf.

[130] A Green Card was a work permit but it was also necessary for refugees to separately obtain a visa to enter the UK.

several different ways. Wealthy British families took to advertising vacancies in overseas newspapers and journals. Conversely, jobseekers posted information about themselves in Britain or used contacts to seek out opportunities on their behalf. Often the individuals were highly educated and over qualified for such work, but it was their only way to escape Nazi tyranny. Each of these approaches could lead to a job offer, which was then advantageous when applying for a permit or visa. However, many applied for entry without such an offer, aiming to secure a position after arrival, and it was a task of the Domestic Bureau to allocate them to available jobs. In this way, tens of thousands passed through Bloomsbury House and subsequently took up work as domestic servants. However, in most cases those jobs were poorly paid and the working conditions were dreadful.[131] Moreover, the refugees often arrived with much more luggage and possessions than domestics were expected to have, which was not only a practical problem but also led to tensions with both employers and other staff. So, despite having got through the pre-selection process, many were ill suited to their jobs and very unhappy working as servants:

> Domestic servants endured some of the worst treatment experienced by refugees, resulting from their lowly status in the households in which they were employed and from the work they had to do there. Many of them were from comfortable middle-class homes and found the indignities of life as a domestic intolerable, though they were probably treated no worse than other servants, including servants in middle-class households in Vienna or Berlin. Underpaid, underfed

---

[131] Jennifer Craig-Norton, 'Refugees at the Margins: Jewish Domestics in Britain 1938–1945', *Shofar: an Interdisciplinary Journal of Jewish Studies* 37, no. 3 (2019): 295–330, https://doi.org/10.1353/sho.2019.0039.

and overworked, they were exposed to callous and inhuman treatment by employers who, ignoring the emotional trauma of their flight from their homelands and their separation from their loved ones, simply saw them as skivvies. Domestics were notoriously at the mercy of their employers, isolated as they were within the confines of a household not their own. Refugees alone in Britain experienced such conditions almost as a form of imprisonment.[132]

A Serendipitous Discovery and an Amazing Coincidence

During and after WW2, the various organisations involved in refugee programmes went through many changes.[133] The Domestic Bureau closed down in 1941. The Central Office for Refugees continued its work into the post-war period but moved out of Bloomsbury House in 1948. GJAC also continued working but reverted to its original name of Jewish Refugees Committee. The CBF gradually extended the geographical reach of its humanitarian activities and in 1995 changed its name to World Jewish Relief (WJR) to reflect the increasingly global nature of its work.

Amidst wartime upheaval, then the pressing problems of post-war recovery and the organisational transformations mentioned, the huge amount of paperwork relating to the refugee caseload was forgotten. For decades, if considered at all, it must have been assumed that the records had been destroyed or lost. All

---

[132] Grenville, 'Underpaid, Underfed and Overworked: Refugees in Domestic Service'.

[133] Tony Kushner, 'An Alien Occupation – Jewish Refugees and Domestic Service in Britain 1933–1948', in *Second Chance: Two Centuries of German-Speaking Jews in the United Kingdom*, ed. Werner Eugen Mosse, n.d.; 'From my Diary', *AJR Information*, May 1948. https://ajr.org.uk/wp-content/uploads/2018/02/1948_may.pdf.

that changed, however, in the late 1980s, when a large number of files were found by chance in cabinets at the back of a garage in London. The garage was at the Heinrich Stahl Home for Aged Refugees, funded by Otto Schiff who had set up CBF in 1933. Initially looked after by the Association of Jewish Refugees, they were eventually handed over to WJR, who in 2012 began a two-year project with London Metropolitan Archives to create a digital archive of over 35,000 case files on individual refugees.[134] That represented just half the total number that fled to the UK to escape Nazi persecution but, fortuitously, one of those files was that of Karola Grünebaum.

The file contents provide an insight into her flight from Germany, her arrival in the UK and subsequent life in Britain. They include a registration card which on the reverse records changes of address until March 1945.[135] There are also three pages of handwritten notes on the headed paper of GJAC, which cover the time from her arrival until August 1943. Clearly, she stayed in touch with GJAC for an extended period. The registration card, completed on 16 August 1939, shows her Case Number as 32060. It confirms her date of birth, home town, nationality and date of arrival in the UK. More interestingly, it indicates that she arrived with a Green Card and that the expiry date of her passport was 19 December 1939. Finally, it gives her occupation as 'Shorthand Typist' and her 'English Address' as 'c/o Mrs D Oldcorn, Lulworth, Iver, Buckinghamshire'.

---

[134] 'Our Jewish Genealogy Archives', World Jewish Relief, https://www.worldjewishrelief.org/news/383-making-it-easier-to-find-your-family-history-our-digitised-archives.

[135] As a refugee, Karola was legally required to notify the authorities of a change of address.

Karola's registration card completed at Bloomsbury House
on her arrival in the UK

It is unlikely that Karola had a passport before it was decided that she should leave Germany, so its imminent expiry might seem surprising. However, the passports issued to emigrating Jews had very limited validity, normally just one year.[136] If that were the case, it suggests that Karola might have started to plan for her departure as early as late 1938. The other details on the card prompt a number of questions. How did she get her Green Card? Did she have a job offer before leaving Germany? And why is her occupation recorded as 'shorthand typist', which does not reflect her previous work? Was this a translation problem or did she deliberately present herself in this way? It will never be possible to answer all these questions with certainty, but the notes provide some clues.

The first half-page includes much of the same basic information found on her registration card. In addition, however, it indicates that she is not 'Orthodox', that she is unmarried and that there is no time limit ('NTL') on her stay in the UK. It also states that

[136] Peter Landé, 'Temporary German Passports for Jews 1938–1940', JewishGen, 2002, https://www.jewishgen.org/databases/Holocaust/0044_TempPassportsForGermanJews1938to1941.html.

her relative or friend in England is a 'Miss Stiefel' who lives at 307 Hendon Way, NW4. Nothing is known about this person, who is not a known relative and whose name, which seems to be German, does not appear in any other documents discovered during the research. Significantly, the notes record that Karola was registered with '*Hilfsverein*', presumably a reference to the *Hilfsverein der deutschen Juden* mentioned above. It must have helped make the arrangements for her escape and possibly issued her Green Card. Under 'Languages' only German is recorded, suggesting she was unable to speak much English on arrival. Again, her occupation is given as shorthand typist, but this time an alternative occupation, 'Domestic', is added and she is shown to have registered with the 'Domestic Dept'. Notes on her 'Experience' include the date '16.6.1939', which is soon after she left her temporary position as a house help for Leonie Löwenberger in Offenbach. Undoubtedly, that helped her to get both a Green Card and a job. Indeed, it is plausible that she took on that job as part of a plan to leave Germany, a conclusion supported by the fact that Leonie provided her with two testimonials, a version in German and another in English.

Testimonial for Karola from Leonie Löwenberger
(German version)

Other notes made on the same date as her registration can be seen in the lower half of the GJAC page. The handwriting of each is different, indicating that she moved from one desk or person to another as she progressed through Bloomsbury House. The first records that she obtained her British visa in Frankfurt and landed in Dover, where the immigration officer 'asked no questions'.

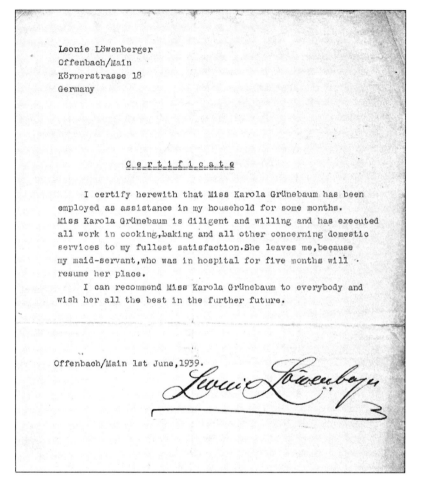

Leonie Löwenberger
Offenbach/Main
Körnerstrasse 18
Germany

                    C e r t i f i c a t e

        I certify herewith that Miss Karola Grünebaum has been
employed as assistance in my household for some months.
Miss Karola Grünebaum is diligent and willing and has executed
all work in cooking,baking and all other concerning domestic
services to my fullest satisfaction.She leaves me,because
my maid-servant,who was in hospital for five months will ·
resume her place.
        I can recommend Miss Karola Grünebaum to everybody and
wish her all the best in the further future.

Offenbach/Main 1st June,1939.

Testimonial for Karola from Leonie Löwenberger
(English version)

It shows that her Green Card was 'surrendered', and finally it notes that Karola has a job and is employed by a Mrs Oldcorn at the Iver address. That she had a Green Card before leaving Germany, and that this first note states she is employed, makes it more likely that she had secured her job before setting off, rather than it having been allocated by the Domestic Bureau after her arrival. A second note relates to money. It records that Karola was given ten shillings, half of which was to cover the cost of either storing or transporting her luggage, while the other five shillings was for pocket money and her fare to Buckinghamshire.

Extract from first page of notes from Karola's GJAC file

Other comments in the GJAC document will be reviewed later. However, there is one further strange twist to the story of the discovery of the Bloomsbury House files to mention here. As already explained, the files were found in a garage at the Heinrich Stahl Home for Aged Refugees, which was in The Bishops Avenue in north London. From the 1920s to the early 1930s, the house and its grounds were owned by the film star, Gracie Fields, but the property was sold when she moved out.[137] The house was then converted to the Heinrich Stahl Care Home and the grounds were divided into smaller plots, on one of which was built The Towers Maternity Annexe. And it was in this unit, in 1951, that I was born, just a few steps away from where my mother's forgotten file had been stored and forgotten for years.

Childminding as an Enemy Alien

Karola left London almost immediately and went to live at Lulworth in Old Slade Lane, Iver, Buckinghamshire. The house was on the edge of Richings Park, an estate developed in the 1920s, when the opening of Iver station made it practicable to commute into the capital.[138] The area was designed as a 'garden village' with 'visually pleasing' properties in a tranquil setting that is now difficult to imagine. Today Old Slade Lane is severed by the M4 motorway and very close to its junction with the M25.

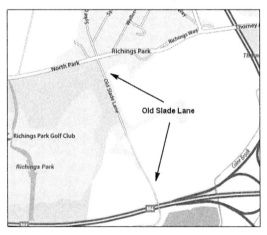

Location of Old Slade Lane, Iver

[137] 'Tower, The Official Gracie Fields', http://graciefields.org/wordpress/tower-2/.

[138] 'The History of Richings Park', http://richingsparkhistory.org.uk/.

Lulworth was the home of Eric Oldcorn, an electrical supply engineer who worked in London, and his wife, Diana. They rented the house soon after marrying in 1933 and by the time Karola arrived they had two sons. David was almost 4½ years old and Richard just 18 months. She was employed at £2 per month as a 'mother's help'.

Karola Grünebaum, thought to have been photographed
shortly after her arrival in the UK

Just a few days after starting work, on Sunday 3 September 1939, war against Germany was declared. The government immediately decided to compile a register of all residents so that National Identity Cards could be issued, and the data was collected in a census on Friday 29 September. Karola was duly recorded as an unmarried single female domestic servant living with the Oldcorns at Lulworth. Interestingly, the enumerator entered her surname using the non-diacritic spelling, 'Gruenebaum'. This was changed, though, in her own handwriting to 'Grünebaum'. Apparently, she did not want to abandon or conceal this facet of her German identity!

Extract from the 1939 England and Wales Register
showing Karola's registration[139]

A potentially much more serious consequence of the war was that all 70,000 UK-resident Germans and Austrians were declared 'enemy aliens' and became liable to internment. Very quickly, the Home Office set up tribunals across the country to examine each individual case and decide whether to impose internment or other restrictions.[140] Karola presented herself to the tribunal in Buckinghamshire on Monday 6 November 1939 and it must have been a nerve-wracking experience. The conclusion, typed on the hearing record card, was that she should be 'exempt from internment' and, unsurprisingly, also

---

[139] Details of individuals still alive are redacted to protect their privacy. The two redacted entries at Lulworth are assumed to be those of David and Richard Oldcorn.

[140] Collar the Lot! Britain's Policy of Internment during the Second World War, The National Archives, http://blog.nationalarchives.gov.uk/blog/collar-lot-britains-policy-internment-second-world-war/.

confirmed that she did not want to be repatriated. The card was then formally stamped on its reverse by Buckinghamshire Constabulary.[141] Not until a later date was her official status changed from 'enemy alien' to 'friendly enemy alien' and restrictions on her movement lifted.

FEMALE ENEMY ALIEN—EXEMPTION FROM INTERNMENT—REFUGEE

923

(1) Surname (*block capitals*) GRUNEBAUM

Forenames Karola Sara

Alias

(2) Date and place of birth 12 May, 1921. Offenbach.

(3) Nationality German

(4) Police Regn. Cert. No. 742310 — Home Office reference if known

Special Procedure Card Number if known

(5) Address prior to Internment "Lulworth", Old Slade Lane, Iver.

(6) Normal occupation Typist.

(7) Present Occupation Domestic servant.

(8) Name and address of employer Mrs. Oldcorn, "Lulworth", Old Slade Lane, Iver.

(9) Decision of Tribunal Exempted from internment — Date 6 November, 1939.

(10) Whether exempted from Article 6(A) (Yes or No) Yes.

(11) Whether desires to be repatriated (Yes or No) No.

[7535] 28717/835 25m 9/39 G & S 704 [OVER]

Record card from Karola's Enemy Alien Internment Tribunal

I set about trying to find out more about the family who had provided my mother with a home and a job at a time when her life had been upturned. Some members of the local Facebook group recalled the Oldcorns and their house and crucially the names of the two sons. Of course, I knew that by then they would have been more than 80 years old. Nevertheless, and without much hope of success, I began a search to find them and, to my amazement, within a few days I had located Richard, the younger of the two brothers, in Sydney, Australia. He must have been astonished to receive my email about someone who had looked after him as a toddler, but he immediately replied, saying that I had reached the

---

[141] The National Archives, Aliens Department, Records of Internees at Liberty in the UK. File reference HO 396/30/409. http://discovery.nationalarchives. gov.uk/details/r/C15203544.

right person, and sent details of his older brother David, who was still living not far from Iver.

Both David and Richard remembered the young German woman whom the family called 'Carol' and, although Richard was too young to remember much more, David recalled details of her life in the Oldcorn household. She was given a room on the first floor that overlooked the front garden on the right side of the house. It had no heating, so in winter was extremely cold, the only warmth outside the kitchen coming from a coal fire in the living room and a paraffin stove at the foot of the stairs.

Lulworth in Old Slade Lane in the 1930s

As a mother's help, her main duty was to assist with the care of the two boys. More of her time was devoted to Richard, since David was already attending a nearby nursery. She often took him there or collected him, sharing this task with Diana. Later, she prepared tea for herself and the boys, which they ate at the kitchen table. The family had a Scottie dog and she sometimes joined them to take it for a walk to the gravel pits at the end of the lane.

Richard and David Oldcorn at Lulworth, May 1940

Despite its relatively rural location, the onset of the Blitz impacted life at Lulworth. Eric Oldcorn was kept busy restoring the electricity supply in London and often came home late, eating his evening meal with his wife off a trolley in front of the coal fire. More ominously, in the dining room he constructed a large 'cage' using wooden battens and wire mesh, and placed steel plates outside the door that connected it to the living room, to create a space that optimistically would be protected from the effects of a bomb blast. The children, and possibly Karola too, slept inside the cage. His concern for their safety was undoubtedly heightened by the proximity of what must have been a high-priority strategic target for the Luftwaffe. On the opposite side of the road to Lulworth were Richings Park Mansion and Lodge, which for a short period was the headquarters of RAF Bomber Command.[142] Anti-aircraft guns were set up in the surrounding fields and smoke generators that burned oil to screen the ground from the air were installed along Old Slade Lane. Despite such efforts, however, in February 1941 (after Bomber Command had been relocated), the building was severely damaged by bombing; and it was demolished after the war.[143]

As already mentioned, life for most domestic workers was hard and unpleasant, especially for those unaccustomed and ill suited to such work. Therefore, although they were subjected to certain movement restrictions, unsurprisingly many found alternative work as soon as possible:

> The vast majority of refugees left domestic service at the earliest possible opportunity, happy to take almost any other position on offer and delighting in their new-found freedom; many found employment in jobs that contributed to the war effort. Though domestic service left bitter memories, the integration of refugees into the war effort and into British society generally meant that it could be consigned fairly rapidly to the past.[144]

However, Karola stayed in her job for 18 months, considerably longer than most refugees endured in their first position. A number of factors point to her having been well treated there

---

[142] 'Bomber Command Structure', Pathfinder Craig, https://masterbombercraig. wordpress.com/bomber-command-structure/.

[143] Allan Williams, *Operation Crossbow: The Untold Story of the Search for Hitler's Secret Weapons* (London: Arrow Books, 2014), 248.

[144] Grenville, 'Underpaid, Underfed and Overworked: Refugees in Domestic Service'.

and developing a close attachment to the Oldcorns, a conclusion supported by comments from people who knew the family. Diana was described as 'a lovely lady', Eric as 'a real gentleman' and the two of them as 'a lovely couple'.[145] Perhaps most telling is that Karola filled three pages in her small photo album with pictures of the house and the children. Several were taken before she arrived and one was taken after she left, suggesting that Diana and Eric had given her the photos as mementos and that she kept in touch with the family after she moved out. Fortuitously, the same or very similar photos are in the Oldcorns' family album, which Diana methodically labelled and dated, enabling Karola's to be similarly catalogued.

The testimonial Karola was given on leaving is, however, rather bland. It referred to her being honest and trustworthy, but made no mention of the quality of her work. It also stated that the start date for her employment was 15 August 1939, the date on which she arrived in England and the day before she completed formalities at Bloomsbury House. Perhaps the testimonial was incorrect on this point or perhaps it is further evidence that Karola got the job before leaving Germany and was considered employed from the date of her arrival. Unprompted, David Oldcorn commented that his mother was not particularly imaginative and would not have been good at composing a personal reference. He believed that she might well have asked Karola what should be included and limited her words to whatever was suggested.

---

[145] Personal communications from members of Iver Facebook Group, 2018.

Karola's testimonial from Diana Oldcorn, her first employer in England

The Oldcorns lived in the same house for the rest of their lives, and Diana was very active in the local community. Eric died in 1977 and Diana in 1996 but both are well remembered. The name Lulworth has disappeared; it is now house number 34 and looks very different. Both David and Richard went on to have successful professional careers, with Richard also excelling in sporting endeavour. Karola probably never knew that the toddler in her care went on to represent the UK in three Olympic Games.[146]

---

[146] 'Richard Oldcorn, Wikipedia', https://en.wikipedia.org/wiki/Richard_Oldcorn.

London, Lyons and the Hindustani

In early 1941 Karola eventually took steps to find an alternative job. The next note in her GJAC file was made on Wednesday 22 January of that year and it records that she came to ask about work. She was sent to 'Women's Emp', the women's employment desk. Two weeks later, on Tuesday 4 February 1941, she finally left Iver and moved to central London. It seems a strange thing to have done during the *Blitz*, but a week later, on Monday 10 February 1941, she began working for J Lyons & Co, who employed her for much of the following 2½ years.

Entries in Karola's GJAC file recording her meeting in January 1941
to discuss changing her job and the start of her employment
at Lyons Corner House (Marble Arch)

J Lyons was a Jewish-owned company established in 1887 by Joseph Lyons and other entrepreneurs. It became one of the largest catering and food manufacturing companies in the world, best known for its more than 200 tea shops, five huge Corner Houses in London (two of them known as Maison Lyons) and restaurants such as Trocadero. The Corner Houses were notable for their 'extravagant, continental and luxurious' Art Deco interior design, and one of my earliest memories is of being in one of them with my parents on a carpeted floor with an orchestra playing.[147] The company was also a technology pioneer, not least through its use of computers to support its business operations. Less well known

[147] 'J. Lyons & Co.', https://www.kzwp.com/lyons1/.; 'The story of J Lyons & Co Ltd', *Westminster Quarterly* VIII, no. 2 (April 2017): 10–11.

is that Lyons was a major supporter of the war effort. It managed one of the largest bomb-making factories and prepared millions of ration packs for troops around the world. It also provided substantial assistance to Jewish refugees who managed to reach the UK. Many thousands were offered jobs in the various Lyons establishments before, during and after the war.[148]

Maison Lyons Corner House at Marble Arch (postcard)

Of course, one of those helped was Karola and the GJAC file note made on 13 February 1941 mentions that she found work 'through us'. Her first position was at the flagship Marble Arch Corner House, where she earned £1 10 shillings per week as a waitress. At its peak Lyons employed more than 7,500 women around the country as waitresses and they were universally known as 'Nippies'. With a distinctive maid-like uniform, including a monogrammed hat, they featured on advertising, product packaging and other promotional activities. The Nippy became

---

[148] C C Aronsfeld, 'The Story of a Cup of Tea', *AJR Information*, October 1954, 7, https://ajr.org.uk/wp-content/uploads/2018/02/1954_october.pdf.

a national icon and Lyons undoubtedly used attractive females in this way to boost its sales. However, the company was keen to present them as very respectable and its businesses as providing a service of the highest standard.

The Perfect Lyons Nippy[149]

---

[149] Image: 'The Perfect Nippy' © London Metropolitan Archives, City of

So Karola became a Nippy, but only for nine months. Later that year she was promoted and on Tuesday 25 November 1941 started work as a cashier, a position that, with the exception of a six-month break, she held until 20 October 1943. In her new role the weekly wage jumped to £2 10s and this steadily increased, so that by the time she finally left her pay had risen to £3 5s. The six months' gap in employment with Lyons was from 23 January to 8 July 1943. What prompted her to leave is unclear, but it led to a very unsettled period, at least as far as work was concerned. Her GJAC file records that on Monday 1 February 1943 she started as a trainee with Dernier and Hamlyn. The company, which was established in the inter-war period, was a pioneer in the lighting industry, designing innovative products and supplying prestigious commercial customers, including Lyons.[150] It is still in business today, based in Croydon. In 1943, however, its offices were in central London at 23 Newman Street W1.[151]

London ACC/3527/201/A, from the J. Lyons and Company Ltd collection.
[150] 'Family of Sidney William Hamlyn and Thirza Maud Barnes', http://www.john-attfield.com/paf_tree/attfield_current/fam3727.html.
[151] Coincidentally, my daughter, Michelle, started work 65 years later just a few doors further down the road in what were the offices of Freud Communications!

Entries in Karola's GJAC file recording her employment with Dernier and
Hamlyn, her move to Arcourt, her release from national service and her
return to Lyons as a cashier

But Karola's employment there was short-lived. Less than
three weeks later, on Thursday 18 February, she began work as an
assembler with Arcourt Engineering, where she was paid 1s per
hour. No company of this name exists today, but one is listed in
the London Gazette for 22 August 1947 after it was dissolved.[152]
She stayed in this post for a maximum of five months, but it may
have been much less, and the final file entry in the GJAC file
explains why she moved on so quickly. Written on Tuesday 31
August 1943, it records that she had 'developed kidney trouble
while working as an assembler. Released from Nat Service &
working as cashier with Lyons'. It seems probable that she had
been called up for wartime work under the 1941 National Service
Act (No 2), which made provision for the conscription of women,
and had been assigned to the engineering factory before becoming
unwell.

---

[152] 'The London Gazette, issue 38052, page 3988', 22 August 1947, https://
www.thegazette.co.uk/London/issue/38052/page/3988.

Karola resumed work with Lyons at the Marble Arch Corner House on Friday 9 July 1943. The file note about this and her illness was actually written seven weeks later and almost certainly her illness and change of job were not the reasons she went to GJAC on that occasion. The note appears at the end of a longer entry about a very different matter. It was whilst working as a cashier that Karola met her future husband and my father, Mohammad Afzal Husain ('Afzal'). He had come in for a cup of tea and presumably, whilst paying, decided that Lyons had more to offer than refreshments, and in that he was not alone. The *Picture Post* reported that 800–900 Nippies got married to customers 'met on duty' every year.[153] And almost certainly it was her relationship with him that prompted her to go back to GJAC in August 1941 because the main part of the file entry is about this.

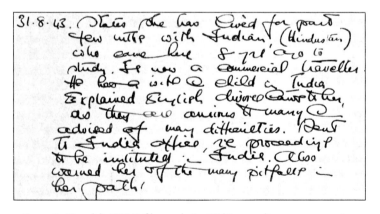

Entry in Karola's GJAC file made in 1943 recording a conversation about living with an Indian

The notes show that Karola reported living for the past few months with an 'Indian (Hindustan)' who had come to England

---

[153] Referred to in P Chrystal, 'Tea: A Very British Beverage (Gloucestershire: Amberley Publishing, 2014).

to study eight years earlier, but who was currently working as a commercial traveller. The reason she wanted to talk about this then becomes clear. He already had a wife and child in India, but they wanted to get married. The GJAC representative, presumably somewhat taken aback, documents their response, which included explaining English divorce laws and alerting Karola to the difficulties she was likely to encounter. Finally, she was 'sent to India office, re proceedings to be instituted in India' and also 'warned … of the many pitfalls in her path'. Clearly, GJAC not only provided practical help with housing and employment, but was also seen as somewhere to turn to for advice and support on personal matters.

Afzal had arrived in England in 1935, so had been there considerably longer than she had, although whether or not he ever embarked on a course of study is uncertain. He travelled to London from India via Montevideo (Uruguay), Buenos Aires (Argentina) and Genoa (Italy) on an adventurous journey which I will come to later.

Staying in Touch

How much contact did Karola have with her parents after she said goodbye to them and left Germany in August 1939? If she received any letters during her first few months in England, they no longer exist but, given that such correspondence would have been treasured, it's more likely that there was none. In any case, in April 1940 the Nazis issued regulations forbidding all communication with hostile countries. So, as German troops advanced through France, forcing the Allied soldiers back on to the Dunkirk beaches, direct contact became out of the question.

In fact, for a long time I believed that Sophie and Friedrich only managed to get one message to Karola. This was a brief note sent through the *Deutsches Rotes Kreuz* (German Red Cross) on a form normally used for messages to and from prisoners-of-war. They were limited to 25 words and could only contain family news.[154] Stamped 'April 1940', it was sent to the Oldcorns' address in Iver, Buckinghamshire. In the note they told her that they were well, that they hoped she was too and that they would send a letter in the future, before signing off with 'Pappa' and 'Mutti'. However, it did include one other rather curious comment. They wrote that, concerning *'Pulover'* (pullover), she should ask *'Lilly'*. At face value, it seems a curious and insignificant matter to mention when wordage was so restricted, but perhaps they were using a pre-arranged code, anticipating that the content would be vetted, and so avoided mentioning anything that might have been problematic. And there is one particular thing to which this might refer.

Fearing for their future, Sophie and Friedrich entrusted his sister Rosette and her husband Friedrich Kühn with RM2100, probably their life savings.[155] As has already been indicated, the two families were close and, as the Kühns were Catholics, Sophie and Friedrich probably thought Rosette and Friedrich would escape persecution and could hold the money safely until it could be returned or passed on to Karola. Perhaps the cryptic words in the letter informed her of this. Unfortunately, though, their assumptions proved to be incorrect. Rosette received notice of her deportation in 1944, but died shortly before it could be enforced.

---

[154] Although the Red Cross mainly carried messages to and from prisoners-of-war during WW2, it also exchanged 23 million letters between civilians when postal communications were interrupted. Personal communication from ICRC Archives, 18 August 2017.

[155] The money is mentioned in letters to Karola from Greta Reusch, 16 December 1951 and 25 April 1958.

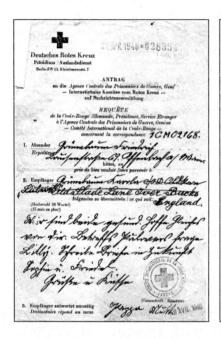

Sender: Grünebaum Friedrich, Luisenstrasse 69, Offenbach / Main

Recipient: Grünebaum Karola c/o Oldkorn "Lulworth" Old Slade Lane Iver Bucks England

We are both well. Hope same with you. Concerning pullovers, ask Lilly. In future will write letters.

Sophie and Friedel

Greetings and kisses
Papa Mama

Friedrich and Sophie's message to Karola in April 1940 (with translation)

Instructions about how to answer Sophie and Friedrich's message were given on an accompanying slip of paper, which stipulated that replies had to be written on the reverse of the original. Karola answered in German that she was well, concealing the mental distress that she was actually feeling. She told her parents that she was working as a cashier and that she had had contact with 'Friedrich', a reference to her uncle (Sophie's brother) in South Africa. She also provided them with her latest address.

4. Antwort des Empfängers:
Réponse du destinataire:
(Höchstzahl 25 Worte!)
(25 mots au plus!)

11. 1. 42.

11 January 1942

I'm well. Hope same with you. Working as a cashier. Have good news from Siegfried. New address: 20 Kendal Street London W2

Greetings Kiss
Karola

Karola's reply to her parents' Red Cross message (with translation)

What is particularly notable about this reply is that it was dated 11 January 1942, almost two years after her parents had written. Why was there such a long gap? Perhaps it was simply a consequence of the difficulties of international communication between protagonists during a war, and maybe Karola had gone to London by the time the message reached Iver, causing further delay while it was forwarded. However, one cannot ignore the possibility that it was deliberately delayed because, by late 1938, the *Deutsches Rotes*

Kreuz was under the control of the *Innenministerium* (Ministry of the Interior) and had essentially become a tool of the Nazi regime.[156] Whatever the cause, it seems that the reply was never sent, since the original is still here.

Having long been under the impression that this was their only contact, it came as a huge surprise when, 18 months into this project, I discovered that correspondence between Karola and her parents actually continued for some considerable time after this message was written. Amongst her surviving papers is a collection of letters from family and friends, all but five of which she received after 1945. The other five were much earlier, written on very flimsy airmail paper and in an old script, which even Germans find difficult to interpret. It was only when a friend deciphered them for me that I learned that they were also from Karola's parents. In fact, they were largely penned by Friedrich, with Sophie adding a few of her own words to one of them. It seemed surprising that both the Red Cross message and these letters were signed off with first names, and with the familiar form of Friedrich ('Friedel'). However, it is clear that this is how they were known to her, for the same names were used in the content of the letters too. But these letters did not just reveal what she called them. It is from this correspondence that I learned for the first time that Friedrich and Sophie had a pet name for their daughter. They called her 'Rola'. This though was just one of the names by which she was known to other family members and friends who, in later correspondence, wrote to her variously as 'Rolus' and 'Kary'.[157]

---

[156] 'Im Klammergriff der Diktatur', Deutsches Rotes Kreuz, https://www.drk. de/das-drk/geschichte/das-drk-von-den-anfaengen-bis-heute/1930/1933/; Birgitt Morgenbrod and Stephanie Merkenich, *Das Deutsche Rote Kreuz unter der NS-Diktatur 1933–1945* (Paderborn: Schöningh, 2008).

[157] In correspondence, her cousin, Katharina (Käthi) Buxbaum, in Bernal (Argentina) addresses her as 'Rolus', while to Evamarie Grünebaum (in Offenbach) she is 'Kary'.

One of Friedrich and Sophie's letters to Karola written in March 1941

Four of these letters were written over seven months between September 1940 and April 1941, that is *after* the Red Cross message was sent.[158] And it is evident from their content that during this time Friedrich and Sophie also received mail from Karola. However, with direct communication banned, it cannot

---

[158] The fifth letter is also from Friedel and Sophie, but this is an undated fragment and addressed to other people, not all of whose names are legible, but they include 'Rina' and 'Fritz'.

have been easy to stay in touch. The post must have been sent through neutral territory, which may explain why it took an extraordinarily long time to reach its destination.[159] Friedrich and Sophie's letter written on 9 March 1941 mentioned that Karola's dated 18 December 1940 had just arrived. Another took just over two months and a third more than three months. Each letter consisted of just a single sheet of paper, which in most cases was used for multiple messages, probably reflecting the cost of and restrictions on international correspondence. In one, for example, there was a short note to Karola from her parents and a separate one from her Aunt Luise.[160] Another had a second note addressed to Käthie and Albert in Argentina.[161] As this was a neutral country until 1944, the letters to Karola may have been first sent to them for onward posting.

The content of the letters was both anodyne and revealing, but perhaps what Friedrich and Sophie did not say is as notable as what they did. Given the terrifying circumstances in which they were living, it is striking that they make not the slightest reference to the political situation or the persecution they were experiencing. The omission is easily explained by the fact that all mail, even when sent to neutral countries, was subject to extreme monitoring and censorship. Three of the four letters have a number written in a different handwriting in the top left corner of the paper, perhaps added by a censor. Each letter included similar remarks, expressing their joy that Karola was well, requesting her to write to them, sending good wishes for special occasions, such as the new year (1941) and Karola's 20th birthday, and sharing a few words of

---

[159] Justin Gordon, *Holocaust Postal History: Harrowing Journeys Revealed Through the Letters and Cards of the Victims* (Chicago: Six Point Watermark, 2016).

[160] Luise Grünebaum, *née* Jester, was the widow of Friedrich's younger brother, Albert, who had died in April 1938.

[161] Käthi was Karola's cousin, Katharina Grünebaum (daughter of Friedrich's elder brother, Edmund). She had married Albert Buxbaum and by May 1941 they were living in South America.

affection. They also gave reassurances about their own welfare and mentioned events that suggested a life of total normality. It seems inconceivable that their words actually reflected reality or their true feelings. Much more likely, they wanted to avoid alarming their daughter and were concealing much deeper and justified fears.

Nevertheless, each also contains fascinating, and occasionally even amusing, news, which sheds some light on their daily lives and the lives of other family members. In the second letter, for example, which was written on 9 March 1941, Friedrich and Sophie told Karola that they had just heard from Aunt Rosette (Friedrich's older sister) and that she was again suffering from 'one of her 365 illnesses … and had to take to her bed'. Presumably, this was a frequent occurrence. They also reported that Aunt Luise had gone away for convalescence and that, for the first time in 16 years, they had had a visit from Greta (Karola's cousin).

9 March 1941

My dear Rola

Jumbo will soon become a father, he got engaged today.
We received your letter of 18 December 1940 today and learned from
it that you are well. We can tell you that it's the same with us. We were
most pleased to know that you are happy and healthy, because that is the
greatest of all riches. This morning we had news that Aunt Rosette has one
of her 365 illnesses again and had to take to her bed. Aunt Luise has gone
for convalescence. We learned from your letter that you have good news
from Uncle Siegfried. Write and give him best wishes from us all. The same
applies to Norbert. But in my opinion, it is not yet the right time for me
to go there. One thing I almost forgot. That is, we had a visit. Greta, who
hadn't been to see us for 16 years, was here for three days. You can imagine,
the whole house was full. In our last letter we told you that the photo had
still not arrived. It would be best to send it to Rina. We will be very happy
when we have it in our hands. There is no other news from us today, except
that we are both in work and, thank God, also healthy and happy.

Best wishes and kisses for today
Friedel and Sophie

Translation of Friedrich and Sophie's letter of 9 March 1941

It is also apparent from this letter that by September 1941
Karola was in contact with family members and friends in other
countries, and had been passing on their news to Friedrich and
Sophie. They asked her to pass on their best wishes to Uncle
Siegfried in South Africa and to 'Norbert', her friend Norbert
Stiefel who had gone to Southern Rhodesia. There is a further
noteworthy comment relating to these contacts. Friedrich and
Sophie wrote *Ich meine aber, es wäre jetzt noch nicht die richtige
Zeit für mich daran zu gehen*' (But in my opinion, now is not yet

the right time for me to go there). Could it be that Siegfried had suggested that they join him in South Africa?

Karola's parents mentioned that they were still awaiting a picture. Probably a photo of their daughter, whom they had not now seen for 18 months. They suggested sending it to Karola's cousin Rina, (the daughter of Ferdinand and Maria Grünebaum), who was still living in Offenbach. Rina had been raised in a Protestant household, so they may have felt that international post was more likely to reach her. Surprisingly, they wrote that they were both in work, an assertion repeated in their next letter. This seems unlikely to have been the case, given other evidence that Friedrich's income was limited to earnings from doing occasional jobs for Georg Hellwig.

Understandably, they were eager to learn about their daughter's new life in England. In the third letter, written just one week after the second, they asked about her Christmas and whether she was given nice presents. In the fourth letter, written almost a month later on 13 April, they expressed astonishment (verging on shock) that she had changed her job and wanted to know what she was now doing. This must refer to Karola leaving her position as a mother's help in Iver and starting work with Lyons in London in February 1941, details of which she apparently had not previously shared. Clearly this was a concern to them because they returned to the matter later in the letter, asked why she had moved and expressed hope that she had not fallen out with her employer.

It is difficult to imagine Friedrich and Sophie sitting in their apartment and continuing this 'normal' conversation while war raged across Europe and North Africa, and while increasing numbers of Jewish citizens were being transported to concentration camps. The contrast with the outside world is even more conspicuous when set against exchanges about what seem the most trivial of matters. In the second letter, Friedrich and Sophie commented on Karola's stockings. Their advice to her was that, if they could no longer be darned, she would have to buy new ones, even if they were expensive. The issue of clothing arose in the next letter too. They asked almost accusingly whether she had looked after her things properly, so that no moths had got into them. They even engaged in some light-hearted banter. Apparently, and for reasons unknown, Karola wrote that she could make use of a violinist! Friedrich replied that this was a bit too much to ask as she was so far away, and said he would have to take a shortcut across country roads to get there. The implication is that Friedrich could play the violin, something which I had no knowledge of previously, but why she felt she needed a fiddler remains another unanswered question.

Nazi Oppression and Murder

Deportation and Degradation by the Gestapo

While these largely banal exchanges were taking place, and as Karola settled into life in the UK, the oppression of Jews in the Third Reich steadily intensified. In April 1939, shortly before her emigration, the Nazis had introduced regulations for the eviction of Jews from their rented homes and their concentration in segregated housing.[162] During the subsequent months, more and more Offenbach Jews were forced out of their accommodation and into a grotesquely overcrowded *Judenhaus* (Jews' House), more often referred to today as a '*Ghettohaus* (ghetto house). As the situation worsened, a number chose to take their own lives rather than submit to such treatment.[163]

However, as their rent book shows, Friedrich and Sophie were allowed to remain in their apartment for three years after Karola left, that is until September 1942. Why were they so fortunate? One reason is that Friedrich's wartime service provided them with some protection, since Jewish WW1 veterans were initially exempted from some of the more barbaric Nazi actions.[164] But it

---

[162] Gesetz über Mietverhältnisse mit Juden (Law Concerning Jewish Tenants), 30 April 1939. Teil I, S. 864.

[163] Hauschke-Wicklaus G, E Katusić and B Leissing (eds, 2021). *Offenbacher Stolpersteine – Gegen das Vergessen*. Geschichtswerkstatt Offenbach, 3.

[164] Michael Geheran, *Comrades Betrayed: Jewish World War I Veterans under Hitler*, Battlegrounds: Cornell Studies in Military History (Ithaca, New York: Cornell University Press, 2020).

must have also depended on their landlord, Georg Hellwig, who had already taken a risk in giving Friedrich casual work, permitting them to continue living there. Nevertheless, when the 1939–40 edition of the official Offenbach address book was published, their names (and the names of many other Jewish residents), which previously had been listed every year, were no longer included. Either they or their landlord had made their presence less visible by not submitting their details for inclusion.

On 1 September 1941, the Nazi authorities decreed that all Jews aged six years or older had to wear an identification badge. The regulations about this were specific. It had to be worn on the chest and have the word *'Jude'* (Jew) inscribed inside a yellow Star of David on a black background. Friedrich and Sophie were forced to wear the badge. But much more ominously, implementation of the so-called 'Final Solution', the Nazis' plan to annihilate the Jewish people, gathered pace. In October 1941, the deportation of Jews to concentration camps, which had started in countries annexed by the Nazis, was extended to cover Jews in Germany itself.[165] In spring 1942, Jewish representatives in Offenbach were ordered to compile a list of all Jews in the city and submit it to the district authorities. It included 344 names, Sophie and Friedrich's among them.[166] War veterans were again initially exempted from this barbaric act, but the relief was temporary. Within a few months, Friedrich and Sophie were notified that they too were to be deported. There is no testimony from them personally about what actually took place, but evidence from other Jewish and non-Jewish citizens in Offenbach and across Hessen provides a

---

[165] 'German Jews during the Holocaust, 1939–1945', Holocaust Encyclopedia, https://encyclopedia.ushmm.org/content/en/article/german-jews-during-the-holocaust.

[166] Werner, 'Juden in Offenbach am Main 1933-45. Gemeinderleben – Sozialstruktur – Verfolgung und Vernichtung', 137

consistent story of what followed.[167] The process began with a knock on the door by local officials who delivered a chilling notice issued by the Gestapo in Darmstadt.

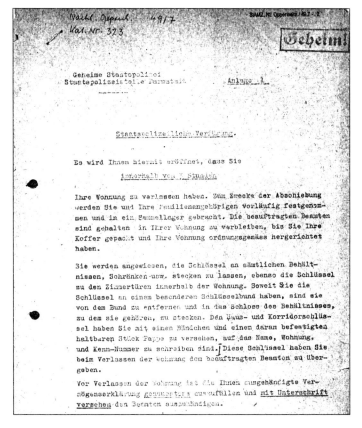

Extract from the deportation order issued by Darmstadt Gestapo[168]

---

[167] Hess, Nichtweiss, and Zahedi, *Juden-Deportation aus Darmstadt 1942/43,* 17; Renate Dreesen and Christoph Jetter, *Darmstadt als Deportationsort: Zur Erinnerung an die unter Dem Nazi-Regime aus dem Ehemaligen Volksstaat Hessen Deportierten Juden und Sinti* (Darmstadt: Initiative 'Gedenkort Güterbahnhof Darmstadt,' 2004).; 'Transports to Extinction: Holocaust (Shoah) Deportation Database', https://deportation.yadvashem.org/index.html?language=en&item Id=5092509&ind=2.

[168] 'Deportation ("Auswanderung")', Stadtarchiv Mainz: Nachlass Oppenheim,

Almost identical wording was used across Germany for this notice, which was based on a template issued in Berlin. However, as far as is known, in no other area was the wording so stark and direct. Elsewhere the Nazis used terms such as *'Wohnsitzverlegung'* (residential relocation) or *'Evakuierung'* (evacuation) for what they were doing. The Darmstadt Gestapo did not bother with such euphemisms and bluntly informed recipients of their *'Abschiebung'* (deportation).

It ordered the occupants to leave within three hours and set out precise rules for their departure. There were, for example, specific instructions for the labelling of keys, what they should take with them and what to do with money and valuables to be left behind. It required them to go out on to the street with a cardboard sign hung around their necks displaying their name and identification number. The orders combined the attention to detail and the inhumanity that characterised so many aspects of the Nazi regime and it is impossible to appreciate the scope of its content or the fear it must have instilled in its recipients without reading it fully.

File NL Oppenheim/49/7, 1942.

Secret State Police, State Police Station Darmstadt
Order of the State Police

You are hereby informed that you must leave your flat within three hours. For the purpose of deportation, you and your family members will be temporarily arrested and taken to a transit camp. The appointed officials will remain in your apartment until you have packed your suitcase and prepared your apartment according to the rules.

You are instructed to leave behind the keys to all containers, cupboards, etc, as well as keys to the internal doors of the apartment. If you have the keys on a special keyring, remove them from the ring and put them in the locks to which they belong. The house and corridor keys must be tied on a ribbon with a durable piece of cardboard attached to it, on which your name, apartment address and identification number are to be written. These keys must be handed to the appointed official upon leaving the apartment. Before leaving the apartment, the asset declaration form given to you must be filled out in detail, signed and handed over to the official.

You must take with you:
1. RM50 cash
2. A suitcase or a backpack, total weight not exceeding 50 kg, containing: linen, clothing, other items needed for a simple lifestyle
3. Two blankets with bedding (not in suitcase, but rolled and tied up)
4. A full set of clothes (you can also put on two coats and two layers of underwear)
5. Food for 3 days, spoon, plate, bowl, cup, (not packed in the suitcase)
6. Identity card, employment and all other identification papers, all food ration cards, potato and coal ration coupons. All special vouchers.
(The items listed in Section 6 must not be packed, but must be kept on the person).

Not allowed to be taken:
    Securities
    Foreign currency
    Bank and savings bank books
    Valuables of all kinds, gold, silver, platinum
    Livestock

You may take with you your wedding ring and a simple watch (nickel and steel watches only). Cash, valuables, jewellery and precious metals should be placed in a cloth bag and handed over to the officials. Your exact address and identification number must be shown on the bag. An exact list of the contents must be drawn up and signed by the officials and the owner, and enclosed with the contents of the bag.

The suitcase to be carried must have a durable label that clearly shows your name, date and place of birth, home address and identification number.

You yourself must hang a sign around your neck, which will show in clearly legible writing your name, date of birth and identification number.

You must unconditionally comply with all orders of the officials and give them any requested information. If you disobey, you can expect the most severe response from the state police.

This order shall also be deemed to be an identity card for the holder.

Darmstadt, 18th March 1942
Secret State Police, Secret State Police Station
Signed by Dr Achenauer-Pifrader
Colonel and senior government official

Translation of deportation order issued by Darmstadt Gestapo

The Grünebaums probably received this order in mid-September 1942. Their rent book shows that a payment was made shortly before this, but entries then come to an abrupt end. Having anticipated that their already grim lives were likely to become even more terrifying, they had already handed over to Rosette and Friedrich Kühn their savings of RM2100 for safe keeping. Now with their deportation confirmed, Herr Kühn returned RM300 to them, which they paid into a bank with the intention of withdrawing it at their destination. It is highly unlikely that they were ever able to do this. On the day of their departure, their apartment in Luisenstrasse was locked up. Sometime later, Friedrich Kühn saw their possessions (as well as those of other Jewish families) for sale.[169] The furniture was on display in the Feistmann factory building, and the linen in the Werk-Öhler horse-riding hall, overseen by members of the *Nationalsozialistische Volkswohlfahrt* (National Socialist People's Welfare).

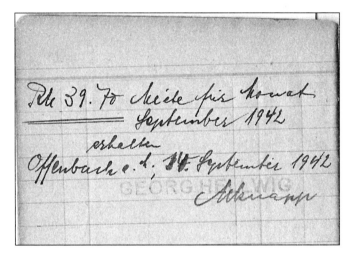

The final entry in Friedrich and Sophie's rent book,
recording the payment made in September 1942

The order from the Gestapo informed Sophie and Friedrich that they were being temporarily arrested and would be taken to a transit camp. Deportees were expected to buy in advance a one-way rail ticket to their destination, a third-class fare being charged if they were to be transported in freight waggons. On leaving their apartment, they may have first been relocated to a *Ghettohaus*, but before long were instructed to assemble in the square behind the synagogue near 110 Kaiserstrasse.[170] From here they were

---

[169] Statement submitted to Landgericht Darmstadt by Friedrich Kühn, 4 September 1952.

[170] This was either the site of, or adjacent to, the previously mentioned factory building once owned by Adolph Merzbach, before his business was relocated

transferred the 30 kilometres to Darmstadt in the back of a truck, before completing the last stretch of this journey on foot.

Darmstadt was the departure point for Jews from across much of Hessen and further afield. They were brought there by train from Mainz and Giessen, as well as by truck from Offenbach. But Sophie and Friedrich, like all the others, were not immediately deported. They were first taken to an assembly point and held there for up to three weeks. That assembly point was the Liebigs Schule, a boys' secondary school made available to the Gestapo by the city authorities and probably selected because of its proximity to the railway station and relative seclusion. While being used to process Jewish prisoners, the school was closed, the boys were strictly forbidden from going near it and armed police stood guard to keep onlookers away. Nevertheless, several pupils and other children who lived close by did see what was happening.[171]

One such pupil, Bernd Krimmel, recalled a ghastly image of Jews, dressed in black, shuffling silently along Kasinostrasse into the school, in what he described as like a funeral procession. Karl Vogt remembered lines of men, women and children, six abreast with armed escorts on both sides. Otto Tramer noticed that many of the prisoners were elderly and all wore Jewish stars, while their escorts wore jackboots and military hats. Marianne Flöring saw crowds of people in the school playground and, on asking what was going on, was told that they were Jews and they were being taken away. In a perverse twist of fate, this school where Friedrich was now to be held as a prisoner was just a few hundred metres from the barracks where he had served his country as a soldier in the army.[172]

---

to Obersinn (Bavaria) and then sold to Friedrich Kühn.

[171] Hess, Nichtweiss and Zahedi, *Juden-Deportation aus Darmstadt 1942/43*, 23–29.

[172] 'Kasernen in Darmstadt bis 1945', DFG-VK, https://dfg-vk-darmstadt.de/Lexikon_Auflage_2/Kasernen_in_Darmstadt_bis_1945.htm.

The buildings and playground of the Liebigs Schule in Darmstadt,
where Jews were brought before their deportation[173]

Inside the school, Sophie and Friedrich had to endure conditions
that were degrading and disgusting. On arrival they underwent a
series of checks by various local agencies, including the finance
department, the land registry, the bailiff and the town council,
to ensure that their assets and liabilities had been taken care of,
and that all taxes had been paid.[174] Their luggage was searched
and they were forced to undress for intimate body searches by
Gestapo officers or their assistants, who included civil servants
and cleaning ladies, in a hunt for undeclared valuables. Others
counted confiscated money and recorded seized belongings. Their
ration cards had to be surrendered and they were made to sign an
authorisation for the transfer of their property to the state. They
were fed on thin watery soup, slept on straw mats in a single large

---

[173] Image © Stadtarchiv Darmstadt. Taken in 1911 on the opening of the
school, which was then called the Liebigs Oberrealschule (High School). It was
renamed in 1937 the Liebigs Schule and is today known as the Justus-Liebig
Schule.
[174] Hess, Nichtweiss, and Zahedi, *Juden-Deportation aus Darmstadt 1942/43*,
17.

room with all the other detainees, and were required to stand erect as soon as a member of the SS entered. Some older detainees were too weak and collapsed, while others were beaten with sticks. Several did not make it out of the school alive. Sick and frail, they died there. The Nazis disinfected all the rooms before the school reopened.

The main deportations from Darmstadt were made in four trainloads. The first, on 20 March 1942, carried 1,000 Jews to Piaski and Lublin (Poland). The second left for Theresienstadt (Czechoslovakia) on 27 September and was due to carry 1,288 prisoners.[175] Three days later, on 30 September, another took 883 to the General Governate, the term used by the Nazis for the occupied area of Poland. Finally, on 10 February 1943, 53 more Jews were sent to Theresienstadt. Friedrich and Sophie, together with 96 other citizens of Offenbach, were on the second and largest of these transports, designated DA 520 by the *Reichsbahn* (Imperial Railway) and Transport XVII/I in the camp's records.

---

[175] Theresienstadt is the German name for the town known in Czech as Terezín.

Extracts from a list compiled by Darmstadt Gestapo of people who had been 'relocated' to Theresienstadt, including Friedrich and Sophie Grünebaum[176]

On the day of their deportation, they assembled with the other deportees in the school playground and were then marched one kilometre to the nearby station goods yard. Anyone who slowed or lagged behind was beaten with sticks by the guards. Although

---

[176] Document 1.2.1.1./11201597 ITS Digital Archive, Arolsen Archives.

the group included a few children and young adults, it mainly comprised the elderly, the reason being that Theresienstadt was being presented to the world as a model settlement for older people.

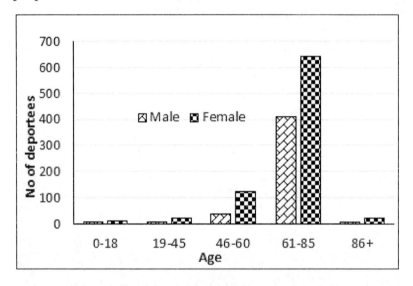

Age profile of the 1,288 men and women deported
from Darmstadt on 27 September 1942[177]

In keeping with Germany's punctilious bureaucracy, the administrative loose ends relating to the Grünebaums' disappearance were neatly tidied up. A month after their deportation, on 22 October 1942, a note was added to their index card in the *Jüdische Meldekartei* which simply, but disingenuously, stated *'Abgemeldet ohne Angabe des neuen Wohnsitzes'* (de-registered without providing a new address).

---

[177] 'Transports to Extinction: Holocaust (Shoah) Deportation Database'.

Entry on Friedrich and Sophie's index card recording their departure
'without providing a new address'

From Darmstadt to Theresienstadt is 600 kilometres and the
train travelled through the night, arriving the next morning at
Bohusovice, the nearest station. By then there were only 1,287
prisoners, one person having died even before reaching the
destination. In groups of 100 people, they then had to walk the
three kilometres along a country road to the camp carrying their
luggage. It was a hot day and they were very thirsty, but there was
no respite. Some simply dropped the few possessions they were
carrying.

Theresienstadt (Terezín) Camp

Theresienstadt is a town about 60 kilometres north of Prague.
Originally a holiday resort for Czech nobility and subsequently a
garrison town, it developed within the walls of its historic fortress,
and within these walls the Gestapo established a camp.[178] From
1941 to 1945 around 150,000 Jews and other prisoners were
incarcerated here, some of them for several years. More than one
in five died there.[179] Despite this, Theresienstadt was not classified
by the Nazis as a *Vernichtungslager* or *Todeslager* (extermination

---

[178] For an in-depth analysis of life in Theresienstadt, see Anna Hájková, *The
Last Ghetto: an Everyday History of Theresienstadt* (New York: Oxford University
Press, 2020).
[179] Of the 1287 deportees on Transport XVII/1, only 89 survived the war.

or death camp) because its primary function was not genocide. Instead, it was categorised as a ghetto or transit camp, where deportees were confined under terrible physical conditions and strict regulation.[180]

Daily life in the camp was administered by a Jewish Council of Elders and there was also a 'police' force partly made up of Jews, but set up and controlled by the Gestapo. The Elders and police took decisions that effectively determined whether individual prisoners lived or died, for example, by controlling the allocation of food and selecting prisoners to be transported to other camps. Unsurprisingly, its members were controversial figures from the outset, condemned by many for their collaboration.

Those brought to the camp were housed in the former barracks, as well as buildings from which the residents had been evicted. Men and women were separated from each other and from their children, who were accommodated in boys' and girls' dormitories. There was extreme overcrowding. Fifty inmates were forced to live in the space previously occupied by ten soldiers. People lived in the roof spaces, entrance ways, courtyards, cellars, fortress gun emplacements and crates. They slept in three-tier bunks or on the floor, often with multiple people sharing each straw mattress. When Friedrich and Sophie arrived, the available space was just two square metres per person, a figure that included lavatory, kitchen and storage space. The living and sleeping areas were infested with rats, fleas, flies and lice.[181]

Communication was severely restricted. Husbands and wives were not allowed to speak to each other and the sending of letters was prohibited. Detainees were not permitted out of the camp. Smoking was forbidden and all inmates were required to have

---

[180] 'Daily Orders from the Terezín (Theresienstadt) Ghetto', https://blog.ehri-project.eu/2016/05/18/daily-orders-from-the-terezin-theresienstadt-ghetto/.
[181] 'Theresienstadt: The "Model" Ghetto', Jewish Virtual Library, https://www.jewishvirtuallibrary.org/theresienstadt-the-ldquo-model-rdquo-ghetto.

their hair cut short. Anyone breaking the rules was at risk of receiving the death penalty.

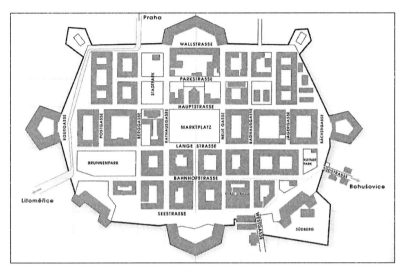

Plan of Theresienstadt Camp within the town's walls

The overcrowding, poor sanitation, severe food shortages and unhygienic conditions meant detainees had little resistance to illness and infectious diseases spread rapidly.[182] It is estimated that 30–35,000 men, women and children died in the camp from illness, malnutrition or other causes. By 1942, the death rate was so high that the Germans built a crematorium able to handle 200 bodies a day. One of those to die was Salomon Reiss, Sophie's eldest sibling. A death notification was completed by the Council of Elders and, as in other matters, the record keeping was detailed and revealing.

---

[182] David Cesarani, 'Life Inside the Theresienstadt Concentration Camp', The History Reader, 2016, https://www.thehistoryreader.com/military-history/theresienstadt/.; Ivan Brod, *From Auschwitz to Du Pont* (Createspace Independent, 2009).

Notification of the death of Salomon Reiss prepared by the
Theresienstadt Council of Elders, July 1943[183]

[183] Image © National Archives, Prague, Registers of Jewish religious communities in the Czech regions, Death certificates – Ghetto Terezín, volume 103, https://www.holocaust.cz/en/database-of-digitised-documents/document/97196-reiss-salomon-death-certificate-ghetto-terezin/

As well as a host of personal data, the notification showed that Salomon was actually transported to the camp on the same train as Friedrich and Sophie in September 1942 and then housed in Room 23c of Building L504. Moreover, that was where he died just nine months later at 16:30 hours on Tuesday 6 July 1943, aged 60. After carrying out a post-mortem, Dr Viktor Kosák, a Jewish doctor who worked in the camp, gave the cause of death as heart failure.[184] But Salomon also had lung and liver cancer, and other serious medical conditions. No date or place was given for his burial.

In some respects, Theresienstadt was quite different from other camps. It had a distinctive demographic profile, being used to incarcerate war veterans and older people, as well as well-educated and prominent Jews, some with international reputations. They included academics, philosophers, scientists, doctors, artists and musicians, and despite the constraints of imprisonment and subjugation, a rich cultural life continued. Musicians performed, poets composed, artists drew, professors lectured and children were educated. Rabbis conducted religious services and there was even a library with thousands of books, many with an emphasis on Jewish subjects. Such activity was tolerated because Theresienstadt actually served three purposes. First, and most obviously, it was used to concentrate and control Jews from annexed states, as well as from within Germany itself. But second, and uniquely, it was a tool of deception, used for propaganda to deceive the outside world and conceal the Nazis' real intentions for the Jewish people. It was portrayed as a model settlement, a retirement town, a spa resort and somewhere with a vibrant cultural tradition. Extreme measures were taken to create the illusion, including a

---

[184] Dr Viktor Kosák was a Czech physician from Prague. He survived the war and died in 1993, aged 81. Hájková, *The Last Ghetto*.; 'MUDr Viktor Kosák, Mudr (1911 - 1993) - Genealogy', https://www.geni.com/people/MUDr-Viktor-Kos%C3%A1k-Mudr/6000000021438317378#/tab/overview.

beautification programme ahead of a Red Cross inspection, which included deporting 28,000 people to extermination camps to reduce overcrowding.[185] But it was the camp's third function that was most chilling. It served as a transit camp for Jews on their way to the gas chambers.

The Last Journey to Auschwitz

Beginning in January 1942, an estimated 87,000 prisoners were transported out of Theresienstadt, principally to concentration camps in occupied Poland. The Council of Elders played a significant role in selecting them, adding to Jewish hostility towards its members. Initial destinations included Baltic and Polish towns where ghettos had been established, but these were usually just temporary stops.[186] From September 1942 almost all trains went direct to Treblinka and then from January 1943 to October 1944 to Auschwitz. Both were extermination camps where gas chambers had been constructed. Four months after arriving in Theresienstadt, Friedrich and Sophie were put on to one of the first trains to Auschwitz. As before, their move was carefully recorded, this time in the Camp's Central Card File and in Czech. As well as their name, date of birth and number of the train that brought them to the camp, the entry logged that on 29 January 1943 they were *'Deportace na východ'* (deported to the east) on Transport 'Ct' as prisoners 43 and 44.

---

[185] 'History of Terezin', Terezin: Children of the Holocaust, http://www.terezin.org/the-history-of-terezin/; 'Theresienstadt', Holocaust Encyclopedia, https://encyclopedia.ushmm.org/content/en/article/theresienstadt; 'Stories from Terezín: The Nazi Transit Camp with a Musical Legacy', https://www.theguardian.com/world/interactive/2013/apr/05/stories-terezin-nazi-concentration-camp-music-interactive.

[186] As with transports into Theresienstadt, the Terezín Initiative has compiled a listing of transports out of the camp. http://www.porges.net/Terezin/TransportsToFromTerezin.html.

File record card of Sophie Grünebaum's deportation
from Theresienstadt to Auschwitz[187]

In Auschwitz they disappeared. How long they survived is
unclear since most camp files were destroyed by the Nazis, and
Friedrich and Sophie's names are not amongst those that have
been preserved.[188] A record card in the Arolsen Archives states
that 'There is some evidence that they were alive in Jan 1945', but
there is nothing of substance to support this.[189] It appears to be
based on an enquiry about them submitted by Luise Grünebaum
in November 1945. In this she vaguely mentioned that they were
thought to have been alive at the beginning of the year, but gave
no reason for believing that.

---

[187] Document 1.1.42.2/5036233/ITS Digital Archive, Arolsen Archives.
[188] 'Auschwitz-Birkenau', https://www.auschwitz.org/en/museum/archives/.
[189] Personal communication with ITS, 8 March 2019.

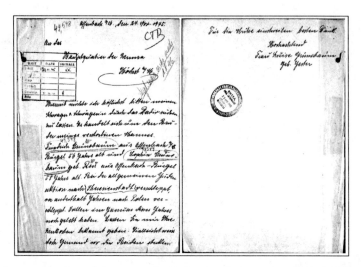

Luise Grünebaum's letter sent in November 1945 to the UN Relief and
Rehabilitation Administration enquiring about Friedrich and Sophie[190]

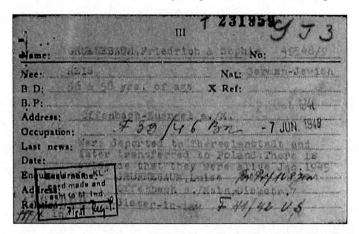

International Tracing Service record of enquiry about Friedrich and Sophie
made by Luise Grünebaum in 1945 mentioning evidence that they were alive
in January 1945[191]

[190] Document 6.3.1.1./86190313/ITS Digital Archive, Arolsen Archives.
[191] Document 6.3.3.2./89590128/ITS Digital Archive, Arolsen Archives.

Given that they were both well over 50 years old, it is improbable
that they were put to work in a labour camp. Nevertheless, there
is one other fragment of information that suggests one or both
might not have been sent to the gas chambers immediately. It
came from Wilma Feick, Karola's childhood friend, whose uncle
was deployed during the war as a motorcyclist in Poland. At the age
of 95, she still clearly remembered that on one occasion, when he
was at home on leave, her uncle spoke about having seen Friedrich
in Poland wearing work clothes. It was an incredible coincidence
and they recognised each other but were not allowed to speak.
Later legal papers show their presumed date of death as Tuesday 8
May 1945 and their names are recorded in the Memorial Book for
the Victims of Persecution under the National Socialist Tyranny
in Germany 1933–1945. There is nothing to suggest that this was
actually the date they were murdered, it is purely notional.

Grünebaum, Friedrich Julius

born on 10th April 1889 in Offenbach a. Main / - / Hessen
resident of Offenbach a. Main

Deportation:
from Darmstadt
27th September 1942, Theresienstadt, ghetto
29th January 1943, Auschwitz, Konzentrations-and extermination camp

Grünebaum, Sophie

née Reiss
born on 21st March 1888 in Bürgel / Offenbach a. Main / Hessen
resident of Offenbach a. Main

Deportation:
from Darmstadt
27th September 1942, Theresienstadt, ghetto
29th January 1943, Auschwitz, Konzentrations-and extermination camp

---

Extracts from Memorial Book for the 'Victims of Persecution under the
National Socialist Tyranny in Germany 1933–1945'[192]

---

[192] 'Memorial Book', Das Bundesarchiv, https://www.bundesarchiv.de/
gedenkbuch/introduction/en.

Also amongst the Auschwitz victims were Salomon Reiss's wife, Lilli, and two of their daughters. Selma was abducted in Frankfurt in April 1940, Hertha in Berlin in February 1942. They were not taken to Theresienstadt but transported direct to Poland. A few months later, their two sisters, Irene, and Gertude, were also arrested, transported, and then murdered, although their final destination is not known.

It seems possible that Karola learned about her parents' deportation from non-Jewish family members soon after it happened. However, when she found out where they had been taken and what eventually happened to them is much less clear. In a letter to Karola dated 16 May 1951, her solicitor (J M Schül) mentioned that they had been taken to Theresienstadt, and asked if she had any information about what had subsequently happened to them. In her reply dated 13 June she stated that she believed they had died there, so she may never have known that they were in fact subsequently transported to Auschwitz.

Nevertheless, amongst the documents in Karola's old suitcase was one item which showed that she was very aware of how grotesque the extermination camps were. It is a gruesome 78-page 'Album' of photographs related to Dachau Concentration Camp. Published in 1945/46 by the International Information Office for the Former Concentration Camp, it detailed its horrors, trials of former SS officers and the lives of those recently liberated, with captions in English, French, Polish and German. How she acquired this chilling record of brutality, we will never know.

Pages from the 'album' of the Dachau Concentration Camp

There is one other family connection to the Holocaust to record here. It concerns Karola's cousin, Wilhelm Kühn (the son of Friedrich and Rosette). In November 1944 he received a *Verpflichtungsbescheid,* a letter ordering him to report to Rossitz bei Altenburg with clothes, tools and provisions for two days' work.[193] On the allotted day, he was taken to Buchenwald concentration camp, where Friedrich had been detained in 1938. It was by then one of the largest camps in Germany and many thousands died there in the months before the war ended, some the victims of medical experiments, many others succumbing to typhus and other epidemics. The work Wilhelm was given was the construction of ovens for the cremation of their bodies.

---

[193] Document and related information kindly provided by Roland Kühn.

Order to report for work sent to Wilhelm Kühn in November 1944

As has already been mentioned, a small number of Karola's family members and friends did manage to escape the concentration camps by getting out of the country. They dispersed around the world to Africa, Europe, and North and South America. Over the next few years contacts between them were gradually rekindled and many letters written in the post-war period from them to Karola survive. But before considering what they had to say to each other, I will turn to events in a very different part of the globe.

Muslim Roots in India

The Marriage House

My father, Afzal, was about 33 years old when he met Karola in London, about 12 years older than his future bride. I say 'about', partly because the date of their first meeting is not known, but also because there was uncertainty about his age. He had no birth certificate and, although his passport showed his date of birth as 19 December 1909, his mother maintained that it was 30 June 1908. He kept his own signed note of that date, written in English in the Gregorian calendar and in Urdu in the Islamic calendar. However, the 30 June 1908 is in Islamic year 1326, not 1325 as he recorded, adding to the confusion.[194]

---

[194] On the same note Afzal recorded the date of his mother's death, but the year is incomplete (it should be 1959). And in 2022, to my surprise, I was shown pages of a notebook kept by Afzal's grandfather in which he had recorded family births and deaths. This showed yet another different date of birth for Afzal.

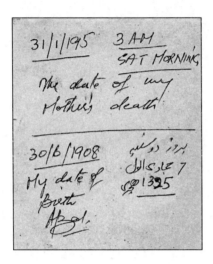

Afzal's note of his mother's death and his own birth date
(according to his mother)

As his name suggests, Afzal's family was Muslim and their first language was Urdu.[195] Both his mother's and father's family originated in Kashmir, but they migrated to Punjab in the early twentieth century. Many thousands made that journey from the early nineteenth century onwards to escape the poverty, famine and harsh treatment by Sikh and Hindu rulers that differentially affected the Muslim population. Afzal's mother, Vilayet, came from the town of Batala, where her father was a railway station master. She had a younger sister, Fatima, and after their mother died in childbirth, Fatima was brought up by her older sibling. As a result, a very strong bond developed between them. Afzal was born in Batala, since it was customary for mothers-to-be to return to their own family to give birth, but he grew up in his father's family home in Amritsar.

---

[195] From the late nineteenth century, languages in Punjab became increasingly linked to religion, with Sikhs speaking Punjabi, Hindus speaking Hindi and Muslims speaking Urdu.

That home was located at 3257/10 Kucha Sai Katra Dullo, just inside the ancient walled city near Lohgarh (Lagar) Gate. And although the family were Muslims, they lived very close to the Golden Temple, the spiritual centre of Sikhism. It was also just a short distance from Jallianwalla Bagh and in 1919 they would undoubtedly have heard the shots fired there in the Amritsar Massacre, when British troops turned their weapons on unarmed Indians. Some were just celebrating a spring festival, and some were protesting peacefully about the arrest of pro-independence leaders, but hundreds were killed and many hundreds more were wounded.

Although built in about 1910 by Miran Bakhsh, Afzal's paternal grandfather, the property and an earlier house on the site may have been owned by the family for much longer.[196] It was a very large modern three-storey brick residence situated in extensive grounds. There were tiled floors and 15 rooms, with several bathrooms and three kitchens, and it was connected to mains water and electricity. The house and grounds were used by the community for wedding celebrations and other big events, as a result of which it became known as the 'Marriage House'.

---

[196] This is based on a confusing comment made by Afzal's father, Mohamed Ismail, in a letter dated 9 July 1935, in which he writes that 'the house has been in the family's possession since the time of my grandmother'. Since the then existing house was built around 1910, this may refer to an earlier dwelling that was subsequently demolished.

میر احمد ملک شٹا

Miran Bakhsh, successful businessman and my great-grandfather

Miran Bakhsh was evidently a successful businessman, although there is some ambiguity about how he made his money. One document states that he was a jewel merchant and government contractor.[197] However, he was also said to be a trader in *kutch*, intricate wood carvings from Gujarat State.[198] Even after the house was completed, he continued to spend periods in Kashmir, dividing his time between the capital, Srinagar, and Anantnag, a smaller town 35 miles to the south-east. Correspondence was sent

---

[197] This is stated in a Court Order made in 1957 awarding compensation to the family for the loss of property at Partition.
[198] Kutch is a district in Gujarat State with a distinctive cultural tradition, including wood carving.

to him there until at least early 1911. From early 1912, however, all known communications were directed to Amritsar, where he started another business in gold thread, which was traditionally woven into fabrics for women's clothing. At some point, though, his fortunes took a serious downturn. He was defrauded by a business associate and left with a substantial debt that evidently became a very serious family concern.[199]

Miran Bakhsh and his wife had five children, two sons and three daughters. The three daughters would have moved into their husbands' family homes after their weddings, as was customary, but the two sons continued to live in the Marriage House. The older one was my grandfather, Mohamed Ismail ('Ismail'), whose adventurous life I will come to shortly. The younger brother, Nazir Ahmad, was married at a young age – perhaps 14 or 15 years old – to Zaheer Begum and the couple had five children.[200] Tragically, he was killed when trying to break up a violent altercation outside his house.[201] After the murder, Zaheer and the children were looked after by her brother Khawaja Ghulam Mohyuddin, a yarn dyer.

---

[199] Personal communication from Asif Hussain and a letter from Mohamed Ismail, 27 March 1911.

[200] Their only son was Bashir Ahmad. In his later years he came to be known to all the younger family members as Uncle Bashir. He built a highly successful carpet weaving business in Lahore and was generally regarded as 'head of the family'. The other four were daughters, named Shamin Akhtar, Nasim Akhtar, Tasmin Akhtar and Parveen Akhtar. Following her marriage, Nasim Akhtar had four children, three sons and a daughter, Naila, who would marry Afzal's eldest son, Asif, and so become Afzal's daughter-in-law.

[201] This incident probably took place around 1935 in Amritsar. The date and location are indicated by the ages of his children in a funeral photo and a mention in a letter from Afzal to his father, 27 August 1934. According to one account, he was stabbed in the leg and died from his injuries.

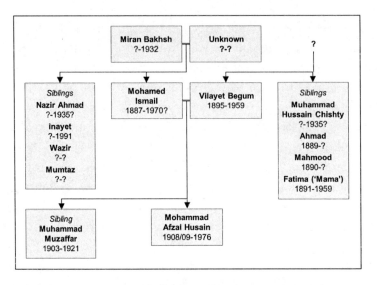

Afzal's ancestral tree

A Mysterious Emigration

Ismail, my paternal grandfather, was born on Thursday 31 March 1887. He was highly educated, having completed high school and possibly a master's degree, and was well versed in Urdu, Farsi and English. He dressed smartly in western clothes and, in the absence of an iron, would press these overnight by placing them under heavy stones. Perhaps surprisingly, since he was a Muslim, Ismail had a job with the Bible Society of India, no doubt in the office rather than in any proselytising role. It is not known when he married, but his wife, Vilayet, gave birth to two sons. My uncle, Muhammad Muzaffar Husain ('Muzaffar'), was born in 1903 and my father, Mohammad Afzal Husain, five or six years later. Afzal never really got to know his father. In August 1910, when his younger son was at most two years old, Ismail left Punjab and travelled 10,000 miles to South America, never to return. Why he went and why he chose that destination when he could have gone unhindered to anywhere in the British

196

Empire, remains a mystery. But there is much more to write about these matters and his life there and I will return to this topic shortly.

Growing Up in Punjab

With their father having disappeared, Muzaffar and Afzal grew up in the care of their mother, Vilayet, with support from her in-laws and other family members. Particularly important was her sister, Fatima, and her husband Abdul Haq. It has already been mentioned that, when very young, Fatima had been looked after by her older sister when their mother died in childbirth. Now the roles were reversed. Fatima, who came to be known as 'Mama', and Abdul Haq lived in Lahore. The three Punjabi cities of Batala, Amritsar and Lahore were close to each other, with Batala situated 25 miles north-east of Amritsar and Lahore 30 miles to the west. There was a lot of contact between them and at that time many families had relatives in each.

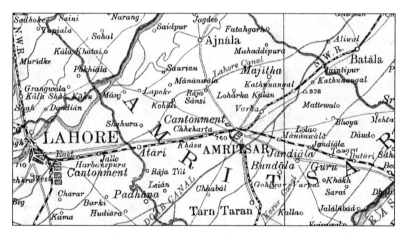

Location of the Punjabi cities Batala, Amritsar and Lahore[202]

---

[202] Image: 'Punjab' © Bibliothèque Nationale de France - Gallica, https://gallica.bnf.fr/ark:/12148/btv1b53209950b.r=punjab?rk=21459;2.

Abdul Haq was a senior civil servant in the colonial government, a job that came with a good salary and an enviable package of benefits. The family was well-off and could afford a large family residence in Model Town, a prestigious planned garden suburb to the south of Lahore's historic core. This became almost a second home for Vilayet, Muzaffar and Afzal, who divided their time between here and Amritsar. Afzal occasionally reminisced about his childhood. He spoke about the fun he had playing marbles and flying homemade kites from the roof. He told a story about going to stay with his maternal grandfather (the station master), where he took in a bear cub that had got separated from its parents, although he hadn't had it for long before it escaped. But amidst these happy recollections, he also talked about the untimely death of his older brother in 1921, undoubtedly a traumatic experience for a small boy.

Afzal completed his matriculation in 1926, leaving school aged 16 or 17 after what would have been a lengthy education for that time. Then for three years from 1927 he supervised the family business in Amritsar, although it is not at all clear what type of business that was. At the end of that period, he relocated to Lahore and for about a year was employed as a Temporary Clerk in the Public Works Department (Buildings and Roads Section) before starting up his own business there in 1931. That was also the year he got married. He was 22, while his wife Masuda was just 16 years old. Like his father, he married his cousin, the daughter of his mother's brother, Muhammad Hussain Chishty (known as Mr Chishty). Masuda and Vilayet probably also moved to Lahore when he set up in business, all of them living with Mama and her family in Model Town.

Constructed in 1921, Model Town is an extremely unusual urban development.[203] It was conceived by Advocate Dewan

---

[203] Shama Anbrine, 'The Co-operative Model Town Society; History, Planning, Architecture and Social Character of an Indigenous Garden Suburb in

Khem Chand, whose belief in the values of self-help, responsibility, democracy, equality and solidarity led him to propose a scheme based on cooperative principles to solve housing problems and improve living conditions. This was reflected in its design, with the town originally divided into ten blocks, each with its own market, playground, place of worship and triangular park. The Cooperative Model Town Society was formed to maintain its services and amenities, which included sports facilities and schools. It became the most desirable residential location in the city and the spacious dwellings with extensive grounds were occupied by the elite, including judges, businessmen, doctors and professors.[204] Mama and her husband lived initially in a house in A Block.

Colonial Lahore' (PhD thesis, Liverpool, 2014), http://livrepository.liverpool. ac.uk/2010879/1/AnbrineSha_Dec2014_2010879.pdf.

[204] The Model Town Society still exists 'to promote the social and economic interests of its members and more particularly to lay out, establish and maintain a garden town,' http://www.mts.com.pk/index.php.

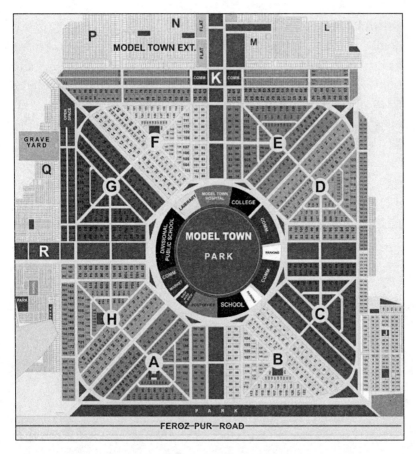

Layout of Model Town, Lahore

Self-Imposed Exile in South America

Immigration to Argentina

Encouraged by its government, many millions of immigrants travelled to Argentina in the late nineteenth and early twentieth century from across the world.[205] Almost all landed at Buenos Aires and entered the country through the *Hotel des Inmigrantes* (Immigrant Hotel), which was situated on the waterfront adjacent to where ships docked. Here new arrivals were given free meals and accommodation for up to five nights. Today this same building is the *Museo de la Inmigracion* (Immigration Museum).[206] Many of the original 'landing lists' of the thousands of ships that brought settlers to the port are housed in the museum.

---

[205] Encouragement of European immigration to accelerate development of the country was written into the Constitution at that time.

[206] 'Immigration Museum - Buenos Aires', https://www.welcomeargentina.com/ciudadbuenosaires/immigration-museum.html.; 'MUNTREF - Museo de La Inmigración', http://untref.edu.ar/muntref/en/museum-of-immigration/.; 'Arcón de Buenos Aires: Hotel de Inmigrantes', n.d., http://www.arcondebuenosaires.com.ar/hotel_inmigrantes.htm.

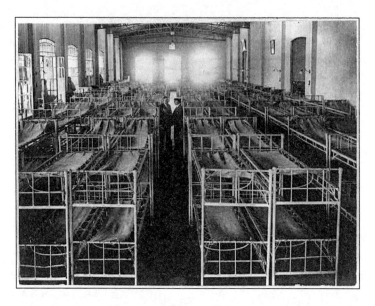

Dormitory accommodation in the Immigrant Hotel, Buenos Aires[207]

When and how did Ismail travel to South America? According to an entry in a notebook where significant family events were recorded, he left Amritsar on 7 August 1910 and travelled to Bombay. Several days later he boarded a steamship that brought him to Europe, a journey that would have taken at least 10 days. Here he may well have had to wait a few days before travelling onward. There were several shipping companies operating regular transatlantic crossings at this time, making multiple stops in Europe to collect passengers and deliver them to Brazil, Uruguay and Argentina, with Buenos Aires often their final destination. So that leg of his journey could have taken three weeks or longer, meaning that he would have arrived in Buenos Aires towards the end of September. A search through the lists of the thousands of passengers who arrived at the port during that period resulted

---

[207] 'Cots in Immigrant Hotel, Buenos Aires, Argentina', Library of Congress, http://loc.gov/pictures/resource/cph.3a26893/.

in an intriguing discovery. A Mohamed Ismail did disembark there on 23 September 1910.[208] Together with more than 1,350 other immigrants, he arrived on the SS *Siena*, which had set sail a month earlier from Genoa, the port most likely to be used by a traveller from India, and he was 23 years old, the age of Afzal's father at that time. This passenger is listed as 'Turkish' but, as will be shown later, there were many errors in the records and nationality data is particularly unreliable, having sometimes been determined more by perception than fact. So it is quite possible that this was his arrival record.

List of passengers who disembarked from the SS *Siena* in Buenos Aires on 23 September 1910, including a Mohamed Ismail

---

[208] Two information sources were searched. One was the CEMLA online database, already described in connection with emigration from Germany, which has a searchable name index. The other was a collection of reports prepared by maritime inspectors following the arrival of each ship. These are in the Argentine National Archives, but have been scanned and are accessible online. Many include passenger lists, but they have not been indexed. Consequently, each list had to be examined individually. It was in one of these lists that a Mohamed Ismail, age 23, was found, https://www.familysearch.org/ark:/61903/3:1:3QHV-FQN1-LF3J?view=explore&groupId=TH-7755-123291-13591-49.

A Life Viewed through Correspondence

Ismail started writing letters to his family in India soon after reaching South America and his correspondence continued intermittently for at least 37 years. During that time, he moved from Argentina to Uruguay, then to Bolivia and then, perhaps finally, back to Uruguay. I have been able to draw on 17 of his letters, as well as a few sent to him and some other documents that touch on his activities and reveal his thoughts about life in South America. Although the collection is incomplete, it is evident that he initially wrote frequently – he says 'almost weekly' in one letter. Later, however, communication became very irregular and at times the gaps between contacts stretched to many years.

The letters were posted to his father, his sons, his brother-in-law and other contacts, but none were sent to his wife Vilayet who, in contrast to his own high level of literacy, could not read or write.[209] And rather than address letters to her that others could read out, he chose to ask others to convey his messages to her. At first, he wrote only in Urdu, but by 1915 most correspondence was in English. In October 1931 he began a letter in Urdu but had to give up after one page, admitting that he had forgotten his mother tongue and had to revert to English. A few of his letters were typed, but most were handwritten. Some were extremely long, one extending to eight pages. They show an exceptional command of both Urdu and English. His Urdu was described as 'poetic' by the person who translated them, while his English was fluent and correct, using a wide vocabulary and complex sentence structures.

A lot can be learned from these documents, but they also

---

[209] This would not have been unusual. The 1911 Census of India showed that only 0.1% of 'Muhammadan' (Muslim) women in Amritsar District were literate, 'Census of India, 1911, Vol. XIV; Punjab; Part II - Tables: Education by Religion and Age', https://archive.org/details/in.ernet.dli.2015.62718/page/n113/mode/2up

make his departure from India more puzzling. They show that he was very worried that people outside the family might read his letters or obtain information about him, and he was suspicious of unusual or unexpected events. He initially said very little about what he was doing in South America and this, taken together with cryptic references to his departure and evident unwillingness to return, suggests that he may have fled from his country of birth. Noteworthy too is that none of the letters written over the 37-year period revealed anything about his domestic circumstances. He never gave a residential address or wrote about his life outside work. A few were sent from offices where he was employed but most provided only a mailbox number for replies. That would not have been particularly unusual, since at that time sending mail from workplaces, which could be done without cost, was commonplace. Moreover, mailboxes were frequently used, especially by immigrants who lived in temporary accommodation and may have moved frequently. Nevertheless, it is surprising that this continued over such a long period and that his lengthy communications made no reference at all to his living arrangements. Combined with other mysteries relating to his emigration, one cannot but wonder whether he deliberately concealed his residential location and his domestic life from his correspondents.

The Early Letters

The three earliest surviving letters were written over four weeks between 27 March and 24 April 1911. Beautifully scripted in Urdu, they include a Farsi honorific and other expressions that reflect his familiarity with that language. These, though, were not the first he wrote after reaching Argentina, since in the earliest of these he referred to correspondence sent on 1 January 1911, indirectly confirming that he must have left India no later than 1910.

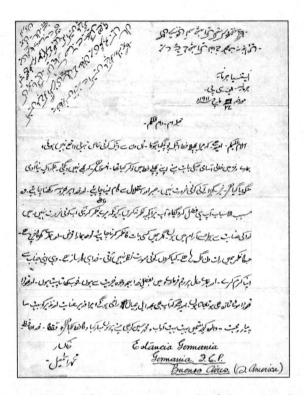

Letter sent by Ismail from Buenos Aires to his father in March 1911

A translation of this letter provides some insight into Ismail's anxieties and the problems besetting the family back in India:

27 March 1911 My revered sir. I am badly trapped. Peace be upon you. I hope that my previous letter will have reached you by now. Since then there has been no significant change. The vacancy in my office, that I mentioned to you in my last letter, has been filled by some new person and the post has sadly not been given to me. Well, please do not worry. We have to be patient and have faith in God. He is Gracious and will grant us with His blessings. Do not worry at all about me. Because there is no need to worry. With God's blessings, I am quite comfortable. If we have to worry about anything, it is our debt. And our household expenditures. I worry about that day and night. What can I do? I cannot see any solution. Only God can help. Only He can grant Mercy and show kindness towards our circumstances. I am alright and am eating well. And have gained weight. I hope that you too as well as all the others in the family are keeping well. Give my love to Wazir, Inayet and Nazir. And my greatest respects and salaams to mother. Day before yesterday, I also wrote a congratulatory letter to Meher Hussein. May God look after you. Yours obediently. Mohamed Ismail. (T)

It is evident too that by this date he had already been in employment for a while, although probably at a junior level since he expressed disappointment at not having been offered a higher position that had become vacant in his office. The letter also includes some intriguing remarks about his and the family's financial situation. They suggest that a significant debt had been incurred, and that the family was struggling to find enough money to meet that obligation and pay their household expenses. His words convey continuing affection for the family, making it clear that his departure was not because of a family rift. One might conclude that his emigration appears to have been prompted by economic hardship, perhaps as a consequence of the fraudulent behaviour of his father's business associate. That, however, does not explain his decades-long concern about others gaining information about his presence in South America, further described later in this account. Moreover, the letter referred to 'our debt' as something for the family to worry about (rather than a business), suggesting a large financial obligation for something specific. Could this have been a debt of honour or compensation (*Diya* in Islamic Law)?[210] Equally plausible, though, is that he left to evade the British colonial authorities, whose treatment of anyone considered a subversive was very widely feared.

A curious postscript was added to the reverse of this letter. Ismail mentioned that he intended to post it on 31 March, which would be his 24th birthday according to the 'English calendar'. He then asked his father to work out his age in years, months and days according to 'our calculation', probably referring to the Islamic calendar. This concern about his birth may be connected to a request made 23 years later, when he asked for information from his mother about the day of the week and 'exact hour' of his birth, so that he could have a horoscope drawn up.

It is very apparent from these early letters that he and his family members missed each other enormously, and that they were very worried about him. Returning home, however, was evidently not a realistic option in the short term, and he had ambitions to travel further to a country where he felt there were opportunities to study and acquire new skills; ambitions that would never be fulfilled:

> *20 April 1911* Only God knows how much I long to embrace you and be close to you. I am trying my best to return home as soon as possible. I don't know where I am fated to live but I hope that my dear mother would now have found some comfort and strength and be in good health. (T)

> *24 April 1911* I know you are all sad that I am not there, but I feel the same here without you. Please console mother for me. Neither you nor I have any solution for our separation. We have to be patient and

---

[210] 'Blood Money in Islam', Learn Religions, https://www.learnreligions.com/blood-money-in-islam-2004418.

have faith in God and have trust in Him that, if he wills it, we will be together one day. I am thinking about this day and night, that somehow I will be able to go to North America so that I can acquire a new skill there. As I wrote to you in my last letter, there are no opportunities for acquiring a new skill in South America. England, Japan and North America are the only countries where I can get this opportunity, where students can go and learn a new skill. I hope that one day I will achieve this ambition. I am determined to see this through and hope that God will grant me my ambition. Please remain hopeful and keep praying. Stop worrying as it is not productive. So please don't distress yourself and remain optimistic. And also, console mother and other relatives. God willing, everything will be alright. I cannot stress this enough, as your sadness has an impact on me and I feel very sad all the time. If I get this assurance from your side that you all are not endlessly worrying about me and are contented and hopeful about me, then it will benefit me a lot. In order to achieve my goals, I need to remain strong and optimistic, but your desperation and sadness make me lose hope and have a negative effect on me. Please remain hopeful and patient and have faith in the Almighty. (T)

One of the earliest letters was written on headed paper that carried two names: Germania Estancia Ltd and Germania FCP 'La Germania'. Germania lies in Buenos Aires Province, about 350 kilometres west of the city with the same name. At the beginning of the twentieth century it was predominantly ranching country owned by La Germania Estancia Compañía Limitada (Germania Ranch Company Limited). FCP is the Ferrocarril al Pacifico

(Germania Pacific Railway).[211] Connecting the Atlantic to the Pacific, it was routed through the area and after La Germania station opened in 1905 settlers were attracted and a small town developed. The correspondence suggests that Ismail was employed by the railway company in Germania, a supposition supported by the fact that he was working for another railway company a few years later.

Suspicion, Remorse and Self-Pity

There followed a period of 10 years from which only one letter survives and during which in all probability he wrote very few. However, on at least two occasions, it seems that he remitted money back to Amritsar. In May 1912, £10 was transferred via London to the Chartered Bank of India, Australia and China for collection by his father, Miran Bakhsh, whose address was given as the family home in Katra Dula. Then in January 1914, a Thomas Cook Money Order for 105 rupees (Rs) was sent by post. A second postal payment is suggested by a further surviving, but empty, envelope also addressed to Miran Bakhsh. I have written that 'it seems' the money came from Ismail because it arrived anonymously. The bank branch in Amritsar informed Miran Bakhsh by letter that 'the remitter's name or any further details were not given …' although the posted items definitely came from Buenos Aires. It is another example of Ismail concealing his exact whereabouts.

Airmail was almost non-existent before WW1, so post from South America to Asia went by steam packet and took a long time to get there. The envelopes used for the money orders were addressed to '*India Británico*' (British India) and '*por vapor via Genova u Brindisi*' (by steam via Genoa and Brindisi), the first

---

[211] Later this became the Ferrocarril Buenos Aires al Pacífico (Buenos Aires and Pacific Railway).

on the SS *Principe Umberto* and the second on the SS *Principe di Udine*.[212] It probably took more than a month for them to arrive.

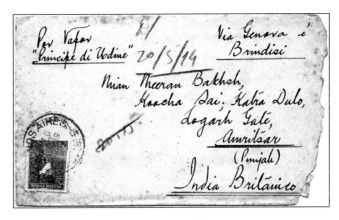

Envelope sent by steam packet from Buenos Aires to
Miran Bakhsh, May 1914

The sole surviving letter from this period was written on Monday 25 October 1915. By this date, war had spread across Europe to the Middle East and Africa, troops from the Indian Army Expeditionary Forces were fighting alongside the Allies, and my maternal grandfather Friedrich was writing letters to his family from the trenches on the Western Front. Argentina, though, remained neutral despite considerable German provocation through the sinking of its ships. This three-page typed letter was the first of a series of very intriguing communications. As before, Ismail gave only his work address, this now being *Gerencia, Ferrocarril de Sud* (Manager's Office, Great Southern Railway) in Plaza Constitución, Buenos Aires. Like most of the early railway companies in Argentina, this was British owned, so perhaps

---

[212] Both vessels were Italian passenger and cargo steamships. The SS *Principe Umberto* was used as a troop carrier in WW1 and sunk by a U-boat in the Adriatic in 1916, with the loss of 1,926 lives. The SS *Principe Udine* was scrapped in 1929.

English was the office *lingua franca*, which would clearly have been advantageous to Ismail since he spoke little Spanish. It was addressed to Dr A C Mannan in Bazar Takrian, Amritsar, who must have passed it on to the family.

From what he wrote, it is evident that in the preceding years Ismail had received multiple letters from his father and friends, and even one from 'my own dear eldest boy', but had replied to none of them. As a result, his parents had evidently enlisted the help of Mr Mannan, who had contacted the YMCA in Argentina to try and locate their silent son. The first few paragraphs not only illustrate his style of writing, but are also very revealing, providing a foretaste of themes that recurred many times in subsequent correspondence. The opening words show just how cautious he was about engaging with someone he did not recognise:

> *25 October 1915* In the first place, pardon me if I say I am unable to tell the real from your very mysterious sounding name – A. C. Mannan. I have puzzled myself considerably with the object of tracing its owner, but for the life of me I cannot remember who amongst all of my acquaintances and friends at home could it possibly belong to. I am afraid you will have to write to me again and disclose your identity.

Nevertheless, despite not knowing his correspondent, he went on to talk emotionally at great length about how he felt after not having kept in touch with his family. He expressed contrition and shame, blaming himself for causing his family anxiety, and reaffirming a strong desire to return. It was, he explained, his own perceived failure that kept him from writing, a failure he attributed to the state of the wider economy. Poor harvests and the effects of the 'European War' had resulted in the people of Buenos Aires suffering 'untold misery', from which he had not been immune, and as a result he had endured much hardship and misfortune:

> *25 October 1915* I am not only sorry but truly ashamed of myself for having been the cause of such unnecessary though cruel anxiety to my dear father and mother, and only wish that they will, with their usual loving kindness, forgive their prodigal and unworthy son. Nothing should have ever prevented me from continuing to write to them now and then, but the fact that I feel ashamed to do so, on account of my having been a hopeless failure in what at the time of leaving home I thought I would probably be able to accomplish.
>
> … First through inexperience of the outside world, and then through lack of knowledge of the Spanish language (the mother tongue of the Continent of South America), and pecuniary difficulties, I have during these past five years that I have been in this country, had to suffer many a hardship. Argentine is an agricultural country, which means that she is chiefly, if not solely, dependent on harvest; and, unfortunately, since a year or two before my arrival here the country has been having bad crops through either excess of rain and floods, or draught, with the consequent poor business, which the European War has only made worse. The result of this yearly repeated misfortune for a period of over five years has been appalling; thousands of people in the city of Buenos Aires alone have been and are out of work, suffering untold misery. Unfortunately, in spite of all my efforts, I could not remain an exception to the epidemic, and had to suffer equally with the rest.

... I have received all my father's letters, and, not long ago, one from my own dear eldest boy. Oh the joy of receiving the first letter from my own son, and written so nicely too! Believe me, I was so overjoyed at reading such a sweetly written letter that, in spite of my being seriously ill at the moment, I wanted to jump out of bed and dance gleefully and hug the nurse that handed it to me. I could hardly contain myself with joy. But, alas! the moments of happiness, as is generally the case, were only short-lived, for, soon the vision of my own helplessness and unworthiness as a father of such a dear boy arose before my eyes, and made me feel ashamed of myself. It must have touched his dear little heart and made him feel awfully sad to have received no answer to his loving letter to his Daddy, but he can rest assured that my unworthy silence (due to the same cause as that in the case of my parents and other friends who have been writing to me from time to time) has grieved myself none the less. I cannot but admit that it was very wrong of me to have suddenly become silent and not written a word home to any body, above all to my parents and my family, during a whole year. I know the suspense must have been cruelly hard for them, and they must have suffered terrible anguish. I shall never forgive myself for all the anxiety and grief I have unnecessarily caused my loved ones, and God help me to act as a dutious son, and a loving husband, and father henceforward. I need not have been ashamed of my misadventure – having left home and kindred to come so far away and then failing to show any results – to such an extent as to have completely severed all connection with those to whom the news of my welfare were a matter of life and death. If I was unable to do better, I should have at least continued to send them a word now and again just to say I was alive. Yes! I admit I have been very foolish. And I wish you to kindly offer my most sincere apologies to my dear parents, and through them (for the time being, till I am able to write to each one of my friends and loved ones direct) to all those good people who have from time to time kindly written to me, but have failed to receive an answer from my unworthy-self. Kindly assure my beloved father and mother that never again shall I cause them any worry and anxiety about myself, and shall write to them regularly once a month.

Probably, in my next letter to my father, I shall enlighten them as to what I intend to do. God knows how I am longing to go back home, and to once again look upon all the dear faces I love, but, unfortunately, my present circumstances do not admit of any such thing as the luxury of going home soon. I must, therefore, per-force stay here for a while longer till I can feel my way about.

It seems odd that Ismail opened up to this extent to someone whom he did not know and asked that person to convey very personal messages to his family, rather than write to them direct, although he indicated that he planned to start doing that regularly in the near future. His health problems were clearly serious, since they necessitated a long stay in hospital, and illness took a heavy toll on his physique, prompting him to delay sending his parents a photograph of their son. And undoubtedly, financial difficulties adversely affected his welfare:

25 October 1915 Believe me that during the past year and a half it has been a cruelly hard struggle for me to keep body and soul together, and after all that I have gone through during this time, I really cannot tell how I am still alive. Such privations as I have had to endure have driven many a fellow out here to his premature grave; but, thank God, I have pulled through the worst and am once again able to stand on my legs, though I have not yet completely recovered from my recent illness consequent upon the effects of the terrible privations on my already poor constitution, as a result of which I was obliged to be laid up in a local hospital for over three months. It is not yet a fortnight when I was discharged from the Infirmary.

... As soon as I look better, I shall send my parents a photo of myself, but, in the meantime, pray, assure them, they need have no anxiety about my health, as I am quite alright now, and out of every danger.[213]

The sentiments in the letter seem genuine and heartfelt, but his words also convey a degree of self-pity. And the same apologies, remorse, wish to return and tales of woe were expressed repeatedly in later communications, not least because he failed to keep his promises and because the interval between some of his letters stretched into years. Moreover, even when he eventually had the financial means, he did not take the opportunity to go back to India. How can that behaviour be explained? Were his feelings and commitment to family really as strong as he expressed them to be? Was it a lack of willpower? Was there another reason not mentioned for staying out of India?

After this letter there is a gap of nearly six years to the next

---

[213] It is likely that he had tuberculosis, which very severely affected his health a few years later.

surviving correspondence, and it is evident that during this period Ismail had again 'disappeared'. This time it was his brother-in-law, Mr Chishty, who initiated enquiries about his whereabouts by writing to the British Consulate in Buenos Aires.[214] Mr Chishty was a well-educated and prosperous entrepreneur. Having had a good job with Sun Life of Canada, he set up his own successful business, The Japan House, in Commercial Buildings, Lahore, selling goods he imported from the Far East to British and local people. As Afzal's mother's brother, he was of course Afzal's uncle, but he would later have an even more significant involvement in Afzal's life, not least as his father-in-law.

Following Mr Chishty's approach, the consulate placed advertisements in the local press asking for information about Ismail. Then, on 13 June 1921, the Consul-General wrote to inform Mr Chishty that Mohamed Ismail had presented himself at the consulate, indicated that he was well and would write soon. He also provided a contact address, which was probably only a work address, since it began 'c/o'. Intriguingly, although that consular correspondence sent to India survived, the rest of the address was torn off, perhaps in another attempt to conceal Ismail's whereabouts, this time by his family. For their missing person search service, the consulate charged a fee of five shillings.

The day after the consulate wrote, Ismail finally also sent a letter to a family member in India. It was a long one, four pages in length, handwritten in his elaborate English. But it was not to his wife or sons, it was to his brother-in-law, although he addressed him as 'My dear cousin'. In fact, both Ismail's wife Vilayet and her brother Mr Chishty were cousins of Ismail, marriage between cousins being extremely common both in India and elsewhere in

---

[214] The identity of the sender is inferred from the address shown on the Consulate's reply, which is Mr Chishty's business address. The name of the person to whom it was sent was not given.

the world at that time. Once again, he was apologetic and full of remorse for the lack of contact with his family, acknowledging that the fault was his, promising to write again in 10–14 days and to keep in constant touch in future. He repeated his wish to return, whilst at the same time explaining that it was out of the question in his present circumstances. As before, he attributed his silence to his hardship and lamented that he was suffering more than those he had abandoned, not least because he had again experienced serious health problems.

His long disconnect was perhaps best reflected in his comment that 'I don't even know whether my father and mother are alive'. He asked for news about his family and requested his older son Muzaffar to write to him. However, there was a marked change of tone in the content of the last few paragraphs of his letter, revealing his suspicion of unexpected contacts and concern that his presence might come to the attention of authorities in India or Argentina:

> *14 June 1921* It seems like resurrection, this getting in touch with some member of the family after years' silence! The fault lies with me, I know; and I have no excuse to offer for it either, except, perhaps, this that life has taken me through such strange and unexpected vicissitudes during the past few years that I feel an entirely different being, totally alienated from old ideas and associations. For a year and a half I lingered between life and death through consumption, which had affected both my lungs, in a Tuberculosis Sanatorium situated in the hilly province of Cordoba in this country. I feel quite well now, but will have to be very careful about my health for the rest of my life.
>
> You will have gathered by now that I am both alive and well. But don't reproach me for the mortification

which I know I have caused you all, more especially to my poor old parents, through an unreasonable and long death-like silence, because my self-mortification is more than enough. My poor mater! What anguish of torture she must have gone through all these years for love of me, an unworthy son! I want to shut out the painful vision, because I feel so unutterably ashamed of myself. Would to God I could undo it!

I don't even know whether my father and mother are alive or dead. Will you tell me? If one or both of them are living, then I beseech you to convey to them a message of love and remembrance from me, and ask them to forgive me for the utter lack of duty and loyalty which I have shown towards them ever since I left home. May God pardon me, too. I feel more ashamed of myself than any words of mine can convey, for the utter disregard of the feeling of my loved ones so brutally manifested by ungrateful me through such long silence, in spite of their repeated reminders and entreaties to at least keep in touch with them by letter. I must have grown very callous, through the years' sufferings and hardships in this country! But God is my witness that in spite of all my callousness, and in the midst of my apparent heartlessness, I have not remained without severe pangs of conscience. My conscience has rebuked me, and rebuked me harshly at times, until my forced callousness has compelled me to shut out the unpleasant vision from my mind's eye. It is a miserable confession to make to one's family, but however disagreeable it is, I do it, that through various causes connected with my life of adventure or a lust for aimless wanderings, call it what you like, I grew too callous to realise the pain my silence was causing to my loved ones at home. I seem to be such an unnatural being for having acted the way I did. But I beg to ask for forgiveness of all those whom I have thus aggrieved, if they can find it possible to pardon a sinner like me, on my solemn word of honour that I will endeavour to atone the past by keeping in constant touch with the family in future. I would give anything to be with you all once more, and wonder sometimes if the gods will be kind enough to afford me such an opportunity! My present circumstances look too black to entertain hope to realize my heart's desire, and the outlook like a dark forest where I can see nothing ahead.

Anyway, let us leave the future alone for the present and talk of something else. Tell me something else; about yourself, home, family, your business and all the rest of it, do, for I'm just hungry for news, any news you care to give me.

Ask Muzaffar to write to me about himself, his mother and his brother. Tell him to give me all the news he can. I shall eagerly look forward to his letter.

Did you write that letter to the British Consul here enquiring for me? Do you know that you forgot to sign it? I saw the letter, it had no signature on it. Well, anyway, the Consul got in touch with me, and you will probably hear from him to that effect by this mail.

Now that you are once more in direct touch with me, may I ask you to write to no one out here about me, as it is not very pleasant to see a third party intervene in one's private affairs, such as the present case, where you felt obliged to employ the services of the local British Consulate in order to trace me up.

> When answering, tell me if this letter has been opened by the Indian Government Censor, or anybody else, before being delivered to you; and, also, how long it takes to get to you. This for my guidance.

The address given at the top of the letter is Paseo Colon 161, Buenos Aires. This is in the city centre on the main artery through the historic core. It is one of the most prestigious avenues, which at the beginning of the twentieth century was largely occupied by railway companies and government offices. Between 1907 and 1910 those companies, mostly British, together built the first skyscraper in Latin America, the famous Art Nouveau Railway Building, on plot 181. It seems highly unlikely that Ismail was living a few doors away from here and more likely that the address was his place of work, probably a railway company office. So, again, he did not disclose his residential address and, despite the length of the letter, and apart from descriptions of his travails, he revealed absolutely nothing about his life and what he had been doing in Argentina.

A Sudden Death in the Family

Despite his assurances, more than six months passed before Ismail wrote to his family again. When he did, he was in a state of shock. He had received another letter from his brother-in-law, Mr Chishty, written in August 1921, as well as two from his father, from which he had learned that his older son Muzaffar was dead. It is not clear how or when he died, or whether it had occurred recently or during the years of lost contact.[215] At the same time he also learned about his parents' dire financial situation and failing health, and that his younger sister, Inayet, was not only married but also had a family.

---

[215] My recollection is that Afzal said his brother became ill and died.

Afzal with his deceased brother, Muzaffar

He was evidently grief-stricken by the loss of his son and it is this, he explained, that had stopped him from writing sooner. It was not until more than three months later, on Christmas Eve 1921 when he was probably on holiday from work, that he eventually put pen to paper again and replied to Mr Chishty. Over three pages he described how sad and bad he felt, mentioning that he had sent a small sum of money to his father and that he had hoped to do it again in the current month. But, he regretted, it had not been possible and he himself had to bear the pain of not being able to do this: 'I had to resign myself to the circumstances and await a more favourable opportunity'. With the demise of Muzaffar, he eventually turned his thoughts to his remaining son:

24 December 1921 Afzal must write to me. I haven't
yet heard from him. Get him to drop me a few lines,
telling me all about himself and his mother.

He also wrote in a very remorseful, respectful and even ingratiating
way about his father-in-law, admitting that he had not 'played
the game' with regard to how he had treated his own wife. He
expressed the hope that he could 'undo the past and make amends',
seemingly alluding to something specific that had happened, but
there is no clue as to what that might have been:

24 December 1921 I wish to send my grateful respects
to my uncle, your dear old Dad. Every time I think
of him, figuratively speaking, my hat goes off to
him in deep admiration for his sterling qualities of
a gentleman of the true Indian type. His culture and
refinement, his manly character and consistency of
purpose and principal stand out before my mind's eye;
to this day he is my hero and model of a truly cultured
Indian gentleman. I know I have not played the game
by his daughter, but that thought in itself is sufficient
remorse and punishment to me. He has acted nobly
throughout, and whatever his inner feeling, to my
knowledge he has never demeaned himself by uttering
a word of complaint or remonstration for my unmanly
behaviour, which has been solely responsible for his
eldest daughter's unhappy married life. What a brave
soul he is, and the daughter too, follows in her father's
footsteps and his noble example. I pray that it may
soon be possible for me to undo the past and make
amends for all my many shortcomings, and make my
wife and her son, <u>my</u> son, happy by faithfully serving
and loving them, is the sincerest wish of my heart.

Whenever these thoughts crowd my mind I feel, I just feel, a miserable wretch, who has been instrumental in bringing nothing but pain, misery and affliction on whosoever I have come in contact with. Methinks I must have been born under a very unlucky star, to be unhappy and unsuccessful in all departments of life, social, material, physical and every other way.

Yet again he restated his wish and intention to go back to India, but remained unwilling to take that step, even when presented with a real opportunity. His brother-in-law's offer to pay his passage was declined, again raising questions about the reason for his being out of the country and his reluctance to return:

24 December 1921 Thank you for offering me money to go back with to India. You are awfully kind, and your generous offer has touched me deeply. But must decline it for the moment, as I cannot yet see my way to return home. Of course, I intend returning there some day, but the dawn of that auspicious day is still enveloped in the dark, through which it is difficult for vision to penetrate.

This, though, is the longest of all the surviving letters, running to eight pages, and whilst several of them are devoted to his despair, Ismail was able temporarily to put those thoughts to one side and give attention to more materialistic matters. Perhaps prompted by news of his cousin's business success in Lahore, he pondered the possibility of starting up some sort of enterprise, importing goods from India:

24 December 1921 I am thinking that while I must remain here for some time to come, perhaps it wouldn't be a bad idea to establish some sort of business relations with India. This is an agricultural and pastoral country; its chief exports being cereals, hides, skins, bones, cold storage meat (beef and mutton), wool, milk by-products, such as butter and cheese, and some sugar. And it imports raw jute and manufactured gunny bag material from our country, and all kinds of manufactured articles from Europe, North America and Japan.[216] I believe that Amritsar carpets (which I read in a North American magazine article the other day are bought almost entirely by some North American firm) and perhaps some Kashmiri shawl goods, together with some real Indian silks (if such are manufactured) and gold cloth, would have a market here. I am not sure but some Indian spices might also find some demand. I am going to get in touch with somebody who might enlighten me a little on the subject, and will then write you more fully.

At the same time, he recognised that the Argentine economy was in extremely poor shape, with international trade stagnating, unemployment rising and all the forecasts pointing to recession ahead. It would not have been a propitious time to start a business and, whether for that or another reason, there is nothing to suggest he did anything to bring his rather vague idea to fruition.

The most incongruous paragraph in a letter, which is mostly concerned with the death of his son and his own misfortune, comes towards the end. Feeling cut off from political happenings at home, he asked Mr Chishty to supply him with reading matter in Urdu and English, and to take out subscriptions for him to two journals, the *Modern Review* of Calcutta and the *Indian Review* of Madras starting in January 1922, promising to send the money for these as soon as he was able. Clearly, despite his circumstances

---

[216] Gunny is a coarse fabric made from jute.

and unhappy state of mind, Ismail retained a thirst and perhaps a budget for intellectual stimulation.

What he did not explicitly reveal in this letter was that his fortune had actually begun to change earlier in the year. On Friday 15 July 1921 he had started a new job with the Mexican Petroleum Corporation, a subsidiary of Pan American Petroleum and Transport Company, in turn a subsidiary of Standard Oil of Indiana, one of the largest companies in the world. Then, at some point in the late 1920s, he began regularly remitting money back via London to his father in Amritsar through the Chartered Bank of India, Australia and China. Payments included £130 in October 1929, £26 in July 1930, £10 in October 1930 and £30 in December 1930.

How much contact, if any, he had with his family during the following years is uncertain, but the next surviving letter is a whole decade later. Dated 4 October 1931, this was to his father and, while the first page was in Urdu, he evidently struggled with the language and completed it in English:

> *4 October 1931* This is a very poorly written letter,
> but the truth of the matter is that not having written
> a letter for so long or conversed with anybody here,
> I have forgotten Urdu to such an extent that I find
> extreme difficulty in expressing myself in even a
> rudimentary manner; hence beg your indulgence.

Moreover, when he wrote it, he was no longer living in Argentina. He had relocated across the estuary of the River Plate to Montevideo in Uruguay, where he would spend most of the rest of his life. But before continuing with Ismail's story, I need to return to what was happening in India.

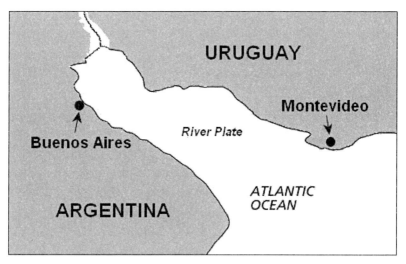

The location of Buenos Aires and Montevideo[217]

[217] "Plata Buenos Aires Montevideo Map" by Roke-commonswiki licensed under CC BY-SA 3.0.

Father and Son Reconnected

More Contrition and a Grand Plan

On Thursday 17 March 1932 Afzal wrote for the first time to his father.[218] That letter has not been found but, based on the reply from Ismail, it is evident that it was long, written in Urdu and conveyed very mixed feelings. Afzal was bitter and angry with his father for having abandoned his wife, children and parents, emotions undoubtedly heightened by the recent death of his grandmother and the knowledge that his grandfather did not have long to live. He castigated his father and accused him of a lack of affection for the family. But at the same time, he told him he wanted to meet and even join him in South America. It was his determination to do this, above anything else, that set the course for the remainder of his life.

Assuming it would have taken several weeks for that letter to arrive, Ismail's reply was unusually prompt, written on Wednesday 27 April 1932. It was typed and sent from Montevideo, but contained no address, just a mailbox number: Casilla de Correo 851. Unlike earlier correspondence, he was able to send this at least part of the way by airmail. It would go by air, he wrote, from Buenos Aires to Paris, then on to Marseilles by train, before being put on a steamer bound for India.[219] The content seems

---

[218] It can be concluded that it is the first time because (a) in his reply to Afzal's next letter, Ismail writes that he has received a second letter and (b) if he had written earlier and had a reply, he would have known not to write in Urdu.

[219] Ismail was almost certainly incorrect in suggesting that the letter would be

quite insensitive, albeit probably unintendedly. In its opening paragraph he implicitly reproached his son for writing in Urdu because he himself had forgotten the language. He then went on to deny his son's accusations, whilst acknowledging his own guilt in causing the family pain. Yet again, he hinted that, despite his wish to return, there were circumstances beyond his control that prevented this from happening, although he did mention making desperate efforts over the previous two years to 'find a way back':

> *27 April 1932* I was truly glad to get your letter of March 17. It is certainly a long epistle and an interesting one. I only wish that you had written it in English, for then I would have enjoyed reading it much more than I have done. You see, I have been living away from home for so many years that I have almost completely forgotten our language – not only as regards speech but also the reading of it. So much so that I had great difficulty in following you as fully as I should have liked. I seem to have completely forgotten the meaning of many of the words you write, and was compelled to half guess it. Still your letter, though it caused me much pain at some of the things you said in it – pain caused not by your words but by the recollection of my own behaviour during the past years – also made me very happy because it was a touch of home and loved ones.

carried all the way to Paris by air. A pioneering transatlantic flight carrying mail from west Africa to Brazil had been made in 1930, but regular crossings did not start until 1933. Although the service was provided by *Aeropostale*, until that date letters were flown within South America to Natal (Brazil) and then transported by 'aviso' ships to Dakar (Senegal), from where the journey to France was completed by plane. See David Crotty, 'Development of Transatlantic Airmail Services 1928–1945, Part I: The South Atlantic', *Postal History Journal* 149 (June 2011): 17–35, https://americanphilateliccongress. org/wp-content/uploads/2021/03/PHJ149.pdf.

You are mistaken when you think that I feel no affection towards any one of you, for I do; it is only the unfortunate circumstances that I lack being demonstrative in my feelings. In addition, due to causes beyond my control, it has never been possible for me to return home once in all the years I have been away. You don't know how much I long to be with you all once more, particularly to see my Dad before he passes into a better world. Your letter also brought home to me strongly the death of my dear mother who, literally, died pining for such a prodigal and unworthy son as me. It made me very sad, indeed, utterly ashamed of myself, for there was neither need nor justification for the way I acted while she was alive and pining for me. May the Lord forgive me for it!

I agree with every word you say about your own dear mother. She is unquestionably a most noble woman. I know she is the sort who would not utter a single word of complaint no matter how heavily sorrow laid upon her heart and how much hurt she felt. Don't think for one moment that I do not feel ashamed of this, too. The truth of the matter is that no matter which side of my conduct I look at only shame and regret are my reward. I am trying to make some amends for my past behaviour by making the last days of that poor old man a little happier with a small monetary help each month. I know this is but a poor effort to right a great wrong done over many years to all members of the family; but for the moment nothing else is within my power, except to assure you that for the past two years or so I have been making, and continue to make, desperate efforts to get away

for even a short visit to India. And who knows but
that I may yet succeed, and that before long.

One further remark in this extract is of interest. It is his
exhortation 'May the Lord forgive me for it'. This is an expression
more associated with Christianity than Islam, and brings into
question whether he used it simply because he had become
habituated to such language in Argentina or whether he had
actually converted, and whether this was in any way connected to
his work in India for The Bible Society. A very similar expression
was used again in a letter written in September the same year,
whereas in earlier letters he had frequently invoked 'God'. There
is, though, nothing in any of his later correspondence to indicate
adherence to either religion.

At greater length, however, Ismail responded enthusiastically
to Afzal's proposal to come to South America. Despite having
dwelt so heavily on his hardship and misfortune in earlier
communications, here he extolled the virtues of living there, and
drew interesting comparisons between the geography, population
and architecture of Buenos Aires and Montevideo:

> *27 April 1932* So you want to join me in South
> America! To tell you the truth, Afzal, I have often
> thought of that myself because in these new and
> wonderful countries in South America one has so
> much more chance of making good than is possible
> to our people in the old country amidst all its
> poverty and misery and lack of opportunities. You
> cannot imagine what life is like here! So free, so full
> of opportunities for the man who is willing to work
> hard and make good! The laws of these countries are
> so utterly generous and benevolent that no foreigner
> need feel the least bit stranger here.

All are equally welcome and enjoy equal privileges with sons of the soil; not the least difference is made between the two. Life here is so totally different from what you are accustomed to in India that you would be amazed. You think that Europe is great, but let me tell you that life there is stunted compared to life in these countries. Unlike in Europe, there is no narrow outlook on life here; everything is new, broad outlook, vast and far reaching vision. Under these skies you feel a different being; want to do something; want to be some-body, to accomplish and be a success!

... Buenos Aires is about 130 miles from here across the River Plate. I go across frequently – about twice a month for a couple of days at a time. Buenos Aires, or BA as the English speaking people call it for short, is a very large city, with a population of over 2¼ millions and many beautiful modern buildings and parks. On the other hand, Montevideo is a much smaller city, with a population of less than, or about half a million souls only. But it is a much prettier place than BA, for while the latter is absolutely flat and uninteresting, Montevideo is built on hilly ground and right in its immediate vicinity is surrounded by beautiful countryside. It also has wonderful roads for hundreds of miles throughout the country, roads such as BA completely lacks outside the city proper.

People in both these countries are of Spanish descent; they are very polite and hospitable to everybody, and in their social intercourse make no difference as to colour or race of their visitors. They are very well informed people, both men and women, and follow world events with keen interest. They are also very understanding and sympathetic towards the people of India in the latter's present political struggle.

The reason for this reversal in his outlook on life was a radical transformation in his circumstances. As already mentioned, Ismail had got a job with the Mexican Petroleum Corporation in July 1921 and over the following 11 years had gradually worked his way up until he was managing the company's entire business in Uruguay. His regular travel between Argentina and Uruguay appears to be evidenced by passenger lists of the ferries that crossed the Plate estuary. Between 1924 and 1938 at least 17 include a traveller with his name (or a spelling variant, such as Mahmud Ismael)), who had British nationality and an age that matched his own.[220]

Ismail was understandably proud of his achievement, and especially that he, an Indian, was overseeing workers from the USA and the UK:

> *27 April 1932* [I have] about 130 men working under me. Of these, about 40 are in the office and the rest at the Company's depots in the city of Montevideo and interior of this republic. Of the men in the office, there are four Americans (from USA), about half a dozen Englishmen, two English women stenographers, and the rest are natives of this country. I sit in a beautifully furnished, large, office by myself, and have a private secretary.

He explained that he was frequently required to travel to Buenos Aires and described enthusiastically the enjoyment and technicalities of the novel experience of a 'voyage' in a large plane.

---

[220] As a citizen of the British Indian Empire, Ismail had the status of British Subject. The passenger lists are handwritten, casually completed and likely to include many errors, especially for non-Spanish travellers, so name variations are to be expected.

27 April 1932 I often fly in an aeroplane across to BA, and back; it takes an hour and a quarter, whereas by boat it is a journey of nine hours. You see an American Company runs aeroplane service twice a week from Miami, Florida, USA, to Montevideo and intermediate ports of call (including BA) via the Pacific Ocean route, and once a week from the same point to BA and intermediate ports of call (including Montevideo) via the Atlantic coast. Thus Montevideo has plane communication to and from BA three times a week. The planes that come over via the Pacific coast are what they call land planes, that is they fly over land; whereas the one coming along the Atlantic coast is what they call a hydroplane, that is, it flies over water. All three of them are large planes, the first mentioned two can carry 12 passengers, two pilots, a radio-telegraphy man and another employee who waits on the passengers during the voyage and helps with their baggage, etc. The hydroplane is larger still. She can carry as many as 20 passengers, in addition to four or five members of the crew.

Flying is a most delightful experience. I first flew about three years ago, and liked it from the beginning, to such an extent that now I always make use of the plane in my frequent journeys to and from BA, and seldom, if ever, go by boat. I suppose you would like to fly too; won't you. May be that like most people you are afraid of flying. The highest altitude I have flown at has been 5,000 feet, and many times above the clouds which is a truly wonderful sight, to see the clouds from the other side.

However, whilst he was enthusiastic about Afzal and his wife,

Masuda, joining him, he expressed concern that his own wife, Vilayet, might feel even more abandoned unless she came too, which he did not expect her to be willing to do:

> *27 April 1932* But the one thing that has so far prevented me from sending for you has been the thought of separating you from your dear mother. Her life has been sad enough without my now adding another grief to it, and such a heavy grief, too, as your separation from her would undoubtedly cause her. This has been the sole impediment so far in my calling you over here. Now you may tell me how we can overcome it. I know the best way would be to bring her over too; that would solve the problem; but would she come? I doubt it very much. Write and tell me whether your mother would permit you to leave home to join me. Personally, I fear it would break her heart and kill her, the same as happened to <u>my</u> poor mother, I should never consent to now also being the cause of the death of <u>your</u> mother, or even to cause her further grief and make her more miserable than she has been for years past and continues to be.
>
> However, should it be possible for you to come over here I should also insist on your wife accompanying you. I can take care of you both until such time as you find your own feet and are able to support yourself. Alone you must not come; I would never consent to it. But even before we talk of your wife accompanying you, you had better find out whether she would be willing to accompany you. She may not want to leave home and family to come to the far off land of South America. Ask her about it, and let me know before we make any plans.

In so far as permission of the Argentine Immigration Authorities for your landing at this end is concerned, I entertain no difficulty in securing this. Of course, the best plan would be for me to take a trip to India and bring you over with me, but this is problematical and cannot be considered seriously at present.

The letter adds weight to the notion that Ismail was not at liberty to return to India. His elevated position, and his offer to support his son and wife if they came over, suggest that he could now afford to travel. His comment that he had made 'desperate efforts' to get away points to another obstacle, but there is still no clue as to what that was.

Later that year, in August or September 1932, Ismail received news from Afzal that his father, Miran Bakhsh, had passed away. His response, written on Friday 30 September, reveals that he was very upset not to have been present or able to see him before his death, and he expressed grief and remorse. However, his remarks were characteristically self-centred, perceiving that his parents 'breathed their last with my name on their lips and pining for the sight of me' and maintaining that he had suffered more than other members of his family through his absence:

> *30 September 1932* I have received both your letters, from the first one of which I learned the sad news of your grandpa's death. I know he had not been quite well for some time past; but I confess that I did not expect to receive the news of his demise.
>
> The death of my father and mother has been particularly sad for me, for they both wanted ever so much to see me at least once again in their life; but alas, it was not to be! Both they and I were denied that satisfaction. We have been the victims of circumstances

and of a cruel fate. I have felt, and am feeling, very sad at the thought of it all.

Convey my deep sympathy and condolences to my brother and sisters, and tell them that their loss is my loss. They at least had the consolation of being near their parents at the time of their death, and had the satisfaction of rendering whatever help or service they could. But such a satisfaction and consolation were denied me; and not only that but also I have the added remorse and mortification to remember that they both breathed their last with my name on their lips and pining for the sight of me! Language is too poor to convey the remorse I now feel at all my shortcomings where my parents were concerned! May the Lord have mercy on their souls and grant them eternal peace in his kingdom!

Every time I think of them (and the thought is almost constant, I can assure you), and the pain and grief I caused them through my separation and long years' silence, I feel like shooting myself. I feel mean and despicable, to think that I responded to their great and wonderful love with such ingratitude and despicable behaviour! And I also feel it is too late for me to beg forgiveness of either my parents or God, for the wrong I did them was unpardonable; my attitude and my behaviour towards them and their constant supplications was un-natural, unworthy of a son loved with such deep and sincere love.

Around the same time, Ismail also learned that Afzal had become a father for the first time. His guidance on Afzal's future behaviour after this significant event indicates that, despite their separation, he had somehow become aware that his younger son was not the most responsible of young men:

> *30 September 1932* My congratulations at your having
> been raised to the dignity of a father. You will now
> have to behave and act more seriously than before,
> and realize your responsibilities.

The baby was a boy and given the name Munir. However, he died at a young age and was never mentioned again in any of the correspondence.

Despite Ismail's apparently comfortable financial circumstances in April 1932, it is evident from letters written in July and September of the same year that global economic trends were beginning to have an adverse impact. Having promised to remit money back to the family each month, he was unable to do so because of currency exchange restrictions introduced by both the Uruguayan and Argentinian governments in late 1931 in response to the deepening worldwide Depression.

Nevertheless, he tried to keep his word. On 22 July Ismail enclosed three cheques with his letter to Afzal. One for £2 was made out to Miran Bakhsh, another for £4 5s 3d was for Afzal, and a third for $12 75c was payable to Ismail but endorsed in favour of his son. Then in July and August he made three bank transfers totalling £34 to his father's Chartered Bank account in Amritsar. After the remittances were sent, though, he received news of his father's death and subsequently arranged for the money to go to Afzal instead. He then started making more frequent payments direct to his son with the aim of building up a kitty for Afzal, Masuda and Vilayet to travel to South America.

Date	Amount	Bank	Branch
08 July	£14 approx	Unknown	Buenos Aires
17 August	£22 approx	Unknown	Buenos Aires
22 August	£10 approx	Midland	Montevideo
08 September	£10 approx	Midland	Montevideo
15 September	£14 13s 7d	Anglo South American	Buenos Aires

Remittances made by Ismail to his father and his son in 1932

With the money came strongly worded guidance on how it was to be used. He recommended that it not be withdrawn or converted into local currency. Instead, he advised opening a sterling account and depositing the payments there, converting only the small amounts needed for essential living expenses. Writing on 30 September 1932, he was extremely blunt in instructing his son not to divert the money to other uses, adding to the view that he perceived Afzal to be somewhat wayward. Events later that year proved that such a perception was well justified:

> *30 September 1932* … the money I have already sent you, and what I will remit you each month hereafter, is not to be squandered by you or any one else in needless expenditure on fine clothes or entertainment, or anything else. On the contrary, only strictly necessary sum is to be spent on household needs of the family and the rest saved and kept in deposit (in pounds sterling) in the bank, so that it will gradually accumulate for the steamship passages of you, wife and mother. Now remember that, Afzal, for I have no other means of providing for your passages, etc. You will not be able to join me here.

Adversity, Airships and Astrology

Paradoxically, at the same time as Ismail was proudly telling his son how successful he had been, storm clouds were already gathering, and his fortunes were about to take a severe downturn. As the global Depression intensified, Uruguay's economic and social situation worsened dramatically. Britain, traditionally the major buyer of the country's exports, began restricting purchases of meat, prices of agricultural products plunged, the currency was devalued and unemployment grew rapidly. Before the end of 1932, the petroleum company for which he had worked for more than 10 years, and which was also affected by a corruption scandal, withdrew from South America and he lost his job.[221] A *coup d'état* the following year did nothing to improve conditions and Ismail again found himself in a perilous economic position.

Sometime after September 1932 Afzal relocated to Mussoorie, a hill station in the Himalayan foothills. Located 250 miles southeast of Amritsar and at an altitude of 6,500 feet, it was known as the 'Queen of the Hills'. It was a popular destination for expats and overseas visitors, as well as Indians. The main promenade and shopping area, as in other hill stations, was called The Mall and it was here that Afzal was to be found working in the Carpet and Fur Store, a business owned by his two cousins (also his brothers-in-law), the sons of Mr Chishty.

---

[221] 'The Conservative Adjustment, 1931–43', in *Uruguay: A Country Study* (Washington: Government Publishing Office for Library of Congress, 1990), http://countrystudies.us/uruguay/14.htm.

The Mussoorie Mall in 2010, still a textile shopping street[222]

Afzal continued to write to his father before and during his time in Mussoorie, but Ismail again cut himself off and did not answer for almost two years. It was not until Tuesday 31 July 1934 that his father replied to a letter received the previous day and, with air transport having become more developed and affordable, he sent that reply for the first time all the way to India by air. The letter was delivered in Mussoorie on 18 August, over two weeks later, but this was much quicker than the four weeks it had taken Afzal's mail to reach him. This, though, is not the only reason for this correspondence being noteworthy. The franking on the envelope indicates that it was carried across the Atlantic in the *Graf Zeppelin*, the largest airship in the world at that time. It was the first to make a circumnavigation of the globe and it provided the first scheduled, nonstop, inter-continental air service in history, operating primarily between Friedrichshafen (Germany) and Recife (Brazil).[223]

---

[222] Image: 'Library Bazaar' (in The Mall Road) by Paul Hamilton licensed under CC BY-SA 2.0.

[223] 'Graf Zeppelin history', airships.net, https://www.airships.net/lz127-graf-zeppelin/history/.

The *Graf Zeppelin* over Recife (Brazil) in the early 1930s[224]

Ismail's letter would have been taken by plane from Montevideo to Pernambuco State (Brazil) and there transferred on to the dirigible, which departed for Germany on Saturday 4 August.[225] The flight took about 10 days and on arrival the letter would have been put on to another plane and carried to India. The airship's route may well have taken it over Offenbach, where Karola had recently enrolled in the *Jüdische Bezirksschule*. She recalled seeing airships flying overhead during her childhood.

[224] Image: 'Graf Zeppelin, Década de 1930 - Recife, Pernambuco, Brasil' by Oscar Maia. https://commons.wikimedia.org/wiki/File:2_-_Graf_ Zeppelin,_d%C3%A9cada_de_1930_-_Recife,_Pernambuco,_Brasil.jpg. By [1933] the Nazi tri-colour and swastika were painted on the airship's fins, so this photo is earlier.
[225] 'Correo via Zeppelin', Club Filatelico del Uruguay, n.d., www. clubfilatelicodeluruguay.com/Marcofilia/MarUyCap09_04a.pdf.

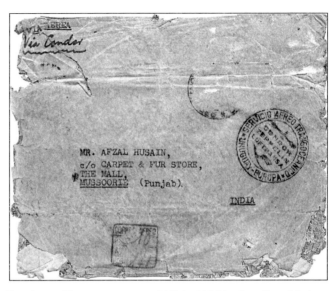

Envelope of letter written on 31 July 1934 by Ismail to Afzal
franked 'Servicio Aereo Transoceanico Uruguay-Europa'
and 'Condor Zeppelin Lufthansa'

The correspondence address given in this letter by Ismail was 4th Floor, Rincón 438, Montevideo. Situated close to the waterfront in the old town at the junction with Misiones, the imposing building on this site was constructed in 1929 and served as the headquarters of the Banco de Montevideo. As before, he appears to have given his work address, for even if the building also offered residential accommodation, it is improbable that he could have afforded it. The original building still stands and is now occupied by another financial institution, Scotiabank.

This time Ismail attributed his failure to respond to previous correspondence to his 'most regrettable habit of procrastination'. But it is also evident that, in the two years since losing his well-paid job, he had experienced serious financial difficulty and been forced to accept employment 'in a capacity considerably less important than in the old firm'. Nevertheless, he was optimistic that his fortunes would improve, writing 'I have hopes that before the middle of next year most of my troubles shall be over', without giving any reason for that optimism.

Towards the end of this letter Ismail raised two other matters that are particularly intriguing. First, he asked for information about the timing of his birth, which he hoped his wife might be able to provide. He wanted this so that he could commission his own horoscope. What prompted this apparently sudden interest in astrology after so many years is not clear. There is no further mention of it in his later correspondence, although it seems doubtful that Afzal sent him the requested details:

> *31 July 1934* When you see your mother, would you mind asking her if she, by any chance, knows or remembers having heard from my mother the day of the week and the <u>HOUR</u> I was born. I am anxious to know not so much the day as the <u>exact hour</u> of my birth, and whether same was am or pm. She may have possibly heard my mother speak of it some time, and remember it. I know my birth date: March 31st 1887; but never found out the hour I was born. I now need this important detail for having my horoscope made. I can have one made for you as well if you send me your date, month and year of birth, as well as the exact hour you were born, stating whether it was am or pm. Will you do that, Afzal?

The second matter reflected ongoing anxiety that he might be under investigation. He asked Afzal a volley of questions to find out whether anyone had been making enquiries about him:

> *31 July 1934* Tell me, also, whether any body has recently made any enquiries about me at home,

officially or unofficially, from you, your mother or any other member of the family. Enquiries of any kind: who I was, where I lived, who were my relatives at home, etc, etc.

Presumably something specific triggered this heightened concern. There is nothing to indicate what that might have been, but it adds weight to suspicion that his emigration was prompted more by the need to escape from India than an attraction to South America. Yet, in contrast to his efforts to remain hidden, he sent with the letter a photo of himself so that, he wrote, 'you can see what I look like at present'.

Photo of Mohamed Ismail sent in 1934 from Montevideo to his family in India and a photo of his wife, Vilayet, taken around the same time in India

This was the first time since leaving India 24 years earlier that he had sent a photo and Afzal could not contain his excitement, as his reply, written in Mussoorie on Monday 27 August 1934, revealed:

> *27 August 1934* I received your Air-Mail letter of 31st
> July on the 18th August. I was very glad to read that
> and as soon as I saw your photograph my joy knew no
> bounds. It was a novelty for me and for which I was
> hankering for the last so many years. This photograph
> of yours has refreshened our remembrance of the
> passed twenty four years. And I feel so much joy
> which is beyond the pen power to be explained.

In his reply, Afzal reciprocated by sending his father a picture of himself. Having been admonished for writing his first letter in Urdu, this one was in English, but evidently his command of the language was not at the same level as his father's with regard to both syntax and spelling. Nevertheless, the wording reveals that, to some extent, Afzal had overcome his earlier feelings of anger and bitterness, and was feeling more affectionate and desirous to spend time with his father. It was written as he was about to return to Lahore and he requested that future correspondence be directed to his cousins' shop there, where he presumably continued to work for them.[226]

Two Foolish Adventures

Afzal's yearning to see his father continued undiminished. Probably realising that Ismail would never actually return to India, he decided that the only option was to go to him. In a rather reflective (but at times confusing) paragraph in his August 1934 letter, implicitly acknowledging his father's age, he argued the case for making the journey as soon as possible:

> *27 August 1934* Now I want to delay upon a different
> subject which concerns our daily life. The short span
> of a human life is passing on with rapid strides and

---

[226] This is the only surviving copy of a letter that Afzal wrote to his father.

finally comes to an end. For instance, I would not go a-far and refer to your life. That since twenty four years you are trying hard for securing some better opportunity for a sojourn to India. But God knows when it will be fulfilled. Consequently I opine that one should not keep one's desires with him and the thing that is possible should be accomplished as soon as it can be. Therefore I have my strong determination to reach you in no time.

Before this letter was written, probably in 1932, Afzal had already made the first of two unsuccessful tragicomic attempts to do just that. What prompted him to embark on that journey, apparently without the involvement of his family, we will never know. What is known is that somehow he managed to reach Singapore. That seems a surprising destination when the most direct route to Argentina would have been westwards through the Suez Canal. However, he would have been able to get to the Far East using a British Indian Passport, to which he was entitled as a British subject and which cost just one rupee. Unfortunately for him, such passports were only valid for travel within the Empire. Consequently, for the onward journey to South America he had to obtain a full passport and his application was referred back to Amritsar, at which point his family discovered his whereabouts. His uncle and father-in-law, Mr Chishty, set off for Singapore and hauled him back, broke and with his tail between his legs.

Ismail was probably never told about Afzal's abortive venture, although he knew of his wish to join him. However, in his July 1934 letter Ismail explained to his son how the state of the global economy had severely impacted his own financial circumstances over the previous two years and, reading between the lines, had forced him to stop remitting money to India. In addition, he emphasised significant obstacles to anyone coming to South

America, most notably the indefinite ban on immigration that several countries had imposed. Against this background, he made clear to Afzal in no uncertain terms that he had no choice but to stay put, get on with his life and make the best of his lot:

> *31 July 1934* … due to the general economic depression and unemployment all over the world, practically all South American republics have prohibited immigration. There is no work for the thousands that are already living here; so they don't want more people coming in to swell the ranks of the unemployed and destitute. Special laws have therefore been passed by these Governments to restrict immigration for an indefinite period. Under the circumstances, you have no other choice but to remain where you are and make the most of your opportunities. Work wholeheartedly in whatever activities you are engaged; don't feel despondent or dejected, for that will get you nowhere. There is no other alternative, for the present at least.

But neither his ignominious Singapore escapade, nor his father's discouraging and blunt remarks, dampened Afzal's determination. In his August 1934 letter he made clear that he did not just want to come to see his father or be dependent on him. He also planned to set up in business, drawing on his experience to date and identifying a number of Indian handicrafts that he could import and trade over there.

> *27 August 1934* But I want to explain you about my aim of arrival there. In the first place, as I have mentioned you time and time again in my previous letters, that I have my utmost desire to see you. Secondly it is not so, as you have explained about my livlihood. For, I have not so much idea for service,

but I have my inclination to carry on business over there. Because I have gained sufficient experience in it as I have spent part of my life in business. Now, the question is that my present business of Gota and Salma is of no use there. Therefore I have arranged some other business for that country.

A friend of mine, Sheikh Mohd Bukhsh Jeweller of Lahore, whose visiting card is also enclosed here with, is a respectable and trustworthy gentleman, who is carrying on the business of old curio, and real jewellery. He wishes to accompany me there, and I will get half the profits on the proceeds. And as regards the goods, it is undoubtedly novel. Therefore I hope that if we were to get a single chance over there we would not hanker after more. Because he who comes from foreign countries to India searches after these things. In addition to this I can also manage for the following businesses to be commenced there:- Kashmir embroidery and general works, Hoshiar Pur wood works, Moradabad brass works and Persian Carpets, etc. So you will not have to bear any botheration regarding myself. Hence I hope it will be a beneficial sojourn for me. Now I think it expedient to consult you on the above matter.

The letter indicated that selling *gota* and *salma* had been Afzal's main business activity to date. These are types of embroidery originating in Rajasthan, which involve weaving copper, silver or gold thread into fabrics.[227] But he was obviously very confident about developing into other markets and disinclined to go into 'service', by which he presumably meant taking a salaried job. This entrepreneurial attitude, characteristic of so many south

---

[227] 'Rajasthan Textiles', http://www.rajasthantextiles.com.

Asian citizens, was evident throughout his life, but sadly he never managed to fully realise his ambitions or build the successful business he hoped for.

Despite confidence about his future prospects, Afzal was only able to accumulate sufficient funds to pay for his own passage. He therefore proposed to come alone with the expectation that his wife and mother would follow when circumstances allowed. Notwithstanding what his father had already told him about the immigration ban, Afzal asked him to obtain from the relevant authorities 'permits for landing' in Uruguay for himself and a business partner named in his letter.

One other matter was mentioned in this correspondence, which had evidently been raised several times previously. It was a request from Afzal to his father for a power of attorney relating to the property owned in Amritsar:

> *27 August 1934* Yes! One very important matter, is to be asked for which I have requested you time and again in my previous letters, has suddenly dawned upon my mind. Please send me by return mail your property's power of attorney.

The wording conveys a degree of frustration and prompts one to speculate why the power of attorney was requested. Was it simply a sensible precautionary action, given that it seemed increasingly unlikely that Ismail would ever return or was something more specific – perhaps the sale of the Marriage House – under consideration? Ownership of the property seems to have been shared between Ismail and his brother, Nazir Ahmad, who was still living there with his family.

Soon after writing this letter, Afzal relocated from Mussoorie back to Lahore, where he started or resumed working in a '*Silma* and *Bankry* merchants' in Kinari Bazar, inside the ancient walled city. It was to this address that he asked his father to send future correspondence. Before the end of the year he would learn that his wife, Masuda, was expecting their second child.

The following year, 1935, was a momentous one for Afzal. It was the year in which he finally realised his ambition to travel to the other side of the world and reach South America. However, he set off without his father's approval, perhaps even without his knowledge, and without telling some of his close family in Lahore. Moreover, although he had previously indicated that he could afford his own passage, he had to sell his mother's jewellery (with her permission) to raise cash for the venture. Leaving his pregnant wife behind, Afzal made his way to Bombay. There, bookings were made by the local office of Balmer Lawrie & Co Ltd, a London agent specialising in steamship travel, and on Thursday 23 May he embarked for Italy on the SS *Conte Rosso*, occupying economy berth 60-D.[228] Noted for its lavish Italian decor, the *Conte Rosso* served the Shanghai-Bombay-Trieste route and was operated by Italia di Navigazione (Italia Line). That company was formed after a merger involving Navigazione Generale Italiana, which was probably the company that had brought his father to South America several decades earlier.

---

[228] Built in Glasgow in 1922, the SS *Conte Rosso* was torpedoed and sunk in 1941 when operating as an Italian troop carrier.

The SS *Conte Rosso*

Working backwards from the start of the next leg of his journey, one can estimate that the voyage to Italy took about 10 days. He spent one or more nights there and then made his way from Trieste to Genoa by train. Balmer Lawrie had written in advance to an Italian travel agent, Compagnia Italiana Turismo, asking them to 'render him every possible assistance with his baggage, rail, hotel, and steamer reservations'. Afzal's first experience of a European city must have been quite overwhelming. In a period when few in India had access even to a radio, awareness of life in the 'West', including behavioural norms, languages, the built environment and everything else, was limited.[229] So his first landing in Europe must have been a huge cultural shock, as it would have been, and even more so, for his father all those years earlier.

From Genoa Afzal was booked on another Italia Line ship, the MS *Augustus,* for his passage to Montevideo.[230] Decorated in

[229] The Indian State Broadcasting Service started radio broadcasting experimentally in 1930 and permanently in May 1932.
[230] The MS *Augustus* made its maiden voyage in 1927. After a period as a cruise liner, it was converted into an aircraft carrier for the Italian Navy during WW2,

the Baroque style, it was the largest diesel-engined passenger ship of its time, able to carry 1,675 passengers. Afzal kept a picture postcard of the vessel, which he presumably received on boarding.

Afzal's picture postcard of the MS *Augustus*

Remarkably, the shipping company's timetable printed on ultra-thin tissue paper also survives. It shows his booking clearly circled and the route taken by the ship. After leaving Genoa at 11am on Thursday 6 June 1935, the *Augustus* called at Nice (Nizza Villefranche, France) on the same day and Barcelona (Spain) the following day. It then crossed the Atlantic to Brazil, calling at Rio de Janeiro on the 18 June, and Santos (Sao Paolo) the following day, before docking at Montevideo (Uruguay) on Friday 21 June.

---

scuttled in 1944, then raised and finally scrapped in 1946.

ESPRESSO SU...

"ITALIA ,, Flotte Riunite
Cosulich, Lloyd Sabaudo, Navigazione Generale
ANONIMA - SEDE IN GENOVA
CAPITALE SOCIALE L. 175,000,000 INTERAMENTE VERSATO
AUGUSTUS - CONTE GRANDE - C. BIANCAMANO

ITINERARIO GENERALE P...
(Salvo varia...)

N.	NAVE	Genova	Trieste	Nizza Villafranca	Spalato	Napoli	Marsiglia	Algeri	Gibilterra	Las Palmas	Dakar	Pernambuco	Bahia	Rio Janeiro	Santos	Rio Grande	Montevideo	B. Aires
1	Oceania	—	3/1	—	3/1	5/1	—	6/1	7/1	—	—	14/1	15/1	17/1	18/1	19/1	20/1	21/1
2	Augustus	19/1	—	19/1	—	20/1	—	—	—	—	—	—	—	31/1	1/2	—	3/2	3/2
3	Neptunia	—	31/1	—	31/1	2/2	—	3/2	4/2	—	—	11/2	12/2	14/2	15/2	16/2	17/2	18/2
4	Conte Grande	14/2	—	14/2	—	15/2	—	—	—	—	20/2	—	—	26,2	27,2	—	1/3	1/3
5	Oceania	—	21/2	—	21/2	23/2	—	24/2	25/2	—	—	4/3	5/3	7/3	8/3	9,3	10/3	11/3
6	Augustus	7/3	—	7/3	—	8/3	—	—	—	—	—	—	—	19,3	20,3	—	22/3	22/3
7	Conte Grande	28/3	—	28/3	—	29/3	—	—	—	3/4	—	—	—	9/4	10,4	—	12/4	12/4
8	Neptunia	—	4/4	—	4/4	6/4	—	7/4	8/4	—	—	15/4	16/4	18/4	19/4	20/4	21/4	22/4
9	Augustus	18/4	—	18/4	—	19/4	—	—	—	—	—	—	—	30/4	1/5	—	3/5	3/5
10	Oceania	—	25/4	—	25/4	27/4	—	28/4	29/4	—	—	6/5	7/5	10/5	11/5	12/5	13/5	13/5
11	Conte Biancamano	9/5	—	9/5	—	10/5	—	—	—	15/5	—	—	—	21,5	22/5	—	24/5	24/5
12	Neptunia	—	23/5	—	23/5	25/5	—	26/5	27/5	—	—	3/6	4/6	6/6	7/6	8,6	9/6	10/6
13	Augustus	6/6	—	6/6	—	7/6	—	—	—	—	—	—	—	18/6	19,6	—	21/6	21/6
14	Oceania	—	13/6	—	13/6	15/6	—	16/6	17/6	—	—	24/6	25/6	27/6	28,6	29/6	30/6	1/7
15	Conte Biancamano	27/6	—	27/6	—	28/6	—	—	1/7	—	—	—	—	9/7	10/7	—	12/7	12/7
16	Neptunia	—	11/7	—	11/7	13/7	—	14/7	15/7	—	—	22/7	23/7	25/7	26/7	27/7	28/7	29/7
17	Augustus	25/7	—	25/7	—	26/7	—	—	—	—	—	—	—	6,8	7/8	—	9/8	9/8
18	Conte Biancamano	8/8	—	8,8	—	9/8	—	—	12/8	—	—	—	—	20,8	21/8	—	23/8	23/8
19	Neptunia	—	29/8	—	29/8	31/8	—	1/9	2/9	—	—	9/9	10/9	12/9	13,9	14/9	15/9	16/9
20	Augustus	12,9	—	12/9	—	13/9	—	—	—	—	—	—	—	24,9	25,9	—	27/9	27/9
21	Oceania	—	19/9	—	19/9	21/9	—	22,9	23/9	—	—	30/9	1/10	3/10	4/10	5/10	6/10	7/10
22	Conte Biancamano	3/10	—	3/10	—	4/10	—	—	9/10	—	—	—	—	15/10	16/10	—	18/10	18/10
23	Neptunia	—	17/10	—	17/10	19/10	—	20/10	21/10	—	—	28/10	29/10	31/10	1/11	2/11	3/11	4/11
24	Augustus	29/10	—	29/10	—	30/10	—	—	—	—	—	—	—	10/11	11/11	—	13/11	13/11
25	Oceania	—	7/11	—	7/11	9/11	—	10/11	11/11	—	—	18/11	19/11	21/11	22/11	23/11	24/11	25/11
26	Conte Biancamano	19/11	—	19/11	—	20/11	—	—	25/11	—	—	—	—	1/12	2/12	—	4/12	4/12
27	Neptunia	—	5/12	—	5/12	7/12	—	8/12	9/12	—	—	16/12	17/12	19/12	20/12	21/12	22/12	23/12
28	Augustus	12/12	—	12/12	—	13/12	—	—	—	—	—	—	—	24/12	25/12	—	27/12	27/12
29	Oceania	—	27/12	—	27/12	29/12	—	30/12	31/12	—	—	7/1 1936	8/1	10/1	11/1	12/1	13/1	14/1

La motonave Augustus ed i piroscafi Conte Grande e Conte Biancamano portano I, II, e III Classe - Le Motonavi Nep...

| ORARIO DI PARTENZA | da GENOVA e da TRIESTE ore 11 |
| | da BUENOS AIRES: 22 |

Printed in Italy

Italia Line timetable showing Afzal's route to South America, 1935

Everything went smoothly until the ship reached Montevideo, but that is where his plans unravelled. Despite having previously asked his father to obtain the necessary permit for entry to Uruguay, he had no visa and had only been allowed to travel after assuring the shipping company that a close relative living in Uruguay would sort out the necessary documentation on arrival. That proved to be wildly over-optimistic. The immigration authority refused Afzal permission to land and a few hours later the *Augustus* sailed on to its final destination, Buenos Aires.[231] Ismail, who by then was aware of what was happening, flew to Argentina, where he was able to go on to the ship and meet his son. It was the first time they had seen each other since Afzal was under two years old, 25 years earlier. They were able to spend some time together but Afzal was not allowed to disembark here either. So four days later, at 10pm on Tuesday 25 June, the *Augustus* set off on its return journey, calling at the same ports, with Afzal still on board. The two did meet again very briefly on deck in Montevideo but that was the last time they would ever see each other.

> PASAJERO RECHAZADO POR LAS AUTORIDADES DE MONTEVIDEO.
>
> AFZAL KUSSAIN: Indú, de 26 años de edad, pasajero de 3ra.clase procedente de Génova, con destino a Montevideo, cuyas autoridades le impidieron su desembarco por carecer de documentación alguna.—
>
> Los dos mencionados pasajeros rechazados han quedado a bordo a disposición de la Superioridad.—

> PASSENGER REJECTED BY THE MONTEVIDEO AUTHORITIES
>
> AFZAL KUSSAIN: Indian, 26 years old, 3rd class passenger from Genoa, bound for Montevideo, whose authorities prevented him from disembarking because he lacked documentation.
>
> The two aforementioned passengers have remained on board at the disposal of the Authority.

Report on Afzal 'Kussain' prepared by an immigration inspector in
Buenos Aires on 22 June 1935 (with translation)

---

[231] Afzal is included in the list of third-class foreign passengers who reached Buenos Aires. It states that he could read, write and speak English, that he was a businessman and in good health. But it also gave his surname as 'Kussain' and his religion as 'Catholic', glaring examples of the errors that permeate the passenger records.

As will become clear, during their time on board together they spoke about matters which Ismail wanted to keep secret, and which undoubtedly related to his departure from India or his activities in South America and his efforts to remain 'invisible'. There are cryptic comments in subsequent correspondence (reproduced below) about that conversation, but they add to the mystery, rather than solve it.

Anger and Anxiety

However amicable their face-to-face conversations may have been, Ismail was upset and furious with his son for making this futile trip. Understandably, he was particularly irked by the financial costs. Although the shipping company had no option but to take Afzal back to Genoa, since it had been responsible for bringing him to South America without a visa, a ticket had to be bought for the onward return to India. As Afzal had no funds left, his father knew he would have to find the money for that and the train journey from Bombay to Lahore. So, when he received a letter from Afzal a couple of days later, in which he requested that his father remit 200 dollars to support his family, he received short shrift. Ismail's reply to Afzal was written on Friday 5 July and delivered by the shipping company after the *Augustus* docked in Genoa. In it he vented his anger about the ill-fated journey and pointed out that, if the family was in such straitened circumstances, Afzal should never have wasted Rs900 on an 'absolutely foolish adventure' that was 'disastrous from every point of view'.

But it was not just the costs of a senseless adventure that provoked his anger. His ire was heightened by something else. Soon after departing from Montevideo, Afzal actually wrote two letters to his father, the first on 27 June and the second the following day. He would have been able to mail them in Sao Paulo and Rio de Janeiro respectively, but he did not personally place the letters in a mailbox. Instead, he entrusted them to a member of the crew to post on his behalf. Unfortunately, the first went astray and, when Ismail received the second, he immediately suspected that the first had been intercepted. Assuming it contained details he wanted kept confidential, he feared that this information was now in the possession of third parties and that his situation had been compromised. His suspicion was compounded by the fact that a letter Afzal had sent weeks earlier from Bombay had also gone missing.

In his reply he expressed extreme anxiety at the loss of the letter, which he believed put him at some unspecified risk. His words verged on paranoia, including unfounded accusations about the crew member and instructions to Afzal to destroy his own letter once read, not by tearing it into small fragments, but by burning it. As with much other advice from his father, Afzal chose to ignore this:

> *5 July 1935* Your second letter from [on] board the AUGUSTUS, dated June 28, reached me, but not so your first of June 27, which, you say, you posted me the day before. I wonder what became of that! I suppose that Commissar friend of yours on board whom you must have handed it for mailing, kept it instead – just out of curiosity to see what you were saying in it to me. I am sorry I failed to say good bye to him just before leaving the ship; but I was feeling so perturbed at the time that I completely forgot about the man, though now I recall he stood very close to us at the head of the gangway all the while we remained there talking, and I suppose he also heard all that we were saying. He understood English, didn't he?
>
> If you find time before leaving Genova for Bombay, write to me, telling me more or less all that you said

in that missing letter. But this time please mail the letter yourself and not leave it with anybody else or at the Steamship Company's office to mail it for you. If necessary, buy stamps at the Company's office, but drop the letter in a mail box with your own hands.

The fact that a letter of yours mailed to me from aboard the AUGUSTUS has failed to reach me is a renewed source of worry for me for what it might have revealed to whoever read it. In handing it to the Purser you, of course, could not imagine that he or anyone else charged with the mailing of it would be mean enough to keep it to learn of its contents, instead of mailing it for its destination. And, Afzal, I am, frankly, apprehensive of the consequences.

Your absolutely foolish adventure of coming to South America has been disastrous from every point of view, and it may yet result tragic, for all I know at the present moment. You have wasted a considerable sum of money that you were not in a condition to afford, in venturing out to this part of the world the way you did, and have caused me a needless expense of sending you back to India, 25 pounds sterling, money I could ill afford at the present time. And in addition to all this, I am passing sleepless nights thinking of what might yet happen as a result of the revelation that your coming here has made – you know what I mean – particularly as a result of your letter from aboard the AUGUSTUS having been intercepted by some one, as I feel sure it has been intercepted, for otherwise I feel sure it could not have failed to reach me. And you are entirely to blame for all this waste of money and for the needless anxiety that is now being caused me.

I do not know what you said in your first letter from aboard the ship, but in your second you ask me to send your family a check for 200 dollars. I am sorry, Afzal, I simply cannot do that, as I have not got money at the present moment; but I will certainly do so at the earliest possible opportunity. If your family was in such straightened circumstances as you say, then might I ask why you took 900 rupees and spent that considerable sum on your passage to Montevideo? Don't you think that it would have been more manly of you to have stayed where you were and employed that money to better advantage, instead of throwing it away on a senseless adventure?

Do you recall from what port that missing letter of yours was supposed to have been mailed to me, and did you give it to the Purser on board, or did you just ask some one to mail it for you from shore?

I may also tell you that to this day I have not received that other letter of yours which, you said, you mailed to me by air mail from Bombay just before taking ship for Italy.

This letter will be handed to you personally by the Steamship Company at their central office in Genova. Once you have read it, destroy it carefully, for there is no sense in keeping it in your pocket. Instead of tearing it up into small fragments, burn it with a match.

As you will see from the attached copy of letter I have addressed to the Shipping Company, I am sending them a check for £16/- with which to pay your passage to Bombay. Enclosed in this letter are two checks drawn to your order: one for 2 pounds and another for 7. The £2/- check you may cash in Genova, because you will need some money in liras to pay for your way about Genova until you board ship for Bombay. The other check you better hold on to carefully and cash it in Bombay. It should fetch you over 91 rupees, which will buy you a third-class ticket to Lahore, and leave you a fair balance in hand for other incidentals. This is the best I have been able to do for you at the present moment. I tried my best to send you a little more, but circumstances do not permit. So you will have to be content with it for the present.

Don't forget all that we talked about on board the AUGUSTUS in Buenos Aires. Should need arise, acquaint your mother, as well as any one else that you deem necessary, with the details of the whole thing, to avoid disagreeable consequences at this end. Do you understand? For the present say nothing to anybody; let us leave things as they are, and hope for the best. But you can see how I shall have to keep on worrying about it, and all thanks to you!

Acknowledge receipt of this letter at once to me, and tell me that you have carefully destroyed it. Did the Commissary on board ask you any questions after I left the ship, or during the voyage? I have a strong suspicion that that fellow purposely failed to mail your first letter to me. His curiosity must have been aroused by the whole circumstance of the way we met in Buenos Aires and the way we parted from each other in the port of Montevideo, and must have wanted to dig a little deeper into the what must have appeared rather mysterious to him; hence his failure to mail that letter. And I would not be [at] all surprised that on his ship's next voyage to this port he brings that letter with him and shows it to somebody here – just to create trouble for me, I suppose. I wish I could have written you this letter in urdu so that on its by chance falling into other hands than yours no one would be any the wiser for what I am saying here; but unfortunately I cannot write urdu any more. However, I am taking the precaution to not only close this envelope well, but also sealing it with wax, as well as asking the Company to see that it is delivered in your hands personally when you call at their central offices on arrival at Genova.

In the event, his anxiety about the letter having been intercepted and fallen into the wrong hands was ill-founded. He confirmed in his next communication, written on 9 July 1935, which also reached Afzal in Genoa, that to his immense relief it had eventually been delivered. At the same time, as well as again promising to write occasionally, he made further cryptic comments about his inability to return to India and the need to keep secret the matters he had discussed with Afzal:

> *9 July 1935* About going back to live in India, don't for one moment think that I would not like to do so; but for the present this must remain only a dream, impractical, or impossible, to realise. Some day, I might fulfil this wish; when that day comes I shall be delighted to return home and be with my loved ones.
>
> … About that other matter we talked about in Buenos Aires & Montevideo, I think you had better say nothing to anybody unless it becomes necessary to do so someday.

In this letter, after having received repeated requests for a power of attorney, he finally enquired why his family needed it and expressed his reservations about selling their property:

> *9 July 1935* And about that Power of Attorney, too, I promise to send you one at the earliest possible date. Does my brother (and sisters) want to sell the property and divide the proceeds among the heirs? Remember, the house has been in the family's possession since the time of my grandmother. For my part, I think it would be a pity to sell it, unless, of course all the heirs desire to do so.

Whether as a result of procrastination, a shortage of money or deliberate resistance, the power of attorney was not forthcoming. Further requests for it were made but it is not known whether it was ever provided.

Rerouting and a New Destination

Ismail's July letter reveals that, after the *Augustus* had set off for Europe, he had airmailed three cheques to the Genoa offices of the Italia Line. The first, made out to the company for £16, was to pay for Afzal's third-class passage from Italy to Bombay. Perhaps with growing awareness of his son's tendency to do the unexpected, and keen to ensure he did not deviate or dally, Ismail instructed the company to 'issue him with a ticket to Bombay and place him on board the first steamer of your Line sailing for that port from Genova, advising me to that effect ...'.[232] He was, though, characteristically distrustful of the company, fearing that they might retain the £16 in payment for the voyage back from Montevideo.[233] The second and third cheques, for £2 and £7, were

---

[232] The steamer probably sailed from Trieste, not Genoa.

[233] This concern was the main subject of Ismail's letter to Afzal dated 9 July 1935.

to be handed over to Afzal on his arrival, together with the letter, which gave strict instructions on how the money was to be used.

Afzal reached Genoa on Thursday 11 July 1935 as scheduled and was handed the two cheques and letter from his father. But what then happened bore no resemblance to his father's expectations. For instead of making the crossing to India for which his father had sent payment, he encashed his own cheques and used the money to buy a ticket to England.

What prompted such a radical change of direction? There was, of course, time during the transatlantic crossing for his imagination to wander and maybe he simply decided to transfer his business plan from South America to the UK. Reaching the centre of the Empire would certainly have been alluring and such maverick behaviour was consistent with his previous adventurous exploits. Whatever the reason, it would have far-reaching and long-term consequences.

Afzal never again entered India and when he eventually returned to the sub-continent, many years later, the area of Punjab to which he came back had just become part of the newly created state of Pakistan.

From Genoa, Afzal booked a passage to the UK and arrived there some days later. Then, on Friday 26 July 1935 he wrote to his father to break the news that he had not returned to India after all but had diverted to London. Having explained his intention to go into business there, he once more asked for financial help. One might have expected Ismail to again have been livid with Afzal for his irresponsible behaviour, but his response was slightly more measured.

He sent two letters, the first of which was to the Italia Line. Concerned that he might have wasted his own money, he asked for the £16 that he had paid for the passage from Italy to Bombay (that had never been used) to be forwarded to his son in London.

The second was a reply to his son.

Writing on Thursday 8 August 1935, he wished him well in his new venture. Nevertheless, he described the whole situation as 'a thorough mess', made clear that it was 'materially impossible' for him to send any cash, expressed reservations about Afzal's prospects for success, and voiced grave misgivings about Afzal's wife and mother being left without support.

It is a sentiment that seems particularly inappropriate, given that he had abandoned his own wife and children decades earlier:

> *8 August 1935* I do not wish to act as a damp blanket on your scheme of going into business in England, but for my part I do not feel so optimistic about its success. Still, I do not want to dissuade you from your purpose. Go ahead, and Good Luck to you. I hope you succeed. I do, however, feel concerned about the welfare of your mother and family; they are both without YOU and without any means of subsistence, with only the Lord to look after them! This isn't right, Afzal.

Today there are more than one million people living in London whose ancestral roots are in the Indian sub-continent. However, when Afzal arrived in July 1935 there were probably fewer than 10,000 Indians in the whole of the UK.[234]

He was one of quite a small group in the capital at a time when racial prejudice was commonplace and supportive community networks were still in their formative stage. He may have had some contacts in London but, having decided to go there while on the high seas, he could not have made any arrangements in advance.

---

[234] C Kondapi, *Indians Overseas, 1838–1949* (New Delhi: Indian Council of World Affairs, 1951), https://archive.org/details/indiansoverseas10000kond. According to Kondapi, the Indian population in the UK was estimated to be 7,128 in 1932.

Moreover, he had very little money and his prior knowledge of life in the capital would have been extremely limited. One has to wonder how he managed in the first few days.

Nevertheless, he quickly found somewhere to live and gave the address to his father, who sent the August 1935 letter to him at '31 Great Alic Street, Ald Gate, E1'.[235] Its location in the East End, close to Whitechapel High Street and Commercial Road, placed Afzal at the centre of the nascent Muslim population of London. Here he would have been able to find help and support, and although there was as yet no permanent mosque, regular prayer meetings were held in various temporary settings, and these provided opportunities to develop contacts and find out about work opportunities.

Great Alie Street, 1934[236]

---

[235] Presumably this was intended for Great Alie Street, subsequently renamed Alie Street.

[236] Image "Great Alie Street" © Tower Hamlets Local History Library and Archives.

Only one other letter between Afzal and his father survives and that was written by Ismail almost 13 years later. From this it is evident that there had been very few exchanges in the intervening years. So maybe his father's disapproving words had fractured their already fragile relationship. However, I will return to that final correspondence later. Very little is known about how Afzal 'found his feet' in London or how he spent the next ten years. The only insight comes from a brief note in a job application made in June 1949 that covered the period from his arrival to early 1948, during which time he seems to have done a little bit of everything.

> Activities in England – An all round business experience, such as buying, selling, commission Agent, manufacturing toilet goods and fancy goods. Worked for other firms. Had own business in partnership under the name BRIT-INDO Ltd, at 13 D'Arbley Street, London, W1. Later opened up an other office for Imports and Exports and on account of partition of India I had to wind up my firm.

Extract from a job application submitted by Afzal in June 1949

Birth of a Baby and a Nation

Just as Afzal was settling into London, a significant family event took place back in India. On Monday 5 August 1935 his wife, Masuda, gave birth to a baby girl. Nusrat Bibi arrived when her father was 5,000 miles away on a different continent and she would be almost a teenager before she saw him for the first time. In the meantime, the family had to manage without him, through a period of rising political tension and then extreme social and economic turbulence.

Prior to the Partition of India, Amritsar and Lahore were referred to as the 'twin cities' and both had cosmopolitan populations. Although Amritsar was the spiritual and cultural centre of Sikhism, almost 50 per cent of its population was Muslim.

Conversely, more than one-third of the population of Lahore was Hindu and Sikh and, 'until the beginning of the 1940s, Lahore was celebrated as a paragon of communal harmony'.[237]

There had been discussion since the early twentieth century about dividing Punjab (and other states) on religious lines, but the complex demography meant that this was always going to be highly problematic. However, with the post-war British Labour government committed to Indian independence, demands for division of the country and the creation of a separate Muslim state intensified. Communal tensions escalated as religious and political groups jockeyed for power and sought to influence the final decision. It proved impossible for Lord Mountbatten, the last Viceroy, to achieve agreement to a unified India, despite support from Mahatma Gandhi. Reluctantly, in a broadcast on 3 June 1947, he accepted a two-state solution. With Independence Day set for 15 August, there were just two months in which to determine how the country should be divided. In fact, the boundary maps were not released until two days after independence, on 17 August 1947.

When the 'Radcliffe Line' was finally published, placing West Punjab, including Lahore, in Muslim Pakistan and East Punjab, including Amritsar, in secular India, it triggered the largest migration in history and extreme violence as huge numbers of families moved across the border to be with their own religious group.[238] An estimated 10 million of the 14 million who moved from India to Pakistan or vice versa, were living in Punjab, and the state accounted for an equally high proportion of the estimated

[237] Ishtiaq Ahmed, 'Forced Migration and Ethnic Cleansing in Lahore in 1947. Some First Person Accounts' (Department of Political Science, Stockholm University, 2004), www.sacw.net/partition/june2004IshtiaqAhmed.pdf.
[238] 'Report of the Punjab Boundary Commission (Radcliffe Award)', Wikisource, 1947, https://en.wikisource.org/wiki/Radcliffe_Award/Report_of_the_Punjab_Boundary_Commission.

one million people killed. Some of the worst atrocities were perpetrated in the cities of Lahore and Amritsar, and the corridor between them. Around 4,000 houses in Lahore were gutted and in Amritsar almost 10,000 buildings were burned down.[239] More than 3,000 people were murdered in a single incident, an attack on a train in Amritsar.

3,000 Dead In Indian Train Massacre

Australian Associated Press

NEW DELHI, September 25.

In what is reputed to be the worst train massacre of Indian refugees yet to occur, 3,000 Moslems were killed and 1,000 wounded on Monday when a train was attacked by Sikhs for three hours at Amritsar. All seven trains which have left Lahore since Thursday have been attacked, says Reuter.

Newspaper coverage of Amritsar train massacre[240]

Serious violence in Lahore actually began some months before Partition, precipitated in March 1947 by a political crisis.[241] Afzal's family members there escaped involvement, but the next day it spread to Amritsar, where other relatives were still living in

---

[239] Ian Talbot, *Divided Cities: Partition and its Aftermath in Lahore and Amritsar, 1947–1957*, The Subcontinent Divided: A New Beginning (Karachi: Oxford University Press, 2006).

[240] '3,000 Dead in Indian Train Massacre', The Advertiser (Adelaide, SA, 26 September 1947, https://trove.nla.gov.au/newspaper/page/2661923.

[241] Ishtiaq Ahmed, 'The "Bloody" Punjab Partition VIII', *Daily Times (EPaper)*, 15 April 2016, https://dailytimes.com.pk/90505/the-bloody-punjab-partition-viii/.

the Marriage House. On that day or shortly after, they received a warning from Khawaja Ghulam Mohyuddin (Uncle Bashir's mother's brother) that a Sikh mob was on its way to attack their neighbourhood. He instructed them to leave immediately, taking nothing with them but the clothes they were wearing. That same night the house was burned down and soon afterwards they made their way to Model Town, Lahore. Until 1947 Sikhs and Hindus owned the majority of Model Town properties, but at Partition about 1,100 of the 1,300 members of the Model Town Society emigrated to India.[242] The house first occupied by Afzal's aunt (Mama) and her family was located in A Block, but when the house across the road in B Block was vacated, they were able to move into 84B.

---

[242] Of 1,366 members of the Model Town Society at the time of Partition, 277 were Muslims and Christians and 1,089 were Hindus and Sikhs. Qasim Khan, 'Model Town Society', Lahore History, http://lahore.city-history.com/model-town-society.html.

London Life

Together during the War

Back in England, Karola moved from Iver, Buckinghamshire into central London in February 1941, during the *Blitz*, and a week later started work at J Lyons. It was here, after her promotion to cashier in November of that year, that she first encountered Afzal. Their first meeting would have been well before August 1943, which is when she told someone at GJAC about their relationship.

Information about where she lived in London is patchy, although most of her known addresses were concentrated in a small area close to the West End. The Red Cross communication to her parents discussed earlier indicated that in January 1942 she was staying at 20 Kendal Street W2, very near to Marble Arch where she was working. The first London address entered on her Registration Card at Bloomsbury House, dated 2 February 1943, was 93 Hereford Road W3. However, this postcode was probably mis-recorded and should have been W2, which is in Notting Hill, much closer to her workplace and previous accommodation.[243]

---

[243] This assertion is supported by Ordnance Survey maps dating to this period. The highest house number in Hereford Road W3 was 49, but the highest number for a street with the same name in W2 is 107.

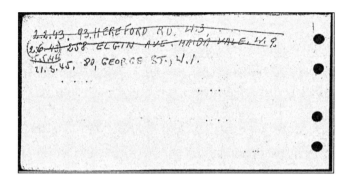

Reverse of Karola's registration card completed at
Bloomsbury House on arrival in the UK

Her next recorded address is 258 Elgin Avenue in nearby
Maida Vale W9, where she moved just a few months later and
stayed for almost two years. Given that the note in her GJAC file
records that by August 1943 she and Afzal had been co-habiting
for a few months, this must be where they started living together.

258 Elgin Avenue where Karola was living in June 1943

Sometime during the war Karola and Afzal left London because of the bombing and went to live temporarily in Goodrington Sands (near Paignton, Devon). However, it's not clear when that happened, since there is no gap in her employment history and no record has been found of any bomb landing in Maida Vale after 1941.

Karola finally gave up her job at Lyons and in December 1943 began working as a general help for a family at 49 Comeragh Road W14.[244] She stayed in that post for four years until December 1947 but, according to her employer, 'as she did not keep very good health, she received only £3 per month for the whole period'. Quite possibly this was a continuation of the kidney problems that had led to her release from national service a few months earlier. Anyway, by the time she moved on from this position, the war was finally over.

Before and throughout the war, Afzal maintained his connection with the Muslim community, continuing to worship at the East London Mosque.[245] However, his Muslim Association membership card shows that by April 1945 (AH 1364 in the Islamic calendar) he had moved out of the East End and was living at 80 George Street W1, again close to Marble Arch. In fact, Karola's Registration Card and her GJAC file papers confirm that they moved there on Wednesday 21 March 1945.

---

[244] Testimonial from employer, 30 June 1959.
[245] Muslims gathered for prayer meetings at various temporary locations in East London from 1910, but in 1941 the original East London Mosque opened in converted houses at 446–448 Commercial Road.

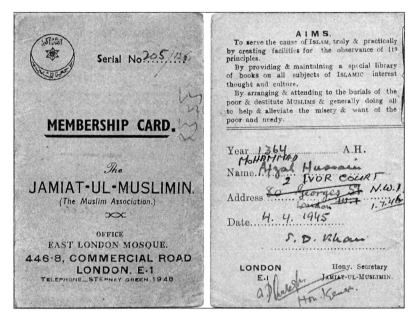

Afzal's Muslim Association membership card, 1945–46

Their accommodation up to this point must have been furnished rooms, probably bedsits. However, their next move was to somewhere more spacious and unfurnished. Their new home was Flat 2, Ivor Court, Gloucester Place NW1, very close to Regents Park.

Ivor Court, Gloucester Place

The address change on Afzal's mosque membership card is dated July 1946, but almost certainly they moved in late December 1945 or early the following month, for on Thursday 3 January 1946, they bought a considerable quantity of furnishings from S. Z. Shah Ltd. in Cavendish Square W1. Their purchases included a light oak bedroom suite, dining table, French settee and armchair, a carpet, wireless table, bed linen, bedspread and towels.

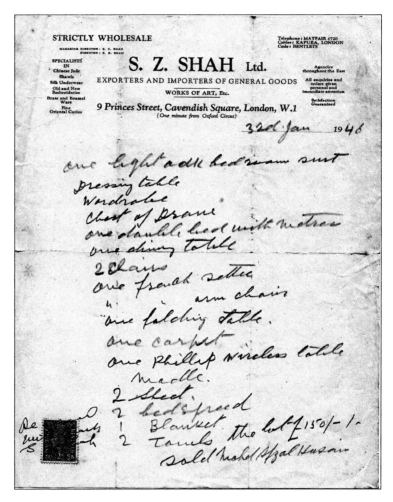

Receipt for furnishings bought in January 1946

The total bill came to £150, a substantial amount in those days, and the furniture was not their only acquisition around that time. They also bought Peter, a black and white pedigree cocker spaniel, who became a much-loved member of the household.

LONDON 1946

Afzal and Karola with Peter the spaniel in London, 1946

There was further expenditure as Afzal started learning to drive. He obtained a provisional licence in June 1946, but more than 15 years would elapse before he finally passed his driving test.

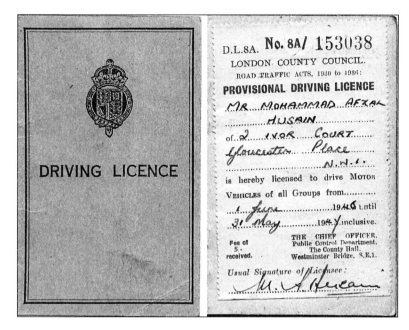

Afzal's provisional driving licence, issued June 1946

Earning a Living in Street Markets

Taking on these financial outgoings (rent, furniture, dog, driving) suggests that both were earning quite well. However, the reality was the opposite and it is difficult to explain how they matched income with expenditure. In fact, comments in later correspondence confirm that they struggled to make ends meet. Karola's pay as a general help would not have been generous and, as already mentioned, it was reduced because of her poor health. Afzal's wages would also not have been high. He took jobs in various firms, sometimes as a 'commission agent', but they would all have been at a low level. However, he never gave up his ambition to go into business.

It was during the war that Afzal, with help from Karola, started working the London street markets. At this time, he traded at

Upton Park Market, and probably Brixton, Leather Lane, Wentworth Street and others.[246] However, he never held a licence to trade regularly at any of the locations, which meant that he had no guaranteed or regular pitch. Competition for such licences was fierce and 'inducements' probably had a significant influence on their allocation. He only held 'casual' or 'temporary' permits, which enabled him to take over a pitch when a licence holder did not turn up on any particular day.

Taking possession of a vacant pitch was often a determining factor. Casual permit holders would try to find out in advance which regular traders were not going to appear and then 'occupy' their spaces early in the morning. It was then a case of waiting, perhaps until around 10am, at which time a reallocation could be made if it was still free. Much later, in the 1950s, I remember being sat on a vacant stall with a parcel or two in Petticoat Lane to stake a claim on it, while my father took possession of another nearby, in the hope that one of them would eventually be assigned to him for the day. A key person in this process was the market inspector, who had the power to make that reallocation, and it was common for them to solicit a 'sweetener' (a 'dropsy' or 'treat') to reach a favourable outcome. Inevitably, Afzal had to pay such bribes. However, it was an uncertain existence and not unusual for casual traders not to get a pitch and have to return home without any earnings, and that certainly happened to him from time to time.

In developing his business activities, then and during his later life, Afzal drew on his experience of trading and his cultural heritage, which he sought to exploit with British customers. All his early ventures involved buying and selling 'fancy goods'

---

[246] Upton Park Market is mentioned in a letter from Afzal to Karola dated 5 February 1948, but he is probably referring to Queens Market, which is in the Upton Park area.

imported from or associated with India, such as joss (incense) sticks.[247] These actually were popular in the 1940s and 1950s, perhaps as a consequence of Britain's historic involvement in India, long before they became associated with the hippie culture of the 1960s. He also sold costume jewellery, bought from mainly Indian and Jewish wholesalers.

At some point he decided that there was money to be made in Indian perfumes and began 'manufacturing' these himself. Production involved mixing essential oils with alcohol (or spirit), then using very small metal funnels to decant from large containers into tiny (one or two dram) glass bottles, before finally adding a descriptive label. Attributing the term 'manufacture' to this process probably gives the wrong impression. It was by no means a factory line, but was done on the kitchen table or in a rented garage. It is doubtful that he had much prior knowledge of how to do this, but with characteristic Indian chutzpah, he never let a lack of expertise deter him from trying anything. Perhaps he learned from another member of the community, but maybe he simply followed the instructions in his book entitled *Indian perfumes, essences and hair oils.*

---

[247] Fancy goods were chiefly ornamental items.

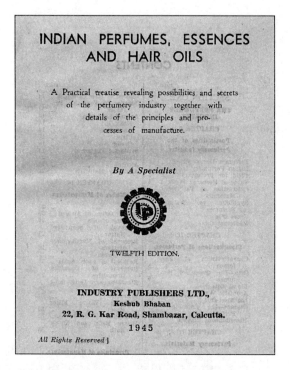

INDIAN PERFUMES, ESSENCES
AND HAIR OILS

A Practical treatise revealing possibilities and secrets
of the perfumery industry together with
details of the principles and pro-
cesses of manufacture.

By A Specialist

TWELFTH EDITION.

INDUSTRY PUBLISHERS LTD.,
Keshub Bhaban
22, R. G. Kar Road, Shambazar, Calcutta.
1945

All Rights Reserved]

Title page from Afzal's book on Indian perfumes, essences and hair oils
revealing 'secrets of the perfumery industry'

As well as learning how to make the perfumes, there was a
bureaucratic obstacle to overcome. During and after the war,
the manufacture and sale of cosmetics was strictly controlled,
initially limited to 25% of pre-war levels, so that labour, raw
materials and factory space could be used for the war effort and
then post-war recovery. In 1946 the relevant regulation was
the *Toilet Preparations (No 3) Order, 1943* and to develop his
business legitimately, Afzal obtained a licence from the Board
of Trade to manufacture and supply what were defined as
'controlled goods'.[248]

---

[248] Ina Zweiniger-Bargielowska, *Austerity in Britain: Rationing, Controls, and
Consumption, 1939–1955* (Oxford: Oxford University Press, 2000), 186

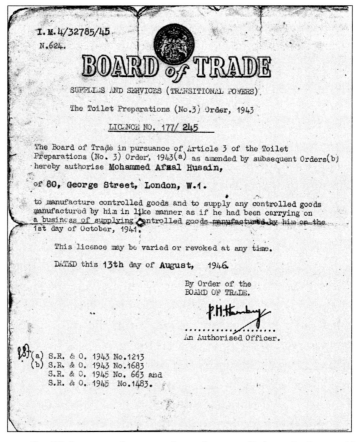

Licence for Afzal to manufacture and supply controlled goods, August 1946

Going into business was and is commonplace for men in the south Asian community, either because of blocked alternative opportunities or perhaps because it is in their DNA. Many started by selling off stalls in street markets, but then went on to create much bigger enterprises. These entrepreneurs included some of Afzal's closest contacts. The Muslim Suterwalla family comprised a patriarch and five sons who set up a business in Southall importing Indian foodstuffs that were marketed under the TRS label. It was still family owned until 2019 and had grown to be one of the largest suppliers of ethnic foods in Europe.[249] Their products can be seen in the largest supermarkets and most Indian grocery stores.

Another was Akbar Mullick, who established a jewellery business, manufacturing chains in a Sussex factory. The family of Pandit Gulhane, who were Hindus and lived in Tufnell Park, became importers of Indian products, principally joss sticks. These were not just business acquaintances, but good friends who had in common the experience of living away from their homes in a foreign country and who almost unquestioningly supported and helped each other.

Market life, though, was very hard. Apart from the challenge of getting a pitch from which to trade, getting to and from the markets was physically demanding. Without a car, sale goods had to be moved across London on public transport or rarely by taxi, and then back again with what was left at the end of each day, which was everything if the search for a stall was unsuccessful. Afzal had a small folding trolley to help with this, but it still required a lot of back-breaking lifting and carrying. Not having grown up in a cold climate, he was outside in all weathers and the returns were not only uncertain, but also low. It was a constant struggle and later, referring to his plans for the future, he writes 'I'll try and get out of this gutter life of markets'.[250] He never really succeeded and market trading remained his occupation for the rest of his life.

The war and its after effects obviously had many impacts on everyday living at this time. With the housing stock reduced by wartime damage, a shortage of building materials and increased

---

[249] TRS Group was sold in 2019 to a private equity company, when it had a turnover of £110m.
[250] Letter from Afzal to Karola, 2 February 1949.

demand for homes from returning soldiers, the control of rents introduced before the war by the Rent and Mortgage Interest Restrictions Act 1939 continued after it ended to prevent excessive increases. So when Afzal and Karola moved into Ivor Court they paid £7 5s 10d per month, including electricity, plus 6s 3d every six months for water rates. And when Karola left 20 months later, it was still the same, although a 6s per month rent increase was due in April 1948. Without rent control, such high-quality accommodation in that prestigious location would have been well beyond what they could afford.

They had a rent book and paid promptly whenever rent was due, and in this respect, they would seem to have been model tenants. However, this is an illusion because their occupancy was actually unlawful! The legitimate tenant of the flat was a Mr Emery Bardos, who sub-let it to Karola and Afzal. How they managed to stay there for so long without problems is a mystery but, in April 1948, the landlord's agent, L E Manousso, wrote to Karola advising that the owners considered her to be trespassing and giving her notice to vacate the property immediately.

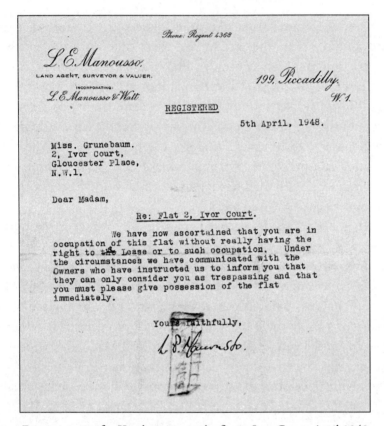

Eviction notice for Karola to vacate the flat in Ivor Court, April 1948

However, a forceful eviction was not needed. After staying there for two years, Afzal moved out in January 1948 and Karola in April of the same year. Both of them would make their next home on another continent, in the new state of Pakistan.

A Good Friend and a Remarkable Woman

Before turning to the next eventful phase in their lives, I need to make a brief digression, the origin of which is a single aerogramme found amongst Karola's papers. Written on Tuesday 2 September 1947 and posted from Salisbury (Southern Rhodesia), it was sent to her by Herta and Norbert Stiefel, each of whom penned part of the letter. I had absolutely no idea who this couple were but, since there were photographs of Norbert taken in Africa and of Herta taken in London in Karola's album, and from the warm words in the correspondence, it was very clear that they were all good friends and that Herta had been in London before joining Norbert in Salisbury six months earlier. Although it seemed a trivial note, I was intrigued and set about trying to find out who Norbert and Herta were. After many days of fruitless searching, I finally found someone who through a strange coincidence had discovered he himself had a very tenuous connection to them. Despite that tenuity, it was a link that would lead to discoveries that added to the story of my mother's life both before and after she left Germany to an extent that I could never have anticipated.

Through the contact, I was able to ascertain that Herta and Norbert had returned to London from Southern Rhodesia and that Norbert had died there in 2004. He also told me that Herta's maiden name was Sichel but, disappointingly, supposed that by then (2020) she too would have passed away because of her age. Despite this, I made further searches and found a profile of her in the newsletter of Hampstead Garden Suburb Synagogue that had been published in 2014.[251] It told her life story and revealed that, although she was alive and well when it was written, she would have been at least 100 years old in 2020. Nevertheless, I optimistically made enquiries about her at that synagogue and was thrilled to be told she was still alive and 'not only looks 20 years younger than her outstanding age but acts it and is fully engaged with life'. I could hardly believe that someone who had been a friend of my mother when they were both teenagers was

---

[251] 'Herta Stiefel – A Story Completed', *The Norrice Leader*, December 2014, https://docplayer.net/34698701-The-vibrancy-and-strength-of-our-community-has-been-much-in.html.

still so alive and perhaps could tell me something about her.

At a subsequent meeting with Norbert and Herta's son, I learned that Herta had indeed recently celebrated her 100th birthday. Moreover, she had told him that she remembered Karola and would be very happy to talk to me about her. Unfortunately, in the midst of the COVID-19 pandemic, it was impossible for us to get together, but a virtual meeting was arranged and I got to speak to her in June 2020. Herta was warm and engaging, and her memory was lucid. Much of what she had to say was news to me and, although some of it was quite disturbing, it was incredibly interesting. The conversation was not just about my parents, as she also told me about Norbert and her own remarkable life story, and how it connected her to Karola and Afzal. What follows is mostly based on that conversation, supplemented by a few details from other sources.

Norbert Stiefel was born in November 1919 and grew up with his brothers in Mühlheim, a village about six kilometres upstream from Offenbach, where he would go to meet up with other young Jewish people and play football. After the Nazis came to power there was very little interaction between Jews and non-Jews and, as Jewish persecution increased, he spent more and more time in the town where he felt less conspicuous. It was during these visits that he and Karola became good friends, but by January 1941 he had left Germany and sought refuge in Southern Rhodesia, from where he continued to write to her.

Herta Sichel was born in April 1920 and as a young girl lived with her parents and two brothers in Schlüchtern, a village 70 kilometres north-east of Offenbach. But the family was torn apart by the Nazis. In 1935, one of her brothers, accused of being a communist, was interned in Dachau. Released after two years, he fled to Columbia and her other brother left Germany for South Africa. Herta came to Offenbach. Her mother's brother and his family, the Bacharachs, lived there and they employed her as a live-in domestic. Around the time of the November 1938 pogroms, her parents also relocated to Offenbach in the expectation that they would be safer in the larger urban centre, but it was a tragic move. A few days later their apartment was ransacked and her father was taken away to Dachau, where he was murdered.[252]

Herta was advised to leave Germany for her own safety and, with the help of a cousin already in England and a testimonial confirming her experience as a domestic, she was soon given a work permit and in April 1939 arrived in London. Her mother, her aunt and her uncle were transported to Theresienstadt in September 1942, three days after Karola's parents had been forced to make that same journey, and ultimately they too were murdered in Poland.[253]

Although they lived in Kaiserstrasse almost opposite the Offenbach synagogue, the Sichels and Bacharachs were Orthodox Jews and worshipped in Frankfurt. However, the young people from both denominations socialised together; the boys often played football and the girls handball. This is where Herta first met Karola and possibly also Norbert, although she could not be sure about this. There was, though, another connection. Herta's uncle's sister-in-law was Leonie Löwenberger, the same woman who employed Karola as a temporary domestic in early 1939, and it was Leonie who put them in touch with each other in London, where they became close friends, often going out together after the war. During this time, Herta got to know Afzal, and Karola talked to her and other friends about going to Pakistan with him, even though he was already married. Several friends advised her

---

[252] Hauschke-Wicklaus and Geschichtswerkstatt Offenbach, *Jüdische Bürgerinnen und Bürger Erinnern Sich*, 52.
[253] Klaus Werner and Offenbach am Main (Germany), eds., *Zur Geschichte Der Juden in Offenbach Am Main* (Offenbach: Der Magistrat, 1988), 139, 180, 190.

not to do it but Karola was, in Herta's words, 'very much in love' and felt that she would be able to get on well with Afzal's wife. Moreover, she was enthralled with the idea of being able to help children with eyesight problems there, most likely motivated by the ocular difficulties she was herself experiencing.

At some later date, pressure was put on Herta and other Jewish friends to cut themselves off from Karola, whose behaviour – to some members of the Jewish community – was outrageous and totally unacceptable. Not only was she going out with a non-Jew, but she was also co-habiting with a married oriental man involved in what they believed was an illegal activity, namely making Indian perfume. Almost certainly because of this, there is hardly any evidence of Karola having contact with Jewish friends in the years after she started living with Afzal. Herta, though, was not put off and, although they could no longer go out together, she continued to visit them in their Ivor Court flat.

It was during one such visit that Karola was writing a letter to Norbert and, struggling to fill the page, she invited Herta to add a few sentences. When he replied to her some weeks later, it was the start of a correspondence that eventually led to a meeting in South Africa in July 1946 and to their engagement. The following year Herta set off on a flight from London to Southern Rhodesia to join her fiancé and get married, but it was a hazardous and eventful journey. The plane crash-landed on the border between the Belgian Congo (now Democratic Republic of Congo) and Northern Rhodesia (now Zambia), and it was only after trekking for five days through the bush that she was able to reach Salisbury, where the wedding took place one week later. Over the next 30 years, Herta and Norbert played a lead role in the Jewish communities of Rhodesia and South Africa, until they returned to London in 1997. However, by 1948 Karola had lost contact with the Stiefels and it was never resumed.

Through the letter and our virtual meeting, it was evident that, although they came from very different family backgrounds, Herta and Karola had much in common. Both sets of parents were murdered by the Nazis, both found work as domestics in Offenbach, both escaped to London in 1939, both left the UK and, as will become apparent shortly, both were married just a few days after reaching a distant and very different country. Talking to Herta was one of my most memorable experiences during the course of my research and so it was with much sadness that I learned of her passing in November 2020, just a few months later.

A Return to Punjab

A Man of Letters

On Sunday 18 January 1948, with a return ticket in his hand, Afzal boarded Pan American (Pan Am) Flight 002 from London (Heathrow) to Karachi. It was 12½ years since he had left India, during which time he had not seen his mother or wife, nor his daughter, Nusrat Bibi, who was born after his departure. In the intervening period, the family had been forced to abandon their home in Amritsar and, leaving all their possessions behind, they had become part of the largest mass migration in history, which was accompanied by racial and religious violence in which a million people died. What prompted him to go at this particular moment? He later wrote that he 'Hurriedly returned to Pakistan to assist my people who were refugees from Amritsar and had lost everything', but whether this was triggered by something very specific or a more general concern will never be known.[254] What is known is that three months later, on Sunday 11 April, Karola also left London to join him.

---

[254] The quote is from a speculative employment enquiry dated 7 June 1949.

Afzal with trunk packed says goodbye to Peter, the spaniel,
before his departure for Pakistan

In those three months, Afzal became an avid correspondent. He wrote and sent 22 aerogrammes and airletters to Karola, as well as a number of telegrams. He wrote letters to friends in England and to Karola's relatives in Germany. Perhaps most surprisingly, he even wrote two letters to his father in South America, to which I will return later. Twelve letters were sent to Karola in the first four weeks. By the time he landed in Karachi, he had already written two, one for her alone and another to be shared with friends, and he wrote two more a few days later on the short flight from Karachi to Lahore. Her replies to this torrent of mail were less frequent and, unfortunately, have been lost. However, with delivery times of 3–5 days, there can have been few occasions when the postal services were not carrying their letters in one direction or the other.

His handwriting was small and initially neat, fitting many words on to each page and, as was his habit throughout his life, he utilised every bit of blank space. After filling the page in the usual way, he would first turn it sideways and write along any margins, then turn the page upside down and write above the opening sentences where a little more space might be found. The end result was often a very confusing letter with handwriting in several directions, although distinctive asterisks and arrows were sometimes added to help the reader move from one segment to the next. He probably did this initially to maximise use of the limited space in aerogrammes and to reduce the number of pages – and therefore the weight and postage cost – of air letters. As the weeks went by, however, the nature of the correspondence changed significantly. His handwriting deteriorated and the later letters appeared hurriedly written. The content became more muddled and he repeated himself multiple times on several matters. The change was undoubtedly caused by stress and anxiety about the issues he had to confront, and with which he was struggling to cope.

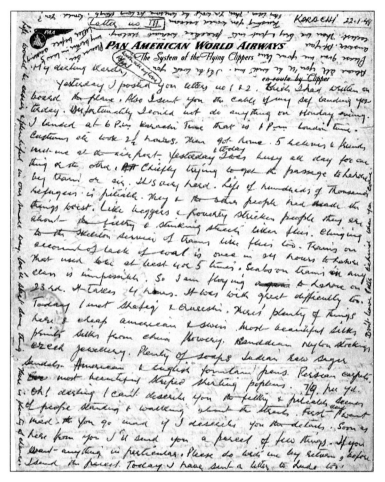

Page from a typical letter sent by Afzal with writing in multiple directions

Reading and writing about these letters from Afzal to Karola has been the most difficult part of this whole project, and not just because of their legibility and layout. It is mainly because of the nature of much of the content, which is poignant and emotional, but also upsetting. They reveal a mindset that was misguided, if not delusional, as well as being in turmoil, perhaps unsurprising in the circumstances. To make consideration of this correspondence easier, the discussion below is divided into two broad themes. The first can be described as reportage. It covers what Afzal saw and experienced as he travelled to, moved around in and then lived through the turbulent infancy of this new country. It includes a great deal of interesting observation and commentary. In places, this was a conscious description to Karola, but elsewhere what he wrote unintendedly provides a fascinating insight into his surroundings.

This provides the backdrop for the second theme, which is much more personal. It concerns all that happened to Afzal as he tried to build a life in Pakistan that would include both Masuda and Karola. It covers his relationship with his wife and other family members, his attempts to find a way to earn a living, his efforts to persuade Karola to join him and his struggle to overcome obstacles to her arrival. Particularly notable is how his feelings, perceptions and views changed in that short period and, as becomes apparent later, how mistaken he seems to have been about the possibility of a comfortable future life in this new country.

Travel and Troubles in Early 1948

Afzal's reportage starts with commentary on his journey by air to Pakistan at a time when inter-continental passenger flights were still a novelty. He took the bus from Victoria Terminal to 'the aerodrome', arriving there at 2pm and after passing through customs went on board for takeoff at 3:40pm.[255]

The aircraft, with registration NC88858, was a Lockheed Constellation, named *Clipper Empress of the Skies*.[256] This was a

---

[255] Details of the journey are taken mainly from the two letters Afzal wrote to Karola during the flight on 19 January 1948.

[256] Three months later, on Thursday 15 April, the same aircraft crashed when attempting to land at Shannon Airport. The aircraft was destroyed and all but one of those on board died. See 'Investigation of Aircraft Accident: Pan American Airways: Shannon, Eire', US Department of Transportation. Repository and Open Science Access Portal, 1948, https://rosap.ntl.bts.gov/

propeller-driven, four-engined airliner and the first in widespread use with a pressurised cabin. With a speed of 250–300 mph and a cruising altitude of 15,000–20,000 feet, the plane flew south of Paris, over Rome, Athens and the Sea of Marmara, before landing at Istanbul and then Damascus. The final leg took him over Baghdad, across the Indian Ocean and along the coasts of Baluchistan and Sind, before reaching Karachi at 6pm on Monday 19 January 1948. The total actual flying time was over 19 hours.

Afzal's postcard of Pan Am's Flying Clipper

It was Afzal's first experience of flying and he wrote 'when I got into the plane I was a bit nervous, wondering what it would be like'. However, the takeoff and flight went smoothly and, seated over the wing on the port side, he soon relaxed and was able to look out of the window and wonder at the 'glorious snow-white mountain peaks', the stars at night and then the sunrise. In the northerly latitudes, though, the cabin was extremely cold and at times he found breathing difficult. In a later letter, Afzal suggested to Karola that she 'take a nip of Scotch (Three Feathers American

view/dot/33338.

is supplied)' on the plane to keep warm on her journey, and informed her that 'you get chewing gum at take off, also some cotton wool to push into your ears to avoid the terrific noise'.[257]

Passengers did not go hungry. Afzal reported that early in the evening he had 'quite a big meal' on board. Then in Istanbul, Pan Am treated passengers to Turkish coffee, and he also enjoyed 'a lovely bottled beer', while breakfast in Damascus consisted of bread and butter, scrambled eggs, bacon and oranges. Finally, on the final leg he had an in-flight 'beautiful lunch [of] fresh orange juice, roast chicken with peas and new potatoes, real chocolate ice cream two lots and coffee'.[258] Interestingly, although he declined the bacon, he much appreciated the beer and advised Karola to have a Scotch, despite consumption of both pork and alcohol being forbidden in Islam.

Surprisingly, although this journey took place long before the age of mobile phones, it was possible for people on the ground to communicate with the passengers. When still some distance from Karachi, Afzal received a welcome message transmitted to the plane by his relatives. It seems unlikely, though, that this was a common occurrence and they probably had some inside contacts who made it possible:

> *19 January 1948* Just this minute the stewardess handed me in a radio message of welcome from my brother-in-law and 2 cousins who are awaiting me in Karachi aerodrome. How nice of them! And I was the only one on the plane to receive a message.

After the long flight and landing in Karachi, it took Afzal another 2½ hours to get through custom checks. But when he

---

[257] Letter from Afzal to Karola, 2 March 1948.

[258] Chocolate was rationed in the UK until 1953, hence chocolate ice cream was something special.

eventually emerged, relatives and friends were waiting there to welcome him and provide him with overnight accommodation, almost certainly at the home of Abdul Hameed Khan ('Hameed'), his brother-in-law.[259]

It was evidently difficult for Afzal to come to terms with the fact that what had been India when he left the sub-continent was now Pakistan, since in several letters over subsequent weeks he still referred to being in India. However, he quickly became aware of the consequences of the momentous change that had taken place. The next day he tried to arrange his onward travel to Lahore and was immediately confronted with the dire reality of a country trying to cope with massive political, demographic and economic upheaval. He was shocked by the flood of refugees, the widespread manifestations of poverty and the disruption to basic services. With train services particularly limited by a shortage of coal, he eventually managed to buy a ticket for a flight to Lahore on the Friday:

> *22 January 1948* (from Karachi) Yesterday and today I was busy all day for one thing or the other. Chiefly trying to get the passage to Lahore by train or air. It's very hard. Life of hundreds of thousands refugees is pitiable. They and the other people have made things worst. Like beggers and poverty stricken people they are about the filthy and stinking streets like flies. Clinging to the skeleton service of trains like flies too. Trains on account of lack of coal is once in 24 hours to Lahore. That used to be at least 4 or 5 times. Seats on trains in any class is impossible. So I am flying to Lahore on 23rd. It takes 4 hours. That was with

---

[259] In a letter to Karola dated between 25 February and about 11 March 1948, Afzal gives his brother-in-law's full name and address, which confirms that he lived in Karachi (at 41/3 Jutland Lines, Karachi Cantonment).

great difficulty too ... I can't describe you the filthy and pitiable scenes of people standing and walking about the streets. First day I went mad. You go mad if I describe you the details ... All inland posts and telegraph services are topsy turvy.

26 January 1948 (from Lahore) Refugees lying all over the place. Simply makes you sick. Hygiene is unknown.

2 February 1948 (from Lahore) I can't describe you the miserable situation which is due to new changes. Unrest. Refugees.

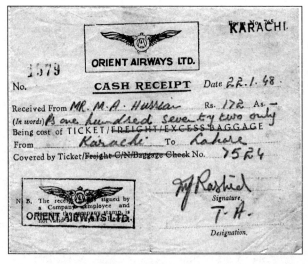

Receipt for Afzal's flight payment from Karachi to Lahore

It is difficult to imagine that anything could have made the situation in the country worse. But amidst this unimaginable chaos and upheaval, an event took place that shocked the world and threatened to further destabilise both India and Pakistan. On Friday 30 January 1948, seven days after Afzal arrived in Lahore,

Mahatma Gandhi was assassinated in New Delhi. Gandhi had initially opposed Partition but came to accept division as the only way to avoid civil war. To many Indians, however, he was over-sympathetic to Muslims, which led to his murder by a Hindu nationalist. His commitment to peace meant that he was mourned throughout Pakistan as well as India. Nevertheless, the regional turbulence prompted Karola's relatives in Germany to write to Afzal, expressing anxiety about the risk of violence erupting between the two countries.[260] Afzal was unperturbed and dismissed their concerns, countering their questions by asking about the growing tensions in Europe:

> *2 February 1948* And new management with the situation not quite under control. Mr Gandhi as you have heard the same day was shot dead in Delhi (India) on Friday. Even the whole of Pakistan is mourning on Sat. like India.

> *11 March 1948* They [Karola's relatives in Germany] seem to be worried about the dangers of Pakistan-India troubles here. I'll write and ask them if and how much peace prevails in Europe. While Russia getting stronger on one side and the western allies on the other.

In contrast to the hardship being endured by so many, Afzal was also struck by the ready availability of most basic and luxury goods, unobtainable or rationed in Britain, although their cost made them unaffordable to most people. The one exception was cotton goods, especially towels and handkerchiefs, which were in short supply, and so he asked Karola to bring with her as many of

---

[260] By early 1948, Karola had re-established contact with her non-Jewish relatives in Germany, most notably with her cousin, Greta Reusch, and her family in Mittelsinn, and had introduced them to Afzal.

these as she could when she eventually came to Pakistan:

> *22 January 1948* There's plenty of things here and cheap American and Swiss. Most beautiful silk prints. Silks from China flowery. Canadian Nylon stockings. Czech jewellery. Plenty of soaps. Indian raw sugar. Sandals. American and English fountain pens. Persian carpets. Most beautiful striped shirting poplins. 7/9 per yard.
>
> … Most gorgeous things of all kinds are obtainable here. One goes crazy. After spending years of utility in London.
>
> *26 January 1948* Plenty of things all that you would love to wear and eat. No shortage.
>
> *10 February 1948* Cotton goods here very scarce.
>
> *15 February 1948* Every mealtime in a large dining room we are about 12 on the dining table. Food is plenty. Four or five varieties to eat. One doesn't know what to eat and what not to eat. Plenty of rice chapatis, various curried meat dishes. Sometimes fish too. Fish is from the fresh water.
>
> *8 March 1948* Life here nowadays is very expensive.

With so many everyday items in short supply in post-war Europe, Afzal not only sent food and other provisions to Karola, but also despatched parcels to friends and relatives in London and Germany:

> *2 February 1948* Long and finest rice are so plentyful that I could send tons. About 10d a pound. Shall soon send you a parcel. Please advise me. Also to send one your home … Soap etc plenty tin fruit and food,

standard bedspread Indian. Most gorgeous colours. Let me know.

8 March 1948 Tomorrow I am sending a food parcel each to (1) Eve and Stan (2) Harry (3) Asgar (4) Pandit (5) Greta (Germany).[261] Each parcel contains one lb butter 1lb cheese craft 1lb marmalade 1lb tea and some sweets. For Greta it will be coffee instead of tea. And tin of milk instead of jam. 50 cig. instead of sweet. The whole parcels' nett weight must not exceed 5lbs. Few days later I am planning to send more with different articles. Rice and sugar is not permitted. But brown sugar can be sent and syrup etc. Everything is in tins.

There was one other difference between living in London and living in Pakistan that he really noticed. It was the weather. In his first few weeks there, he was effusive about the clear skies and warm days, even though it was the cooler season, and he contrasted the conditions with the cold and snow in London. Very soon, however, when the rains started and the days got hotter, his attitude changed somewhat as the mosquitoes started to bite and he realised how challenging the extreme summer heat would be:

23 January 1948 No more nasty English weather

26 January 1948 This gorgeous weather you would love it.

5 February 1948 Temp here 80°. Hot sunshine all day.

6 February 1948 Weather is marvellous and strange here. Continuous sun shine without a break ever. Clear

---

[261] Eve and Stan Vigdor were Karola and Afzal's neighbours in London, living at 3 Ivor Court. They became very close friends and are mentioned in almost all of Afzal's letters sent to Karola while he was in Pakistan without her.

sky. Burning sun at 72°in day 36° at night after sun set
ie bitter cold. It's going into summer. In another 2–3
months it would be 120° in shade.

15 February 1948 It's getting very warm here and the
sun is one stillness from morning till the evening.

… We'll buy some mosquito nets as mosquitoes
are starting. I am only wondering how you [Karola]
and I in particular are going to stand the mid-summer
heat of 120° in the shade.

20 February 1948 What's the weather like in London
these days. Below freezing, I guess. Here it had got
quite warm. But for three days it had been rain cloudy
and cold. It first started though with dust storm that
lasted 15 minutes only. Mosquitoes too have started
biting at night. We'll buy some nets at Karachi when
you come. With rain its pools of water and dirty mud
all over.

27 February 1948 We had another couple of days and
nights rain (continuous) again. Cold too. It's dry and
sun shining today.

2 March 1948 Weather is getting hotter and hotter
every day. Hope you are enjoying the London snow.

10 March 1948 There have been heavy rains for days.
It has ruined crops. Otherwise bumper crops were
expected.

11 March 1948 Heavy rains continued till today. Sun
is shining now.

An Extremely Complex Situation Develops

The more personal content of Afzal's correspondence with Karola in the three months after he left Britain reveals that this was a very difficult time for both of them, as well as for his family. He was severely conflicted, torn between a sense of duty to his family in Pakistan and his love for his soulmate in London, both of whom probably wanted his undivided presence and affection. To square the circle and satisfy all sides, he proposed a solution that was both naïve and unrealistic, and he soon realised that a way forward was going to be much harder to achieve than he had ever imagined. Ultimately, his plan was doomed to fail, but that point was not reached until much later. In the meantime, his letters touched on many different issues, practical and emotional, and they reflected the mental confusion that he was undoubtedly going through.

Afzal did not intend to go to Pakistan permanently, but planned to help his family through the post-Partition difficulties and then come back to Britain. For this he had a return ticket. However, there is no doubt that Karola resisted the idea of him going on his own. Apart from not wanting to be separated, she probably feared, rightly, that he would be pressed by his wife and other family members to stay. In addition, there are comments in his letters which indicate that her state of mind was also fragile. After all, she had lost all her close family in the Holocaust, was living in a strange new country, did not have a job and was not in good health. It seems that, as he was intent on returning for a short visit, she was keen to go with him, an idea he rejected at the time but came to regret later:

> *11 March 1948* I can't curse myself enough for not bringing you with me. You had said that all the time. It was only me who couldn't think right.

Certainly, even before he went, she had concerns about how she would be able to survive, reflected in repeated references to her worries and anxieties in his later correspondence. It is therefore understandable that she did not want him to go and that there were very emotional and tearful scenes in the days before his departure and at Victoria Station as she saw him leave. He seems to have been equally distraught by their separation. His first letter, written on the flight, was full of endearments, concerns for her welfare and reassurance. He was at pains to convince her that she alone was the one he wanted to be with and that he would soon be back:

> *19 January 1948* I know it's your love for me that made you feel that way. And this is my love for you which is making me write you now. My love I shalln't be long when I am back to you soon. You are the very part of my life. You are my life. We can not now remain apart for long. Sweetheart these are words from the very bottom of my heart. Hoping they might console you. Please darling don't let yourself go like you did until yesterday, anymore. I do realize how much I have hurt you. I feel as if my heart has been continuously bleeding ever since I left you crying so very desperately. Your last words 'Afzal come back' when I got into the bus at Victoria Terminal are still ringing in my ears. It's high time sweetheart for you that you must try and pull yourself together in full faith that I'll be back with you.
>
> ... I had not slept a wink last night on the plane ... partly because of the deep and very sorrowful thoughts for you and you alone. My darling! I am and have been wondering throughout the journey, just one thing ie How are you? Untill I hear from you I

shall not be at peace my love.

… It has been so very painful for me ever since I left you because I made you very painful. You don't deserve to be made so, my love. I most sincerely believe that you are a perfect angel. We are not two but one. You understand me darling. Don't you? You and you alone can. No one else can.

… Every time I think of you I see you only in the saddest picture of the last moments in crying. And how, darling, this has made me cry inwardly for I know it will not stop until I come back and kiss you and embrace you with my heart. I shall have no peace until then…

… I shall only live again when I hear from you soon. So hurry up and write me.

From Karachi, Afzal sent a telegram to let her know of his safe arrival. It was the first of the many communications she received over the following weeks. He also made a trunk call to Lahore to tell his family there that he had landed.

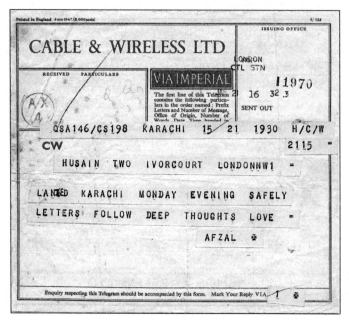

Telegram sent on 21st January 1948 by Afzal to Karola

A recurring topic in his early letters was Karola's poor health. As already mentioned, she had been sick at various times from 1943 to December 1947 whilst working as an assembler at Arcourt Engineering and whilst working as a general help at Comeragh Road. And when Afzal departed in January 1948, she was still unwell with a condition that was affecting her eyes, a problem compounded by the breaking of her glasses. It is quite possible that this was connected to her earlier ill health since certain types of kidney disease are associated with eyesight problems.[262] After taking medication, and possibly after surgery, her eyes did eventually get better. However, the separation, the subsequent weakening of Afzal's commitment to return and worries about her trip to Pakistan had a serious impact on her general well-being:

---

[262] 'Kidney Disease, Dialysis, and Your Eyes', National Kidney Foundation, https://www.kidney.org/newsletter/kidney-disease-dialysis-and-your-eyes.

19 January 1948 The most I feel concerned is your eyes. How you feel with them after all that crying and with no glasses … Darling I am frightfully worried about your eyes. It will keep me very restless untill I hear from you in detail.

… Now darling I want to remind you about your glasses above all, so that they get repaired at the earliest. Secondly, about your general health. Do take regularly your red medicines and small tablets and act upon Dr Guna's advice and phone him every week as he asked you to do. Drink plenty of milk. Take a regular walk in fresh air.

… Your health is my greatest anxiety. I won't be there for a while to tell you to take care and take medicine though with that you hardly ever took any notice. So this is how I feel about you, my love, every moment since I left you. I think I go crazy until I hear from you that you are ok.

22 January 1948 I am very worried about your general health. Particularly about your eyes.

26 January 1948 And the news of your own health was like a stab.

2 February 1948 I must ask you first as how you are. Your health and your feeling are the pressing factors of my life. I want you to be well … My mind had been seriously disturbed over your health ever since I had the first letter from you and then this second … If Dr thinks you must go to hospital, please do so.

5 February 1948 You don't know how glad I am to learn that you are at last better in your health.

7 February 1948 [In your last letter] you told me that you have got your eyesight back after 36 hours and that you are better …

27 February 1948 I was sorry to learn about your ill health in your last letters. I hope you have picked up by now. It must be due to the visa affair that you got worried.

Afzal's first few letters were full of affection and devotion. But gradually the content changed so that, although still present, such sentiments became a smaller part of each, and more pragmatic matters took up an increasing amount of space. Much more significantly, all mention of a return to London disappeared. On the contrary, in the very first letter he wrote after landing in Karachi, Afzal put forward a very different proposition. Towards the end, almost as an afterthought, he asked Karola whether she would be willing to leave London and start a new life in Pakistan:

22 January 1948 My darling I ask you a very important question in brief. Also my brother in law would be writing you in connection with the same question. If I ask you to sell the flat and everything, pack up and come to Pakistan. We start a new life here.

This will have come out of the blue for Karola. The wording indicates that it is not something they had discussed before. Indeed, in letters written during his flight from London, Afzal repeatedly affirmed his intention to return. However, on his arrival he was confronted by his brother-in-law, Hameed, who was very unhappy about Azfal's long separation from his wife and daughter. Moreover, although Afzal had not told anyone in Pakistan about Karola, they evidently knew about her and even expected her to arrive there with him. They left him in no doubt that this situation could not continue and gave him an ultimatum: either stay in

Pakistan or return to London with Masuda and Nusrat Bibi. He explained all this to Karola in his next letter, written on the flight to Lahore:

> *23 January 1948* So far what news I got from my brother in law and cousin, they all know about you for a long time. He told me point blank that either I should be asked to stay here or if I must go to London I must take Masuda and Bibi with me. I said to him I can not live without you or my Peter. I would die if I don't see them before long. So he said there is a very simple [way] out of it. We have nothing against it. What he suggested I wrote you darling in my last letter … Infact he never expected me to come alone. He was most shocked when he saw me alone landing from the plane. I told him all about you. Shafiq also spoke very high about you. My brother in law was so very impressed about you.

Afzal was also significantly affected by what he saw and heard on arrival there, most obviously the reunion with his wife and mother, and a first encounter with his daughter. His mother, who was then in her early 50s and had herself been separated from her husband, Ismail, for around 38 years, was in poor health:

> *2 February 1948* Mother does not keep good health. On her elbows and certain parts of her body there are indescribable large sores. She doesn't sleep well.

But perhaps he was most moved by the realisation of what his wife had endured through his absence, about which she and other family members left him in no doubt. Over subsequent weeks, he explained to Karola how, despite feeling so badly treated, she had remained stoic and faithful to him:

6 February 1948 …[Masuda] most sacredly awaited with full honours for the best 13 years of her life. Which she not only spent in utter lonesomeness, but under the continuous bickering of her relatives.

11 February 1948 She as you know had waited for me 13 years like a saint.

Faced with these realities, Afzal concluded that his future lay in Pakistan and he tried to convince Karola to join him there. He appreciated that this would be a difficult decision for her and, to persuade her, his messages focused on two particular matters, about which she would have had considerable concern. The first was what it would be like to live there and the opportunities to earn an income. Perhaps it was the sight of the merchandise for sale and the pleasant climatic conditions that, despite the chaos and poverty, made him feel very optimistic in those early days. He repeatedly highlighted the excellent job prospects and business opportunities, and the expectation of a quality of life much higher than they could possibly achieve in London. However, he wrote much more about her employment than about how he would secure an income for himself:

22 February 1948 Life would be easier and plentiful in our small way. We'll start something. There is plenty of chances.

23 January 1948 Sweetheart, if you decide to come over you will begin to enjoy a good health. A good business or a fine job. No more markets. No more nasty English weather. A comfortable life for good. I would love you to come here darling. You'll here begin to enjoy a new life here. We will live in a peaceful atmosphere no more anxieties like one has while living in England.

26 January 1948 We will all have peace and can begin a new life. I think I'll be a success in doing so … We will try and get you a nice job in an office or smart shop.

2 February 1948 For that love of mine for you I want to make our lives better. If I can help I'll try and get out of the gutter life of markets. I see here there are great many fine and paying prospects. Many opportunities here are in view. And believe me very bright ones. My people are very very influential. So far everything is in the air. My people suggest while I am here I should try and see if I can find some favourable opportunity.

6 February 1948 I aim to get a nice job for you. Either in the Government office [or] in business houses. We will see. At first when you land at Karachi we might look around for some German firms. Perhaps. Otherwise there'll be something for you. Don't worry. One thing certain. A new life. A pure life. No more markets. No more standing in gutter and cold.

7 February 1948 My darling everything would be ok here for you. Scope is plenty. A job in Govt office, in business or anything else we'll be able to get for you. You'll be able to learn shorthand type free of charge. A cousin of mine teaches in spare time. … No more hardships and anxieties at every step of London life.

15 February 1948 I'll be very glad that you too will start seeing some happy days. No more of the gutter life of the markets in London.

The second matter was how she would be received by family members, and especially by his wife, Masuda. He made clear from the very first invitation to join him that it would involve living with his mother, Masuda and Nusrat Bibi, so Karola would surely have been apprehensive about what must have seemed a very unconventional arrangement. In response, while still in Karachi, Afzal assured her several times that she would be welcomed by everyone, avowed that she was the one he loved, and tried to provide some clarity about their future domestic arrangements:

22 January 1948 We start a new life here, of course with Mother, Masuda and Bibi together who would most heartily welcome you, I can assure. Trusting you would welcome this idea.

23 January 1948 Sweetheart do believe I am lost without you and my Peter. I have now actually cried many times during my stay at Karachi, while talking and thinking about you and Peter.

... [My brother-in-law] said he could tell us with confidence that Masuda would take you as her own sister. Everybody else would give you a hearty welcome.

... I can assure you darling that Masuda mother and Bibi and every one in the family would do everything to make you feel happy and comfortable ... One thing is certain darling though everyone here would love you and have you here among them. You'll have the warmest welcome of your life. Please do realise that for economical reasons we'll have to live together with Mother Masuda and Bibi. Of course in separate rooms.

26 January 1948 Mother and many relatives tell me off for not bringing you along and for leaving you there alone.

2 February 1948 I can assure you darling once again that you are still mine and always will be. I love you with all my heart.

5 February 1948 Anxious eyes of the family are awaiting to see you and to give you a homely hearty and warm welcome. I can assure you it would be no less than mine.

5 March 1948 You are deep in my thoughts every moment of the day and night.

8 March 1948 So please darling don't let anything worry you. Just think that you are the very heart of my life. We can not part.

10 March 1948 You as well as I know too in our hearts that one thing is unalterable. That is our love for each other.

Afzal was not the only person who wrote to Karola about his plan. His brother-in-law, Hameed, also sent a letter and Afzal asked her not to come to any decision until she had read it. Unfortunately, that letter no longer exists. One can surmise, though, that it would have been intended to provide further reassurance and may also have set out conditions or details about what her future life there would be like.

Karola, though, was distraught that Afzal was now suddenly not planning to return. She feared losing the one person around whom she had started to rebuild her life, and the anxiety took a further toll on her health. Initially, she was lukewarm to the idea of moving to Pakistan. In response, Afzal sent a letter to his friend in London, Aziz, and enlisted his help in consoling and reassuring her about their relationship:

2 February 1948 Reply to Aziz is quite detailed one.

I have written him quite a bit about you too. Have asked him to read it personally to you too. Trusting he would. Pray it would help to console you and give you a clearer and truer understanding, as far as you and I are concerned.

However, with no hint that Afzal would come back to England if she refused to follow him, despite her reservations and even before she learned what was in the letter to Aziz, Karola relented. On Thursday 29 January, just a week after he wrote to ask, she confirmed her willingness to go.

A Rude Awakening

Afzal must have discovered very soon after arriving in Lahore that the assurances he gave Karola on both matters were just wishful thinking. His initial optimism about finding a business opportunity proved totally unfounded. He had his own business cards printed, but had no success whatsoever in finding an opening, as he made very clear in his letters:

Afzal's business card

6 February 1948 I have not been able to start any business yet. Quite a few favourable schemes. Yet everything is in the air.

7 February 1948 All my present anxiety is to find a good business here ...

10 February 1948 I am still extremely busy in finding some business. Not successful yet. But soon I shall by the Grace of God.

11 February 1948 I haven't been a success in making any start yet. Perhaps we'll be luckier [when] you come.

15 February 1948 Everything is still in the air, as far as any business is concerned.

27 February 1948 I am out all day. Simply running from one place to another. Trying to find something. No luck yet.

2 March 1948 I have been very busy in finding some business. Now since the 25ᵗʰ I have been running about for your permit. Result is I have not been able to pay much attention towards getting some business.

8 March 1948 I haven't got any business yet.

11 March 1948 So far I have not secured any business here.

Perhaps in desperation, he asked Karola to speak to Rahmen, a contact in London, about setting up a joint business venture with him in Pakistan. However, that does not seem to have led anywhere either and, while he remained forever hopeful that his fortunes would change, he soon discovered that this failure to secure an income was a major obstacle to the fulfilment of his plans:

24 March 1948 Please contact Rahman and tell him I would very much like to deal in Pakistan all the goods he manufactures or handles. Please ask him to treat this as serious and vital and if possible get the necessary particulars and catalogues and price lists ... And tell him that I am most certainly counting on him. Also please ask him to give a letter of introduction for me to his elder brother in Karachi. Perhaps I'll be able to do some business with his brother here.

As far as his wife was concerned, Afzal quickly realised that he had totally misjudged how she would react. It seems that she was one of the few people who did not know about the relationship with Karola and she was truly shocked to find out. Unsurprisingly, she was extremely unhappy about her coming to Pakistan and Afzal eventually had to tell Karola not to expect a pleasant welcome from her:

6 February 1948 There's still a great deal of anxiety about you joining me. Particularly where Masuda is concerned ... Her joy didn't last for long when she found out that there's some one else too. And that some one is going to be the shareholder of her only treasure and hope in life. What would be the outcome and response? This vital question she puts me and herself. You would naturally appreciate her feelings. As woman to woman. She is obviously trying to persuade herself to let you be her shareholder.

10 February 1948 Everybody else is quite contended about you joining me. Except Masuda. Which is quite natural. I have already written you all about it. She agreed too about your coming but with great sorrow. You only can realise that. As a woman to woman. I don't think personally that you'll get a pleasant welcome from her. To start with anyway. Later I can assure you, she'll be ok. I am giving you these details so that you know beforehand what to expect.

11 February 1948   One thing sweet heart is that
Masuda is no more happy about my coming home.
For your coming here she gave me the consent though
but inside her she feels it a big blow. And is most
unhappy…

Sorting out this tangled situation became a priority and it
occupied a lot of space in Afzal's letters during February. Initially
he explained to Karola that two conditions needed to be met for
her to be able to come to Pakistan: first, she had to be willing
and, second, the idea had to be acceptable to the family. By early
February he wrote that 'Consent from you and here is 100%
…', curiously referring to the family, and specifically Masuda, as
'here'. But then he had to add a third condition, agreement on
the arrangements for a life of 'peace and harmony' or 'mutual
understanding', phrases he used over and over again to describe
the nirvana he was hoping to achieve.

His 'solution' to this predicament was to ask Karola to write
to Masuda to reassure her and set out proposals for their future
together. He seems to have had very few, if any, ideas himself
about how this would work, except for one thing. He asked
Karola to tell Masuda that she, Masuda, would 'come first' and
that Karola would 'come after'. At the same time, though, he
assured her that this would not make any real difference to her
status and entreated her several times to be 'understanding' and
'broadminded'. He was convinced that, if she did this, everything
would work out well within a short time after her arrival:

5 February 1948 Consent from you and here is 100%
by now. The only thing remains concerning this is
mutual understanding. As you would appreciate
you and her are both strangers to each other. That is
why the responsibility on me would be tremendous.

All I want a clear understanding in mutual domestic life when you come over. The vital responsibility of justice peace and harmony falls on me. So I would like to settle up first and make sure. Every day I speak high about you. I assure Masuda and others of your sincere devotion to them all. I speak of your generous kind, true and sincere nature which is rare. Your simplicity and simple outlook on life is also another very beautiful part of your life. Trusting when you come you will prove your worthy and thus honour my prestige that I have created here for you. By your very nature of putting others first.

... Now I want you to write me and Masuda and Bibi and all as what ideal plans for a mutual cooperation plans you got in your mind. Please write and assure them now. They are naturally very anxious about it. You as a woman would appreciate, won't you? Masuda and all were naturally aggrieved when I first broke this news about you. I convinced them. Thank God they are contended now. But more they would be when you reassure them of the coming mutual life. So let us see what you write them in this vital matter.

6 February 1948 I try my best to assure her and convince her that Karola will prove herself most faithful to you. And that you would put Masuda first. Which is only natural. And that you would do everything to plan a mutual life of peace and harmony. I am confident that you'll agree and honour my prestige when you come. But Masuda will only be convinced if you write her a personal letter and disclose her your own very feelings, thoughts, respect love that you possess for her. And how you propose your plan for a mutual life of peace and harmony. By now I believe you must have one. I myself or some one else would read it out to her. Masuda is extremely worried and upset over this issue. Only your personal assurances and letters would probably help her to over come it ... Pray God Almighty alone can content her and give her the courage to be able to take it. So let me see what you write her to console her.

7 February 1948 ... a life full of peace and harmony and free from any domestic anxieties when you come and join Masuda. You alone can assure me and her. Please write soon.

10 February 1948 I am sure now at this stage and under these circumstances you'll prove yourself to be thoroughly understanding and thus broadminded. As time goes by everything will smooth down.

... I gave your message and love to Masuda and all. She cried the whole day. So you better write a detailed letter direct to her and tell her that you (Masuda) come first and I (Karola) come after. It won't reduce you. You know that, Don't you? Just for harmony and peace. Tell her how you intend to spend a life of mutual association with sincere wishes for each other.

11 February 1948 Perhaps you can help me to write her. I want you both to be equally happy with me as well as with each other. I wrote you and asked you before too about this. Please see what you can write her and me.

20 February 1948 I have had all your letters. Also one for Masuda. At times she still cries and feels most upset about you joining me. Don't let this worry you

my love. Within few days of your arrival she will get
over it. I am sure.

2 March 1948 Masuda saw a picture [film?] yesterday
of domestic life like ours that upset her once again.

It was an unconscionable request and, understandably, Karola,
did not acquiesce to it immediately. But he asked several times
and eventually she did send a letter, which others then had to read
to Masuda. What she wrote and whether it made any difference
is difficult to know. As late as 2 March, Afzal was still saying how
upset Masuda was about the proposed arrangement. However,
one day later he wrote again and told Karola that even Masuda
had become reconciled to her coming:

3 March 1948 As far as the home people are concerned
there is not the least bit objection. Not even from
Masuda now. She would most welcome you.

A Different Type of Proposal

Afzal's initial invitation to Karola to join him in Pakistan made
no mention of getting married and, of course, he already had a
wife and child. However, the note in Karola's GJAC file written
in 1943 made it clear that they had discussed marriage five years
earlier and that she anticipated that he would first divorce his
then wife. In fact, every letter he sent to her from Pakistan was
addressed to 'Mrs K Husain' (at Ivor Court), suggesting that
they had been living as man and wife in London, something that
would probably have been more socially acceptable than overt
cohabitation.

Whether Afzal ever seriously contemplated divorce is doubtful.
It is never mentioned in his correspondence and it is clear from the
first mention of Karola going to join him that his intention was to
have two wives, polygyny then and now being legally permissible

for Muslims in Pakistan.[263] Whether they had discussed this possibility before he left or whether she was expected to infer what was being proposed is unclear. But once Karola had agreed to travel, he suggested that they should wed immediately after she had landed in Karachi ('there and then'). He did not ask her in any direct way whether she would consent to marry him. What he did ask about is whether she would be willing to become a Muslim and participate in the *nikah* ceremony.[264] He suggested she do this 'only if you want to live a holy pure and sacred new real married life'. To this end he recommended that his friend in London, Aziz, provide her with lessons on Islam and how to prepare for life under the new domestic circumstances.

It has to be assumed that at some point she agreed to this proposal too and on Wednesday 11 February he wrote that she should share the news with all her 'people', whilst also alerting her that, unlike most marriages in Pakistan, theirs would be 'a quiet wedding':

> *10 February 1948* When you land at Karachi we will get married there and then. I am confident that Aziz will kindly give you few lessons about Islam. As you would have got my letter by now in which I said that it would be most welcome that you first accept your religion ISLAM, then we'll have an Islamic marriage with NIKAH. Please ask Aziz to explain you all this. I hope you'll agree to all that. Only if you want to live a holy pure and sacred new real married life with me. What do you say to that?
>
> … Please ask Aziz to explain and prepare you not

---

[263] Polygyny is the practice of a man having more than one wife at the same time.

[264] In the *nikah* the groom or his representative proposes to the bride in front of at least two witnesses and the marriage contract is signed.

only to become Muslim but how to prepare yourself for this new life under these prevailing domestic circumstances of ours.

11 February 1948 Please congratulate all your people everywhere and tell them we are getting married in Karachi. When you land. That would be our first major affair. It will be a quiet wedding. You only can appreciate that. And that's all that matters.

On the Move

As the address on Afzal's business card shows, when he reached Lahore, he and the rest of the family lived at 84B in Model Town, the home of his aunt (Mama) and her family. It seems that this was where he too wanted to stay and develop his business. However, by late January that plan had clearly changed and his intention then was to move to Karachi. Perhaps he was influenced by Karola's cautious consent to come to Pakistan and the difficulties she would experience fitting into the wider family. However, there is ambiguity in his correspondence about whether he foresaw living there with Karola alone or with his mother, Masuda and Nusrat Bibi too:

> *23 January 1948* If you come we will all live in Karachi.

> *26 January 1948* I intend to plan then either you or all of us to live in Karachi.

A few weeks later, though, his plans changed yet again. On 8 March 1948 he wrote excitedly about having secured what he called a 'big bungalow' in Lahore:

> *8 March 1948* But I have a very big bungalow. It's almost next door to this one. It's two story. About a

dozen rooms in all. Big garden. Two large steel gates. Soon as I get a camera I'll send you pictures. Two large verandas on two sides. Balconies at the back and side. Rent only 75/- per month. Furnished too. There are three ceiling fans alone. It's next to nothing. It's simply beautiful. Roses and all kinds of trees flowers plants are there.[265]

This was 98B in Model Town, which abutted corner to corner with 84B. It was a large corner plot on which there was an imposing mansion. Previously, it had been occupied by a wealthy Sikh family, headed by Bishan Singh, but they had relocated to India at Partition and the house had been taken over by the government.

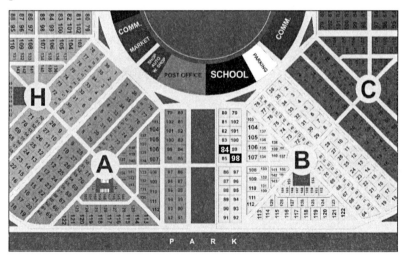

Location of houses 84B and 98B in Model Town, Lahore

In keeping with other dwellings in Model Town, the mansion was large, well designed and built to a high specification. It had

---

[265] The dwellings in Model Town, most of which were substantial two-storey buildings, were known as bungalows.

three floors, shaded verandas, extensive grounds and connections to mains services. Along the drive outside the house was a channel into which water was diverted through tunnels from a canal, enabling the gardens, which were built at a lower level, to be flooded on a monthly cycle, allowing flowers and lawns to survive the hot dry summers:

Model Town 98B (side entrance) in 1978

24 March 1948 We have our large private gardens all round. Full of narcissus, red and pink roses, sweet pea and gardenia. Roses are beautiful and in bloom. We pick dozens every day. Sweet peas are nearing finish. And it's too early for gardenia. We have five trees of lemons. You can see little lemons all over. Not ripe yet. They will be in another three weeks. There are many fruit trees like mangoes, pomegranates, sour oranges etc.

Just three days after first telling Karola about it, on Thursday 11 March, Afzal together with his mother, his wife and daughter moved into 98B.[266] It was to be the family home for the next 50 years but, as will become apparent, the time he spent there over those five decades amounted to no more than a few weeks. Even though he had moved, Afzal instructed Karola to continue to address letters for him to 84B, perhaps in the unrealistic hope of concealing them from close family members.

Money Matters

While Afzal was working in the UK, he may have remitted some of his earnings back to his mother and wife, who were also being supported by other family members. Once in Pakistan that income stream dried up and his outgoings were probably much higher than he had anticipated. For example, he had to pay for an air fare to Lahore, rather than buy a train ticket.

Moreover, as someone returning to the sub-continent after working for years in a country perceived to be very wealthy, family members would have expected him to have brought back considerable savings and to be generous in distributing them. He would not have wanted to lose face by disabusing them. As a result, most of the money he brought with him from London was spent before he even reached Lahore:

> *10 March 1948* You would remember when I left England I had £100 travellers cheques. By the time I reached Lahore I had £25 left.

---

[266] 98B was initially rented but Afzal's mother, Vilayet, later reached agreement with the Government for its purchase. Paying for it took many years and was financially challenging. The price was set at approximately Rs60,000 and the agreement required monthly repayments of Rs750 (reduced later to Rs400), which was well beyond the regular household income. To raise the money Vilayet bought up discounted compensation claims from people who had lost property in India, but who could not afford to buy in Pakistan; rented out the ground floor of the building; and used contacts in Government to get assistance. It was not until the mid-1960s that the final instalment was paid and the Permanent Transfer Order, finally confirming ownership, was handed over.

11 March 1948 I have hardly any money left. I wonder how much you would be able to bring.

15 March 1948 Bring as much money in cash as possible.

Inevitably, his financial situation quickly became unsustainable and worsened as each day passed without him finding a 'business opportunity'. It must have been worrying and he would have become even more stressed when he later learned that his lack of money and income was a major obstacle to Karola being allowed to enter the country. It was only by borrowing and getting financial help from friends and family that he was able to overcome that particular difficulty.

Understandably, once Karola had agreed to come to Pakistan, realising as much cash as possible from anything that was to be left in London became a priority. That, though, was not much: their material possessions comprised some modest business assets and some furniture in their flat. As Afzal was out of the country, it fell to Karola to deal with all the arrangements. The business assets included their market licences, stalls and covers (tarpaulins). She was also to dispose of unsold stock comprising some costume jewellery and Indian perfume, as well as 1-dram and 2-dram perfume bottles. Afzal asked Karola to count these up and expected either his supplier to take them back or friends and contacts to buy them:

5 February 1948 Regarding business. Jewellery from Akbar if there be any, please ask him to buy it back together with emties and filled if he can. Otherwise contact Pandit and ask him to help you. I am sure he will. First count all the empties at home, room and market ones. Whomever Pandit wants the Lane stall to take over, he can ask him to buy some stock.

RE Upton Park Nazeer would surely like to take over Kavrana's and perhaps your stall too. Please ask him to pay you for stock stall covers etc. The best he can. Tell him that I shall consider it a great favour.

10 February 1948 So you have sold Kavrana's stall for £8 to Asgar. Is it complete with the cover? Then how do you stand with Mr. Kavrana? You must have informed him. You must darling count the empty bottles of one dram and two dram. Then count the filled ones. Try and dispose them off as best you can. Jewellery too whatever you got on hand. Try and sell it to Akbar Asgar or Pandit.

15 February 1948 We shall be losing a good deal in bottles. Never mind!

Disposal of their flat contents seems to have been more complicated for, although they were apparently living at Ivor Court illegally (as explained above), Afzal not only wanted her to sell its contents, but also the tenancy. The post-war housing shortage probably meant that people were prepared to pay for access to accommodation, even if the transaction was not strictly above board. The intricacies of the deal are a little difficult to untangle. Afzal was of the view that they should be able to get at least £300 for the flat and its contents and it seems that an acquaintance, Harry, wanted to take over the lease. However, they needed to get the consent of Mr Jackson, whose identity is a mystery, since that was not the name of either the owner or the managing agent named in the rent book and eviction notice. Afzal proposed that Mr Jackson should be told that Harry was taking over temporarily while he and Karola were in Pakistan and that Harry should pay him £50 to encourage him to make the right decision. Afzal fretted and fussed, especially over the prices she achieved, and his messages became quite repetitive and muddled. Eventually, though, a sale was agreed:

> *5 February 1948* Re. Flat. Don't you think you should at least get 300 pounds. It cost us in all lot more. See what you can get best. Would Mr. Jackson agree? Let Harry treat him to £50. Under no circumstances you should pay him if you sell the flat. Jackson must be paid too in Harry's own interest. One thing good they already know each other. Also known to Eve and Stan too. I don't think they would object. If Jackson objects please tell him you are joining me for a few months. And Harry will be staying in the meantime. That would be the best to say. Then they can carry on.

> *7 February 1948* Regarding disposing of business goods and flats to Harry. Please settle everything best you can. Please try and get £300 for the flat at least. And if Harry or anybody else takes it please see that Mr. Jackson is also persuaded and treated quite separately by the one who takes over. This should be done, of course through you.

> *10 February 1948* Have you talked to Jackson about the flat, that Harry is taking it over while you are away to India for few months to join me. Ask Harry to treat him to a lump sum. But you must get hold of the full money from Harry before you even disclose anything to Jackson.

> *11 February 1948* Have you settled about the flat.

> *15 February 1948* You said you have settled about the flat with Harry and Jackson. You never said, how much?

20 February 1948 I am glad you have arranged about the flat with Harry and Mr. Jackson. But you didn't say how much? I hope it's £300.

27 February 1948 With regards to business and flat. Please thank Akbar and Charlie for helping you. How much you shall be getting for the lot of goods and the flat. I hope the business transactions with Akbar etc would have been finished by now.

Tied Up in Red Tape

Alongside negotiations over living arrangements, searching for a business opportunity and selling up in London, Karola and Afzal had to give attention to the paperwork needed for her to come to Pakistan, and to her travel arrangements. It turned out to be yet another challenge that was much more difficult to overcome than expected. As already mentioned, Karola's German passport expired soon after she arrived in the UK. Moreover, by taking up residence in a foreign country, she was stripped of her German nationality under Nazi legislation. Consequently, she became 'stateless' and could not enter another country without some form of recognised documentation issued by the UK. As a stateless person, she was not entitled to a passport but had to apply to the Home Office for a permit to travel, which she did in early February 1948.

To support her application, Karola asked Afzal for a letter, which he sent to her on 16 February. Addressed to the Home Secretary, and rather untidily handwritten on flimsy aerogramme paper, it was for her to take personally to the Home Office. In it he explained that she was his fiancé and that he was 'anxiously awaiting her arrival by air when I have arranged to marry her'. Nine days later, in a letter to an official in Pakistan, he wrote rather cryptically that 'she has intimated that she has secured the Passport', which is not unequivocal confirmation that she had it and, in the light of what followed, it seems more likely that it had not been granted.

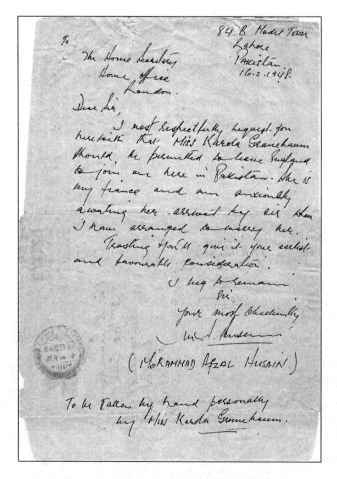

Afzal's letter to the Home Secretary in support of
Karola's application for permission to leave the UK

But Karola did not just need British documentation. She also had to have a visa from the Pakistan authorities and obtaining this was much more difficult. To get this moving, on 10 February

Afzal wrote direct to the Pakistan High Commissioner in London asking him to give her permission to enter the country.

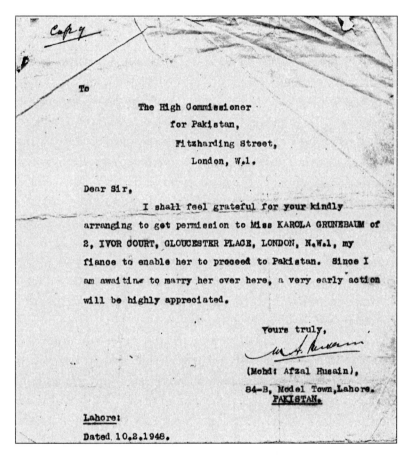

Afzal's letter to the Pakistan High Commissioner in London
in support of Karola's application to enter Pakistan

This, though, was not a decision that could be made in the UK; visas were granted in the then capital of Pakistan, Karachi. Accordingly, the High Commission cabled the application to the relevant government department there and the British

Passport Office also wrote to ask for the visa to be issued, perhaps indicating that Karola's permit to travel was actually dependent on the visa too. However, Pakistan's central government officials were unwilling to make a decision without approval from the Government of West Punjab.

On 19 February Karola wrote to Afzal to update him on this situation and he then visited the Lahore Passport Office for advice on how to proceed. He learned that one of the key considerations in reaching a decision was his economic circumstances. Given the parlous state of the country, the authorities wanted to be sure that Karola would not make any demands on the country's finances or public services, apparently assessing her as they would a refugee. Consequently, on 25 February Afzal submitted another letter, this time to the Under Secretary of the Government of West Punjab. It was a longer document which affirmed that he would be responsible for her maintenance during her stay and for the cost of repatriation, should that be necessary. Also attached was a 'personal guarantee attested on a stamped paper in original duly attested by a First Class Magistrate'.

Rather boldly, he asked that the matter be given "immediate attention' by the West Punjab Government, that its decision be communicated 'telegraphically' to the Karachi Government and that a visa then be sent by 'cablegram' to the High Commissioner and the Home Office in London. This, he stressed, was important because Karola's passage had been booked for the 14 March and 'any delay would cause personal inconvenience'!

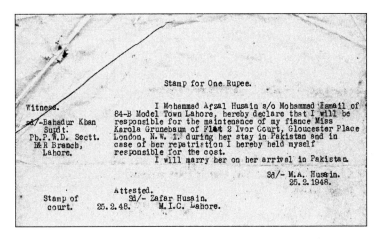

```
                    Stamp for One Rupee.

Witness.                    I Mohammad Afzal Husain s/o Mohammad Ismail of
                     84-B Model Town Lahore, hereby declare that I will be
sd/-Bahadur Khan     responsible for the maintenance of my fiance Miss
     Supdt.          Karola Grunebaum of Flat 2 Ivor Court, Gloucester Place
Pb.P.W.D. Sectt.     London, N.W. 1. during her stay in Pakistan and in
 B&R Branch,         case of her repatriation I hereby held myself
  Lahore.            responsible for the cost.
                            I will marry her on her arrival in Pakistan.

                                                    Sd/- M.A. Husain.
                                                       25.2.1948.
                        Attested.
     Stamp of           Sd/- Zafar Husain.
      court.    25.2.48.    M.I.C. Lahore.
```

Attestation of financial responsibility submitted by Afzal
to the Government of West Punjab

Two days later there had been little progress. Afzal learned that, before being sent back to Karachi, the visa application had to be considered by the 'the Inspector General CID's Office' in Lahore. To apply some pressure there, he visited that office on 27th and was assured that a decision would be made by 4pm the same day. But by 2 March there was still no movement. He wrote again to Karola, assuring her that the file would be sent back to the Passport Office that afternoon, clearly still hopeful that everything would then quickly fall into place. But ominously he mentioned that something unfavourable had come to light in the CID's enquiries and later that day there was still no progress to report:

> *2 March 1949* My application for your permit which I made in Passport Office Lahore is still till this morning in CID's office. I am after it. Today it will be returned to the Passport Office from CID's Office. I have been after this affair since the Feb 25th when I first heard about it from you. I have made personal contacts

everywhere. This afternoon I shall know a step further about it. CID's report has been quite favourable. Although at one stage during the enquiries about me it had taken a rather unfavourable form. Which before going any further I had it made better so today as I said we are expecting the application back into Passport Office. Pray it all goes well then would cable Karachi and would ask Karachi authorities to cable permit to London. The very moment I too shall cable you and I myself shall proceed to Karachi at once. So that I can expedite the matter in the offices there.

... It's 2 PM now I am writing this, sitting in my cousin Riaz's office in Civil Secretariat where all the offices are too. I just went again to find out if CID's office has sent your application back to Passport Office or not. It still isn't. Because so many have to sign same thing. Again I have put a man in CID's Office on its tail. To see it goes out today. I'll write you again tomorrow now. And tell you about the progress. Lahore Passport Office has not received yet any intimation of London office's cables from Karachi Foreign Office.

As the days passed, Afzal became increasingly frantic, frustrated and concerned, and Karola extremely anxious that she might never be allowed to travel. He repeatedly told her not to worry, that everything would work out fine and that she would be able to come to Pakistan soon. But his words of optimism and expectation of a quick resolution to the problem appear more and more misplaced:

> *25 February 1948* ... so please don't worry. Everything would be OK I have no doubt that you will be able to

leave on the 14th as arranged.

27 February 1948 Please don't worry. It's nothing serious. It's just a matter of formality.

3 March 1948 But please darling don't let this worry you. It's only a matter of little extra delay which has unfortunately been caused through present difficult times … Needless to say again that please sweetheart don't let this temporary delay worry you. Let me worry for you. I am running about every day in this connection. The delay seems to have been caused by the nature itself.

On 3 March Afzal finally admitted that it had become impossible for formalities to be completed in time for Karola to travel on the 14th as planned. He was either naively hopeful or given false assurances but, whichever was the case, he told her that she must postpone her departure. He also discovered that one of the main reasons why a visa had not been approved was his failure to find work and his lack of money to support his family:

3 March 1948 One of these reasons is particularly my own. As I have not started any business here yet. That's what's so far stands in my opinion candidly against me, because the question of your maintenance by me is concerned.

10 March 1948 An other thing which is most vital and that very weakness frankly speaking has spoilt the whole thing so far. That is of course my own financial position … In fact this very vital weakness has, I have come to know spoilt the matter from the very beginning.

With this obstacle seemingly blocking his path, Afzal reverted to what was normative behaviour in the sub-continent. He drew on help from family and friends, and used social networks to reach people who could exert influence on his behalf to get what he wanted, even if it meant bending the rules.

To strengthen his financial position, he borrowed money from his mother and asked Karola to cable as much as she could afford to his Lloyds bank account in Lahore. He then implied that she could ask their friend Harry for money, if she did not have enough:

> *10 March 1948* By the time I reached Lahore I had £25 left. I opened the account at Lloyd's Bank Limited The Mall Lahore, with this little amount. Mother has only £400 left in deposit in an other bank. Tomorrow I shall get this from her and put it in my a/c. Then to strengthen the matter through my own bank balance which would obviously prove most helpful in getting the permit.
>
> … This I will definitely get done tomorrow. Strangely enough (11.3.48) tomorrow is the mother's deposit's renewal date. On this date it can either be put back for another year or taken out. Though it won't be all that enough. Still something is better than nothing. I wonder therefore if you too could cable into my Lahore account some money most you can. That indeed would be most timely and needed help. But it only depends if you have got it. I would suggest this that keep your P.O. etc money, bring that in traveller's cheques. And what money if you have already got for flat etc., you may cable to my a/c here. Darling only if you have already got flat money in hand. Please cable me at your earliest. If not please state the whole thing to Harry. If I had in my account

here at least 7 to 800 pounds I have been told by the
Lahore Office today that there will be not the slightest
hitch in getting the permit. So darling you can see the
importance of it. Please don't think I am forcing you.
I am only suggesting.

To try and encourage decisions in his favour, Afzal had already
been taking family members with him to meetings with officials.
Now, though, he sought help from someone who operated at a
different level. He visited Sheikh Mahboob Alam, an influential
individual who lived in The Mall, one of Lahore's most prestigious
addresses. After the meeting, buoyed with renewed optimism, he
wrote to Karola for a second time on the 3 March, and this time
recommended that she delay cancelling her flight until the last
moment, contrary to his earlier message:

> *3 March 1948* I have met Sheikh Mahboob Alam. He
> knew everything before I told him about this delay.
> He assured me not to worry. He will help me to get it
> done within the next two or three days. If there is any
> guarantors needed he will stand for you and me. He is
> the most influential personality. Now we will see about
> it tomorrow. He will contact the topmost man in the
> Political and Passport Office Lahore Civil Secretary.
> God willing everything would soon get straightened
> up. I suggest you shouldn't cancel the seat yet. Wait till
> the last day ie 13 March. Now I am certain that within
> the next few days you'll hear the signal for okay.

There was, though, one 'small' matter that was limiting Sheikh
Alam's goodwill. He had met Afzal and Karola previously in
London and something had occurred there to which he had taken
great offence. It was to do with Peter, their cocker spaniel, and
Sheikh Alam had not forgotten the incident. To smooth things

over, Afzal encouraged Karola to write to him and apologise:

> *3 March 1948* Mr. Alam is very kind and helpful. He
> told me before in joke when he heard first few days
> ago from Mrs. Mullick that you were coming that he
> was still cross with you. Unless you apologise when
> you come, he won't have anything to do with you.
>
> I want you to write him personally and thank him
> for this act of kindness. This would be like thanking
> him in advance. In his letter please be brief and to
> the point. Also ask him if you could be of any service
> to him while you are still in England and before
> leaving for Pakistan. Also tell him how sorry you feel
> for offending you when he was in London. It was
> nothing personal but only because of Peter. And that
> you would also make a personal apology and thank
> him for his kindness when you reach here. With love
> to his wife and kiddies.

Perhaps she did do this because, from then on, Sheikh Alam
became a central figure in their efforts to extract a visa from the
government. On 9 March he and Afzal went to visit the Under
Secretary of the Government of West Punjab. He was working
from home because of leg injuries sustained in a motorcycle
accident, but conveniently also lived in Model Town. Sheikh
Alam provided him with an indemnity bond 'drafted out on a
court paper' confirming that he would personally underwrite any
costs related to Karola. Even this, though, was not enough on its
own and the Under Secretary advised them to submit a further
application to the Passport Office, together with the bond. Afzal
did this the very next day and then revisited the Under Secretary
in his home the following evening. Afzal told Karola 'I am
personally pretty hopeful' but hopes for a speedy resolution were

dashed yet again. Days passed and she had no choice but to cancel her travel reservation for the 14th and rebook for a later date. In fact, as the days extended into weeks, Karola had to rebook her flight at least three times. But finally, at some point later in the month, a favourable recommendation did get forwarded from Lahore to Karachi and Afzal sent a telegram to Karola to share the good news.

Telegram sent on 15 March 1948 by Afzal to Karola

He prepared to go there himself to ensure that a positive decision was sent on to London immediately. That would however have been premature for on 22 March he learned that the Karachi officials had requested yet more detail about his financial circumstances. So more than six weeks after Karola made her first visa application in London, on 23 March 1948, Afzal submitted another even longer request to the Under Secretary of the Government of West Punjab, again attested by a magistrate. He emphasised that Karola was coming to Pakistan to get married and would embrace Islam,

339

so 'her position would be quite different to the ladies who come out to India in similar circumstances whose cases are viewed by government from a different angle'. He highlighted the fact that he had possession of a large bungalow in Model Town, and so was well able to accommodate all his family members.

In this latest submission he also set out in greater detail his financial position, which had somehow become surprisingly strong. Not only did he now have a substantial cash balance in the bank, but he had also become a partner in his cousin's Persian carpets and textile business, into which he had apparently invested a substantial sum of money. This, he asserted, was generating a monthly income and, moreover, further business developments were imminent. Given other indications that he was short of money and struggling to get any business started, one has to wonder how this transformation had come about.

Finally, Afzal mentioned that he was 'well connected' and that his relatives were ready to offer any help he needed. He listed four of them, providing their names and job titles. All were men who held or had held senior positions in the civil service, raising questions about whether these were really provided to demonstrate respectability and give reassurance or, alternatively, to exercise some gentle coercion by making it clear that he had friends in high places. Whatever the reason, the following day the Punjab Government finally confirmed to Karachi that his finances were 'sound'.

> To set at rest any further doubts that Government may have, I submit that I am very well connected and all my relatives, some of whom are mentioned below, are whole-heartedly willing to render any help I may seek...

Extract from Afzal's attestation about his status and connections

It must have been with huge relief that he learned that a permit had been granted on the 27 March and that the High Commission in London had been informed the same day. He sent a telegram to Karola to give her the news and added a postscript to a long letter written over the previous days to say that she would finally be able to leave London the following Sunday.

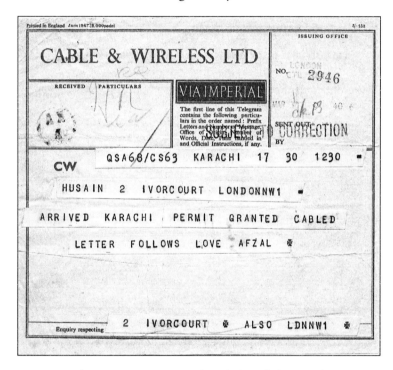

Telegram sent on 30 March 1948 by Afzal to Karola

Afzal finally felt sufficiently confident to head for Karachi and set off on Monday 29 March, this time travelling between the two cities by train. The journey, which lasted 30 hours, took him through 'dusty desert'. He arrived looking like 'a sand man, unrecognisable' and suffering from a fever. In Karachi the reality of the poor living conditions and limited access to health services was brought home to him much more directly than before. His brother-in-law was away buying a cow so that the family could have fresh milk, which was needed for his daughter who had been ill with typhoid for over a month. But once again Afzal's expectations were over-optimistic and another week passed before Karola was able to send a cable to confirm that she had at last received a visa to enter Pakistan.

Telegram sent on 3 April 1948 by Karola to Afzal

The protracted visa process caused Karola significant difficulty. She had to survive in London without any income for several weeks. By mid-February, the market stalls and stock were sold, so she had to use the money received from those sales for living expenses. Afzal was concerned and understanding, but he suggested she contact various friends to see if they could help out by offering her some casual work:

> *10 February 1948* And I understand how much you are spending and what the expenses have amounted to. Sweetheart you can't help that.

> *3 March 1948* I am wondering now that you have given up business and nearly the flat too. To sit idle and wait you need money for regular expenses. There's no alternative I am afraid. That you'll have to do so. I know that you shall make manage for the waiting period with the minimum of expenses.

> … If you darling can do something to meet your weekly expenses at least. Please do so. Talk to Asgar Ali and see if he can help you in that respect. I know business at this time of the year is terribly slack. Or ask Akbar and see if can't fix you up somewhere temporarily. Or can get in touch with Pandit if he can put you in the store for the time being. I think if Pandit can do so that would indeed be most helpful.

All Work and No Play?

Afzal's correspondence covered a range of topics, but by February it was mostly concerned with the problems relating to his and Karola's future in Pakistan. He generally gave the impression that resolving them occupied most of his time and that his days were spent negotiating with his family, searching for business opportunities or chasing government officials:

> *22 January 1948* Yesterday and today I was busy all day for one thing or the other.

> *10 February 1948* … I am still extremely busy in finding some business.

27 February 1948 As I'm out all day. Simply running from one place to the other. Trying to find something.

2 March 1948 I have been very busy in finding some business. Now since the 25th I have been running about for your permit.

3 March 1948 All day I am out after this permit affair. Going from one office to the other ... I am running about every day in this connection

But it was not all work. Occasionally, he did reveal that some of his busyness arose, not from dealing with the problems, but from more pleasurable social engagements. Admittedly, attending weddings, family celebrations and other functions was such an integral part of Pakistani culture that attendance was almost obligatory. Nevertheless, despite the stresses and frustrations that he was experiencing, he was also enjoying this side of life in the new country:

2 February 1948 I've been extremely busy. Last weekend's there was another marriage in the family. This was in town which is 7 miles from this Model Town. There was one the day I reached Lahore. Not far from our bungalow. Soon after my arrival we went over to this marriage. We came back from town late last night.

3 March 1948 Within few days of my arrival at Lahore we at the bungalow gave him [Sheikh Alam] and his family a big feast. Few days ago he gave a grand ... party. Till 4 in the morning. Drinks and snaks all night. Mrs Mullick was there too. About 25 people in all. All big gentry. With two singing and dancing girls for all night. I thoroughly enjoyed it. There's another one tonight. I am invited tonight too. I will let you know tomorrow how I got on.

Afzal recuperating or relaxing in Lahore

Preparing for the Off

At the same time as the initial visa application was submitted, and clearly confident that all the formalities would soon be completed, Afzal gave attention to the practical arrangements for Karola's journey to the sub-continent. There was some discussion about whether she would travel by air or by sea, but eventually it was decided to go ahead with a flight booking. Afzal visited the Thomas Cook office in Lahore and asked for the refund on his return ticket to be credited against the cost of Karola's passage to Karachi. Accordingly, on 10 February the Lahore office wrote to Thomas Cook (London), enclosing the unwanted ticket. He told Karola to expect a credit of about £96 and that she would need to pay the balance of £25.

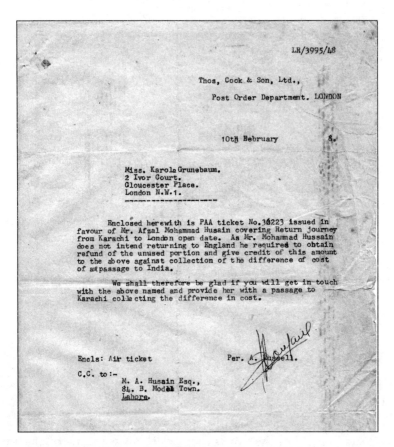

Letter from Thomas Cook (Lahore) to Thomas Cook (London)
requesting refund for Afzal's unused return ticket

The transaction was completed smoothly and just over two
weeks later Thomas Cook (Lahore) confirmed that the London
office had made a provisional reservation for her to travel by 'Pan
American Airways plane' on the 14 March. Perhaps still not used
to the partition of the country, the agent referred to her passage
to India, not Pakistan.

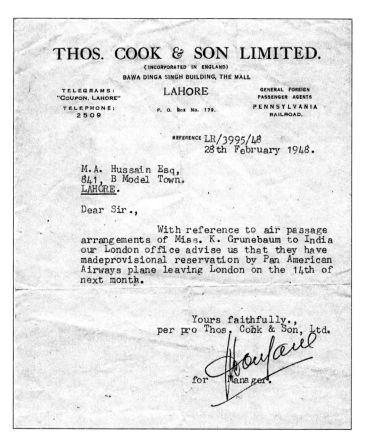

Confirmation from Thomas Cook (Lahore) of provisional booking
for Karola to travel to Karachi

However, having agreed to move to Pakistan, Karola asked
Afzal if he would mind her first making a one-week 'flying
visit' to see family members still in Germany. It was somewhat
surprising, not only that she would want to go there so soon after
the end of the war, but also that she would ask permission to
do this. It was perhaps an indication of her attachment to, and
maybe dependence on, him, at a time when she was undoubtedly
feeling alone, insecure and fragile, given all that had happened.

Nevertheless, without hesitation he encouraged her to go, although he warned her that she would need to get permission for this trip, just as she was having to for the one to Pakistan:

> *7 February 1948* You asked my consent if you could pay a week's flying visit to Germany. My darling if it's the possible, please do so at the earliest.
>
> … Under these circumstances I don't think the authorities for Pakistan British and Germany should have any objections. Quite the contrary. I am confident, they will give you every possible assistance. They should any way. So do try and take a week's trip home first before leaving London finally for Pakistan.

Whether it was the difficulty of getting a travel permit or for some other reason, the visit did not go ahead and it would be another 11 years before she eventually returned to her country of birth. Meanwhile, her preparations continued and these included getting inoculated against diseases prevalent in the sub-continent. For her smallpox vaccination, which required three treatments, she went in late February to St Mary's Hospital, Paddington, while yellow fever immunisation was delivered at the Wellcome Research Institute in early March. She felt quite unwell for some days afterwards and wrote to Afzal about this.

An early discussion point between them was what she should bring with her or send to Pakistan from London. She did not want to leave behind some of the personal things that she had managed to escape with from Germany, especially the linen and towels. Afzal wanted her to bring some of his clothes and possessions from the flat, and to buy certain other items. He seemed particularly concerned about 'hanks', presumably handkerchiefs, which he mentioned repeatedly. Bizarrely, he told her not to bring the 'pistols', but did want her to get a 35mm Leica camera with an f2 lens, although he also hoped this might come direct from Germany.

These goods could not all be transported by air; they had to be shipped, and so Azfal provided detailed instructions on how to pack them and send them via Thomas Cook. Special treatment, however, was to be given to what seems to have been a particularly prized possession, their pepper grinder. This he asks her to take with her, rather than send by steamer, if at all possible:

> *5 February 1948* I don't mind, how [you travel]! I don't want you to lose your linen and towels etc. There's extreme [shortage] of all cotton goods here. And you can't bring them by air either, I know.

> *7 February 1948* By the way if you do happen to go to Germany I think you perhaps be able to buy Leica (f2 lens or better) camera from there. Which would cost little. In that case please don't bother Harry. It must be of 35mm film.

> *10 February 1948* Regarding your linen I wrote you before to lock in the big trunk. Aziz will help you to tie it with a thick strong cord and ask Thos Cook to collect it. Then call at their office, fill the form. Get it insured for at least £100 pay towards the freight and put it for direct shipment to Lahore via KARACHI only. Don't forget to make and take to Thos Cook the list of the contents like I did. Put everything used. Keep a copy too. Don't buy anything except towels and Hanks. I wrote you before too about the Hanks. You have plenty of towels at home. You may buy a few more. As cotton goods here are very scarce.
>
> … Don't forget camera 35 mm. Either from London or from Germany if you go there.

11 February 1948 When packing big trunk please don't forget my big over coat. Moth balls. If big trunk alone is not enough. Please send the small one too. Don't forget to buy through Pandit or else some more Hanks and towels. Bring the Hanks with you. Many as you can. Not forgetting the camera either like Harry's from London or if you go over to Germany then Leica.

15 February 1948 … you must bring all the linen. Pack the new pair of curtains your aprons all towels. Buy more if possible and the Hanks from Pandit or Shah Bros. Don't bother about pistols. Bring as much money in cash as possible. If one big trunk is not enough. Pack the small one too. Don't worry then about the camera from London.

20 February 1948 I do pray and hope that you won't have much pains in packing dispatching and settling everything. Do buy some Hanks. Please don't bother to buy anything else. Don't forget to bring with you all the big knives and grinder your set [of?] spoon and above all the pepper grinder. Bring these things with you. If possible. At least the pepper grinder. Please pack my top coats with your linen to be sent by the steamer. I have advised you before how to pack.

The Man's Best Friend

There is one other recurring topic in Afzal's letters that was interwoven with the serious familial, economic and bureaucratic issues that he was confronting. Although personal, it was not focused on the complexities of their future lives and in some respects seems incongruous when set alongside the challenges they faced. It was about dogs! During his first three months in Pakistan, Afzal was tormented by his separation from Peter, the cocker spaniel, whom he seemed to miss almost as much as he missed Karola:

> *19 January 1948* How is my darling Peter. I do miss him very much darling. Please darling console him for me too. Don't let him worry about me. Bless his little heart.

> *22 January 1948* Please darling do hurry and write me all about you and my darling Peter …

> *23 January 1948* Sweetheart do believe I am lost without you and my Peter. I have now actually cried many times during my stay at Karachi, while talking and thinking about you and Peter … I said to him [brother-in-law] I can not live without you or my Peter. I would die if I don't see them before long.

> *26 January 1948* I have been crying for Peter every day without a miss. Poor soul what has become of him.

> *11 March 1948* How is my darling Peter. I have never known to love a dog before. But Peter is my darling. I do miss him and you terribly. I can't bare to look at his picture. In every picture his innocent face looks so devotedly at me, as if he knew I was going away from him. And, goodness would only know when if I do see him again. Please give him my love.

In the absence of his favourite dog, he even wrote about getting another and took a close interest in a different family pet, which reportedly spent much of its day at 98B. He told Karola, probably not flippantly, that the family was expecting her to look after it when she arrived:

> *11 February 1948* I am planning to get a pair of
> AFGHAN dogs. Still nothing can replace my darling
> Peter. Bless his soul.
>
> *15 February 1948* Uncle has a 3 yrs old Alsatian called
> 'Dempo'. Nice big dog.
>
> *24 March 1948* Did I write you ever about Dempo
> uncle's Alsatian dog. He is 3½ years old. He is out in
> the garden barking. All day he does that barking to
> sparrows, birds and squirrels on the trees. They watch
> him too. At night he becomes a watchdog in both
> the bungalows. We all love him. He has become very
> much attached to me. He always reminds me of Peter.
> Ever since we have moved in our new bungalow he
> doesn't care for his own place. He just comes to his
> place at meal times and back again to us. We all laugh
> at this. Uncle jokes that he has deserted them. If he
> stays with you, you must feed him too. No body has
> combed or brush or bathed him lately. Zia's youngest
> brother Kami usually attends to that. He is a student
> and is too busy with his college exams. And everybody
> is awaiting that when you come you take charge of
> Dempo and all his looking after.

But as plans for her journey to Pakistan took shape, he saw
a possibility to be reunited with Peter. Even though they had
previously agreed to her travelling by air, he asked her to reconsider
making the journey by sea, so she could bring the dog with her:

> *20 February 1948* Before I forget please give my love
> to Peter. I wonder if he would get over the shock of
> parting of you from him. If you had come by boat to

Karachi (as the steamers do go to Karachi now) could Peter be allowed to travel with you?

27 February 1948 How is my darling Peter? Had you come by sea, could you then possibly bring him along or not? What would have been the fare?

5 March 1948 Also I must request you that is only for the sake of my darling Peter. If he can also come by sea, please darling when permit comes for Peter's sake do travel by sea and bring him along too. Don't leave him behind. It would be a tragedy if he's left behind. Journey will be longer. No doubt. But we'll have our Peter with us.

11 March 1948 And if he can come by boat, please do travel by sea, only for his sake and bring him along. Darling don't leave him behind.

Even after her flight had been booked, he still tried – without success – to find a way to make it happen. He sent a telegram, followed up with a letter, to suggest that she could arrange for Peter to travel by sea with a friend if she could not bring him herself.

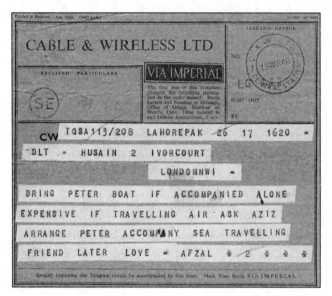

Telegram sent on 18 March by Afzal to Karola

24 March 1948 So Peter's coming seems to be out of the question for the present. I never thought Peter could never travel in a passenger boat. If you could arrange for him to travel later when permitted to travel accompanied with some friends coming to Pakistan. Perhaps Aziz could help in that matter. I am not going into long details about it, I do hope you understand me fully.

But Peter never did get to Pakistan. A clue to what happened to him is provided by a strangely worded signed document dated 6 April 1948. This attested that the signatory had consented to post Peter's pedigree and licence to a Miss Rowe and had also given up the dog's custody. The signature is difficult to decipher, but the initial looks like 'H'. So this might be Afzal and Karola's friend Harry, who took over their flat. Perhaps he agreed to look after Peter until a new owner was found. It is odd, though, that

Karola was still in London when this was signed and odd too that it was not handed over to the intended recipient.

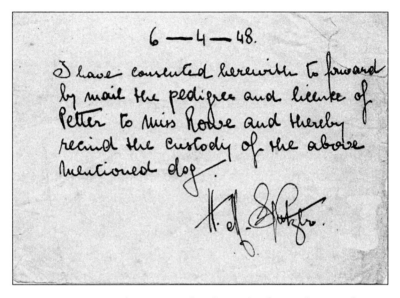

Document confirming transfer of custody of Peter the spaniel

Marriage and Married Life
in Pakistan

Another Journey into the Unknown

On Sunday 11 April 1948, as London was preparing for the first post-war Olympic Games, Karola finally set off for Karachi. Like Afzal three months earlier, she took Pan Am Flight 002 with just one suitcase, her remaining baggage having been sent on by sea. Her ticket cost £120 2s, so Afzal's estimate of the balance she would have to pay was probably correct. She was the only female passenger on the plane.[267]

Karola's ticket for her flight to Karachi on 11 April 1948

---

[267] Mentioned in a letter from Mya Davis to Karola, 5 May 1948.

She would have been happy to leave behind the austere economic climate and food rationing, but it must have been a journey into a world that was totally alien to anything she had ever experienced. Apart from the differences in culture, climate, language, religion and general living conditions, this was only five months after the Partition of India and the country was still in the aftermath of the horrific violence that had accompanied the creation of the state. Her journey certainly aroused a lot of curiosity amongst her friends in London, who subsequently wrote frequently to ask about her new life and how she was enjoying or coping with the food and other lifestyle changes.

With hindsight, it was a remarkable thing to have done for at least three reasons. First, having been forced to leave Germany, and apparently having started to settle down in London, she was willing to uproot herself again to travel to this distant, very different and turbulent part of the world. Second, having been brought up as a Jew, she was ready to marry a devout Muslim, at a time when interfaith marriages were uncommon and controversial in Judaism. Third, and perhaps most extraordinary of all, she went to Pakistan knowing that Afzal was already married and that she would become his second wife, as was permissible in Islam. One has to conclude that it was their devotion to each other – and perhaps a sense of adventure – that made her want to take that astonishing step.

Karola reached Karachi on Monday 12 April and was met by Afzal at the airport. Their wedding took place just four days later at 3pm on 16 April 1948 after the regular Friday prayers in a *shamiana* (marquee) at Jacob Lines Mosque. Immediately before the ceremony, she converted to Islam and took the name Khadija, which was recorded on their marriage certificate.[268] By

---

[268] Curiously, in the scores of letters that Afzal wrote to her over the next 25 years, he always addressed her as Karola, even though some friends called her

relocating to Pakistan, Afzal had acquired Pakistani citizenship. Through marriage, Karola lost her stateless status and also became Pakistani.

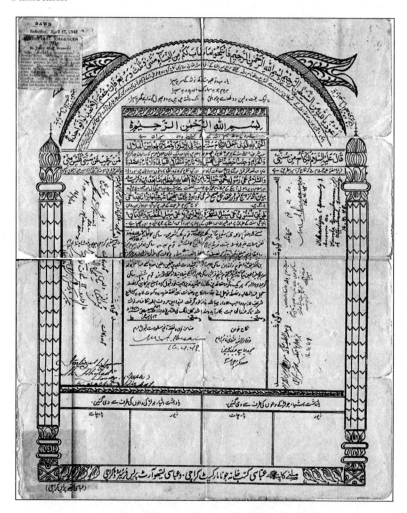

Afzal and Khadija's wedding certificate

Khadija and she had to use that name in any formal or legal document. When referring to her in the remainder of this narrative, the name most appropriate to the context is used.

The unusual conversion and subsequent wedding attracted considerable media attention. There were articles in *Dawn*, Pakistan's main English language newspaper, before and after the event, and it reported that thousands of Muslims gathered at the mosque to witness the ceremonies. The number is rather difficult to reconcile with Afzal's earlier assertion that it would be 'a quiet wedding'.

Friday, April 16, 1948

German Jewess to embrace Islam today in Jacob Line mosque

By Dawn Staff Correspondent

Miss Karala Grunebaum, a Jewess from Offenbach, Germany, will embrace Islam at the Jacob Lines mosque, Karachi, on Friday after the prayers.

Miss Grunebaum sought refuge from the Nazi tyranies in London shortly before the war. In London, she met Mr. Mohammad Afzal Hussein, a Pakistani, and was engaged to the latter.

She arrived in Pakistan last week in response to a call from her fiance who had preceeded her, and will marry Mr Hussein on Friday after she has embraced Islam.

Saturday, April 17, 1948

JEWISH GIRL EMBRACES ISLAM

By Dawn Staff Reporter

Miss Karala Grunebaum a Jewess from Offenbach embraced Islam on Friday April 16 after the Friday prayers in the Jacob Lines mosque. Thousands of Muslims ga thered to witness this ceremony after the prayers in a shamiana. Miss Karala was given the name of Khadija and was married to Mr Afzal Hussain at 3 p.m. Miss Karala read the kalma in English.

Clippings about Karola's conversion and her marriage that appeared in *Dawn* before (left) and after (right) the wedding[269]

Having got married, Afzal and Karola, now Khadija, remained in Karachi probably until the end of April. At some later date they went to Model Town (Lahore), where she met his mother, his first wife, his daughter and other family members.

---

[269] The *Kalma* (mentioned in the second newspaper clipping) is the Islamic declaration of faith.

Khadija and Afzal on their wedding day in Karachi, 16 April 1948

What Karola would not have known when she set off for Pakistan, but would have learned soon after her arrival, was that Afzal's first wife, Masuda, was by then expecting another child. On Wednesday 27 October 1948, she gave birth to a son, Muhammad Asif Hussain ('Asif'). However, echoing what had happened with his daughter, Afzal was not going to be around to share this child's childhood either. As I will shortly come to, not long after the birth Afzal left Lahore and Asif did not see his father again until almost two decades later.

And an absent father was not the only difficulty he had to confront. Like his older sister, Asif was born with oculocutaneous albinism, a genetic disorder resulting in very poor eyesight and a light complexion highly susceptible to sun damage. It is a condition more common in populations where there are cousin marriages.[270] But with incredible resolution and determination, he would in time overcome both these challenges to educate himself and build a successful business career.

Desperate for Work – The Only Way Was Up

At the time of Khadija's arrival in Pakistan, the new country was facing massive economic problems. Around 90% of the people were living in the countryside and most existed on subsistence agriculture. Karachi was the only relatively modern city with substantial trading and business activity. Earning a living to support a family was extremely difficult, especially for someone without qualifications. Not having been successful in developing his own business, Afzal looked for a job, but his position was made more difficult by health problems. No longer accustomed to the climate or living conditions, he became very ill and was in bed with a fever for several months. Even after he had recovered, he was unable to find work, employers seemingly unwilling to take on someone who had been in England for so long.

Khadija too found it difficult to adjust to her new environment. In letters to friends and family, she shared some of her concerns.

---

[270] Sajjad Ali Shah et al., 'Oculocutaneous albinism in Pakistan: a review', *Journal of Cancer Science & Therapy* 10, no. 9 (2018), https://doi.org/10.4172/1948-5956.1000552.

Having reached Pakistan as summer was approaching, she found the heat intolerable. Like Afzal, she was unwell for several months after her arrival, most likely because of the unhygienic conditions and new diet. Moreover, as a guest she was not expected or allowed to do anything, and found just sitting around all the time extremely frustrating. And, although only hinted at in her correspondence, she could not get used to the domestic arrangements, which meant sharing her husband with another wife.

It is difficult to track Afzal and Khadija's activity and movements through the rest of 1948. It is unclear whether either found any work and they may have moved between Lahore and Karachi more than once. Some letters from family and friends were sent to them in Model Town, others to the address of Afzal's brother-in-law, Hameed, at 41/3 Jutland Lines, Karachi Cantonment, and another to the Indian Merchants Association Building in Nicol Road, Karachi.[271] In early 1949, however, they were both appointed agents of the Eastern Federal Union Insurance Company (Lahore office) to sell life assurance policies. The positions came with no salary, only a modest commission and were conditional on three new clients being signed up in the first two months.

Whether they were able to achieve this target is doubtful and any money earned was insufficient to support the family, so they continued to be dependent on the generosity of relatives. They tried to make it pay for several months but, in a final effort to improve their economic situation, Afzal and Khadija relocated to

---

[271] Cantonments at that time were wholly garrison areas, so Hameed may have been connected to the military. The Indian Merchants Association Building was an impressive example of Anglo-Mughal architecture that today accommodates the Karachi Chamber of Commerce and Industry, 'KCCI or Karachi Indian Merchants Association Building. a Fabulous Example of Anglo-Mughal Architecture', Pakistan Travel & Culture, http://blog.travel-culture.com/2010/05/17/kcci-or-karachi-indian-merchants-association-building-a-fabulous-example-of-anglo-mughal-architecture/.

Karachi in the first week of June 1949, renting accommodation at 81 Ellander Road. The street was in the central area close to the main station, and not far from Karachi Cantonment where his brother-in-law lived. Masuda and Nusrat Bibi remained in Model Town.

Khadija at her typewriter, perhaps preparing a job application

Soon after, Afzal received the offer of a job as a salesman with Buckwell & Co, a company actually headquartered in Lahore which sold imported engineering and consumer products. With a three-month probationary period, he started work on Thursday 23 June 1949 on a salary of Rs250 per month, 'inclusive of Dearness Allowance'.[272]

---

[272] Dearness Allowance is a cost-of-living allowance paid to public sector employees and pensioners in Pakistan, Bangladesh and India. It is calculated as a percentage of a basic salary to mitigate the impact of inflation.

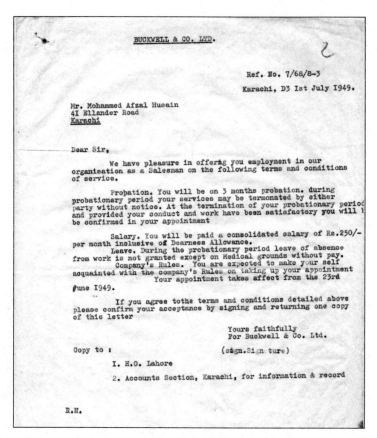

Afzal's job offer from Buckwell & Co

Afzal and Khadija moved home again soon after this appointment. Their new address was Block 30, House No 1 Jehangir Quarters, Bunder Road Extension, which was located about 6 miles north-east of the docks.[273] Correspondence and other paperwork indicates that this happened between July and

---

[273] Bunder Road was renamed M A Jinnah Road after the death of the nation's founder. It is one of the city's main thoroughfares. Jehangir Quarters was one of several colonies built by the federal government in 1947 for its employees. They provided a high-quality residential environment, calm and peaceful with wide streets, greenery, huge playgrounds, parks and other facilities.

September. But how they came to live here is a mystery. As far as is known, Afzal never was a government employee in Pakistan, so perhaps they stayed here with someone who was.

Khadija's career now took a very different direction. She secured a one-year appointment as an air hostess with Pak Air. Founded in 1948, it was one of the first private airlines in Pakistan and had a small fleet of American Douglas and British Handley Page aircraft. Her job offer, sent by Captain S L Wilson, stated that her initial salary would be Rs200 per month, with an entitlement to an efficiency bonus of Rs50 per month after completion of training, plus Rs5 for every hour flown in excess of 65 per month. She started work on Thursday 16 June 1949.

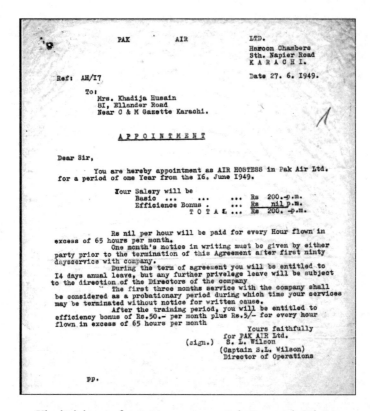

```
        PAK         AIR        LTD.
                               Haroon Chambers
                               Sth. Napier Road
                               K A R A C H I.
  Ref: AH/I7                    Date 27. 6. 1949.

        To:
          Mrs. Khadija Husain
          8I, Ellander Road
          Near C & M Gazette Karachi.


          A P P O I N T M E N T

  Dear Sir,
          You are hereby appointment as AIR HOSTESS in Pak Air Ltd.
  for a period of one Year from the I6. June 1949.

              Your Salary will be
                  Basic   ...    ...    ...  Rs  200.-p.m.
                  Efficience Bonus .    ...  Rs    nil p.m.
                              T O T A L ...  Rs  200. -p.m.

              Rs nil per hour will be paid for every Hour flown in
  excess of 65 hours per month.
              One month's notice in writing must be given by either
  party prior to the termination of this Agreement after first ninty
  daysservice with company.
              During the term of agreement you will be entitled to
  14 days anual leave, but any further privelege leave will be subject
  to the direction of the Directors of the company
              The first three months service with the company shall
  be considered as a probationary period during which time your services
  may be terminated without notice for written cause.
              After the training period, you will be entitled to
  efficiency bonus of Rs.50.- per month plus Rs.5/- for every hour
  flown in excess of 65 hours per month
                                        Yours faithfully
                                        for PAK AIR Ltd.
                    (sign.)   S. L. Wilson
                              (Captain S.L. Wilson)
                              Director of Operations

  pp.
```

Khadija's letter of appointment as an air hostess with Pak Air

With no previous experience of such work, Khadija went through a short training programme. The 12 pages of notes she made during the course indicate the range of topics covered. They include names of different parts of a plane and its technical details, such as dimensions and fuel consumption; duties on first boarding, such as spreading passengers around to maintain the aircraft's centre of gravity; emergency procedures; and the ten rules of conversation. The latter include avoiding 'argumentation', not being bossy, avoiding risqué conversations, never discussing politics or religion; and never sitting on the arm of a passenger's seat!

Rules of Conversation
1. avoid arguementation
2. avoid flipancy both in manner & remarks
3. avoid being bossy or giving orders to passengers always be tactful.
4 avoid conversation which may be connected risque.
5. Never discuss politics - religion
6. Never give preferential treatment to passengers.
7. avoid turning ones back to a pas. always face the rear end of the plane.
8. Very important avoid talking about yourself
9. Be a good listener.
10. Never sit on the arm of a pas chair

An extract from notes made by Khadija during her
air hostess training on 'rules of conversation'

Her first flights were on Wednesday 20 July 1949. She flew from Karachi to Lahore, Lahore to Delhi and then from Delhi back to Lahore. Probably because of the tensions then existing between India and Pakistan, the High Commissioner for India in Pakistan provided her with a permit valid for six months which enabled her to travel there and included a request to allow her 'to perform journey to India without any let or hindrance'.

Khadija's permit to enter India as an air hostess

In the following five months she completed 167 flights, clocking up over 450 hours in the air. Each one was recorded in her log book and all were made in planes designated Douglas DC-3s or DC-4s, which Khadija always referred to as 'Dakotas'. In fact, these were Douglas C-47s, C53s and C54s, military planes used by the United States Air Force before being converted to civilian use.

Most of her flights were between cities on the sub-continent, but she flew once to Bahrain and a few times to Riyadh and Jeddah in Saudi Arabia. The latter carried Muslims on their Haj pilgrimage to Mecca and she occasionally recalled aspects of those trips that presented unusual challenges. When it was time for prayers, the pilgrims would move to the back of the plane where there was more space, changing its centre of gravity and causing it to pitch severely. Then, on the return journey, she had to stand at the top of the boarding steps and empty the containers of holy water which they wanted to take home with them, so that the plane was not overloaded.

Pages from Khadija's flight log book

Being an air hostess certainly gave Khadija a higher income than she had previously earned. But what she may not at first have realised was that she was putting her life at considerable risk every time she took off. In just 20 months Pak Air's planes were involved in four serious accidents, the last of these on 12 December 1949. On that day a DC-3 with registration AP-ADI crashed at Karachi killing all 26 people on board.[274] Khadija was due to be one of the crew, but at the last minute had swapped duties with a colleague. It was a fortuitous change that saved her life but caused the death of a friend. Following the crash, the Pakistan Ministry of Defence

[274] 'AP-ADI', All Pakistan Aircraft Registration Marks, https://aparm.net/ap-aaa_ap-azz/ap-ada_ap-adz/ap-adi.htm.

stepped in and stopped the company operating and Khadija lost what must have once seemed a promising job.

By that time, Afzal's employment situation was also precarious. His performance at Buckwell & Co did not meet the company's expectations and in October 1949 the Director wrote to inform him that 'we are not entirely satisfied yet with your activities'. The contract was not terminated, but his probationary period was extended for a further three months.

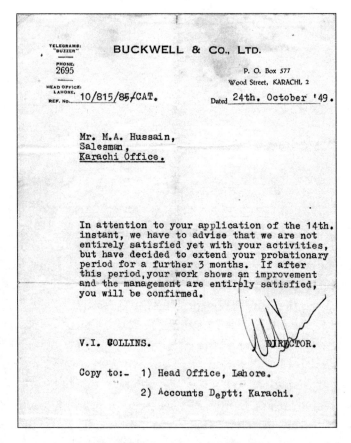

Letter informing Afzal that his work performance was not good enough for his position to be confirmed permanent

Family and Social Networks Rekindled

News from Around the World

Although Karola was an only child, she was part of a large and close-knit extended family. When the Nazis came to power, she had 11 aunts and uncles (including six by marriage), 14 cousins and a considerable number of nephews and nieces. Most lived in Offenbach, while a few were 70 kilometres further east in Mittelsinn and Obersinn (Bavaria), and they kept in frequent contact with each other. Karola was particularly close to some of her nephews and nieces, who were nearer to her in age than most of the cousins. She also had a wide circle of friends in Offenbach, boys and girls mostly of Jewish faith. But over the following years these networks were ripped apart. Some, who were not practising Jews, sought to distance themselves from their Jewish relatives. More significantly, as has already been detailed, family and friends left Germany for other countries in Europe, North America, South America and Africa.

Remarkably, though, within a fairly short period those networks were re-established as kinship and friendship groups coalesced in the destination countries. On arriving in London, Karola was reunited with several friends and similar reunions were taking place in New York and other cities. Letters played an important role in sustaining the contacts and the volume of correspondence is astonishing, even though written communication in the immediate post-war years was not without its difficulties. Postage was expensive, there were restrictions on what could be sent and content was censored. Moreover, there were no airmail services out of Germany for almost three years, so international letters took a long time to arrive. To achieve faster delivery and overcome restrictions, letters to distant countries were sent to nearer intermediaries for forwarding by air to their intended recipients.

Amongst my parents' papers, the only surviving correspondence written during the war is the few letters from Karola's parents that I have previously described. From these, though, it is evident that at that time she was also in contact with her Uncle Siegfried in South Africa. However, in the old suitcase retrieved from the loft there were also 60 letters from family and friends written over the 10 years following the ending of hostilities, many of them sent to Karola and Afzal while they were in Pakistan between April 1948 and March 1950. Around half of this total came from the non-Jewish family members in Bavaria, who had remained there throughout the conflict, the majority penned by Karola's cousin, Greta Reusch, and her younger son, Ludwig ('Ludo'). To get their letters to Pakistan quicker, they first posted them to their friend in London, who sometimes added her own before forwarding them to the sub-continent. Although Afzal had never met his wife's relatives and could not speak German, even he wrote letters to the Reusch family, which Ludo translated and answered in English.

The other half were written by contacts outside Germany. Some were from relatives, such as aunts and cousins in Argentina, but others came from acquaintances around the world. A few were German *émigrés*, amongst them old friends from Offenbach. They included Rosette Kaufmann, her first cousin once removed who had lived with Salomon and Lilli Reiss (Karola's uncle and aunt) in Bürgel and had also come to London. Another was her schoolfriend, Annelies Blumenstein, who managed to survive the war in Germany but emigrated to New York in May 1947.[275] Some were from new Jewish friends whom Karola had got to know in London, such as Hanni Koppel from Halle; Herta Sichel, who also came from Offenbach; and their closest friends and neighbours at Ivor Court, Eve and Stan Vigdor.[276] Rosette, Annelies, Hanni and Herta had all found work as domestics in their new countries, so they had a lot in common. But their circle of correspondents was much more diverse than this, as it included Indians and Pakistanis as well as Britons. Those in London formed a close-knit multicultural group, who knew each other well and socialised together. Indeed, some of the British contacts, such as Doris Asgaralli, were also in 'mixed' relationships or, like Mya Davis from Wales, had somehow become connected with this eclectic group. The letters show just how close they were and how they felt about being separated. Eve Vigdor wrote to Afzal about this even before Karola left London:

> *24 March 1948* Karola and I are very great friends and I shall miss her terribly when she does go. We have grown very fond of her and she is one of the family with us.

[275] Annelies Blumenstein was born in July 1920 in Leipzig (Germany), but in 1934/35 was a pupil at the *Jüdische Bezirksschule* in Offenbach and later found work in the town as a clerk. How Annelies survived the war inside the country is unknown, but perhaps one of her parents was not Jewish and she managed to conceal her mixed heritage. On 5 May 1947 she was registered by the Allied Expeditionary Force as a displaced person and on 29 May she sailed on the SS *Marine Marlin* from Bremen to New York. Sources: School register in Yad Vashem archive, Arolsen Archives and Alien Passenger Lists in myheritage.com.

[276] Hanni Koppel was born in October 1919 into an Orthodox Jewish family living in Halle, Germany. In June 1939 she travelled to the UK by sea, arriving in Southampton. She worked initially as a domestic servant in Andover, but in August found similar work in London. In June 1948 she successfully applied for British naturalisation but later went to the USA and in 1954 became an American citizen. Sources: WJR, National Archives (London) and USA Naturalisation records in myheritage.com.

Mya Davis sent two letters to Karola soon after her departure, remembering the things they did together and expressing regret that they were now apart:

> *5 May 1948* We had some very good times together, didn't we? I keep on saying to myself that we ought to have contacted each other sooner. I wonder when we shall meet again? ... I'll never forget the morning you left England – the time seemed to go so quickly and you had gone before I really realised it. So you were the only female – we would have had fun if we'd been together, wouldn't we???

> *31 May 1948* How I wish we were near each other and I could pop over for curry in the lunch hour – you know my mid-day 'break' is very elastic, usually from about 12.30 to 2.45pm!

And a couple of months later, Doris Asgaralli was still reminiscing and hoping for an early reunion:

> *July 1948* I should also be very happy if you wrote and said you were returning – remember our nice little dinner parties with Afzal as the perfect host and they were very happy memories.

Much of the content of the correspondence comprised news about family members and friends. Even when scattered across different continents, staying in touch and sharing the latest gossip seems to have been a powerful driver for writing, perhaps reflecting an emotional need to cling on to what was left of their previous worlds. An extract from a letter sent from New York by Annelies Blumenstein to Karola is an extreme example of this, but illustrates the size of their networks and the extent to which the German escapees managed to regroup abroad:

16 January 1948 Now, about our mutual acquaintances. I recently went to a reunion. Frankfurt and Offenbach reunion. There were others there too. It was very nice. I met Eugen Marx and Seppel Weil, Lolo Löwenstein, Rina Feibuschwitsch and others. Ernst Feibuschwitsch lives near me and brought me home in his car. I get together most often with Lore Weil, she's already got two children. Recently I had a call from Rudi Loeb and we met up. I also go and visit Ellen and Ruth Rozanski. I already told you that Ellen married Leo Katz from Bürgel. Ruth is married to Norbert Nussbaum from Frankfurt. They live together not far from me. I often go to their place. We celebrated New Year there. There were 14 of us. Ellen and Leo, Ruth, Norbert, Lore with her husband, Erich Grünebaum with his wife, an American. She is very nice. Berthold Wolf with his wife, Gustav Katz, Leo's brother and me and another young American couple. It was very nice and we celebrated until the next morning. So it's not boring here just now! Heiner Abraham was also here again. We often met up. He's coming again in the spring. I'm looking forward to that. Hans Hirschhorn has also got engaged to Margot Grünebaum. Kurt Rosenberg should also have been invited to Ellen's for New Year but he is a partner of Erich Grünebaum and they don't seem to enjoy going out together. Kurt is getting married soon. I also meet Otto Hirsch. He is still studying and has a Turkish girlfriend. Recently, when I was at Lore's, I met Herbert Gutenstein from Usingen. You know, he was my boyfriend at one time. He is also married. Lotte Hirschhorn is married to an Egyptian.

Inge Grünebaum is also married. I'm telling you all this because I am sure you will be interested. What a pity that you can't be here too. We Offenbachers generally stick together. (T)

The letters also included observations about contemporary political, economic and social events, providing a contextual and sometimes poignant backdrop to the more personal news. Herta Stiefel, writing to Karola from Southern Rhodesia just two weeks after Partition, commented on developments in the sub-continent:

2 September 1947 Has Afzal gone to India? He must be pleased with the political situation there. He always wanted it – I mean the separation.

In May 1948 Hanni Koppel wrote to her about the creation of Israel:

25 May 1948 What do you say about the new Jewish state? Isn't it marvellous. If only there would not be so much bloodshed. But I hope soon peace will come and the Jewish people will build their land after 2000 years.

A month later, and eight days after the MV *Empire Windrush* had docked in Tilbury, bringing the first large cohort of Caribbean citizens to settle in Britain, Hanni observed how London's population was changing through immigration and the arrival of people in advance of the first post-war summer Olympics:[277]

---

[277] In 2018 the children of migrants who arrived on the MV *Empire Windrush* became the focus of a huge political scandal in Britain. Many of them, and thousands of other Commonwealth citizens' children (the 'Windrush Generation'), were threatened with deportation as illegal immigrants as a result of the UK Home Office's 'hostile environment' policy, for which the Government subsequently was forced to apologise and provide compensation.

30 June 1948 There are quite a lot of Indians here now, and the women look so lovely in their marvellous saris. In any case there are a lot of foreigners here now. Next month the Olympic Games are starting. I got a ticket for the close of the games on August 14ᵗʰ.

In the same month Rosette Kaufmann experienced a rather different sporting occasion:

18 June 1948 On 5 June, Khadija, by chance [I] was in Epsom on the day of the great horse race [the Derby]. Where even their majesties themselves, the King and Queen, and Princess Elisabeth, were spending the day. Oh, it is beautiful there. (T)

Later that year and 15 months after India's first independent Prime Minister was elected, Doris Asgaralli wrote to Karola:

1 November 1948 We went to Conway Hall, Holborn about a fortnight ago to hear Nehru. I think the whole of the Indian population in London were present. Lady Mountbatten was there. I was very impressed by him, not his speech so much as by his sincere personality.

A limited international airletter service out of Germany finally restarted in May 1948.[278] Greta Reusch, writing to Karola and Afzal, looked forward to using it, comparing the eight days that it took their letters to reach her from Pakistan with the eight weeks it was taking hers to reach them.[279] And in June her cousin in New York, Rosette Katzenstein (*née* Grünebaum), sent

---

[278] Walter Farber, 'Air Mail into and out of Germany from the End of WWII to 1948', The Collectors Club, https://www.collectorsclub.org/air-mail-into-and-out-of-germany-from-the-end-of-wwii-to-1948/; M C Gilhousen and R Anders, *German Philatelic History from the End of WW2 until the 1950s* (unpublished manuscript, n.d.).

[279] Letter from Greta Reusch to Khadija and Afzal, 14 May 1948.

her an International Reply Coupon that enabled her to do just that.[280] The resumption of airmail services was a development of such significance that it was mentioned by most of Karola's correspondents. Writing from Buenos Aires in September of that year, her cousin Käthi Buxbaum (*née* Grünebaum) told her that the previous week she had received a letter from their Aunt Luise which had for the first time been sent direct by air from Frankfurt to Buenos Aires.

She also described how little awareness Argentinians had of the differences and divisions between the groups of immigrants that had entered their country, and was evidently frustrated by their inability to grasp this:

> *27 September 1948* Here a high percentage cannot distinguish between a Jew and a German. They believe they are one, don't know that we are Jews like others are Catholics or Protestants, and that this has nothing to do with nationality. They use 'Aleman' to mean Nazi and lump everything together. It's often difficult to clarify this because they just don't get it. (T)

Economic Crisis in Post-War Europe

One topic was mentioned by almost everyone in their correspondence – the parlous economic situation in the countries of western Europe. Initially, the focus was on the shortages of food and other commodities in Germany. Greta Reusch repeatedly wrote to Karola and Afzal about this:

> *14 May 1948* I would like to go to another country because it is terrible in Germany, I do not want to

---

[280] Until October 1948, airletters had to be prepaid with International Reply Coupons (IRCs) because carriers would not accept payment in Reichsmarks, which had very little value. For this to happen, a contact in another country first had to buy the IRCs with foreign currency and then send them to Germany.

complain and you know that I have never done it before, but if it goes on like this the outlook is bleak, we will all perish miserably. Think about it, dear children, we haven't had a gram of meat or fat here in six weeks. Hunger is spreading and sending people to their grave, it is unimaginable. (T)

18 August 1948 There has been nothing to buy for many years ... We just have to live on what is earned each week. Nobody has any money, the earnings are not much if you have two boys going to school. But we are satisfied, at least it is peaceful and you are no longer being followed. (T)

Family and friends overseas tried to alleviate the problems by sending provisions to the Reusch family. Even before Karola arrived in Pakistan, Afzal had started making shipments of food, clothing and other supplies. These continued for several months and their appreciative remarks leave no doubt about how important they were for the family's welfare:

14 May 1948 from Greta Reusch I am so grateful to both of you for providing my two children with clothes so that they won't have to go naked or walk around in tattered rags, like so many. There is nothing to be had here. I'm so looking forward to Afzal's package, even though I don't know what's inside, I'm very, very grateful to you for all of it, because there is a huge shortage of everything. (T)

13 June 1948 from Greta Reusch Just think, today on my birthday your dear little package arrives, how happy we all were with the contents. Thank you all so much, you made it a wonderful birthday, extra thanks from Michel and Edgar for the fine cigarettes, they both feel like kings and wealthy people, this is definitely a very good contribution to our very scarce food rations. (T)

13 June 1948 from Ludo Reusch Many thanks for your so nice parcel which arrived at Mittelsinn yesterday. We were very happy about [that], for we thought it to be lost. All things were all right and they gave us much pleasure. It arrived on mother's birthday, a week after my birthday, which I celebrated not at home but with my class at the River Rhine ... Of course Dady and Edgar most delight in the cigarettes. Afzal seems to have a good nose for the troubles of a German smoker. I must say that the condensed milk gave me most pleasure. So we had much fun this day.

25 July 1948 from Greta Reusch My dears, this week we received two packages from dear Afzal, which must have been underway for a very long time, oh they made us so happy. Everything inside was fine. My dear Afzal, you really knew what we needed, we could smell the quality of the soap before even opening the package. For everything, my dears, I would like to express my sincere thanks. You have already done too much for us, how can we repay you. (T)

Food shortages were just one symptom of an economy in ruins. After the war, the Reichsmark was almost worthless and an estimated one-third to one-half of all transactions took place on the black market or through barter. The situation, however, was transformed by a combination of radical measures: the lifting of price and production controls, the adoption of policies to create a social market economy, support from the USA through the Marshall Plan and the currency reform implemented in June

1948. It was this last development that was most often mentioned in the letters sent out of Germany, and it was a cause of much concern. Ludo Reusch, then aged 17, attempted to explain to Karola and Afzal how it would work and suggested that there was widespread scepticism about its impact. Writing first in English but struggling with the terminology, he reverted to German:

> *25 July 1948* As I indicated in one of my letters we have got an inflation (Geldentwertung) in Germany. Dear Karola, I will briefly explain this to you because it is very difficult for me to write it in English in a way that you will understand. [continues in German]. Right, all money has been collected up; we are getting DM40 (Deutschmark) per person in new money, which has been printed in America. The old money will be converted at a ratio of 1:10, that is for 10 old <u>Reichs</u>mark, 1 new <u>Deutsch</u>mark. But nobody believes in this today. Prices have remained generally high and everyone now has to make a living through hard work. Thank God, Papa isn't unemployed like many others. (T)[281]

Ludo's explanation was a simplified account of what actually occurred. Individuals did immediately receive DM40 in cash in exchange for RM40 and a further DM20 a few weeks later at the same exchange rate. Subsequently, however, RM540 per person was deducted from their bank accounts (if their balance allowed), so effectively the conversion rate was 10:1. Of the remaining money, up to RM5,000 per household was converted at the same rate, but only half the total was released for spending. The other half was held in a blocked account until October 1948, when 70% of it was cancelled, 20% released and 10% retained for

---

[281] Ludo uses the word 'inflation' in English but adds the German term '*Geldentwertung*', which actually means devaluation.

investment in medium- and long-term securities. Balances over the limit were only converted after the authorities had confirmed that no taxes were due. Effectively, this meant that at least 35% of each household's cash became worthless and a further 5% was inaccessible. Both Greta and her older sister, Else, wrote to Karola about the consequences for their families:

> *19 June 1948 from Else Ortloff* Today monetary reform is taking place in this country. We will get 10% of all our savings and will once again be poor people, having to start from the beginning again … The people are all dismayed by the monetary reform and have been thrown into confusion. (T)

> *27 March 1950 from Greta Reusch* My husband's assets, as well as mine and what we had saved, was about RM20,000, from which we are now left with DM500, because only RM5000 per family was taken into account and revalued at 10%. And since then we have become poor people … (T)

And Greta's father, Friedrich Kühn, told Karola what had happened to the RM1,800 that remained from the money her parents had given him for safekeeping before they were transported. He too felt that the reform had caused considerable financial loss:

> *27 March 1950* This RM1800 is still in the bank, converted at a rate of 1:10 or rather 1:6½ and I could withdraw this sum for you, but you wouldn't be able to do much with it here. Everything here is outrageously expensive and 1 English £ = DM12.43 … I had invested my savings in government bonds and for the time being I can't get a penny back, unfortunately … The amount of money mentioned above is hardly

enough for your fare through Germany, let alone for your ferry crossing and shopping. (T)

Despite the concerns of so many people, in the British, American and French zones, which became West Germany in May 1949, the measures taken actually transformed the economy. Investment led to the growth of employment and output, and almost overnight the availability in shops of food and other goods increased, although affordability remained an issue. By 1950 Greta's portrayal of the situation in the country was very different:

17 March 1950 Living costs are quite high, a few examples, pork DM2 per pound, beef 1.60, butter DM3, cocoa DM3.50–4 per pound. One can get everything down to the smallest item, nothing is lacking any more, there is no point in bringing any foodstuffs with you. (T)

29 July 1950 School fees and travel to school cost a lot of money and we cannot afford anything else, even though everything is now available in Germany as far as food and clothing is concerned. That's why I have to do a lot of mending and sewing, because we can't afford anything new. Today, my dears, I am still very grateful to you for what you sent us back then, because Ludo would literally have had nothing without Afzal's shirts and other things. (T)

Greta's letters also revealed how family members earned their living during this difficult period in what was a predominantly rural area with few jobs. It often meant moving to where work was to be found and living away from home:

23 May 1948 This week I am alone. Edgar [her son] has been transferred to a different forestry office, which is at Neuwirtshaus, 50–60 km from here. Michel [her husband] is working on a building site in Lengfurt, and won't be home until Sunday. (T)

12 January 1950 Michel is currently unemployed because of the winter weather … Edgar was at a nearby forestry school but has been transferred to Emmerichstal, which is not too far from here, today he is at home. (T)

1 July 1950 My husband has to get up [at 5am] when Ludo leaves the house [to go to school]. He is a foreman in Gemünden at a construction company, so I have to prepare food for him. Edgar is in Lohr at the forestry school for one year, so until December 31, then he will get a job. (T)

31 March 1954 Michel has been working again for the past fortnight. I'm very happy, he was unemployed for ten weeks because of the cold weather that we had, and when you don't get any money for ten weeks, that is bad. (T)

There were also unimaginable risks in their everyday lives and in August 1951 she wrote to tell Karola and Afzal about a particularly serious incident:

15 August 1951 And now, dear Karola, I have to tell you why you haven't heard from me for so long. On 29 June, my son Edgar had a serious accident. Here we have a lot of wild boar that do a lot of damage to the arable crops. So at 10 o'clock one evening Edgar went up to his father-in-law's field to look for wild boar. It was quite dark and when he was 20m away, a private gamekeeper thought he was a boar and fired

22 shotgun pellets into his legs above the knee. I can't describe the sight to you, dear Karola, when they called us and I saw Edgar bleeding from 22 wounds and lying in a pool of blood. (T)

Meanwhile, in Britain both Hanni Koppel and Rosette Kaufmann also noticed changes as the availability of some goods increased and rationing was eased:

> *30 June 1948 from Hanni Koppel* The rate of coupons has been reduced on several items and an additional 12 coupons have been issued as well. Shoes are only 3½, fully-fashioned stockings 1½, non-fully-fashioned coupon free, so are gloves and ties. Purchase tax has been reduced on radio sets and utility furniture and are available for everybody. But fruit is scarce. Cherries and strawberries are plentiful but terrible expensive.

> *18 September 1948 from Rosette Kaufmann* … a lot of things here are no longer rationed … Bought a pair of blue shoes. No more coupons. Thank God. And a nice jumper. Now I'm saving for a radio. (T)

Curiosity and Concern

As well as sharing information about family and mutual friends, those who wrote to Karola whilst she was in Pakistan bombarded her with questions. Whilst British friends had some knowledge of life in the Raj, for most Germans the sub-continent was a largely unknown world. They had little awareness of the Partition of India and quite unrealistic perceptions of what it was like there at this time, but they wanted to find out and Greta began asking even before Karola had left London:

> *21 March 1948* Once you have reached India and

recovered from the journey, then write a detailed letter
to tell me everything about your new homeland, I am
really interested in the customs and traditions, what it
is like to live there and so on. (T)

In the six months following her arrival, their curiosity was
insatiable. Else Ortloff and Rosette Kaufmann were interested in
the food:

> *19 June 1948 from Else Ortloff* Are you getting used
> to the customs and food? Or do you cook European
> meals? (T)

> *16 October 1948 from Rosette Kaufmann* What is the
> food like there, always curry? (T)

Doris Asgaralli, Mya Davis and Rosette Kaufmann wanted to
know what she was wearing and whether she had adopted the
local dress:

> *17 May 1948 from Doris Asgaralli* How are you liking
> Pakistan? Are you getting used to the different way
> of life, it must all seem very strange to you … Do
> you wear English clothes or sari, I am sure that a sari
> would be frightfully hot around the legs.

> *31 May 1948 from Mya Davis* Yes, I can imagine how
> hot it must be. What do you wear Karola? I'm sure
> there was no need for you to wear two sets on your
> journey, was there????

> *18 June 1948 from Rosette Kaufmann* How are you
> dressing, Khadija? Are you wearing a sari? (T)

Käthi Buxbaum was inquisitive about every aspect of her
personal life: the wedding, family structure, domestic arrangements
and the *lingua franca*. She was clearly astonished that Afzal had

such a large family and was keen to know how they catered for so many:

> *5 June 1948* You mentioned that you were married according to Indian custom. What does that involve? Describe it all to us. You know we are not being nosy, but would like to know everything. Don't you speak English there, since it was under English rule? So what language do you speak with Afzal? Does Afzal only have his mother or his father too, and does he have any brothers and sisters? ... Regarding work, is your husband happier in his homeland than he was in England? Is he doing import and export, like before, or something different? He will be glad not to be dependent on food rationing any longer, since I'm sure you can get everything one needs there, just like here [Argentina]. Do you do the cooking or do you have a black servant? Please write to us in detail. (T)

> *27 September 1948* How come Afzal has such a big family? Does he have so many siblings or how is it made up? You write about more than 100, you cannot get to know them if they come from so many different connections ... Well, I hope you'll write to us about this again some time. When you have a family get-together, can you buy food wholesale and arrange mass catering? I would like to see how that works. Does everyone talk to you in English or have you learnt the local dialect in the short time you've been there. Do you get on with your mother-in-law and does she live with you? Does Afzal have more siblings and are they all married? I am convinced that, after they welcomed you so warmly, nobody will be offended that you are a

European, or even German or Jewish, or do they not know what that is? ... We would like to hear from you about the unrest there, one reads about it so often in the newspapers that we are fearful that you are there at this time. Write to us soon in detail about it, so that we are not in the dark for long. (T)

But more generally they wanted to know how she had adjusted to her new environment, how that compared to life in Europe and what she was doing with her time, as exemplified by questions from Annelies Blumenstein and Doris Asgaralli:

27 July 1948 from Annelies Blumenstein How have you settled into your new homeland? It must be interesting to live amongst a race of people who are totally different to us. Have you now got to know your mother-in-law? (T)

1 November 1948 from Dors Asgaralli You do not tell me how you spend your days and evenings, I would be very interested to hear how does life compare with that of England, is it fuller and more interesting?

The intimate letters that Afzal wrote to Karola following his arrival in Pakistan while she was still in London were testimony to their love for one another. The letters sent to them by family and friends showed that they were very aware of that affection and how painful it was for the couple to be apart. Even before Karola had left, Greta Reusch in a letter to her, and Eve Vigdor in a letter to Afzal in Pakistan, wrote about their longing to be together again:

21 March 1948 from Greta Reusch Your dear Afzal will be quite annoyed about it [Khadija's delayed departure], he is undoubtedly looking forward to your arrival. Hopefully, you will like it in India, you will have to get used to a lot that is different to England and Germany because every country has its own customs and traditions, but people get used to everything. The main thing is that you and Afzal get along well and you love each other very much. (T)

23 March 1948 from Eve Vigdor Karola is with us every day and she is very excited to think she will be joining you soon and can hardly wait for the reunion in Karachi … Well, Afzal, let's hope Karola will be with you very soon. I'm sure neither of you can wait for the day.

Karola's willingness to abandon her life in London and travel across the world confirmed to family and friends the strength of the couple's relationship and they saw her sudden decision to follow Afzal as romantic, adventurous and intriguing. To them it must have seemed like a love story from a film script, and Mya Davis, Greta Reusch and Hanni Koppel all celebrated the happy reunion that they envisaged took place:

5 May 1948 from Mya Davis I was so pleased to receive your letter and to hear that you had landed safely in Karachi – I can just imagine the welcome you had from Afzal.

14 May 1948 from Greta Reusch My dear Karola, you are now with your beloved Afzal and, from what you write, you like it there. I am very happy about that and wish you lots of luck in your new homeland. (T)

25 May 1948 from Hanni Koppel How is Afzal? I imagine he is very happy to be again together with you.

Over time, however, Karola's letters became less frequent and those that she did write began to reveal that life in Pakistan was not working out well for them. It was evident that she and Afzal were encountering multiple problems and she was becoming increasingly unhappy. They experienced difficulty adjusting to the climate, food and lack of hygiene, all of which had an adverse impact on their health. As already mentioned, they both became ill soon after their arrival and were indisposed for several months. Almost all their friends commented on this:

> *23 March 1948 from Eve Vigdor* I am so sorry to know that you have had a fever and we both sincerely wish you much better by now. When Karola reaches India she will be able to take care of you, eh? I'm sure you must miss her as she is most capable.

> *28 May 1948 from Elsie Malcolmson* We hope you have by now recovered from the effects of the fever also your husband – you both must take good care of yourselves.[282]

> *31 May 1948 from Mya Davis* I was very pleased to receive your letter of 23rd May on Saturday but sorry to know that you have been ill. I hope you are now feeling better and able to go about. It is very worrying for you that Afzal is not well but I'm sure that he will get better now that you are with him, especially if you get a flat and do your own cooking.

> *18 June 1948 from Rosette Kaufmann* Thank you very much for your dear letter of 4 June 1948 and I was very sorry to hear that you are so disappointed and that you had such bad food poisoning. Well, that will

---

[282] Elsie Malcolmson lived with her family in Paignton. She was a friend made when Karola and Afzal went to live in Devon for a period during the war.

have pulled you down. It's probably also the water there and you must first boil it before you drink it … (T)

30 June 1948 from Hanni Koppel But I am so sorry that you are not feeling so good. It must be dreadfully hot … Everyone is asking me how you are getting on. I do hope very much you are feeling better now. I suppose [it] is hard to get accustomed to this tropical climate, especially when you come from England.

July 1948 from Doris Asgaralli I am so sorry to hear that India is not proving all that you anticipated, the boiling sun can I know be very trying.

Health, though, was not the only concern that Karola disclosed to her family and friends. Their letters indicate that she also shared with them the strain she was feeling from living in Lahore surrounded by so many family members with the consequent lack of privacy and unaccustomed to their uninhibited curiosity. Greta Reusch, Mya Davis and Rosette Kaufmann commented sympathetically and tried to give her hope that things would improve:

23 May 1948 from Greta Reusch Hopefully, you will soon get your own apartment and then will have your own home. (T)

31 May 1948 from Mya Davis Yes, I can imagine how you feel when you are asked to give full details of everything you do. In the villages in this country it is exactly the same – everyone knows everyone else's business better than their own!

18 June 1948 from Rosette Kaufmann Khadija, hopefully you'll soon be living alone with Afzal again,

which will make it as comfortable as it used to be ...
(T)

Nevertheless, all her contacts realised that life in Pakistan was not what Karola and Afzal had hoped it would be and that the situation was unlikely to improve in the foreseeable future. Karola was very worried about Afzal's failure to secure a salaried job or establish his own business, and she was homesick for London. Rosette Kaufmann, who was considerably older and evidently had tried to dissuade Karola from going to Pakistan in the first place, became extremely anxious and wrote, reproaching her friend for not heeding the advice she had given her. And if Karola and Afzal were not thinking about it already, she left them in no doubt that she thought they should leave Pakistan and move elsewhere. In her agitated state of mind, her writing was frenetic, disorganised and ungrammatical but the message was clear:

> *16 October 1948* My dear Karola, what did I tell you before you left? Karola, you shouldn't give up a beautiful home so lightly. If Afzal loves you, he will definitely return ... but you didn't listen. I'm not your mother, as you once reminded me, and my English may not be good, nevertheless I have worldly experience. But I don't want to give you a lecture, I'm so sorry that Afzal can't find a job, what do you live on, Karola? I'm sure you will have become very skinny. Write to me ... And why do you write that you can't get used to living your life in a room? You told me before you left you would have a government job. Karola what happened to that? I want to hear from you urgently. And what has Afzal got planned? Write and tell me, please. Can you not contact Siegfried [in South Africa], if you can't tolerate the climate there? ... Don't be angry

with me. I mean well … And now my dear Afzal, how is it that you can't find work. That's gone on for months. It's brought you both down. I wouldn't have thought it. You were so hard-working here, you had your nice little shop and such a beautiful home. The mistake has been made. The only thing to do is look for work, save and, when an opportunity arises, to return to England. (T)

In addition to all the above trials and tribulations, there was a further significant development mentioned in a letter written by Greta Reusch, Karola's cousin:

> *12 January 1950* You, my dear Karola, have great things ahead of you this year. Your family will increase in size. Do not let it scare you, because the time will pass and then you will be happy. Afzal will surely grow a bit taller once he is a father. I can imagine how happy you will be when it's all over and I am happy, Karola, that you are going to a hospital. (T)

Clearly, Karola was expecting her first child. However, the pregnancy was never written about again and presumably she miscarried. Also conspicuously missing from all the correspondence was any mention of the horrific events that had taken place in Germany during the period of Nazi terror just a few years earlier.

Tetchy Words and a Bizarre Proposition from a Distant Parent

On 18 May 1948 Ismail wrote what was probably one of the last letters he sent to his son. It was a reply to two he had received, both written by Afzal soon after his arrival in Pakistan four months earlier. The reason for the delay was that Ismail had been in La Paz (Bolivia) for six months working for an Argentinian company, and he had left no forwarding address for his mail. The letter begins 'My dear Afzal' and it ends 'Affectionately yours', but between these opening and closing words, there is little warmth or friendliness towards his son. On the contrary, the tone of his opening paragraph suggests that they were far from being on good terms and that there had been little correspondence in recent years.

Rather than simply saying sorry for his slow response, Ismail tells Afzal that he should pardon his father for the delay, while pointing out that he had not expected to hear from him and, anyway, he had waited much longer for a reply to one of his own letters. He signs off with a business-like 'M Ismail' and, as before, only provided a mailbox number for any reply:

> *18 May 1948* I had left no forwarding address, because I expected no letters to arrive here (and least of all from you) during my absence. You will therefore have to pardon me for the long delay (tho' not quite so long as that incurred by you in writing to me from London – a year and a ½!) with which I'm answering your letter. It was altogether involuntary. I can assure you.

After these barbed comments, he did go on to say how pleased he was that his son had returned to the family. He sent his love to Masuda and other family members, and once more expressed a forlorn desire to see them. Despite that goodwill, however, he was unable to offer them any practical support. Afzal had apparently repeated his earlier request for financial help and Ismail again responded that it was out of the question. He was, he explained, unemployed and getting old, and winter was approaching. He would have been in his 62nd year:

> *18 May 1948* I would gladly help you & the family

> with money if I could; but I'm sorry to say the same
> is totally beyond me, as I'm without work at present
> moment (AND getting old!) I'm faced with the
> problem of keeping body & soul together, and it is
> the beginning of winter in this part of the world (you
> are going into summer!) which makes matters worse.

Whilst he may have been understandably preoccupied with his difficult circumstances, it is evident from the letter that his interest in current and international affairs was undiminished. Referring to Pakistan as 'our new country', although he had not been near the sub-continent for almost 40 years, he was very aware of the chaos and terrible social and economic conditions prevailing there following Partition:

> *18 May 1948* How are things in Pakistan – our new
> country? Newspapers and radios do not report very
> favourably on the situation in general; anything but.
> With the millions, literally, uprooted & transplanted,
> losing everything they possessed, homeless, workless,
> penniless, with thousands upon thousands brutally
> done to death; the chaos and misery must be beyond
> description & rehabilitation of the countless millions
> a truly super-human task. It will take at least a
> generation or two to more or less normalize things.
> God, what a state of affairs.

Nevertheless, he still perceived that developing trade between their countries could be the way to extricate both his family and himself from their predicaments. It was the same idea he had first floated 27 years earlier. That was to set up an import-export business to sell Pakistani products to Uruguay and Argentina, and bring their products in the reverse direction:

> *18 May 1948* But there would be some hope of an

improvement all round if we could develope some trade between Pakistan & Uruguay & Argentina. On this side, for instance, Jute, Hessian (jute cloth for making gunny bags), Cotton, Rubber, Shellac, Textiles, Tung oil (if Pakistan or India produce any), Pashmina from Kashmir, and some tea & spices would be in great demand. The field for exports to India/ Pakistan, on the other hand, would be rather limited, for beyond wheat, corn & linseed, cow hides, sheep skins, a little rice, frozen and canned meat, quebracho extract and butter, I cannot see anything else.

Mindful of the wider business environment, especially with regard to currency issues, he even advised what the payment arrangements should be, and instructed Afzal to get busy and take the idea forward:

18 May 1948 The present day method of business is the opening of irrevocable credit in a Bank in favour of the supplier which ensures the latter a prompt payment of his bills as soon as he takes the shipping documents to the Bank. So get yourself busy & see whether you can do anything to develope any trade in the lines I have suggested above. If Pakistan or India would agree to accept payments in sterling for any commodity they sell us, instead of demanding U.S. Dollars, interchange would be by far easier, for, Dollars are scarce, as all over the world today. I await your answer with interest.

This, though, was not the only idea he put forward to increase his income. In the final sentences of the letter, almost as an afterthought, he floated a much less conventional proposition to his son. He suggested that Pakistan appoint him as that country's diplomatic representative, provided the position came with a payment:

> *18 May 1948* Won't Pakistan Govt. appoint me their Consul (not honorary, of course) either in Argentina or Uruguay? Can you use any influence towards that at your end?

Over subsequent months, Afzal probably did attempt to generate some trade between the two countries. However, the little evidence available not only shows that he acted more as an introducer than a business partner, but also reveals the disruption to commercial activity caused by Partition. In December 1948, at Afzal's suggestion, Khalifa Wahid-Ud-Din & Co, a Lahore-based company, wrote to Ismail to respond to his interest in importing goods from Pakistan. The proprietor explained, however, that, having closed their Bombay office in 1947, they could no longer supply any of the products that Ismail had identified. Moreover, while the company had a base in India, it imported from Argentina tanned leather goods, such as wallets and suitcases in cow and crocodile hide, but they could no longer do this, presumably for economic reasons. He did offer to connect Ismail to an associate in Calcutta, who could supply gunny bags, tea and shellac, and to another exporter in Cochin who could supply spices. However, as far as is known, nothing came of this and, even if something did take off, there was no obvious role for Afzal.

What became of Ismail? There is no later correspondence to provide an answer, nor has conclusive information been found in Montevideo, despite enquiries sent to the city administration, the Islamic Centre, the British Hospital, the British Cemetery, other cemeteries and elsewhere. However, there are two tantalising clues. First, the city's telephone directories for 1964, 1969 and 1970 (copies of which were found in the New York Reference Library) list an 'M Ismail', the only entry with that surname. The name does not appear in earlier or later editions and the accompanying address is an apartment block that was built by a cooperative, providing housing for low-income households. Second, the death of a Mahmud Ismael (the name on some of the Montevideo-Buenos Aires passenger lists) was registered by the city authorities on 8 June 1970. On the death certificate, the fields for date of birth, marital status, nationality, address and occupation are all blank. The only pertinent detail given was the cause of death, namely pneumonia. Given that Ismail would have been predisposed to this illness (with his history of tuberculosis), that his name had apparently been misspelt since his arrival in South America and that he had struggled economically, it is highly plausible that the person named in the telephone directory was the person who died in June 1970, and that this person was my grandfather, Mohamed Ismail. If correct, he had managed to maintain his anonymity until the very end. He would have been 87 years old and been in South America for 60 years, during which time the only close contact he had with family members was a brief passing meeting with his youngest son on a ship 35 years earlier.

Resettlement in London

The Return Journey

Towards the end of 1949, Afzal and Khadija were once again facing a number of challenges. Financially, they were struggling to make ends meet. Employment was difficult to find and new business opportunities elusive. Khadija was still finding it extremely difficult to settle down, especially within the constraints of an extended Muslim family. Moreover, she was now also pregnant and would have been apprehensive about giving birth in Pakistan.[283] It was a difficult decision but they resolved to return to the UK, and soon started to make preparations for their journey. Having struggled for months to get permission for her to enter the country, they now had to find a way through the bureaucracy again before they would be allowed to leave. Still without a passport, Khadija had to obtain a 'Certificate of Identity' which was required by 'Pakistan domiciled persons' before they could apply for a permit to travel out of the country. She would also have needed documentation to re-enter the UK.

---

[283] Although this pregnancy must have ended in a miscarriage, the date when this occurred is unknown.

Certificate of Identity to be produced by Pakistan Domiciled persons,
applying for a Permit for Temporary and Repeated Journey.

Part I.   CERTIFICATE OF IDENTITY.

Valid for one year from 6.12.49 to 5.12.50

Province............. *Karachi* .... District .... *Karachi* ....

Serial No.............. 7224

Name.............. KHADIJA HUSAIN HUSAIN

Father's name.............. MOHAMMED AFZAL HUSAIN
Husband's name (for married Ladies & widows.)

Date of birth.............. 12.5.1926

Place of birth.............. *Offenbach, oldMain Germany*

Domicile.............. *Pakistan*

Occupation.............. *Air Hostess PLA Air Ltd*

Permanent address.............. *Jehangir Road Jehangir Quarts*
House no1 Block No3u Karachi

Signature or thumb
impression of the holder.............. *Khadija Husain*

In case of Displaced persons only.

1.   Original address in other Dominion................................

2.   Date of migration ....

Seal of the
Deputy Commissioner Collector.
..............District.

Signature of the
Deputy Commissioner Collector.
..............District.

P. T. O.

Khadija's Pakistani Certificate of Identity

The certificate, which carried one of the few surviving pictures from her time in Pakistan, was valid for 12 months from 6 December 1949 and with that document in their hands they could make the flight reservations. On 21 February 1950, Khadija wrote to Travelogue, a travel agency based in Karachi Airport, to make the bookings. They replied the same day to confirm two seats on Orient Airways 'special flight' leaving Karachi 'on or about the 16th March'. Why it was special and why no firm date was given is unclear, but on the payment receipts the flight was again described as a 'special charter'.

The travel agency's reservation confirmation letter shows that the fare per passenger, including meals and night stops, was Rs741 or £80. However, four days later Khadija paid an initial instalment of Rs1000 and three days after that the balance of Rs112, making a total of Rs1112, instead of the quoted Rs1482, a discount of exactly 25%. The reason for this reduction was that Khadija worked her passage back, reprising her role as an air hostess because they had insufficient cash to pay both full fares.[284]

---

[284] Letter from Khadija to Otto Stein dated 23 June 1960 mentions that she worked on the flight.

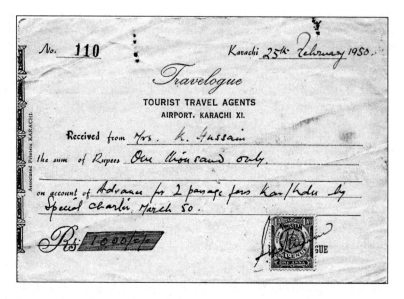

Receipt for deposit paid for airfares from Karachi to London

There were other formalities to be concluded before they could travel. They went to a dispensary in Jutland Lines where Khadija had a cholera inoculation and Afzal a smallpox vaccination. A few days later he had a yellow fever inoculation at Karachi Airport, for which Karola paid Rs15. And just as Karola did when she left Germany, Afzal had to get permission to take their possessions out of the country. In early March 1950 he wrote to the Collectorate of Customs, enclosing a list of the personal effects they wanted to bring to England. His covering letter specifically mentioned some new fabrics in the list, which presumably were subject to export restrictions. He explained that these 'were very recently presented to us by friends and relations' and that there was insufficient time before their departure to have these made into garments.

```
From:-
        M.A. Hussain,
        30/1 Jehangir Quarters,
        Karachi.

To
        The A.C.C.I. & E.,
        Custom House,
        Karachi.

Dear Sir,
              Since I am proceeding to U.K. along with my wife, I have to
    request you to kindly issue necessary permits to enable me to take
    out of Pakistan our personel effects as per list attached.

              On examining the list you would notice some clothing materials
    as well. These were very recently presented to us by our friends and relations.
    Since we are scheduled to leave for U.K. on the 16th., instant, therefore
    in view of the short time we could not have these materials made into garments.

              Thanking you, and hoping that you would do the needfull at
    your earliest convenience.

                                              Yours faithfully,
```

Afzal's (unsigned) application for a permit
to take personal effects out of Pakistan

The personal effects were to be sent to the UK by sea as unaccompanied luggage and the manifest included all manner of items, divided into 'new' and 'old and used'. Amongst the former were woollen fabric for a suit, a silk sari, bedding, ten bundles of joss sticks, 4 lbs of soap and a similar quantity of tea. The latter included large amounts of household linen with at least ten quilt covers, tablecloths, pillow slips, sheets and serviettes, presumably items that were in Karola's trousseau that she had brought from Germany. There was a wide range of men's and women's clothing, plus a dictionary (probably the one Karola had brought out of Germany), a cookery book and six works of fiction.

```
      List of Articles belonging to Mr. and Mrs. Hussain to be taken to U.K.
   as unaccompanied luggage by boat.

   NEW.

   Suit length  woolen   One No.          Gents Clothing Wearing apparels
                ONE No.                                    (Old and used)
      "    "   Palm Beach. One No.
   Costume "   "     "   . One No.         Shoes              2 Pairs.
   Sari   "   Silk.      one No.           Ties              12 Nos.
   Khes Pakistani        Two Nos.          Under Paints       1 Pair.
   Phulkari  "           Two Nos.          Bathing Trunk      1 No.
   Agar Battie Pak:      Ten Bundles.      Summer Shorts      2 Pairs.
   Toilet Soap.          Four Lbs.         Shirts             2 Nos.
   Tea     Pakistani.    Four   "          Tankx Shirx
                                           Pyjamas            1 Pair.
                                           Lungi              2 Nos.
         Bedding (Old & Used)              Suits (Woolen)     3   "
      Bedding consists of necessary        Flannel Trousers   1 Pair.
   bed clothes such as Quilt,Khes,
   Durrie, Dotahi, Sheets and
   Pillow slips

         Household linen.

         (OLD AND USED)
   Quilt covers.        Ten Nos.
   Table Cloth.         Ten   "
   Pillow Slips.        Ten   "
   Bed Sheets.(top).    Six   "
   Bed Sheets (Bottom). Ten   "
   Servietts(Plain)     Fifteen "
      "   (Border).     Twelve  "
   Overall (White).     One No.
   Table mats (X set).  One No.
   Bed Spread.          Two Nos.
   Apron.               one No.
   Towels.              Six  "

   Ladies Clothes Old and Used.

   Two Piece Dress      OneNo.
   Jackets.             Two Nos.
   Top Coat.            One No.
   Dresses.             Two Nos.
   Skirt.               One "X

   Books OLd.

   Dictionery, Cookery book,
   and six fiction books.

   Miscl: Articles Old and Used.

   Electric iron    One No.
   Ladies Winter Boots One Pair.
   Blanket          One No.
```

Inventory of items to be shipped to the UK

If it is true that the fabrics were gifts from family and friends, it suggests that Afzal and Khadija were leaving Pakistan with the support and goodwill of family members. However, on 14 March he received a telegram from Lahore that seems to give a very different impression. Apart from his name – Ahmed Hasan – it is not clear who it comes from and a couple of words are difficult to read, but it does clearly state 'understand you going Europe seventeenth … have mercy your old mother wife daughter child …'.

Telegram sent on 14 March 1950 by Ahmed Hasan in Lahore to Afzal

If the telegram was intended to persuade them to change their plans, it did not succeed. On Wednesday 15 March 1950 Afzal wrote to Buckwell & Co and asked the company to release him from his contract. He only gave three days' notice, but his request was accepted the same day and his final work day was Friday 17 March. On the same day they collected their tickets and, early the following morning, he and Khadija headed for Karachi Airport for the 6:30am take off on their journey back to London. Now aged 29, she left Pakistan, never to return, having been there for just under two years.

Khadija's ticket for her flight back to London, March 1950

The route back to London was different from that on their outbound flight and had more stops. It called at Sharjah, Baghdad, Nicosia, El Adam (Libya), Malta and Nice.[285] They had an overnight stay in the Ledra Palace Hotel in Cyprus, one of the largest and most glamorous hotels in the capital. Occupying room 126, they were woken at 5:30am and an hour later left for the airport, flying first to Nice (where Afzal had docked exactly 15 years earlier on his way to South America), and finally reaching London on Sunday 19 March 1950.

---

[285] Itinerary detailed in booking confirmation letter from Travelogue travel agency, 21 February 1950.

Overnight accommodation voucher for Ledra Palace Hotel, Cyprus

Afzal (third from left) and Khadija (sixth from left)
pose for a group photo at Nice airport

Meanwhile, their personal effects had been packed into four parcels and sent to Bombay, where they were loaded on to the Anchor Line ship, SS *Cilicia*, which transported them to Liverpool.

A Nomadic Existence

A week after arriving back in London from Pakistan, Khadija and Afzal were issued with the ID cards that all adults were required to carry under the National Registration Act 1939. These showed their first address was at 8 Frostic Place E1, a small road off Brick Lane. But this was temporary accommodation, perhaps with a friend, and by early May they had already moved on.

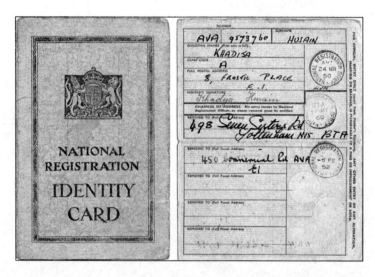

Khadija's Identity Card issued on 24 March 1950

Over the following five years they moved home on multiple occasions from one rented room or bedsit to another. By piecing together details in various documents, it has been possible to compile an indicative record of where they lived and for how long, although there is uncertainty about actual dates and some locations might be missing completely. After Frostic Place, their next stop was in Seven Sisters Road, Tottenham, where they stayed for about 20 months. In early 1952 they moved across London to Commercial Road, Aldgate, into a room above or adjoining the East London Mosque. It was then on to Queens Gate Terrace,

Kensington, where it is unlikely that they could have afforded to rent, but probably stayed with Khadija's friends, Eve and Stan Vigdor. In 1954 they actually moved out of London as far as County Durham for a few weeks, before returning to Maida Vale, the area where they had lived before going to Pakistan. And by early 1955 they were to be found at 2 Talbot Road, Highgate, where they finally settled for a longer period, staying there for four years. One can only speculate over the reasons for such frequent relocations, but they may have included the need for more space, financial pressures and pursuit of work.

From	To	Address
24.03.1950[a]	30.04.1950[a]	8 Frostic Place, Stepney, E1
01.05.1950[a]	10.01.1952[b]	498 Seven Sisters Road, Tottenham, N15
05.02.1952[c]	25.09.1952[b]	450 Commercial Road, Aldgate, E1
27.12.1952[d]	28.06.1954[b]	5 Queens Gate Terrace, Kensington, SW7
17.07.1954[b]	23.08.1954[b]	2 John Street, Blaydon-on-Tyne, Co Durham
13.09.1954[b]	06.10.1954[b]	18 Randolph Road, Maida Vale, W9
05.05.1955[a]	27.11.1959[e]	2 Talbot Road, Highgate, N6

Sources

a   Identity cards
b   Post Office Savings Bank book
c   Identity cards and ration books
d   Letter from solicitor
e   Land Registry record

Addresses of rented accommodation where Afzal and Khadija lived on their return from Pakistan with indicative dates[286]

---

[286] The table shows dates either known for sure or inferred from, for example, locations of Post Office Savings Bank transactions. Probably not all of their addresses are listed.

The accommodation at Talbot Road comprised two rooms in a large house built around 1906, sharing a toilet, bathroom and kitchen with other tenants. Probably for the first time, they also had a share of a sizeable garden with fruit trees and space for children to play. The landlord was a Sikh immigrant, Mr Dharam Bir, who lived in Caledonian Road, near Kings Cross. As a condition of their tenancy, they were also responsible for cleaning the communal areas.

Two Become Four

It was whilst Khadija and Afzal were living at 498 Seven Sisters Road, South Tottenham, that Khadija – at the age of 29 years – learned that she was expecting a baby, and this was still their home on Saturday 3 March 1951, the day on which I was born.

498 Seven Sisters Road, South Tottenham, where Khadija and Afzal were living when I was born (photographed in 2019)

My birth certificate shows that this happy event took place, as previously mentioned, at The Towers Maternity Annexe in The Bishops Avenue, Finchley, a road known then as Millionaire's Row (and today as Billionaire's Row). It was a favoured place for the rich and famous, including for example Shirley Bassey, to have their babies, an association that Afzal never tired of recounting with much amusement. Visits to the unit were tightly regulated. Permits were required to gain entry and, on the back of his permit, Afzal carefully noted that I had arrived at 10.20am, weighing in at 7lb 2oz and measuring 20" in length.

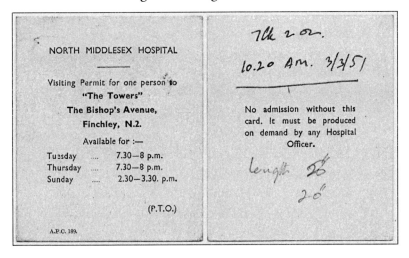

Visitor permit for 'The Towers' maternity unit at North Middlesex Hospital with details of my birth recorded by Afzal

While both parents were delighted with my arrival, it was accompanied by a difference of opinion on a rather delicate matter. My father wanted me to be circumcised in accordance with Islamic custom, something that Khadija was evidently much less enthusiastic about. As he was unable to visit her every day in hospital, they wrote letters to each other and continued exchanging views about this on paper. But his view prevailed and he set about making the practical arrangements. While his preference was for a Jewish doctor or 'a special man' to perform the surgery, the choice of surgeon was ultimately not based on religion or expertise, but on cost, as he explained in the letter written just two days after I was born:

> *5 March 1951* This is to let you know my decision in this matter. It's better to have it done in good time while you are in there for another week or so. It will be all cured by then. I had a chat with Sister on Sunday about this. I told her I would prefer a Jewish doctor for that. She [said we] should wait, as she said the hospital usually does it on 4th day. I saw Dr Roody tonight. He said that Jewish doctors don't do it, but there's a special man for the job who might charge 6 or 7 guineas. So can't afford it. Better go ahead by the hospital doctors. Please talk to Sister or Matron and ask them to arrange for it, for any day they think right to do this. I am writing this in case they want to do it on the 4th day. However, I'll be seeing you in the evening and if it's still not done we'll have a chat.

The same letter reveals that at the time of my birth there was uncertainty about what I should be called. For reasons that will never be known, Afzal refers three times to his new son as 'Cisco'. That seems to have been a provisional moniker, for the final lines indicate that their thoughts were already heading in a different direction and, from a purely personal point of view, I am much relieved that a change was made:

> *5 March 1951* Just to let you know that SOHAIL means a brilliant star (a planet) so for its meaning the name is lovely. Don't you think so.

While they were still in hospital, Afzal was tasked with shopping for his wife and new baby. He bought essentials, such as cotton wool and baby powder, but also some additional food for her, including water biscuits and butter, and – perhaps less conventionally – raw kidneys. These, he was confident, the ward staff would cook for her using the fat that he also intended to provide. As for my own nutrition, at a time when breastfeeding was considered old-fashioned and uncultured, I was soon being fed on National Dried Milk. Once out of hospital, it was given out at clinics together with the standard dietary supplements to keep me healthy: orange juice and cod liver oil, providing vitamins C and D to prevent scurvy and rickets respectively. Whether because of, or in spite of, my diet, I certainly put on the pounds and my birthweight almost doubled inside six months.

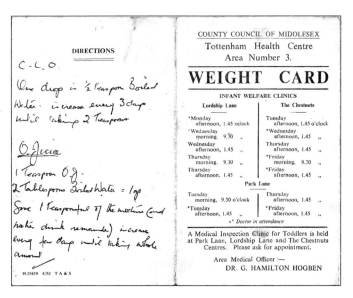

Weight Card issued by Tottenham Area Health Centre
detailing the dietary supplements I was to be given

413

My arrival was followed by congratulatory letters and telegrams from Pakistani and European contacts, confirming that Khadija and Afzal had by then once again established a network of close friends across London and around the world.

Three and a half years later, having returned from the north-east, Khadija was expecting a second child and on Wednesday 22 September 1954 my sister, Marium Bibi, was born. It was probably because of the need for more space after her arrival that the family moved to 2 Talbot Road, Highgate the following year.

It is no exaggeration to say that Khadija and Afzal devoted the rest of their lives to their children. Having both had – for very different reasons – endured extreme hardship in child- and adulthood, it became their goal in life to give their children an upbringing that would lead to a career and a life that was less gruelling than the one they had experienced. That often meant making personal sacrifices so that money could be saved and directed to meeting their children's needs. An early indication of that commitment was the opening of a Post Office Savings Bank account for 'Master M S Husain' when I was only four months old. Although the opening deposit was just 5s, and 12 months later the total had still only reached £1 15s 4d including interest, 15 years later, as England were winning the World Cup, I imagine that I felt very well-off with £238 0s 6d in my account.

After I was born, Khadija initially only took on casual work a few evenings each week, but they found it difficult to manage on her reduced income.[287] So before I was two years old, by which time we were living in Kensington (probably with friends), I was enrolled in Sterling House School nursery in Victoria Road, freeing her up to work more hours. Fees for the autumn term were £15 15s 0d, but an extra 2s 6d per day was chargeable for lunches.

When we moved to Talbot Road, Highgate, I transferred to

---

[287] Letter from Khadija to Otto Stein, 23 June 1960.

414

Highfield School, an independent preparatory school for 2–11 year olds, in Bloomfield Road. There were just four weeks of the term remaining, the fees for which totalled £3 3s with an extra 2s 6d for stationery! Although the Group Mistress and Principal both reported that I settled down well in that first term, I don't think I would have been considered a star pupil. I had made a start at reading single words and learning numbers, but I was struggling with 'cutting out'.

My first school report from Highfield School, 1955

My attendance at Highfield was also short-lived. As soon as I was old enough, I was enrolled in the local state school, St Michael's Church of England Primary, in North Road. Miss Webb, my class teacher, was a stern grey-haired elderly lady who I remember as a disciplinarian. But it was through her teaching that I learned to read and write, and through daily repetition that I learned my 'times tables'. Break times were spent with my friends racing Dinky cars down the sloping playground. It was here too that my sporting prowess first became apparent when I was awarded third place in the Class D Potato Race for Boys. And although I was very happy at St Michael's, my primary education did not end there. In November 1959 my parents moved home once again, this time to west London.

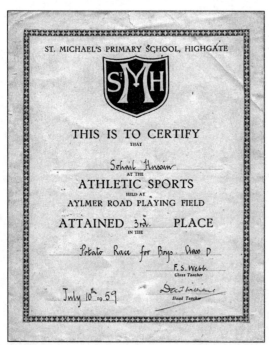

Certificate awarded for my third place in the school sports day
potato race for boys

Making Ends Meet

When Afzal and Khadija returned from Pakistan in March 1950, the legacy of war was still affecting all facets of life in Britain. Basic commodities – butter, meat, tea and coal – were rationed; there was a housing shortage; consumer goods were in short supply; taxation rates were high; many businesses had become bomb sites; and dense smog impacted public health. With so many men killed in the conflict there was full employment, but many people were living in straitened circumstances.

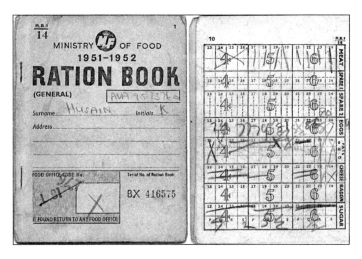

Khadija's ration book

For a while Khadija found work again at J Lyons but, despite the labour shortage, Afzal did not have a salaried job for six months.[288] Perhaps he was still ill, perhaps he had casual work. Undoubtedly, though, Indian and Pakistani immigrants experienced severe discrimination in employment and housing, and maybe this was also a factor.[289]

---

[288] Letter from Khadija to Otto Stein, 23 June 1960.
[289] According to the Census, there were just 111,000 Indian-born people in Britain in 1951. They were a very small and unfamiliar minority. Office

The Indian and Pakistani immigrants formed strong communities and they had limited interaction with white British people. Having been amongst the earliest arrivals, Afzal had a wide network of Muslim and Hindu friends, whom he got to know at the East London Mosque or through mutual contacts, or who came from the same part of India. Just like in their home countries, the men would gather in the evenings and at weekends to sit and talk for hours, while the women prepared food and looked after the children. The network was extremely important socially and economically, providing support and a forum for exchange of information, especially news from 'home' and about business or work opportunities. Almost certainly, it was through that network that Afzal did eventually get a job and on Thursday 16 November 1950 he started work as a Temporary Clerk (Grade III) in the Supply and Stores Department at the Pakistan High Commission (Inspection Branch), initially earning £5 per week. He remained in that post for more than 2½ years, longer than he stayed in any other throughout his life. During that time his earnings increased to £7 18s a week and he managed to remit some of that money to the family in Pakistan. However, for reasons unknown, he did then resign and his employment ended on Friday 31 July 1953.

---

for National Statistics (2013) 2011 Census analysis: Immigration Patterns of Non-UK Born Populations in England and Wales in 2011.'2011 Census Analysis - Office for National Statistics', https://www.ons.gov.uk/people-populationandcommunity/populationandmigration/internationalmigration/articles/immigrationpatternsofnonukbornpopulationsinenglandandwales-in2011/2013-12-17.

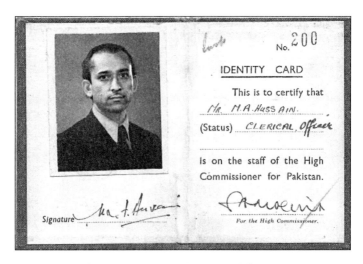

Afzal's employment identity card from the
Pakistan High Commission, London

Afzal (third row, fourth from left) at a dinner in the
Pakistan High Commission, London

What jobs he had over the next few months brought in very little money and they again struggled financially. In a document dated July 1960, his friend Bilal Memon stated that he had been working for him as a travelling salesman since December 1953 on a wage of £10 per week. However, since Afzal had neither a car nor a driving licence, it is difficult to see how that could have worked. He did go to Edinburgh for several weeks one summer, possibly as part of that role. But he certainly wasn't employed when the document was written, because in the mid-1950s Afzal returned to working the London open-air street markets, once more selling Indian handicrafts, joss sticks, sandals and brassware; 'home produced' Indian perfumes; and costume jewellery. And to attract attention he dressed for the role, combining a collar and tie with a turban and long colourful robe, clothes that he never wore in his life away from the stalls.

Afzal selling joss sticks, possibly on a bomb site off Petticoat Lane

Towards the end of the decade, however, this itinerant existence finally came to an end. For years before and after their stay in Pakistan, Afzal and Khadija had eked out a living as casual traders, setting up stalls in different markets on different days of the week. As well as being physically exhausting, their earnings were dependent on finding a vacant pitch and on the weather. In cold, wet or windy conditions, not only was there little demand for non-essential goods, but they were easily spoilt or damaged. But in the late 1950s some of that uncertainty was eliminated when they took over the rental of a lock-up hut in Shepherds Bush Market, one of the most famous street markets in London.

Established in June 1914, the market stretched along Railway Approach, a road running for a quarter of a mile alongside a viaduct carrying the Metropolitan Line (now the Hammersmith and City Line) between Shepherds Bush and Goldhawk Road stations. The railway arches provided premises for large stores and a glass canopy covered the pavement in front of them, protecting customers from bad weather. At the roadside adjacent to the canopy were the market pitches. Some of these were occupied by traditional stalls, not much more than covered tables, but on others traders had built their own lock-up huts. These pitches were let with a longer-term tenancy, thus providing traders with a semi-permanent base; and it was in one of these, Hut 64, that Afzal and Khadija set up their new business. At this stage they did not rent directly from London Transport, who owned the land and managed the market. Rather, the tenancy was in the name of a business contact who wanted to give it up. Sub-letting was against the regulations, but 'sweeteners' to the right people ensured that any such infraction was conveniently overlooked. Irrespective of the legal arrangement, it was the first time they had ever had a fixed business location.

When closed, their lock-up had a very small footprint, about four metres in length and one metre in width. But this was deceptive. The sides of the hut folded down towards the pavement on one side and the road on the other to form flat surfaces, and rows of tables put up in front of them created a large area for the display of goods. This did mean that setting up in the morning and packing up in the evening took a considerable amount of time, and storing the tables and all the stock in the tiny structure was like completing a three-dimensional jigsaw, but at least there was no need to carry everything to and from the market each day. What's more, the hut also provided somewhere to shelter in bad weather and a place to boil a kettle for a cup of tea. The disadvantage of the layout was that it was impossible for just one person to serve customers and deter shoplifters on both the street and pavement sides, so the street side remained closed when Afzal was there alone.

By taking over the hut, they became part of a unique, colourful and multicultural market community. Some of the shops had been in the hands of families with deep roots in London since the market opened, while in the immediate post-war period stalls were given to ex-servicemen. Many premises were also rented by Jewish immigrants from eastern Europe who had settled locally and later they were joined by more recent migrants from the Indian sub-continent and the Caribbean. The incredible variety of cultures, faiths, ethnicities, languages and nationalities of the traders was reflected in the range of wares they sold to meet the needs of the equally diverse local population and to appeal to visitors attracted to the market from around the world. Khadija and Afzal would themselves buy rye bread from an east European baker; sausages from a kosher butcher; ghee (clarified butter), basmati rice and lentils from a south Asian grocer; and 'lady's fingers' (okra or bhindi) from a Caribbean vegetable seller. As for their own stall, they carried on selling the same goods they had always sold.

The market was filled with constant noise. As tube trains rumbled overhead, music blared out from record shops and stallholders cried out their sales patter, whilst continuing a witty banter with customers and fellow traders. Spending most days outside together, they got to know each other at least superficially. Some with foreign origins anglicised their names, either because they wanted to be less conspicuous or because locals found their true names difficult to pronounce. Others were simply given nicknames. I don't think Afzal ever considered changing his name but, for some unknown reason, he was given the sobriquet of 'Jim' by his stallholder neighbour.

Khadija at Hut 64 Shepherds Bush Market waiting for a customer

But a semi-permanent stall did not change the hard realities of market life. Most of the working day was still spent outside, even in the coldest weather. Moreover, the market was an unhealthy environment: sanitary provision was almost non-existent and, although there was a tip where rubbish could literally be dumped, by the end of the day the street was always strewn with waste of all kinds. Conflict between stallholders was not uncommon. Individuals under the influence of drink or drugs, as well as riotous fans going to or from QPR's football stadium, caused a lot of trouble. And petty crime, especially shoplifting during the day and burglaries and arson during the night, were constant concerns.

Afzal worked at least six days a week. The stall would normally be open Tuesday, Wednesday, Friday and Saturday. On one or both of the weekdays when the business was closed, he would go to wholesalers to restock, while on Sundays he would still take parcels to Petticoat Lane and try to get a stall to earn some additional income. On the relatively busier days at the end of the week, Khadija would help out, so that both sides of the stall could be opened. This meant that, whilst we were very young, on Friday afternoons my sister and me were collected from school by a childminder, who took us back to her council flat. Occasionally we slept there too and stayed until collected by our parents on Saturday evening. It was a very different family environment to that which I was used to and I didn't enjoy the food or having to share a bed with her own unruly children. I did learn some new words but, when I innocently used them at home, my parents practically collapsed in shock and told me in no uncertain terms never to repeat them. Overall, it was not an enjoyable experience.

When I was older, my parents would often take me to the market with them. And although they would give me jobs to do and I was allowed to serve customers, spending a day at the stall could be boring. But there was one part of the day that was particularly interesting: the journey from Highgate to Goldhawk Road on the London Underground. As the train left Paddington Station on what was then the Metropolitan Line, it ran parallel to the mainline track and past the Ranelagh Bridge Depot near Royal Oak station. Here up to 15 locomotives might be seen, steam puffing out of their funnels as they were refilled with water, refuelled with coal or rotated on the turntable. This, though, was the era of the government's railway 'Modernisation Plan' and it was the sight of the huge newly introduced diesel engines that gave me the greatest thrill!

Despite now having a semi-permanent market base, Afzal and Khadija's income remained low, with daily sales sometimes totalling less than one pound. In letters Afzal sent to her in April 1959, he provided details of daily takings and outgoings:

> *5 April 1959* Started the market Friday again. Takings: Friday £2 10s, Saturday £12, Sunday £9.[290]

> *13 April 1959* Business was very poor. No Friday. Saturday just over £12 less about 30/- expenses. Sunday [Petticoat] Lane. Scotch crowd … Took £4 less about 15/- expenses.[291]

> *16 April 1959* Yesterday went to the [Shepherds] Bush. Rain all afternoon, and what a rain. Took 4/- … Saturday about £11.

> *20 April 1959* You'll be glad to know that I had a bit better weekend … Friday £5-3-0. Saturday £17-15-0. Sunday £9-16-0.

---

[290] The shop had been closed until Friday because Afzal had flu.
[291] The shop was closed on Friday because Afzal was at Regents Park Mosque for the Eid celebration at the end of Ramadan. There were Scots in Petticoat Lane because the England-Scotland football match had been played the previous day. Afzal could not get his own stall, so he shared one with another trader.

Initially it was a hand-to-mouth existence. Paying all the bills was a struggle and Karola fell behind with her National Insurance contributions. At times Afzal had to borrow money from friends and stock was bought on credit, but that was never a problem because everyone knew that he always repaid his debts. And despite their financial difficulties, we ate well and they scraped together enough money for my sister's nursery fees. Afzal also continued to look for any opportunity to escape market life that would enable them to live more comfortably or, if that were not possible, to at least increase their earnings. It was this determination that in 1960 led him to Brighton, where he took over a kiosk at the end of the town's famous West Pier, selling his usual range of wares. It was enterprising, but the very seasonal business never generated significant profit, and it separated him from the rest of the family for several months, leaving Khadija to run the business in Shepherds Bush alone. It was simply not sustainable and soon abandoned, but there were many other ventures. He could, for example, be found each March on a trade stand at the Ideal Home Exhibition in London Olympia, while at Easter he put up a stall at the Hampton Court Bank Holiday Fair held on the green in front of the historic royal palace.

Gradually, though, their situation did improve and Afzal and Khadija began to do things that had previously been out of the question. Both learned to drive, which Afzal had begun to do in 1946. Having passed their tests, they bought 'UMF 75', a second-hand small blue Ford van. More significantly, when the owner of Hut 64 decided to sell up, they were able to buy it, and so on Saturday 4 May 1963 they finally became the legal tenants. The rent book stipulated that they could sell 'perfumes, oriental wares and jewellery', that they had to open at least four days each week and that the rent of £1 10s was to be paid weekly in advance to London Transport.

Taking over the tenancy was a momentous family milestone that provided further reassurance and stability. But it was not the end of Afzal's entrepreneurial adventures and on the day the tenancy started he was not even in London. His ambition was still to escape from market life, just as it had been before he went to Pakistan. So when his long-time friend Akbar Malik, who had opened a gift shop in the popular South Devon resort of Paignton, suggested he rent a small shop there in the new Adelphi Arcade, it was an opportunity he couldn't let pass by. And that's where he was at the beginning of May. After a few weeks spent fitting out and setting up, India Handykraft opened in June for the Whitsun week trade, selling a range of traditional craft products. Contrary to what the name suggested, these were not just from the sub-continent. Brassware, carved tables, sandals, bamboo flutes and the inevitable joss sticks, perfumes and bangles from India were complemented by African carved figures, animals and masks, and goods that looked as though they might have come from there, such as rugs, cushion covers and table runners, but were actually produced in Europe. All these items were quite fashionable at the time and bought by British holidaymakers both for themselves and as gifts.

Over the bank holiday, the rest of the family joined Afzal in Paignton for a few days, making the long journey on the Royal Blue coach service. For my sister and I, it was the first time we had stayed in a guesthouse and it was our first beach holiday. But for Khadija there was little time for relaxation; she was there mainly to help open the business. Initially the takings were not particularly encouraging, totalling just £74 in the first week. However, that increased to £161 the following week and then continued at that higher level. Additionally, Afzal even managed to sell some goods wholesale to travelling salesmen. After paying £38 per week rent and the additional costs of living away from home, there was still a small profit and he was able to remit some money back to their London bank account most weeks. We returned to Paignton at the beginning of the school summer holidays in July, but it was not possible to leave the market stall closed for more than a couple of weeks. The family was therefore separated for much of the period from May to September, at which point most shops dependent on visitors shut their doors until the next spring and Afzal could return home.

It was, though, a very stressful time for them both. Taking on the business was a big decision, with no way of knowing in advance if it would succeed. The working day was extremely long. Afzal would arrive at the shop around 9am, but would often not go home until 11pm, having cleaned up and prepared for the next day. Moreover, with Afzal in Devon, Khadija had to take over Hut 64 in Shepherds Bush. It could not have been easy being away from her husband, working full time, looking after two children and managing our home on her own. Letters were exchanged almost daily and there were frequent telephone calls, but Afzal commented on how lonely he felt, how much he missed the family and how worried he was, with justification, about whether I would pass the exams at the end of my first year in grammar school. I sat them on our return from Paignton and he was not impressed when I just scraped through.

That cycle was repeated for the next three years. Afzal would go to Paignton in May and run the shop there until September, while Khadija looked after everything else back in London. Then, when the school summer term ended, we would take the coach and travel down to the West Country and be reunited for a couple of weeks. Over those years India Handykraft made a significant contribution to family finances to the extent that in 1965 Afzal and Khadija were able to trade in their Ford van and buy, admittedly on hire purchase, a new Ford Anglia Estate

Deluxe. With its 1200cc engine, blue and white bodywork and comfortable seats, it was luxury beyond our wildest dreams. And the success of the business also gave Afzal confidence to open a second shop in the arcade, China Handykraft, selling *papier mâché* goods, hand-painted fans and lanterns, rice bowls and other items made in the Orient.

It was however a step too far. By then the turnover of India Handykraft was already beginning to decline and China Handykraft barely broke even. Many factors contributed to the downturn. The arcade was well positioned close to the sea front, but the shops were inside and they depended on the 'right' people being drawn in. When the café at the end of the arcade became a bingo hall, the clientele changed dramatically. At the same time, Indian and Oriental wares became less fashionable, while the huge increase in cheap European package holiday offers depressed visitor numbers. Alongside these considerations, the annual summer separation of the family was becoming intolerable, especially for Afzal. He doted on and worried about his children intensely, especially around the time of school exams, even though my performances had improved considerably. And there was one other factor that must have weighed on my parents' minds. Afzal's health had started to deteriorate and managing the shops alone, with all the manual labouring that entailed, was becoming too onerous. Inevitably, the decision was taken to close them both down.

From then on, the stall in Shepherds Bush Market became the family's only source of income. But fortuitously it was not a bad time to focus on London. The capital was at the heart of the hedonistic 'Swinging Sixties' cultural revolution that embraced flower power and hippy counter-culture, and was characterised by radically different design, music, art and fashion. Living standards were rising, unemployment was low, and people had money in their pockets to spend on non-essential goods, including jewellery. London emerged as the 'coolest' city on the planet, attracting visitors from around the world, including to its renowned street markets.

Jewellery became the mainstay of Afzal and Khadija's business and what they now sold reflected those cultural changes. Designs were big and bold, colours were bright and materials modern. Popular lines included huge dangling ball earrings, hoop earrings, thick chunky bangles, long beads and floral hairbands, all made largely from plastic. They not only sold to the local population, but also to celebrities and sports stars who frequently walked through the market on their way to the nearby BBC Studios and White City Stadium. Occasionally props were supplied to the BBC for television programmes, such as *Steptoe and Son*. Customers from other parts of Britain and abroad made up a significant proportion of the clientele, especially around the time of major sporting events. They even developed an ongoing trade with airline crews who came to the market from Heathrow Airport and bought large quantities, mainly of dangling earrings, that they took back to West Africa to sell.

For a few years all was well. But the 1970s were very different. Britain entered a period of economic malaise with soaring unemployment and extreme inflation. As elsewhere, business in Shepherds Bush Market became much more challenging and once again it became difficult to make ends meet.

The Struggle for Compensation and a Return to Germany

Obstruction, Officialdom and Obfuscation

It would have been impossible to put any meaningful financial value on the losses Karola suffered as a result of Nazism, losses which began in her childhood and blighted the rest of her life. Nevertheless, she took the first steps to getting some compensation even before travelling to Pakistan in March 1948. Still grieving for her parents and finding it hard to exist in post-war London, she must have hoped that her case would be dealt with sympathetically and swiftly, but the reality could not have been more different. It took 13 years and hundreds of written exchanges to reach a conclusion on the main issues and then she probably took what was on offer because of exhaustion, not because she felt it was fair.[292] One matter was still unresolved 30 years later.

The main reason for the process being so protracted was that, despite demands for restitution being made as early as 1945, it was not until September 1951 that the first West German Chancellor, Konrad Adenauer, acknowledged Germany's responsibility for reparations, and another five years before comprehensive legislation was in place to compensate victims for their persecution.[293] Not

---

[292] Fortunately, Karola kept copies of most of the letters relating to her claims that she sent to solicitors and authorities in Germany. This is her only surviving outgoing correspondence and it provides considerable detail about her past and present circumstances, as well as her state of mind.

[293] The principal legislative instrument providing for compensation in West Germany was the *Bundesentschädigungsgesetz* (BEG, Federal Law for the

until 1957 was an act passed to enable payments to be made for material possessions that had been appropriated and lost. Based on Khadija's experience, it then took two more years for procedures under that act to be finalised in Hessen.

The resultant arrangements required multiple applications for different types of loss, creating an extremely complex and bureaucratic process. For example, with regard to personal possessions and household goods, if these were expropriated a claim could be made for reimbursement of their value. However, if the owner had been forced to sell them at an unrealistically low price, it was necessary to claim the difference between the sale price and the true value. Many people had experience of both situations, requiring separate claims to be made, which were dealt with by different authorities. With millions of claims being submitted, numerous administrative hurdles to overcome and continuing anti-Semitism, it was inevitable that their resolution took a very long time.[294]

However, it also has to be admitted that Khadija was not as diligent as she might have been in moving things forward. At

---

Compensation of Victims of National Socialist Persecution), passed in 1956. It was modified by the 1965 *Bundesentschädigungsschlussgesetz* (BEG-SG, Final Federal Compensation Law). Both the BEG and BEG-SG were made effective retrospectively from October 1953. Other restitution laws passed included the 1951 *Gesetz zur Wiedergutmachung nationalsozialistischen Unrechts im öffentlichen Dienst* (BWGöD, Act to Compensate Public Service Employees for the Injustices of the National Socialists) and the 1957 *Bundesrückerstattungsgesetz* (BRüG, Federal Restitution Act). The BEG dealt with compensation for persecution, while the BRüG covered restitutions for expropriated property that no longer existed. See United States Department of Justice Foreign Claims Settlement Commission, 'German Compensation for National Socialist Crimes', in *When sorry isn't enough*, ed. Roy L. Brooks (New York University Press, 2020), 61–67, https://doi.org/10.18574/nyu/9780814739471.003.0012.

[294] Robert S. Wistrich, 'Anti-Semitism in Europe since the Holocaust', *The American Jewish Year Book* 93 (1993): 3–23, http://www.jstor.org/stable/23605811.

times she was slow to respond to requests for information and did not always keep her solicitor informed about a change of address. Additionally, there were periods when she was incapacitated by illness and, moreover, she undoubtedly found applying for compensation a daunting task. Providing the evidence demanded to support her claims was extremely difficult and she struggled to understand the complexities of the legal process, its jargon and some of its decisions. For someone not living in Germany, still young and lacking in relevant experience, and having to deal with a range of new and more immediate life challenges, the combination of all the above meant that there were delays in communication and at times she almost gave up. When she did communicate, her words expressed frustration and desperation, and at times she was reduced to pleading for a few pounds to be sent to help feed her family.

Loss of Family Homes and Possessions

At the start of the process, Karola had authorised her uncle, Friedrich Kühn (the father of her cousin, Greta) who had continued living in Bavaria, to pursue on her behalf a claim for loss of possessions. In February 1948, Bundy and Bundy, a firm of London solicitors, drew up for her a power of attorney, giving Friedrich authority to take her case forward. That document, though, was never signed and the reason seems clear. Karola's life was again in turmoil. Just a few days earlier, Afzal had set off for Pakistan and a few weeks later, having struggled to get the necessary travel papers, she followed him there. Over the next few months, she had far more pressing matters to deal with, including getting married and trying to settle into a totally alien country and culture.

Friedrich Kühn was then 71 years old, but still the driving force in the Neeb und Kühn business. He had considerable standing in the community and was a member of the local *Schiedsgericht* (court of arbitration), which would play a role in compensation matters. His letters to Karola were infrequent, business-like and to the point. Perhaps because he was so busy, Greta also became involved and wrote to her cousin on more than one occasion urging her to sign the power of attorney. Eventually, in November 1948, a revised draft was prepared, now in her married name of 'Khadija Husain', stipulating that proceeds from her claim were to be transferred to Pakistan instead of England. However, this too remained unsigned, perhaps indicative of her uncertainty about a future in that troubled country.[295]

Very little happened over the following year and it was late 1949 when Friedrich's solicitor, Emil Halang, finally submitted a claim to the *Wiedergutmachungsbehörde* (reparations office) for the loss of personal items, furniture, fixtures and fittings in the Grünebaums' three-room Luisenstrasse flat.[296] However, the process ground to a halt and it was not until June 1950, three months after Khadija and Afzal had returned to the UK, that the office responded. That, though, was only to make the first of many requests for more details and documents to support the claim, this initial requirement being for a detailed list with prices of all the items for which Khadija was seeking compensation.

At first Greta, and occasionally Friedrich, willingly acted as go-betweens, informing Khadija what was needed by the authorities and giving her advice. He reminded her to include shoes and clothes in the list and suggested that RM800–900 per room might be a reasonable figure to ask for. In August 1950 Friedrich

---

[295] No correspondence survives between Khadija and Friedrich from the time she was in Pakistan. However, the power of attorney is mentioned in letters from Greta Reusch, 18 August and 19 September 1948. In a letter dated 27 March 1950, Friedrich notes that he has still not received a signed copy.

[296] The claim is referred to in letters from Greta Reusch to Khadija dated 12 January, 11 April and 9 July 1950.

went to Offenbach, where Halang had his office, to try and move the claim forward. But he still had no power of attorney and so, whilst there, he wrote yet again to ask her to return it. However, Greta and Friedrich were becoming increasingly wearied by this responsibility, and his age was now also taking its toll. The following year, as he approached his 75th birthday, Greta wrote that he was no longer fit enough to travel to Offenbach and, although they and the solicitor, Halang, continued to be involved, from then on they repeatedly encouraged Khadija to come to Germany so that she could sort out her affairs herself.

Nine months after being asked to submit a list of possessions, Khadija received documents from the *Wiedergutmachungsbehörde* asking for all the same details again. This time Greta advised her to include 'more rather than less', since it was unlikely the claim would be accepted in full, and specifically not to forget the '*Steppdecken*' (quilts)! Around the same time, Khadija heard from Halang that officials also required an inheritance certificate to prove that she was the legal heir to her parents' possessions. Unsurprisingly, it was not something she had taken with her when she fled the country or could easily produce. Another nine months elapsed before, in March 1952, she was given the alternative option of submitting an affidavit witnessed by a notary.

Almost two years after first submitting a claim, Halang was finally asked to attend a meeting at the *Wiedergutmachungsbehörde* in August 1952, when officials decided that further corroboration of the claim was required. Only after Friedrich Kühn provided a sworn statement detailing the contents and value of the furniture and fittings in the Grünebaums' flat, did the state agree in September 1952 that Khadija should be awarded the sum of DM4,000. It must have been a huge relief to have received that decision and she decided to use some of the money to pay for her, Afzal and me to travel back to Germany and visit Greta and other surviving members of her family.

However, any assumption that this particular claim had now been settled would have been completely misplaced. It would be another seven years before Khadija actually received the money. In the weeks after the compensation amount was agreed, her health took a turn for the worse and she was admitted to hospital, where she underwent surgery. It was not until the end of December 1952 that she felt well enough to write to Halang again, complaining that she had heard nothing more about the money and, if it could not all be remitted immediately, imploring him to send £50 and return tickets so that she could come to Germany. But her letter went unanswered and she became increasingly impatient and anxious. Several months later, she wrote yet again and this time he did reply, explaining that the delay was caused by ongoing matters at the international level well outside his control. Regulations for payments by the West German government had not been finalised and, he suggested, these might be linked to the *Londoner Schuldenabkommen* (London Agreement on German External Debts).[297]

Incredibly, another six years passed, during which there was no contact at all between Khadija and Halang. However, in March 1958 she wrote once more to ask about her money and why she had heard nothing from him. His rather terse response was that that he had tried to reach her, but his correspondence had been returned as undeliverable because she had not notified him of her changed address. He had, he claimed, tried to contact her through the Pakistan High Commission in London, but they did not know where she was either. The delay, he asserted, was because the West German government was still not ready to make any payments.

---

[297] The *Londoner Schuldenabkommen* (London Agreement on German External Debts) was a debt relief treaty between the Federal Republic of Germany and creditor nations. It was signed in London on 27 February 1953, and came into force on 16 September 1953.

Before continuing this strand of Khadija's story, I first need to go back in time. For while her compensation application for losses related to the family home was making its tortuous and seemingly unending way through the system, she had also become involved in a second claim. This related to the estate of her uncle, Salomon Reiss, and his family, who had lived in their own house at 7 Offenbacherstrasse, Bürgel. As has been told, he died from illness in Theresienstadt, while his wife, Lilli, and their four daughters had been murdered. This claim had been initiated by Salomon's brother, Siegfried Reiss, who had emigrated to South Africa. Siegfried appointed another Offenbach solicitor, Joseph Maria Schül, to represent him.[298] Like Emil Halang, he had an office in Kaiserstrasse, and they knew each other well. So when Khadija became involved in 1951, they agreed to work together, but decided that Schül would act for both clients. At this time, however, Schül was already 77 years old.

As with her first claim, Khadija now had to prove that she was a legal heir. She was again asked for details of her early life; what she knew about the fates of her parents and the Reiss family; and about her present circumstances. Copies of family birth and death certificates were requested, as well as her own marriage certificate. Of these, she was only in possession of the latter, but this was in Urdu and there was only one copy, which she was understandably unwilling to send. Schül advised that she would instead have to get a certificate from the Pakistan High Commission written in English to confirm her marriage and maiden name. And

---

[298] Schül was a Catholic and, before the war, a prominent politician. In 1921 he was elected as a member of the Hessen state parliament, a position he held until ousted by the Nazis in 1933. After the war, he was appointed head of the district court. Only after he 'retired' in 1948, aged 75, did he start representing Holocaust victims, mainly those who emigrated to the USA, in their compensation claims. 'Ein Verdienste Jurist Starb', Internet Archive: Siegfried Guggenheim Collection, Series C: Letters to Siegfried Guggenheim, https://archive.org/details/siegfriedguggenheim.

seemingly oblivious to the serious content of his correspondence, in the same paragraph he asked Khadija if she would collect for him some postage stamps for his son-in-law's collection!

When they instigated the claim, Siegfried and Khadija had no doubt that they were the only surviving heirs to the family of Salomon Reiss. So they were bewildered to learn that a considerable number of other people were applying for the same compensation and that there were even more other potential claimants. It emerged that these were the seven siblings of Lilli Grünebaum (*née* Löwenstein) and their children, several of whom were then living in New York and being represented by an American lawyer. When Schül asked Khadija if she had any information about them, she told him that she had no idea who they were. Evidently, she had never met or even heard of them, but their involvement would become a continuing irritation and frustrate both Siegfried and Khadija's attempts to get some recompense through this claim. That, though, would not become evident until much later.

This application for compensation also progressed at a snail's pace. However, when Khadija did eventually hear from Halang in March 1958, after their six-year hiatus, she learned that a legal ruling had been made for the return of 7 Offenbacherstrasse to the plaintiffs. As this was to be shared amongst so many, the only option was to sell the property and then divide the proceeds. But, Halang explained, this had been thwarted by just one person, who had refused all cooperation. She was Regine Löwenstein (*née* Baum), a widow not previously mentioned in any correspondence. Khadija again informed Halang that she had no knowledge whatsoever of this person and demanded to know how she was connected. That question was never answered, but it is possible that she was Lilli's sister-in-law or the daughter of one of her three brothers. At the same time, Khadija bluntly asked Halang what he had done to get compensation for the loss of her parents' lives. Other people, she noted, had received £500 per person. She had understood he was working on this too, but had seen no evidence of a claim. It was another question to which she received no answer.

Taking the Fight to Offenbach

Yet another year passed. By now, Khadija had lost all confidence in both Halang and Schül, and had little expectation of ever getting any recompense from either of the two claims submitted. In a last-ditch attempt to change that situation and at the same time see her relatives, she and Afzal decided to use their savings to pay for her, my sister and me to go to Germany.

For this she needed a British passport and to get that she needed to be registered as a British subject. Under the British Nationality Act 1948, and as a citizen of Pakistan who had been living in the UK for 12 months, she already had the status of a British national and was entitled to make the necessary registration. Her application was submitted on Monday 23 February, accepted within the month and soon after she received her first British passport. A few days later, travelling through the night by train and ferry via Ostend, she went back along the same route by which she had escaped from Nazism exactly 20 years earlier, arriving in Germany on Wednesday 1 April 1959.

After spending two weeks with family in Mittelsinn, she travelled to Offenbach on Sunday 12 April. I will write more later about that emotional return to the country of her birth and her family. Here I will focus on her efforts during that visit to advance those long-delayed compensation claims. Both she and Afzal were very aware that what happened there would be critically important and, if she were successful, could transform their lives. He wrote to encourage her and advise her to stay as long as necessary to achieve her goal:

16 April 1959 Sweetheart, please remember, you are
on a very very vital mission. First time in 20 years.
Please see that you see it through completely. You,
under no circumstances leave it halfway. If the children
miss school right up to the half term, doesn't matter.

It is clear from the surviving correspondence that Khadija
approached the task with considerable trepidation, but also a
steely determination. On the day after she arrived in Offenbach,
she had her first face-to-face meeting with Halang. The encounter
was undoubtedly tempestuous. She had not notified him in
advance that she was coming and he was not pleased to see her.
She soon discovered that some time earlier he had received her
share of the proceeds from the sale of the property once owned by
Salomon and Lilli Reiss, but had done nothing to pass that on to
her. Furious, she gave him an ultimatum to hand it over. Within
three days she had received DM500 in cash and DM4,015 in
travellers' cheques, which she immediately transferred to her
Midland Bank account in London. Converted to sterling, it was
the equivalent of £337. Later she wrote to Siegfried:

25 April 1959 Halang sits here forever and thinks
that if no one comes there is no need to worry about
the matter.

8 February 1960 At the time of my visiting him he
had quite a shock. It went so far, that I had to use force
to get the money out of him. I gave him a time limit
to get the money to the bank or else I would take him
straight to court.

No.	Währungs-Betrag	Order	Bemerkungen
899701–715	£: 300.–.–	Khadija Husain	15/20
5532878–880	£: 30.–.–	dto.	3/10
6156828–	£: 5.–.–	dto.	1/5
2041502	£: 2.–.–	dto.	1/2
	£: 337.– –		

Receipt for transfer by Khadija of £337 from Offenbach
to her London bank account

Khadija also learned that the claim for the loss of her own
and her parents' possessions had stalled because Halang had not
submitted the necessary forms. So, the following day she went
to the *Oberfinanzdirektion* (main finance office) in Frankfurt
to complete the paperwork and was assured that a payment of
DM4,000 would follow in 4–5 weeks. She told Siegfried:

> *8 February 1960*   I myself had to go to the
> *Oberfinanzdirektion* and fill up papers which should
> have been done by [Halang] years ago.

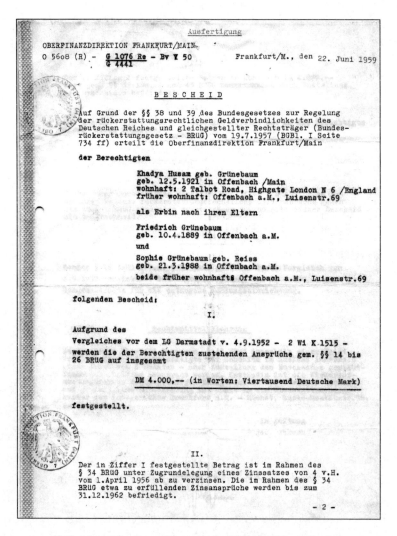

Official notification of the award of DM4,000 to Khadija
for loss of furniture and personal possessions

Unfortunately, the promise to remit the money in 4–5 weeks
proved to be another false dawn. After writing in late May 1959
to find out why it had not been sent, she was told that the relevant

arrangements to enable payment had still not been approved. More exchanges followed and, with understandable incredulity and growing anger, she wrote and demanded to be told which departments or officials were holding things up, so that she could contact them directly. This did not happen. Instead, she was asked to confirm that she was content with the amount promised and would not take any further legal action in connection with this claim. This she did in July and at the same time pleaded with the *Oberfinanzdirektion* for the money to be transferred urgently:

> *1 July 1959* I hope that, with this confirmation, this matter can be brought to an end. As I have previously mentioned, I have two children who cost a lot of money. Also, my husband unfortunately does not earn much. I would be very grateful if you would now transfer the money as quickly as possible. (T)

Eventually, the authority did pay out the DM4,000. Sadly, though, that still was not the end of this particular saga. The money did not reach Khadija's account and seemingly disappeared. Another nine months elapsed before Barclays Bank wrote to tell her that it had been located. The money had not been credited to her because it had been received before her account at the Highgate High Street branch had been opened. Finally, in April 1960, she received the sum of £339 15s 2d in compensation for the loss of her own and her parents' possessions. More than seven years after the amount due was determined, the money reached her account.

Returning to events in Offenbach, Khadija's meeting with Schül was less confrontational. She was shown paperwork relating to the settled claim, as well as his correspondence with Siegfried in South Africa. From this she learned that her uncle had decided not to continue to pursue the claim for what Salomon and Lilli had suffered or for the possessions they had lost. It was a decision that upset Khadija greatly and she was unwilling to go along with it. On Saturday 25 April 1959 and while still in Offenbach, she wrote to Siegfried for the first time in many years. After briefly telling him that she now had two children and was on her first visit back to Germany, she turned to the question of compensation. And her words in this letter, more than in any other document, display the anger, emotion and desperation that she must have felt so often but kept hidden most of the time:

> *25 April 1959* I have read various letters of yours and gather from them that you consider the matter closed. Regrettably, I have to tell you that I do not agree. There is still a whole story to be applied for. My dear Uncle Sally and his family had to do the same as my dear parents. They had to walk around with the Jewish star, they could not go where they wanted, and so much more. One can also claim for the furniture that was there, as well as clothes and linen. I don't know why you don't want to do it. Believe me, I need every penny. My husband is not rich and, with two children, we have to work very hard all the time. Work doesn't bother us, but one must be able to save something so that one has a penny for old age. We still do not have our own flat and that is very important. At that time Herr Schül asked you to make an inventory of the flat. You sent this to him but it was not on a separate sheet of paper and not signed.
>
> ... I hope my dear ones that you will help me in this matter because, as I have written, I need every penny. My dear uncle, if you wish to forgo everything, you can transfer it to me. As I see it, the relatives of my Aunt Lilly will not let the matter rest. Since you are the brother, everything depends on you.

Khadija informed Schül that, despite her uncle's decision, she still wanted to make further claims relating to Salomon and Lilli Reiss. However, in an attempt to dissuade her, he explained that her options were very limited and there was not much to be gained. Although she wanted to claim for the restrictions on their liberty and for deprivation of their liberty, only immediate family members could do this. All she could claim for was reimbursement and compensation for loss of their personal possessions. Moreover, now 85 years old, Schül was understandably reluctant to carry on working and suggested that she look for a different solicitor to represent her. That is exactly what she did and she appointed Dr Otto Stein, about whom more will be written shortly. However, Schül never passed the files on and continued with the case himself, claiming that no one else would take it on. Khadija, now totally disillusioned with both Halang and Schül, suspected the real reason was that he did not want to lose out financially. She wrote to Siegfried:

> *8 February 1960* … he has told me, that nobody will take over, because there is not much to get. In other words he himself wants a bigger slice … both these solicitors are the biggest enemies of ours.

A few days after their meeting, Schül wrote to Khadija to ask for a listing of the contents of Salomon and Lilli's home. He included a copy of the inventory that Siegfried had prepared five years earlier but which, Schül claimed, not only lacked detail but clearly was also inaccurate. It listed furniture in the living room (beds, wardrobe, dressing table, nightstands, chairs), the bedrooms (beds and wardrobes) and kitchen (cupboard, table, chairs), as well as linen and four or five bicycles. Schül asked her to add to it everything that she could remember, and specifically the contents of the individual trousseaux of the two eldest daughters, Selma and Herta, which Khadija had mentioned to him.

```
                    Erklaerung

        des Miterben Siegfried Reiss in Cap- Town
     Auszug aus dem Brief vom 2. Mai 1954
Ich kann Ihnen die Wohnung meines Bruders genau aufstellen.

Wohnzimmer: Hell Eiche, 2 Betten, Schrank, Frisiertoilette,
            2 Nachtschraenkchen, 2 Stuehle,
Die anderen Schlafzimmer waren Stahlbetten, 4 Schraenke.
Kueche: Kuechenschrank, Tisch, Stuehle.

5 oder 4 Fahrraeder waren vorhandem,

Die 4 Toechter hatten ihre ganze Ausstattungswaesche.

                                gez. S. Reiss
```

Inventory of the home of Salomon and Lilli Reiss based on a listing
prepared by Siegfried Reiss, May 1954

On 13 May 1959, having accomplished as much as she could
in Germany, Khadija returned to London. One of the acquisitions
she brought back with her was an Adler typewriter, which meant
that she was finally able to put to use a skill that she had acquired
during her apprenticeship twenty years earlier. All her subsequent
correspondence was typed, with copies made using carbon paper
rather than laboriously writing everything out a second time by
hand.

Anticipating that Schül would need more information, she had
already written to Siegfried to ask for his help. However, when in
late June she had still not heard from him, she decided to compile
the list herself, which she forwarded to the solicitor. Curiously,
this did not provide details of any furniture, but simply stated
that the flat was well maintained and that its contents included
a new sewing machine, as well as linen, curtains and lamps. As
for the two trousseaux, she explained that she did not know
precisely what was in them and based her statement on what was
in her own, although she believed that her cousins had more. The
content of each, she asserted, included 18 sheets, 20 quilt covers,

24 pillows and much more.

It must therefore have been with considerable surprise that on 20 October 1959, six months after writing to him, Khadija received a reply from her uncle, who had undergone surgery two months earlier. There were several reasons, he explained, for discontinuing his own claim: frustration about being asked so many questions he could not answer; anger that so many unknown people were claiming to be heirs; the high cost of his legal representation; and poor health. But he expressed willingness to help Khadija pursue her claim and for this he provided a new list of the contents of Salomon and Lilli's flat. It was longer and more detailed than the previous one, with an additional room and considerably more furniture now including, amongst other items, a sofa and a grandfather clock.

The following day, Khadija prepared yet another listing and sent this too to Schül. At the same time, she made clear to him the frustration and anger that both she and Siegfried were feeling about the competing claimants. It was, she explained, their understanding that Reiss family members were the rightful heirs and that Lilli's relatives would inherit through the Löwenstein line. She questioned how they had been accepted and again suggested that, if the work was too much for him, he should hand over the case to Otto Stein.

```
                    Wohnungs Aufstellung


     Speisezimmer in schwarz Eiche
     I Bueffet
     I Tisch
     6 Stuehle
     I Sofa
     I Standuhr

     Schlafzimmer in hell Eiche
     2 Betten
     I grosser Schrank
     I Waschtisch
     2 Stuehle

     2 kleine Schlafzimmer mit Betten in Stahl
     2 Schraenke

     Kueche
     Kue cheneinrichtigung mit Kohlherd und
     Gasherd.

     4 Ausstadungen fuer die Maedels welche
       alle in gutem Damast.

     I Herrnfahrrad
     4 Damenfahrraeder
     I Neue Naehmaschine
```

Khadija's revised inventory of the Reiss home submitted in October 1959

Schül's reply was understandably sceptical and uncompromising. He questioned how it was that, after all this time, Siegfried was now querying the legitimacy of the other claimants. He bluntly rejected the assertion that only the Reiss family members were entitled to a share of the estate, pointing out that the land registry record showed that Salomon and Lilli each owned half of the property. As for the household items, there was a strong possibility that these were part of Lilli's trousseau and, given that they married in 1906, these would have been well used, reducing their value considerably. He pointed out that Salomon had apparently closed his butcher's shop and sold its fixtures and fittings before the war because of his illness, so there was no claim to be made for this. All in all, he asserted, there was very little to gain from a claim but it would involve a lot of work.

Despite this rebuttal, Khadija decided to persevere and in December 1959 Schül wrote to her one more time, yet again asking her to answer questions that she must have already answered multiple times. Were you born in Bürgel or Offenbach? How many children do you have? What are their ages? What was your previous nationality? What is your current nationality? What was your profession? What is your present occupation? Did you leave Germany because of the Nazis? She replied in January 1960 and four months later he sent her a claim form to complete. It required much the same information again. That was the last correspondence she had with Schül. Six months later, in October 1960, she received a letter from Herr Lutterberg, a solicitor in Stein's office, which opened with a message from Anna Schül to say that her husband had died. He was 86 years old.

In the same letter, Lutterberg informed Khadija and the other heirs that he had reviewed the paperwork concerning the estate of Salomon and Lilli, and confirmed that the claim relating to their household goods and personal possessions remained unresolved. It was his opinion, though, that there was very little to be gained and he urged them to think carefully about whether it was worth continuing the process. At this point Khadija finally decided to call a halt to her pursuit of this particular claim, but it was far from the end of her struggle to get compensation.

Loss of Lives and Livelihood

Although Schül had declined to hand over to Stein the files relating to the Reiss estate, Khadija had nevertheless tasked him with pursuing claims for the loss of her parents' lives and her own 'forced' emigration to London, about which Halang had apparently done nothing. Stein's practice had gained a reputation as one that could be trusted and relied on to get results for Jewish claimants.[299] When Khadija arrived in Offenbach, their offices were also in Kaiserstrasse, between those of the other two solicitors, but before she returned home the firm had relocated to 64 Frankfurterstrasse, less than 100 metres from her erstwhile family home. She wrote optimistically about this new appointment in a letter to Siegfried:

> *25 April 1959* I have taken on a new solicitor. His name is Dr Stein, solicitor and notary, Kaiserstrasse 51. The man who is dealing with these matters is Mr Lutterberg. He worked on the cases of Löwenberger & Scheuer [the Grünebaums' former landlord], Kambergs, etc. All these people have already had payouts.

In fact, although Stein had been the person with whom she first dealt, it was Lutterberg who became her main contact and it was Stein's partner, Otto Schaaf, who signed the correspondence sent to the various authorities.

Seated in their offices, she went yet again through the details of what had happened to her and her parents. It must have been increasingly traumatic, with each repetition feeling like revictimisation. In early May 1959 three applications were

---

[299] Otto Stein became a highly respected figure in Offenbach. Having opposed the Nazis before the war, he conscientiously represented many Jewish claimants seeking compensation in the post-war period and served as the town's mayor for two years.

submitted to the *Entschädigungsbehörde* in Darmstadt, one for each person. Set against the unimaginable horror of their experiences, the details seem understated and clinical. For Sophie and Friedrich, the claim was for limitation of liberty as a result of being forced to wear the Jewish star and then loss of liberty through deportation and death. Additionally, compensation for occupational damages was claimed for Friedrich. Khadija's claim was also for occupational losses and emigration expenses. In his accompanying letter, the lawyer requested that, as so much time had elapsed and she no longer could remember how much had been spent, the authority should estimate the costs of one large trunk, two suitcases and a second-class fare to London. This seems to have reduced the enormity of what had occurred to some trivial shopping and a rail journey. However, a postscript in a later letter to Lutterberg provided a rare insight into how what had happened to her and her family had affected her mental health:

> *5 July 1959* P.S. I must tell you that my income from the end of 1943 was very low. My health at that time was very bad. I was extremely worried about my dear parents and often was not in a state to work. (T)

The claim forms contained only basic information and they needed to be supplemented by supporting detail and documents, which the lawyers now started to collect. For the claims relating to loss of liberty, the authorities required proof that Friedrich and Sophie had in fact been deported and murdered. The lawyers therefore had to apply for certificates to confirm this from the International Tracing Service (ITS) at Bad Arolsen.

Evidence was also required of Friedrich's employment and earnings. The lawyers learned that he had closed his butcher's shop before the Nazis came to power and was self-employed from 1933. At Khadija's suggestion, they contacted Herr Hellwig (the Grünebaums' former landlord) who explained that he had given Friedrich a few odd jobs as a favour, but that this had not amounted to employment and payment had been more at the level of a tip than a wage. Without evidence of him having been forced out of employment and a consequent reduction in income, the lawyers concluded that there was no possibility of an award for occupational losses succeeding and that particular claim was withdrawn.

With regard to Khadija's own claim, the authority wanted proof of her earnings after she had emigrated. So, on returning to London from Offenbach, she obtained statements from Diana Oldcorn covering her work as a mother's help and from Cumberland Hotels covering her employment in J Lyons, which she sent to Lutterberg in July 1959. She did not substantiate any earnings in Pakistan and (incorrectly) informed him that she had not worked after getting married. She could not have foreseen that her failure to mention any income from those periods, which she probably omitted because it amounted to very little and was largely undocumented, would in time prove to be highly problematical.

Six more months elapsed during which Khadija heard nothing from either the lawyers or the *Entschädigungsbehörde*. So she wrote to Lutterberg again, asking why there had been no news and pleading for at least an interim payment:

> *12 January 1960* I am very astonished that I have not heard from you for so long. I sent the papers you requested on 3 July 1959. But you did not confirm their receipt.
>
> ... This matter has now been ongoing for over a year and it looks as if nothing has been done. I have heard from acquaintances the same age as me that they have all received some payment, if not everything.

As you know, I have two children and my financial situation is not good. I could really use the money to give my children a good education. Mostly it is money for having to wear the Jewish star that has been paid. Perhaps you could try to get the same for me. (T)

The delay was caused by the lack of any response from ITS, which was dealing with a huge number of enquiries, and the reply, when it did arrive in December 1959, was not at all helpful. Although there was plenty of proof that Friedrich and Sophie had been transported, initially to Theresienstadt and then to Auschwitz, there was nothing to show that they had died there. The ITS was therefore unwilling to issue death certificates![300]

Sympathetically, her solicitor wrote to the *Entschädigungsbehörde* a few days later to ask that the claims be given priority status because their client was in straitened circumstances. No further requests were made for death certificates but the response was for yet more information. How much did Khadija earn each month when she worked at Alligator? Did she continue her career after getting married? If so, could she provide payslips for that work? She provided Stein with the answers, but in her reply again highlighted the seriousness of her situation:

8 February 1960 Additionally, I would like to inform you that I have taken a loan from my bank. It is for £200 which I now need to pay back. I am finding things very difficult at the moment as this is not the only debt that I have. Please let the relevant authority know this, and if you need a letter to confirm it, I can send you one. I hope you can help me and that I can get the money as quickly as possible.

---

[300] Document 6.3.3.2./89590143/ITS Digital Archive, Arolsen Archives.

Finally, on 9 February 1960 the authority decided on the claims relating to Sophie and Friedrich. For each of them Khadija was awarded compensation of DM6,450. Uncharacteristically for German administrators, the official documents spelt the names of both Khadija and her mother incorrectly.

Decision of the *Entschädigungsbehörde* to award Khadija DM6450 compensation for her mother's loss of liberty (first page only shown)

She was assured the money would be received within a month but not until seven weeks later, on 31 March, was the sum of £1,024 17s 5d credited to her Barclays Bank account in London, DM1,081.60 having been deducted to pay legal fees and expenses and £1 5s 8d for the bank's commission.

Khadija's own claim, though, was still a long way from being settled. The authority was suspicious of the amount she told them she had been paid at Alligator, considering RM458 per month extremely high for someone so young and inexperienced. They wanted proof of her earnings, such as payslips or independent corroboration. Unsurprisingly, payslips were not amongst the items she packed for her escape to England and her reference from the firm did not mention her salary. So she was unable to provide either and instead had again to submit an affidavit, this time witnessed at the German Consulate. At the same time, she wrote and explained that her salary was relatively high because she managed the Despatch and Costing Department alone, a responsible position for someone newly qualified. Moreover, she added, the business owners were close friends of her parents and they knew what hardship the family was experiencing. That, though, proved to be an unfortunate admission, which may have helped to explain the level of her remuneration, but would shortly have serious adverse consequences.

Issues relating to her entitlement to a state pension then arose. Enquiries were made with the relevant government department in Berlin to ascertain what insurance contributions she had made during her employment. There were records of 24 monthly payments between 1935 and 1937. These were Class A contributions, suggesting a monthly salary of RM50, consistent with what she would have received as an apprentice. But there were no records for the 21 months that followed. As a victim of persecution, she would receive some contribution credits, but to qualify for an invalidity pension required 60 contributions, while 180 were needed for a pension at age 60. Without the necessary number, she would only qualify for benefits if she made additional payments. Lutterberg repeatedly urged Khadija to find other ways to confirm her salary and her insurance contributions. Probably realising the potentially serious implications of not submitting such documents, he also asked the *Entschädigungsbehörde* to credit her account for the missing months, arguing that there was plenty of evidence to show that the government department's records were incomplete and unreliable. Although that probably happened, faced with the option of making unaffordable additional contributions, she decided not to pursue further her pension rights, in the hope that this would bring her case to a speedier conclusion.

On 7 June 1960 a decision was finally made. She was awarded DM5,684 compensation for 'damage to her professional advancement', essentially loss of earnings. The calculations made to reach this figure were based on two significant judgements. First, it was concluded that the salary she claimed to have received was far too high for her age and the nature of the job. The Offenbach Chamber of Commerce and Trade had confirmed that the highest paid worker in the leather industry would only have received RM420 per month. Without any insurance contributions or other corroboration, it was determined that the correct salary could not have exceeded RM250. In later correspondence, Lutterberg informed her that the authority believed her actual remuneration was inflated to include a hidden payment to her parents. Second, compensation was only for the period from 1 January 1939, the day after Khadija was made redundant by Alligator, until 16 April 1948, the date of her wedding in Pakistan. No consideration was given to later years because Khadija had indicated that she had stopped work and no evidence had been produced of her husband's earnings. This led to the conclusion that his means of livelihood had provided her with an adequate and sustainable existence.

The final figure was clinically determined by formulae set out in legislation. Khadija was entitled to 75% of her presumed Alligator remuneration plus 20% for lost pension contributions over 9 years and 3 months. This totalled RM28,416 which, converted at the rate of 5:1, totalled DM5,684. After deduction of DM447.20 for legal fees and expenses and DM9.40 for bank charges, the sum of DM5,227.40 was remitted on 18 July 1960 from Offenbach to her Barclays Bank account. In sterling she received £450. This though was still far from being the end of the matter.

Khadija was undoubtedly upset and probably angry with the outcome. Perhaps it brought home to her for the first time how, as far as compensation was concerned, the suffering she had endured and its lifelong consequences were reduced to a simple financial calculation of lost income. Her reaction was understandable. Even within that framework, no allowance was made for career progression or inflation. No consideration had been given to how the trauma she had experienced had affected her ability to work, nor had any award been made to cover her emigration expenses. And, of course, the assumption about the household income and her quality of life after marriage were totally erroneous. She probably now also realised how her failure to mention any earnings in Pakistan and after her return to London had significantly reduced the compensation she was given.

When Lutterberg communicated the decision to her, he too seemed incensed with the findings. He asked her again about her Alligator salary and whether her husband's livelihood really had provided an adequate and sustainable existence such that she did not need to work, as the authority had assumed. Citing case law, he raised the possibility of taking legal action to get her case reopened and applying for a *Lebensrente*, a continuing payment that could be awarded if a marriage brought a woman into a relationship in which it was not usual for her to continue her profession.

Khadija replied to Lutterberg, strenuously denying that her Alligator salary had been inflated, although recognising that probably nothing could be done to challenge the ruling on this. But she did now detail the work that she and Afzal had done in Pakistan, explaining that they did not earn enough to survive there and had had to return to London, where he had been employed in low-paid jobs and she had stopped work after their first child was born. A small number of supporting documents was enclosed with the letter and she subsequently obtained verification of Afzal's employment from the Pakistan 'Embassy' in London.[301] She urged Lutterberg to see if, with all the information she had now provided, he could secure for her a *Lebensrente*, although in the same paragraph she admitted she did not know what that was and asked him to explain.

There followed a flurry of exchanges. Khadija completed an application for a *Lebensrente*. The solicitor submitted to the *Entschädigungsbehörde* a strongly worded appeal, which was both factually detailed and highly emotional. He pointed out that the decision had been based on a lack of evidence of Afzal's earnings, when the wording on the application form did not even make it clear that such evidence was needed. He further argued that it was incorrect to conclude that, because the relevant government department could not substantiate payment of insurance contributions, they had not been made:

> *29 June 1960* In the past, stamps were glued [on insurance cards]. The completed cards went to the

---

[301] Although Khadija referred to the 'Embassy', since 1948 it had been the High Commission.

insurance offices or the representatives of the Federal Insurance Office, who issued the policyholder with a certificate. Now, who believes that, before they fled abroad, Jews would have handed in their partly completed cards, perhaps because they were convinced that the empire which it was proclaimed would last for a thousand years would actually only last for 12 years and that all the injustices would later be put right? The insurance cards had the same fate as all other papers, they were ignored and somehow lost.

Finally, in employment law there was contractual freedom. Is it surprising if a persecuted company paid its loyal and efficient employees a wage that was above the tariff level? (T)

He bluntly told the officials that their reasoning and their decision were both wrong and could be challenged with regard to their classification of Khadija's salary grade and the period for which compensation had been awarded. He closed the letter by threatening legal action if they did not review her case and make a further financial award.

He was partially successful. Within ten days he was told that the authority would consider extending the compensation period. However, with regard to the calculations based on Khadija's salary grade and later financial circumstances, further information was needed. In anticipation of this, Lutterberg had already written to people with links to Alligator, including Joseph Weil in New York, who had appointed her in 1935. However, none was able to confirm her salary. He had also asked Khadija for more specific details about their earnings, especially while in Pakistan:

30 June 1960 I cannot do anything with descriptions of activities. I need income figures and, if these are in a foreign currency, what these mean in purchasing power and, at the very least, exchange rates. (T)

Even though she had pointed out that 12 years had passed since they had been in Pakistan and that the administrative systems in that newly created state were not good, he nevertheless now asked her to write to Afzal's former employers or government tax offices there to get independent corroboration of his income from 1 January 1948. This, he emphasised, needed to be done urgently, using airmail if necessary, because there was a time limit on appeals.

A couple of weeks later, on 27 July 1960, he wrote again, this time to ask that she prepare for herself and Afzal separate listings showing their employers, dates of employment and payments received from 17 April 1948, and to make clear which of the supporting documents she had provided related to each listed activity. Additionally, he needed all the supporting documents to be translated into German and the original plus two copies of everything sent to him. It was seemingly a task that overwhelmed her. In early August, clearly irritated, he wrote again:

> *10 August 1960* With regard to work, I now have English and Pakistani employment certificates for your husband. You haven't given me an exact translation. I will do it myself!
>
> For you, I only have your appointment [letter] as a stewardess with Pak Air Ltd with terms and conditions. You haven't told me from when to when. I need a document!
>
> The attachments cannot be used by German authorities, since they are not originals or officially certified translations. They are also wrong because one does not earn DM abroad.

Please confirm the dates of your employment with Pak Air. This is urgent because there is a legal deadline. (T)

On 17 November 1960 the authority made a new decision on her claim. The previous judgement was quashed, but the ruling on her salary grade remained unchanged. More positively, it recognised that until 1954 her husband had an income below the level considered sustainable and the compensation period was extended to 31 December 1953. Using a similar formula to that applied previously, but with an allowance for career development and covering a period of 15 instead of 9¼ years, the total compensation awarded increased to DM16,258, DM10,574 higher than the previous figure. She also learned that a claim for her emigration expenses would be paid. There was other good news too. Lutterberg also assured her that, with the compensation period having been extended, she would receive enough insurance credits to qualify for a state pension at the age of 60 years.

Der Regierungspräsident in Darmstadt
I/1o (f) - 3 w 02
Reg.Nr. D/34119/21 (A) -Hus.

Darmstadt, den 17. November 1960

xxxxxx 81 Nbst. 695

Festsetzungsbescheid W 7798

In der Entschädigungssache
der Frau

   Khadija H u s a i n geb. Gruenebaum,

   geb. am 12.5.1921 in Offenbach/Main,

   wohnhaft: 6o College Road Isleworth/England,

Bevollmächtigte: Rechtsanwälte Dr. Otto Stein, Horst Schaaf und
   Dr. Gerhard Körner, Offenbach/Main, Kaiserstr. 51,

ergeht auf den Antrag vom 13.3.1958 aufgrund des Bundesgesetzes zur Entschädi-
gung für Opfer der nationalsozialistischen Verfolgung (BEG) vom 29.6.1956 (BGBl.I
S. 559) in Verbindung mit der 3. Verordnung zur Durchführung des BEG (3.DV-BEG)
vom 2o.3.1957 (BGBl. I S. 269 ff) in der Fassung der Verordnung zur Änderung der
Ersten, Zweiten und Dritten Verordnung zur Durchführung des BEG vom 16.12.1958
(BGBl. I S. 941 ff) und der 2. Verordnung zur Änderung der Ersten, Zweiten und
Dritten Verordnung zur Durchführung des BEG vom 25.2.1960 (BGBl. I S. 13o ff)
folgender Bescheid:

1. Der Festsetzungsbescheid W 74o3 vom 7.6.196o wird aufgehoben.

2. Die Antragstellerin hat wegen ihres Schadens im beruflichen Fortkommen nach
 §§ 64, 75 ff und 92 BEG Anspruch auf eine Kapitalentschädigung in Höhe von

     16.258,-- DM

 in Worten: "Sechzehntausendzweihundertachtundfünfzig Deutsche Mark".

3. Auf diesen Anspruch ist der für Schaden im beruflichen Fortkommen bereits zu-
 erkannte und gezahlte Betrag von 5.684,-- DM anzurechnen, so daß ein Betrag von

     1o.574,-- DM

 in Worten: "Zehntausendfünfhundertvierundsiebzig Deutsche Mark"
 zur Auszahlung verbleibt.

4. Die Rückforderung noch nicht verrechneter Vorschüsse bleibt vorbehalten.

5. Die Entscheidung ergeht gebührenfrei. Die der Antragstellerin entstandenen
 Kosten und Auslagen werden nicht erstattet.

Extract from the final decision of the *Entschädigungsbehörde*
on Khadija's compensation claim

At the end of November, Lutterberg wrote to ask whether she
wanted to challenge again the decision made on her salary grade,
while expressing doubt that it would succeed for the reasons
already given. She concluded that it would not be worthwhile.

He also advised her that the money awarded would be released in four weeks but, once again, the payment forecast proved to be over-optimistic. It was not until 21 February 1961 that Barclays Bank confirmed that the money was in her account. After deduction of DM1,164.80 for legal fees and expenses, as well as DM14 for bank charges, a total of DM9,395.20 was received and £808 18s 6d credited to Khadija's bank balance.

The *Entschädigungsbehörde* still needed details of her emigration expenses but, since she could not provide receipts or precise costs, asked for a description of her luggage items, as well as their weight and contents. Also needed was information about her route to London and her mode of travel. In providing this, she explained that she had been forced off the train in Aachen and robbed. However, she was told that without supporting evidence or a sworn statement listing her losses, plus definite information as to whether or not she was inside the German border and whether or not the thieves were employed by the state, a claim for her losses would fail. Unsurprisingly, she decided that this too was not worth continuing. Whether she ever received payment of her emigration expenses remains unknown.

That might seem to have brought all the matters to some sort of conclusion. However, in October 1961, nearly a year after the decision on her case had been made, Khadija received a package of papers from Lutterberg relating to her social insurance. It included receipts and certificates showing her contributions, which she would need to produce when ready to draw her pension. However, he pointed out that it only showed 177 payments and credits, not the 180 that he had assured her would be included and which were needed for pension qualification. Without offering any explanation for this, he urged her to urgently get in touch with the relevant federal office to find out about the three missing contributions.

Certificate from the Federal Insurance Agency showing the periods for which
Khadija received insurance credits (16 April 1938 to 31 December 1949)

Whether or not she did as advised is not at all clear. The
next surviving correspondence is dated 1976, 15 years after she
received that last letter from Lutterberg, and it seems that her
position then was still unresolved. It is possible that, with two
young children and with Afzal becoming increasingly unwell,
she had been fully occupied as a homemaker, mother and
breadwinner. Corresponding with remote bureaucrats about a
pension that seemed almost unattainable could not have been a
priority. It was only after he died in 1976, and as her own pension
age was approaching, that she resumed correspondence with the
Bundesversicherungsanstalt (Federal Insurance Agency). However,
over the following 12 months all she received were more forms to
fill in and requests to resend certificates and papers relating to the
decision of the *Entschädigungsbehörde* because these had been lost.
By that time her cancer had been diagnosed and she again had

more urgent matters to attend to.

At the beginning of the compensation story, I wrote that the process was protracted, complex and bureaucratic, requiring multiple applications and overcoming numerous obstacles, and that has been amply demonstrated. At the end of it all, Khadija had received the equivalent of £379 for her share of her aunt and uncle's home, £339 for her family's possessions, £1,025 for the loss of her parents' freedom and lives, and £1,259 for her own lost income. A total of £3,002. She probably still did not know whether or not she qualified for a state pension. However, even if she had secured the necessary credits, it would have been to no avail. Sadly, she would not live long enough to benefit from that success, passing away two years before her 60th birthday.

The Family Reunion

Pursuing the compensation owed to her was one of main reasons why Khadija made the long-delayed return to Germany in 1959. The other, equally important, was to see again the few surviving family members who still lived there. Without doubt it was an extremely emotional journey with the joyful anticipation of a reunion with relatives tempered by the memory of all that had caused her to leave, and by learning only a few days before her departure that her Uncle Friedrich had died the previous year. Ludo Reusch met us at Frankfurt Station and put us on a train to Mittelsinn, where Khadija was finally reunited with his mother, her cousin Greta, the one person with whom she had been in continuous contact since the war had ended. Year after year they had hoped that such a visit would be possible, but were repeatedly disappointed. Now, it finally happened.

On arrival Khadija immediately sent a telegram to Afzal to let him know that we had got there safely. She was concerned about him being on his own, since he was unwell with flu and weakened further by fasting during the month of Ramadan. He replied to her the same day and his words show how aware he was of what a momentous day it was for his wife:

> *1 April 1959* Received your most awaited telegram at 10.30 this morning. I felt very much relieved and felt happy too thinking that today you are really back in Germany. I wish I was with you to share the joys and the sorrows too of course. If only your parents could have been alive today, what a joy it would have been to see you and with, bless them, Sohail and Marium Bibi. However, this was fate. Fate is nothing but the will of God. No one knows in advance, nor one can alter it.

Over the following weeks, communication between them was a mirror image of what happened when he was away in Pakistan and she was left in London. Correspondence was exchanged on an almost daily basis. In the month after Khadija reached Germany, Afzal wrote to her on 15 occasions, often long letters with up to nine pages, while she sent a similar number to him. He sometimes added separate notes for my sister and me. It required considerable commitment on his part, coming home late from the market to cook a meal and break his fast, reading from the Qur'an, then continuing to write until well past midnight before getting up in the early hours for prayers and a meal before sunrise. He repeatedly wrote how much he was missing us all, how much he was thinking about us, and of his longing to find a letter from us when he came home in the evening. It was further testament of how close my parents were and how his affection for Khadija was undiminished. And as before, he used all available space on each page to tell us this, turning the paper upside down and sideways to fill the margins once the usual areas were covered. But unlike the flimsy aerogrammes sent from Pakistan, most of these letters were written on the double pages pulled out of a school exercise book, which were much cheaper than writing paper!

Greta and her husband Michel accommodated us in their house and a fortnight was spent getting to know each other, meeting other family members, visiting the local cemetery and discussing the compensation claims. They also retrieved some of Sophie and Friedrich's possessions, which had been secreted in the attic for almost 20 years, one of them almost certainly being the rent book for their flat at Luisenstrasse 69.

Although the visit was overshadowed by sombre and serious matters, my sister Marium and I had little awareness of this. She was just four and I was eight years old, and for us this visit was simply a holiday, the first we had ever had. And having only known London before, it was an incredible adventure into a totally unfamiliar world. Mittelsinn was a small village in a largely rural area. Across the unmade road in front of the house, the small River Sinn flowed through lush green meadows. We watched cows being milked, collected eggs from the hens, paddled in the cold water and played with the village children, who were curious about the visitors from England. The lack of a common language was no barrier and I soon learned my first few words of German. Within a few days I was wearing *Lederhosen* (leather trousers) and before we left, I had learned to ride a two-wheeler bike.

We all enjoyed and benefitted from the stay in Mittelsinn. There was a lot of comment in the correspondence about how relaxed and rested Khadija felt, how well we all looked and how much our health had improved since leaving London, and discussion about whether it was breathing the clean air, drinking the mineral water or eating the rustic bread that was responsible. After two weeks, though, it was time for Khadija to relocate to Offenbach where she could speak directly to the people dealing with her compensation claim. There she was able to stay with two other cousins, Friedericka ('Friedel') and Regina ('Rina'), who still lived in the flat where they had grown up at 18 Faltorstrasse, Bürgel. Khadija had had little contact with them since leaving Germany, but they welcomed her warmly and Friedel was the one German relative with whom she stayed in close touch in subsequent years.

Marium went with her to Offenbach. I, however, went to stay with Greta and Michel's son, Edgar. It was the first time I had been away alone and it was the highlight of my holiday. As already mentioned, Edgar was a forester, but he was also a hunter; and in the evenings we would go out together into the woods, climbing up into a hide - he carrying his gun. There we sat silent until darkness fell, waiting for deer and wild boar to appear. They never did, but I can still remember the excitement of sitting high up in a tree in anticipation. My father, who was an inveterate worrier, fretted constantly that I would be lonely. In reality, I could not have been happier. However, my stay with Edgar lasted just one week, after which I joined the others in Offenbach.

Much of Khadija's time in the town was spent dealing with solicitors and officialdom. But one of the first things she did was go to Luisenstrasse and stand outside the building that had once been her family home. She met several people there who had known Friedrich and Sophie, and we all went to the Old Jewish Cemetery in Bürgel, where her grandparents' gravestones were still standing, but where many others had been removed or desecrated. Understandably, it was all traumatic and upsetting, and she wrote to tell Afzal about it. His reply shows how deep an impact it had on them both:

> *16 April 1959* While reading this morning's letter I couldn't hold my tears. The whole thing overcame me. I cannot forgive myself for not being with you, particularly at these stages that you are going through

> now in Offenbach. How I wish I were beside you when
> you visited your dear parents (bless their souls) house
> and met neighbours and your parents old friends. I
> should have been there to share your tears.

On a lighter note, there was time for some shopping. Khadija had soon come to the conclusion that the standard of living in Germany was higher than in the UK, the cost of living was lower and the availability and quality of consumer goods was better. So she spent some of her compensation money on things to take back home, including a down quilt, a watch, an Adler typewriter, bath tablets, some clothes, and silver cutlery for both children, engraved with our initials. Afzal put in an order for an alarm clock with an illuminated dial and another friend in England requested a camera. It seems a fairly random and bulky collection of items to take back on the train.

Never one to let a potential business opportunity pass by, Afzal also tasked Khadija with investigating the possibilities in Germany. He got her to discuss becoming a Neeb und Kühn agent with Greta's brother, Wilhelm Kühn, so that he could resell the bag, purse and case fasteners manufactured in the Obersinn factory. He encouraged her to seek out jewellery makers and send samples of their lines to him for market testing. And he sent a parcel of Indian 'spiral bracelets' – their most popular market offering – to Germany, for Khadija to assess demand for them there. He was being characteristically entrepreneurial, but had no capital to invest and so his ambition was limited by realism. It could only ever have started on a very small scale but, on top of this, Khadija did not have the time, inclination or skills to take it forward. She wrote and told him of the difficulties and little more happened. His whole life, Afzal was on the lookout for a successful venture that would turn his life around, and optimistic about his prospects of doing it, but despite his many ideas and attempts, he would never achieve that goal.

It was expected that Khadija would spend 3–4 weeks in Germany. The trip had begun immediately after Easter in the school holidays, but our return would be after the start of the summer term. This was not a particular concern to my parents or my head teacher, but Afzal was keen that I continue to study while we were away, and insistent that I learn to speak German and find a pen friend with whom I could continue to correspond once back home. He was therefore somewhat annoyed to learn that I was not making much of an effort to do this:

> *10 April 1959* [For] Sohail not to pick up language is
> sheer laziness like me. But I don't want him to follow
> my bad things. Never! He must try and learn some of
> it. It's nice to know other language.

It took a long time to get there, but I am sure he would have been pleased to know that years later I did learn to speak German, formed friendships with German students that have endured for more than half a century and found it invaluable throughout my career to be able to speak the language.

For financial reasons, Khadija made the trip to Germany without her husband. Afzal stayed behind because they could not afford to forgo their meagre income for several weeks. Additionally, he did not have a British passport. However, they had hoped he might be able to earn or borrow money that would enable him to join the rest of the family towards the end of their stay. With this in mind, immediately after Easter he too completed the forms to register as a British citizen in order to apply for a passport. But it proved to be a protracted and very frustrating process, first requiring a sworn affidavit, then the deletion of Khadija's details from his Pakistani passport, after which officials mislaid his citizenship papers, before noticing that details in his old passport were obviously inaccurate. Despite many visits to the Home and Passport Offices, all these obstacles held up the issue of a new passport and it became increasingly unlikely that he would be able to make the trip. So having completed her business and longing to return home, Khadija made arrangements to leave Offenbach on Sunday 3 May.

However, a couple of days before her departure, he finally received news that his citizenship had been registered and, optimistic about getting a passport quickly, he sent a telegram asking Khadija to cancel her booking. There were more delays before he received his documents, but a week later they were eventually reunited. They stayed together in Germany for another week, so Afzal was able to meet the family in Offenbach and Mittelsinn, and he clearly met with their approval. On their return to London, Greta wrote 'Afzal is really such a quiet and good man, of whom you can be proud'. (T)[302]

There is one sad postscript to add to this account of Khadija's return to the country of her birth and it concerns Greta Reusch, with whom Khadija had formed such a close relationship. They had sustained each other after the war, with Greta providing a link to the family and Khadija, with help from Afzal, providing food and clothing when the German economy was in ruins. However, after Khadija returned to London, that relationship came to an end when a vicious dispute erupted over the ownership of two gold coins that had once belonged to Sophie and Friedrich. In October an enraged Greta wrote a blistering riposte to Khadija in which she made it very clear that she never wanted to hear from her cousin again. After being so close over the 20 years they had spent apart, their coming together had ultimately caused bitter division. They never spoke or wrote to each other again.

---

[302] Letter from Greta Reusch to Khadija, 21 June 1959.

A Dream Fulfilled

Through perseverance, determination and forcefulness, Khadija managed to push forward her compensation claims during her visit to Germany. Admittedly, when the family arrived back in London on Thursday 14 May 1959, she had still only received £400. Nevertheless, this seemingly small sum and the expectation that more would follow was life-changing, for it gave Khadija and Afzal the confidence and means to buy a house, something that they had always aspired to do, but which until then had been out of the question. In fact, Afzal made contact with estate agents even before he went to Germany, and by late August they had found their new home, an early twentieth-century terraced house in Isleworth, 10 miles west of the city centre. Since they had no car at the time, the location was strongly influenced by public transport and from here the 657 trolleybuses went direct to Goldhawk Road Station, just a few steps away from the entrance to Shepherds Bush Market.

Number 60 College Road was a large dwelling and this was reflected in its freehold price of £3,250. A holding deposit of £100 was paid to the estate agent and an application for a local authority mortgage submitted to Heston and Isleworth Borough Council, together with a cheque for £5 14s, the fee for a valuation survey. Less than two weeks later they received the offer of a loan of £2,520, repayable over 25 years at a fixed interest rate of 6% in monthly instalments of £16 6s 6d. This offer was £125 less than they had applied for and the estate agent queried whether they would still be able to go ahead with the purchase. But this they confirmed and appointed a solicitor to carry out searches and agree a contract, which he estimated would cost no more than £77.

S H E L L E Y S

F. A. L. P. A.

AUCTIONEERS, SURVEYORS
HOUSE, LAND & ESTATE AGENTS

STATION YARD, ISLEWORTH   *and at*   STATION APPROACH, TWICKENHAM,

Telephone : ISLEWORTH 2321-2322   Telephone : POPESGROVE 1667-6800

No.60   COLLEGE ROAD, ISLEWORTH.

IDEAL FAMILY HOUSE IN THIS POPULAR RESIDENTIAL POSITION.
The property has been modernised, redecorated throughout and
is in really first class condition.

THE SPACIOUS ACCOMMODATION COMPRISES:-

First Floor

BEDROOM 1.   16' x 12' with large bay window, fitted open fireplace
             3 Electric points. Gas point.

BEDROOM 2.   12' x 11' 3 Electric points.

BEDROOM 3.   8' 9" x 8' 9" extending to 12' 6" Electric point.

BEDROOM 4.   7' 9" x 7' 9".

BATHROOM   Fitted panelled bath. Pedestal wash basin. W.C.
             Ascot multi-point heater.

Ground Floor

SPACIOUS ENTRANCE HALL.

LOUNGE.   16' x 13'. Fitted modern tiled fireplace. Gas & Electric
             points.

DINING ROOM. 12' x 11' 6". Electric points. Door to Garden.

BREAKFAST ROOM.   12' 6" x 9'. Electric points.

KITCHEN.   Fitted sink unit. Kitchen Cabinet. Gas & Electric.

INSIDE W.C.

REAR GARDEN WITH BACK ENTRANCE, suitable Garage Space for small car.
GARDEN SHED.

PRICE: £3,250   FREEHOLD

View strictly by appointment through Shelleys Isleworth Off:

The above particulars are supplied ... through ... Messrs. SHELLEY'S. Any further information, or another List, gladly supplied on request.

Estate agent's particulars of 60 College Road, Isleworth

Stability with Strife

Finally a Home of our Own

Despite their improved economic circumstances, Afzal and Khadija were still very aware that their finances were precarious and they had little money to spare. They chose not to pay for a building survey and sought advice on what they could do to ensure that they would not lose their home if their financial situation deteriorated. The solicitor advised them that shared ownership was the best option because they were each contributing to its costs. However, his words do not seem particularly reassuring, explaining that, if the worst happened, Khadija would remain the owner of half the property:

> *25 September 1959* You have asked me to advise how the house can be protected from any creditors whom Mr Husain might have in the future. I advise as follows:-
>
> 1. Mrs Husain should own a half share of the house, because she is bringing in about £750 towards the original cost of purchase.
> 2. Mr Husain should own the other half share of the house because he will have to pay the rates, the cost of repairs and the instalments to the Council, since I understand that Mrs Husain has no separate income.
> 3. There is no prospect of that arrangement ever being upset on a bankruptcy if Mr Husain ever

becomes insolvent. His half share could be taken
by his creditors but not the half share belonging
to Mrs Husain.

After the inevitable delays, contracts were finally exchanged
and the Husain family moved in on Friday 27 November 1959.
If Khadija had looked up as she went through the front door, she
would have seen the name of the house etched in the stained glass
toplight. It was called 'Hill 60' after an area of higher ground near
Ypres (Belgium) where there had been ferocious fighting through
much of WW1. Presumably, it had some connection with the
original owner's family, but it was not so far from where her own
father, Friedrich, had himself become embroiled in that same
bloody conflict.

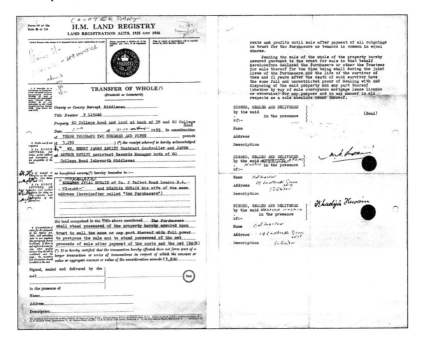

Land Registry record of the transfer of 60 College Road, Isleworth
to Khadija and Afzal, November 1959

Having got the house, they now needed to furnish it. A few items were bought from the previous owners, paying £26 5s for the royal blue stair carpet, three chairs, a tea trolley, chandeliers and curtains. But their main acquisitions came from Bush Furnishers, a second-hand shop on Shepherds Bush Green, where they spent £60 on wardrobes, tables, bedsteads and a chest of drawers, most of which were made from solid mahogany and extremely heavy.

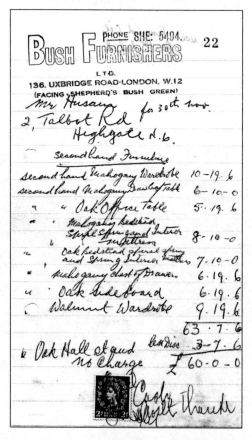

Receipt for furniture bought second-hand from Bush Furnishers

Their happiness and relief at being able to move out of the cramped, rundown, unhygienic and rented Highgate flat, where facilities were shared with other tenants, into their own spacious home was unbounded. With four rooms upstairs, they could give my sister and me our own rooms and still have space for a guest. Downstairs there were another three rooms, a second WC and even a telephone! Outside, the small back garden had flower beds, fruit trees and an area of grass for play. Of course, there was no central heating and, although paraffin heaters were lit in the bathroom and a few of the other rooms, warming such a large house with its high ceilings and no insulation during those first cold winter months was almost impossible. It would also have been peaceful and quiet, had it not been immediately below one of the two main flightpaths into Heathrow Airport, which meant that the deafening roar of Comets, Boeing 707s and other early passenger jets punctuated normal life every few minutes for much of the day.

Having their own property enabled Khadija and Afzal to create a stable family home, which in many ways was no different from others in the area, almost all of which were occupied by households of English origin. But in some respects, it was very different. Although Khadija seemingly had little interest in religion, Afzal was a devout Muslim and became increasingly pious as he grew older. He would pray five times daily, even when working in the market, where he would perform midday and afternoon prayers inside the hut, and on Fridays he would escape for a couple of hours to join the congregation at Regent's Lodge, the Islamic Cultural Centre near Regents Park, which also functioned as a mosque. He read the Qur'an regularly, fasted during Ramadan and never swore or used profanities. He would only eat halal or kosher meat, and never touched pork or alcohol.

He also tried his best to inculcate Islamic beliefs and practices into the lives of his children. At home we were taught the *Kalma*, encouraged us to say *'Bismillah'* before meals and learned why he wrote *'786'* at the start of most correspondence.[303] On the few occasions we were apart, he reminded us to do these things in his letters, which were always peppered with 'please God', 'by the grace of Allah' and exhortations asking for His blessing. He desperately wanted us to be able to read the Qur'an ourselves and for a while took us to Regent's Lodge on Sunday mornings for Arabic lessons. We would also go there as a family to celebrate the festival of Eid al-Fitr at the end of Ramadan.

Afzal, Khadija and Marium at Regent's Lodge, the Islamic Cultural Centre, for the Eid al-Fitr celebration, March 1962

---

[303] The *Kalma* is the Islamic declaration of faith. *Bismillah* means 'in the name of Allah'. The letters of the opening phrase of the Qur'an (*'Bismillah ir-Rahman ir-Rahim'*) have numerical values which, when added together, total 786, which is widely used to represent these words.

It was, however, an uphill struggle and, although he never gave up trying, his efforts fell on stony ground. I took little interest in Islam and was particularly resistant to giving up weekend time to learn a language for which I could see no use. Only much later did I realise what an amazing opportunity I had turned down. In fact, the only time I was enthusiastic about going to the mosque was on 13 May 1966. It was the day when the world heavyweight boxing champion and one of the most famous people on the planet, Muhammad Ali, was going to be there. But unfortunately, it was a school day and I wasn't allowed to go. Afzal, however, met the great man and asked him to sign my autograph book, which he willingly did – three times! A week later Ali fought Henry Cooper at Arsenal's Highbury Stadium and beat him for the second time.

Autograph of Muhammad Ali signed on his visit
to Regent's Lodge, 13 May 1966

Our family was also very different in another respect. That was in the food we ate. Although the weekly menu included traditional English meals, especially Sunday roasts, Khadija and Afzal each brought to the table culinary favourites from their homelands. Typical German dishes, such as *Hackbraten* (meat loaf) and *Hühnersuppe mit Nudeln* (chicken noodle soup), were served up fairly frequently, and ryebread with caraway seed was normally to be found in the breadbin, never the soft sliced white British loaf.

As for Afzal, although he generally left household chores to his wife, that certainly did not apply to cooking. He enjoyed being in the kitchen and was a superb cook when it came to Pakistani food, excelling in making flatbreads (chapatis and parathas), pilau rice, curries and dhals, carrot and vermicelli puddings, buttermilk and *dhai* (yoghurt). Without any recipe books, he would magically combine spices and herbs to produce the most flavoursome dishes, and even grew his own *dhania* (coriander) in the back garden. It was enormously time consuming and labour intensive since many of the dishes required long preparation or cooking times. *Atta* (dough) for flatbreads had to be made several hours before rolling them out, and carrot pudding needed to be on the hob for several days. But the results were delicious. Long before Asian restaurants made such food commonplace, and before many in the indigenous population had even heard of 'lady's fingers' (okra or bhindi) and yoghurt, they were part of our regular diet.

On top of this came special treats: a box of Indian sweets (such as *ladoo* or *halwa*) that a friend had brought back from the sub-continent or, after a visit to Petticoat Lane, an almond ring or cheese cake from Kossoff's, the renowned Jewish bakery in Wentworth Street. On very rare occasions we went out for a meal, perhaps to Bloom's, the most famous kosher restaurant in London, where we might enjoy salt beef, or to Schmidt's in Charlotte Street, renowned for serving the best German food in the capital. These were exceptional events, but all the more memorable because of that.

Khadija and Afzal's social circle also reflected their individual roots. Most of their friends were either business acquaintances from the sub-continent or women who had also escaped Nazi persecution in Austria or Germany. They got on well with indigenous British neighbours, but did not form many close friendships or socialise together. Not that there was much time for such activity. With long working days and the business always open on Saturdays, it was restricted to Sundays and Bank Holidays, and not possible at all during the summer in the years that Afzal was in Paignton. But when the opportunity arose, they would visit friends and sit talking for hours, just as would happen in India and Pakistan.

The demands of the business and financial constraints also meant that a family holiday was out of the question, but having a vehicle did allow Sunday outings to become much more adventurous. If the weather was fine, we would head out to Box Hill or to the south coast for a few hours in the fresh air. The journey was not exactly comfortable when the vehicle was a van with no proper rear seats or windows, but Afzal had had it adapted so that a bench from a railway carriage could be fitted into the back for the day trips, so my sister and I could at least be seated. However, since he often invited the children of friends who lived nearby to join us, there could be seven or eight crammed on to and behind that bench. With hindsight, it now seems incredibly reckless, but it was more than 25 years before wearing rear seat belts became mandatory and relatively little consideration was given to passenger safety.

Afzal, Khadija and Marium on a day trip to Bognor Regis
in the Ford van, May 1962

It was also in this period that Khadija welcomed into her home several young German visitors who were neither family nor Jewish. Given the inhumane treatment meted out by Germans to her and her family, it would have been wholly understandable if she had shunned all such contact. But she was adamant that she did not hate all Germans, and showed a remarkable capacity to distinguish between the Nazis who perpetrated the Holocaust and other Germans who were not culpable, such as a younger generation who were not responsible for the actions of their forefathers. When I opted to start learning German at school, she was happy with that choice and when in 1967 I participated in a student exchange with a school in Mainz, she could not have been more hospitable towards my partner, Reinhold Klüter. When in December 1970 she made her second return trip to Offenbach, to see her cousin Friedel Grünebaum, she went to Mainz and visited the families of those young Germans who had come to visit us.

The 1960s were the happiest years that Khadija and Afzal spent in the UK. However, by the middle of the decade Afzal's health had become a concern. For many years he had suffered from a weak heart and now the symptoms – breathlessness and arrhythmia – became much more worrying. One day when walking home uphill from the bus stop, he suddenly experienced severe chest pains and shortly after was diagnosed with angina. Although not overweight, a non-smoker and teetotal, his high-fat diet was probably a contributory factor to his heart disease.[304] Manual work and anything that was mentally stressful became almost impossible and by 1970 he was experiencing pain even when resting.

A Divided Family Causes Family Division

Afzal had returned to London from Pakistan in March 1950, leaving in Lahore his mother, Vilayet; his first wife Masuda; his teenage daughter, Nusrat; and his infant son, Asif. It would be another 23 years before he returned. Never again would he see his mother, who passed away in January 1959, nor her younger sister, Fatima ('Mama'), who had played such a crucial role in his upbringing. She died just a few months later.

The economic emigration of men from south Asia and their separation from loved ones was nothing new; it had been happening for decades. What was unusual in Afzal's case was that

---

[304] Sandy Gupta, 'South Asian Background and Heart Health', British Heart Foundation, https://www.bhf.org.uk/informationsupport/heart-matters-magazine/medical/south-asian-background.

he returned to Europe with his second wife, Khadija, who was European. But despite this and the geographical distance between them, he saw those left behind and the two of them in London as all being part of a single family, and this was a feeling shared by the relatives in Pakistan. They kept in close contact with him through frequent correspondence and occasionally wrote to Khadija. As was customary, Nusrat addressed her affectionately as 'mummy', treated her as a second mother, and even today she and her brother, Asif, refer to Khadija in this way.

Whether Khadija saw the relationship in the same way is much less clear and she certainly had mixed feelings about some of its consequences. As head of the family, Afzal was responsible for the well-being of all its members and obligated to support them financially, which he did by remitting money from the UK to Pakistan whenever possible. Although the amounts involved were usually small, Khadija felt severely conflicted by this, recognising the need for the cash in Lahore, but unhappy giving away what she and Afzal had worked so hard to earn, which made their life in London even more difficult.

The money he sent was not the only income that those in Lahore received. They also got rent from letting out the ground floor of their Model Town house. But even added together, this was barely enough to live on and for many years they depended on support from other members of the extended family. However, while Khadija was fighting to get compensation for the losses she had suffered in Germany, a parallel process was underway in Pakistan for the loss of the ancestral family home in Amritsar, which had been abandoned at the time of Partition.

A claim was submitted on 14 November 1955 and three years later a court awarded Afzal Rs25,800, equivalent to about £1,900 at that time. It was a significant sum that was collected by Masuda, to whom he had given power of attorney, and provided very welcome financial relief.[305]

Afzal, though, was not content with just supporting those he had left behind financially. He wanted to bring his two children, and especially his young son Asif, to join him in England. In Europe, he was convinced, Asif would be able to get a better education and they would both be able to get better treatment for their albinism, which had impacted their lives so severely. This had long been an aspiration, but it was the prospect of an improvement in their financial circumstances, as a result of having a more stable business base and Khadija receiving compensation in Germany, that seems to have prompted him to try and make this happen. On 20 April 1959, while Khadija was still in Offenbach, he went to see his friend Rahman, who worked for the Travelogue travel agency, and booked a flight for his eldest son to fly from Karachi to London. It didn't matter that he couldn't afford the £68 fare; he put down £8 in cash and arranged to pay the balance by cheque in monthly instalments of £5. In other words, he would be paying for it over the course of a whole year. But so finely balanced were his finances that even this caused financial stress. 'This has naturally made me short on money', he admitted, whilst brushing off the cost as a price worth paying. 'Never mind. It's for a good cause. I shall get over it', he wrote to Khadija.[306]

It was an open ticket with no fixed date for the journey, but Afzal's hope was that Asif would be able to travel in late May, by which time Khadija would be back. And with that date not far away he could hardly contain his excitement, nor let anything get in the way. It was 'like a dream', he wrote. Frantically he started making

---

[305] The house in Amritsar was initially inherited by Miran Bakhsh's two sons. At the time of the compensation award, one son (Nazir) had died and the other (Mohamed Ismail) had disappeared in South America. As a result, Afzal received 50% of the total award, while the other half was shared by Nazir's wife and her children, that is Bashir Ahmad ('Uncle Bashir') and his four sisters. It is unclear why Vilayat (the wife of Mohamed Ismail) did not receive anything.
[306] Letter from Afzal to Khadija, 21 April 1959.

arrangements and, despite having already overstretched financially, did not hesitate to make further spending commitments. He asked Masuda to make plans to accompany Asif to Karachi, where they could stay overnight with relatives, promising to send money to cover their expenses, but advising her to borrow more if it was not enough and assuring her that he would repay it later. He asked a friend with a car to take them to the airport. He spoke to Mr Williams, the head teacher at my primary school in Highgate, to check that Asif could enrol there and get his eyes tested by the school doctor. He got permission from their landlord for Asif to live in their tiny flat. Afzal enthused to Khadija how much he was looking forward to meeting his son at the airport, how they would then need to buy Asif warm clothes, and how happy they would all be once he was living with them in London:

> *21 April 1959* I am sure you and the children will be very happy at the increase in the family. Bless them, Sohail and Asif are only couple of years apart and I'm sure they'll be happy to have each other. And I am sure Asif will be equally happy to see and be with his own little sister too.

Afzal had been discussing his children's relocation with both Masuda and Khadija since long before she went to Germany. Neither seems to have overtly opposed the idea but whether either was actually happy with it is doubtful. It's quite likely that neither thought it would come to fruition. He certainly seems to have been largely oblivious to any concerns they might have had, just as when he proposed to take Khadija as his second wife, and he ploughed ahead with the preparations regardless. For Masuda, though, the prospect of losing her only son so soon after the death of her mother-in-law (who was also her aunt) would probably have been devastating. Afzal did acknowledge that informing her that Asif's passage had been booked would be 'a small shock', but he treated this as a relatively minor consideration.[307] He wrote to reassure her that her son would be well looked after on the flight and well cared for in his new home, and he got Khadija to do the same.

In contrast, Khadija's main concern was about money. Even though she was optimistic about getting compensation, they planned to use it to put down a deposit on a house. Yet Afzal was spending with abandon and seemed not to have considered how they would manage with an extra mouth to feed once Asif was in London. Balancing income with expenditure was certainly not his strong point. He owed various people money, had bought a flight ticket on credit, assured Masuda that he would remit money for her travel expenses and planned to join his wife in Germany. But he had virtually no cash and had to borrow £40–50 from a friend to pay for his fare and some new clothes for that journey.

In the end all the preparations for Asif's visit came to nothing. Masuda became so ill with worry about losing her son that the plan was abandoned and he never made use of his ticket. So Asif completed his education at the English-medium New School in Model Town, after which in 1965 and aged 17 he was taken on by Uncle Bashir as an apprentice. Under his tutelage he learned about every facet of the hand-knotted carpets trade, from their weaving in the homes of rural peasants to their sale in luxury shops abroad. As part of his training, he made multiple road trips to Kabul and in 1967 took his first flight when he went to Hong Kong. As Asif himself recalled, for someone who had never before been in a modern city it was an eye-opening and eventful trip. During an overnight hotel stopover in Bangkok, he had his first experience of a lift and, fascinated by the technology, spent much of his time there travelling up and down in it. Then on arrival in

---

[307] Letter from Afzal to Khadija, 23 April 1959.

Hong Kong the next day he was detained overnight because he had no return ticket and only allowed out of the airport when a local contact agreed to act as guarantor.

In November 1969, more than ten years after the aborted journey to the UK, he did finally make it to London on a complimentary ticket given to Uncle Bashir by Pakistan International Airlines, the main carrier of his exported carpets. There he met his father for the first time since he was less than 18 months old. It was history repeating itself. Just as Afzal had never got to know his father who had gone to South America, so Asif never got to know his until he was 21 years old. But it was not a permanent relocation. He stayed for just three months and then returned to Lahore. Five years later he set up his own company and developed it into a successful business, also exporting carpets around the world. It was a remarkable achievement for someone with severe sight impairment. Apart from having to manage the inevitable paperwork, the essence of hand-knotted carpets is the fineness of their weave and the intricacy of their design, both of which require intense visual examination.

As the years passed, Afzal increasingly felt a longing to make a return trip to Pakistan and in 1973 his wish was finally fulfilled. On Friday 5 January, exactly a quarter of a century after first making the journey from London and now aged 64, he again landed at Karachi Airport before travelling on to Lahore. In some respects, he arrived in a very different country: the carnage and chaos that had followed Partition were in the past. Now, though, the country was emerging from a different territorial division that had also been accompanied by bloody and catastrophic conflict. The 1971 Bangladesh Liberation War had resulted in a humiliating defeat by Bengali militia and Indian forces, as well as the secession of East Pakistan. The Pakistan army stood accused of genocide, torture and mass rape, and almost 100,000 of its soldiers had been taken prisoner. Not until the signing of the Simla Agreement in July 1972 were they released. Few households were untouched by the war and the events were still fresh in their memories when Afzal began his visit.

From his point of view, however, it was a good time to be there. The weeks after Christmas when it was cold and wet in England were a quiet time in Shepherds Bush Market, while the weather in Lahore was much more tolerable than the scorching summer heat. It was arguably his first ever holiday and understandably he planned an extended break. Although no return flight was actually booked, he said that it was his intention to fly back in early April, by which time daytime temperatures would have become unbearable. The following account of his stay is largely based on more than 50 letters that were sent between him in Pakistan and Khadija, Marium and myself in London while he was away.

As in 1948, Afzal received a grand welcome as he was reunited with family and friends. His morning flight from Karachi to Lahore was seriously delayed, and many who came to the airport to greet him were unable to wait. But there were still around 50 people when he arrived in the evening. Over the following days many more came to see him in Model Town. He spent the next few weeks relaxing, sitting in the sunshine and visiting friends. In the mild weather and without the stresses of work, he felt his health improving and his angina attacks became less frequent. Gradually, though, he became more active and in March made a one-week car excursion with his cousin, Uncle Bashir, to the north of the country. After stopping overnight with relatives in Rawalpindi, they drove on to the picturesque district of Swat on the Afghanistan border, renowned for its lush green valleys and views of the Hindu Kush and Himalayan ranges. Unfortunately, it rained heavily for most of the week.

He was inundated with invitations to people's homes and

to social events, including lunches at the prestigious Lahore Gymkhana Club and various wedding receptions. The cooler months are very popular for marriage in Pakistan and celebrations traditionally extend over several days. Families often spent fortunes to make them extravagant occasions that evidenced their wealth and enhanced their social standing. One of the banquets he attended had more than a thousand guests. There was, though, one special wedding in which he took a much closer personal interest. It was the wedding of his son, Asif, to his fiancé, Naila.[308] It had probably been his intention that this should take place while he was there and plans were made for this to happen in early April. It too was a lavish event with several hundred invitees and it was one of the proudest moments of his life. However, it would undoubtedly have drained the family coffers. Afzal had remitted some money to Lahore before he travelled, presumably to help pay for the wedding, but it was not enough and he had to borrow the equivalent of £200 from a friend.

As well as providing the opportunity to see his family again, to relax and to socialise, Afzal's entrepreneurial instinct meant that he saw his visit to Pakistan as yet another chance to do something that would enable his escape from market life. Between social engagements, he spent much of his time meeting potential business partners and selecting goods manufactured in Pakistan that might find a market in the UK. He soon came to an agreement with a local company and in early February sent a letter to Khadija explaining how it would work. Unusually, the letter was typed, indicating the importance he attached to its content and ensuring that there was no misunderstanding arising from his sometimes difficult-to-read handwriting.

The proposition was for Afzal to be the British agent for the

---

[308] He had already missed the marriage of his daughter, Nusrat Bibi, whose wedding took place in 1963.

company, which would export handicrafts and garments to the UK. He would make recommendations about which specific products would be in demand and market them to wholesalers, for which he would receive one-third of the net profits. A major attraction of the arrangement was that the company would finance the consignments, essential since he had virtually no money to invest himself. He foresaw the business building a significant turnover in the UK before expanding to Europe, but Khadija would need to run the business in Shepherds Bush until it was well established. Like many successful entrepreneurs, he never let past failures dampen his confidence or his ambition and was totally convinced that this was a winning formula. He asked her to start looking immediately for a suitable shop or warehouse premises to rent. It would be, he wrote, 'on a very big scale' and 'a lifetime opportunity' with 'a great future'.[309]

To say that his ideas received a lukewarm response from Khadija would be an understatement. One reason was her concern about the financial implications of the deal. Even though Afzal had assured her that they would not be buying and selling the exported goods on their own account, it was clear that they would need to invest, including paying for a shop or warehouse, something that they would struggle to afford. But this was not the only matter causing her unhappiness and distress. In fact, she was anxious, angry and fearful about the whole trip, and had not wanted him to go in the first place for a whole host of reasons. One of these was anxiety about his health. Very aware of the seriousness of his heart condition, she knew that if he became unwell, he would get much better treatment in the UK. The work he was taking on to develop the business plan only increased that concern, and implementing it on his return was, in her view, far beyond what he could manage.

---

[309] Letters from Afzal to Khadija, 31 January and 5 February 1973.

What made her angry was the workload and responsibility that she had to bear during his absence. It was not just that she had to keep the business in Shepherds Bush Market running as normal, as well as looking after the home and my sister, although this was particularly demanding.[310] With just one person, it was only possible to open one side of the lock-up hut and, combined with bad weather, takings plummeted, again making it difficult to make ends meet. Khadija wrote to her husband:

> *16 January 1973* Every time I go to the shop it is cold and wet … In the last 2 weeks it has been impossible to make the expenses. The takings for the week are ⅓ of last year. The house expenses are always the same weather you are here or not and that goes for the shop too. I am not drawing any wages, but still unable to put anything buy to buy some stock. That no doubt is all to do [with] only being open on one side at the weekend.

It was also a period of exceptional national developments that had huge implications, even for small enterprises. On 1 January 1973 Britain had joined the Common Market and, as a consequence, radical changes in taxation were being introduced. Purchase Tax, which had been levied on wholesale prices, was to be replaced by Value Added Tax (VAT) levied on the sales of most goods and services. All inventory had to be counted, the amount of Purchase Tax paid on that stock calculated, each item's price adjusted and various legal documents submitted. The changeover was to be implemented at the beginning of April, so all the preparations had to be undertaken in the first three months of the year, the exact period that Afzal intended to be away. Khadija, who had not previously been that involved in the business accounts,

---

[310] By 1973 I was living away from the family home, having embarked on my doctoral research at Nottingham University the previous year.

now had to manage this process singlehanded. She felt completely overwhelmed and probably bitter about having to work long days in freezing weather, while Afzal was relaxing in the warm sunshine. Matters were made worse by severe back pain, exacerbated by all the lifting, which kept her bedbound for days, while my sister was suffering from glandular fever and requiring extra support as she started her mock A-Level exams.

There was, though, one other worry that affected her more than anything else. It was the fear that Afzal would not return. Despite writing soon after his arrival that he intended to return in April, he did not have a flight booked and she was unconvinced by his words. The combination of the heavy workload, anxiety, anger and fearfulness affected her attitude towards her husband and this was reflected in the correspondence. Letters to Afzal were business-like and dispassionate. She asked few questions about him or family members. Their tone was at times reproachful, at times distraught and, despite wanting him to come back, unusually cold, lacking in real concern for his welfare. Less than two weeks after his departure, she wrote to him:

> *16 January 1973* I am sure this letter will explain how my children and I are feeling and therefore I beg you to let us know weather or not you will be coming back to us. In the last 2 weeks you must have been able to decide on this point. Which ever way you do decide I think it is not asking a lot to let us know. After all the life of these 2 children is in your hands. I have opened my heart to you. If you can give me a satisfactory answer I may be able to put my best foot forward. And pull out of all the difficulties we are facing.

He was very upset by her letter, seemingly unable to understand her agitation and why she had written 'so angrily'. His lengthy reply was generally conciliatory:

> *24 January 1973* Needless to say how sad I have felt
> ever since I got your letter. For I feel this attitude
> of yours was not necessary and uncalled for. When,
> looking back at our matrimonial life, we find ourselves
> devoted, sincere, faithful, straight, hard-working,
> kind and loving husband and wife and father and
> mother full of affections. A couple who has made
> every possible personal sacrifice throughout to raise
> the family in the most decent and noble way, could
> ever either of us become strange to each other, so
> sudden as you have referred so sadly in your letter.
> However, since I feel that so much has fallen upon
> you so suddenly to face single handed, you could
> not hold it and therefore given way to your nerves.
> Karola, darling I have no intention or even thought
> to retaliate, I mean to answer in the same manner as
> yours. No certainly not. My main object at this stage
> is to console you and try and bring before you once
> again the basic facts that I had all along tried to bring
> to your notice. Now that we are advancing in age
> and have advanced too with such state of health as
> mine, perhaps I haven't got many years to go, we need
> creating all the more harmony, so that we hopefully
> have a happy ending.

Nevertheless, he could not help remarking bitterly that she had
shown no real concern for his health, which was not mentioned
until the final sentence in her letter:

> *24 January 1973* But now that I have come and I am
> here, I want to take full advantage of being here in
> warm and sunny atmosphere that we so lack and long

for. Call it a holiday after 22 years as both the children assured me of repeatedly in my depression of parting from you all. If I benefit from it, it would help me improve my health, which to me and no doubt to you all is of paramount importance. Even though, you, in your letter completely ignored this relative factor, until you reached the last closing line. This now to me seemed just a formal touch, as if a matter of no particular importance, but a casual remark, one is likely to make to a stranger ...

His attempted reassurance did nothing to placate her. Although she enquired about his health in the opening lines of the next few letters, there was no warmth in her words and she continued to respond negatively to his business plans. Eventually he lost patience and the untidy scrawl of his next letter suggests it was written in anger and frustration:

> *20 February 1973* ... I feel it's a waste of time to write anything to you for you neither care nor are interested, either in myself, business propositions or anything relevant to that.

His sharp rebuke seems to have been a turning point. Perhaps she realised that her attitude was counterproductive, making it more likely that he would not return. Certainly, her next letter took a very different approach. She apologised for upsetting him and asked him to forgive her for doing this, explaining that she just felt unable to cope with the workload in his absence and could not sleep for worrying about it.[311] He once again replied calmly and tried to reassure her, but over the next few weeks she continued to write repeatedly about how she was overwhelmed by the demands of the changeover from Purchase Tax to VAT, and

---

[311] Letter from Khadija to Afzal, 26 February 1973.

worried that businesses not completing the paperwork on time would be closed. She was minded, she wrote, to simply pack her bags, go to Germany and leave it all behind.[312]

By mid-March the weather in Lahore had already become much hotter with daytime temperatures reaching 35°C and they would rise to 46°C within a couple of weeks. Unused to such heat, Afzal found it unbearable and was forced to stay indoors all day. More seriously, his health began to suffer and his angina attacks increased in frequency. Irrespective of whether or not he had intended to return, he knew that he could not stay there much longer and on 17 March sent to Khadija confirmation that his flight back to London was booked. On Friday 20 April 1973 he landed at Heathrow Airport.

Whether Khadija's fear that he would not return was justified is a matter of conjecture. Her direct questioning of him about coming back implies that it was something that they had already spoken about. However, throughout his stay Afzal's letters – with the one notable exception – were warm and affectionate and they consistently affirmed his intention to return. All his business planning was predicated on him being in the UK. There was nothing to suggest any other possibility. So why was Khadija so concerned? One reason was that he had not booked a return flight. She also feared that, whatever his stated intention, family members would persuade him to remain. But it is also evident that, once Afzal had gone, Khadija felt unable to cope with the workload, stress and physical pain. Her mind was in turmoil and she was not thinking clearly.

Afzal returned to Pakistan one last time for six weeks in February 1975. This time, though, he went with my sister, Marium. It was just for a holiday, but again Khadija became extremely anxious about his going, fearing that he might use the opportunity to

---

[312] Letter from Khadija to Afzal, 3 March 1973.

arrange his daughter's marriage. But after all the tension of the previous visit, this short trip was comparatively uneventful.

The Final Years

Throughout the 1970s, Afzal's health worsened. Coronary artery surgery, which might have given him a new lease of life, was still in its infancy, so he was treated with medication alone, which provided only short-term relief. He remained mentally positive, wanting and trying to continue working, but Khadija had to take on more and more responsibility for the business and for his welfare. He proudly watched me graduate in 1972 and happily attended my wedding the following year. In December 1974 the family celebrated his 65th birthday, which was then the official retirement age. He found it most amusing to get his first state pension payment, never before having received any state benefit and certainly not intending to retire. Then in February 1976 he became ill with flu, which progressed to pneumonia and in the early hours of Thursday 4 March, the night after I had celebrated my 25th birthday, I was woken by the telephone ringing. It was Khadija calling from West Middlesex Hospital to say that Afzal had suffered a heart attack and been taken there by ambulance. Despite the doctors' best efforts, it had not been possible to save his life.

By coincidence, Asif had arrived in Sweden on a business trip that very same day. Soon after landing he received the news that his father had died and immediately flew to London, where he was able to accompany me in the Islamic funeral rituals and subsequent interment in the Muslim section of Hatton Cemetery in the London Borough of Hounslow. Messages of condolence arrived by telegram, letter and phone from around the world, remembering a very kind and gentle man. As was his wish, a gravestone was later made in Pakistan and brought to the UK.

Khadija was devastated. Despite the challenges that their marriage had encountered, she was devoted to her husband. For years she had dedicated much of her life to looking after him and doing the things that he could no longer do. His death left a huge vacuum, but fairly quickly she had to reopen the business, without which she had no income, and adjust to being without him. She was not alone, as my sister Marium was still living at home, and a few things brought her happiness. In July, four months after the funeral, she came to Nottingham for my doctoral graduation and, after I had taken up a post at the University of Southampton in September, we were able to see each other more frequently. But much of her *raison d'être* had gone and over the next few years she seemed to age very quickly.

In spring 1978 my wife, Caroline, and I went to Pakistan on holiday and met many members of the family for the first time. We could not have been made more welcome and it was a truly memorable experience. There were so many relatives that it was at times overwhelming and impossible to remember who each person was, but there was one observation that they all made that I could not forget. It was how much I reminded them of my father. Not only were they struck by how alike we were in appearance, but also by the similarity in our mannerisms and demeanour. I don't think it was something of which I had previously been particularly aware but, after it was mentioned repeatedly, I began to realise just how true it was. We arrived back in London in April to the devastating news that Khadija had been diagnosed with breast cancer. Sadly, she had delayed seeing a doctor, afraid of what she might be told, and it was already at an advanced stage. Despite receiving radiotherapy, the cancer spread and she became progressively weaker. In March 1979 she attended Marium's wedding in a wheelchair, but weeks later was admitted to West Middlesex Hospital and passed away a few days after her 58th birthday on Friday 1 June. She too was buried in Hatton Cemetery next to Afzal, her husband for 31 years.

My parents' graves lie almost immediately below the flightpath of planes landing on the Southern Runway at Heathrow Airport. Many times, returning from trips abroad, I have looked down from my aircraft seat at that section of the cemetery. For a couple whose lives had been so connected to global events and global travel, it always seemed a fitting final resting place.

Afzal's and Khadija's weathered gravestones at Hatton Cemetery

Postscript - A Special Day
in Offenbach

When I retired in 2017, one of the tasks on my 'to do' list was sorting through the contents of a battered old suitcase that had belonged to my parents. I knew that it contained bundles of letters and other papers that I kept after they died, but most of them had been untouched for decades and I knew almost nothing of their content. My intention was to go through the documents in the hope that I would learn more about their lives, not just to inform myself but also my children and grandchildren. As I have already written, at that point my knowledge of our family history could at best be described as sketchy. I had been told some things by my parents, but I hadn't taken much interest and, by the time I was interested, it was too late to ask them questions. I recalled warmly the visit to Germany with my mother in 1959, when I was only eight years old, but had no awareness at the time of its main purpose or its significance for our future lives. As for my father's stories of his past, they were often entertaining but did little to spur my curiosity.

Despite this earlier apathy, I seem nevertheless to have been drawn – perhaps subconsciously – to the countries where my parents were born. As a teenager, I took part in a school exchange to Mainz (not far from Offenbach) and went to Bavaria on holiday. During my professional career, Germany is where I took students on study trips, gave presentations at conferences, conducted research and delivered training courses. I spent a sabbatical there and was a visiting professor at Hamburg University.[313] Some of my closest friends are German and I have learned to speak their language reasonably competently. Contact with the Indian sub-continent has not been so intense, but I have holidayed in Punjab, Kerala and Rajasthan, and made several visits to India for work, including to Delhi and Assam.

Despite this, on only two of these many trips did I connect with relatives. In 1978, when my wife and I went to Model Town, we met Afzal's first wife, Masuda, and numerous other relatives for the first time. The warmth of their welcome and generous hospitality, as well as their interest in and knowledge about us, brought home just how much they saw us as intimate family members, despite living thousands of miles apart. Since then, I have stayed in contact with my half-brother, Asif. We have met many times on his visits to the UK and my visits to Vancouver, where he now lives.

The second connection was in 1981 during a family caravanning holiday in southern Germany. Completely unannounced, we turned up at the Neeb und Kühn metalworking factory in Obersinn, which I knew was somehow linked to the Grünebaums. After explaining who we were to a very surprised and bemused Roland Kühn (the grandson of Friedrich's sister, Rosette), we again received a warm welcome and he took us to meet his cousin, Ludwig Reusch ('Ludo', who had written to Khadija when she was in Pakistan) and his family in Fulda. But despite the friendliness of the contact, it was a one-off meeting and did not lead to any ongoing relationship. In fact, another 28 years would elapse before

---

[313] Coincidentally my sister, Marium, also developed strong connections with Germany. In London she found employment with Lufthansa and she married a German man. They moved to Schleswig-Holstein, where she was again employed by Lufthansa at Hamburg Airport. She is now retired and has lived in Germany for over 30 years.

we had any further communication.

Subsequently, however, two things ignited interest in my parents' and grandparents' life stories. In 2001 when I had some time to spare, I began to examine the letters in the suitcase that my paternal grandfather had sent from South America to his family in India. They made fascinating reading, raising puzzling questions about the reasons for his emigration and his anxiety that authorities in his homeland might discover his whereabouts. They revealed details of my father's early life and his tragicomic exploits to reach his father, which brought him to South America and ultimately to Europe; and included observations about major social, economic and technological changes that were occurring in his part of the world and globally in the 1920s and 1930s. It made me want to know more about all of these topics.

Then, on the evening of Sunday 1 February 2009 I received out of the blue an email from Christiane Kühn, who I now know is my second cousin once removed, Rosette's great-granddaughter. At the request of her father, Roland (who I had met in 1981), she had been trying to trace the son of Karola Grünebaum and, after several abortive contacts, had finally found the right person. A quarter of an hour later we spoke on the phone and a few weeks after that were able to meet for the first time during her holiday in southern England. It was then that she told me about her family research and her efforts to construct a family tree. Over the following months we exchanged information, shared photographs, and discovered that we had inherited many of the same pictures of family members. To my astonishment, she was able to identify many of the people who, until then, had to me simply been anonymous faces. That seemed to bring them to life and, moreover, the details that she had sourced from official records made me realise that there was probably a lot that I could still learn about my side of the family, despite the passage of time.

When I first delved into the old suitcase, I never imagined that it would turn out to be such a treasure trove. However, most of the small bundles of correspondence comprised aerogrammes and air letters written on extremely thin paper, so the number of documents was far greater than I had anticipated. In fact, it contained almost 500, most of them comprising several pages and handwritten in a variety of languages and scripts. With help from friends, they were gradually transcribed and translated, filling large gaps in individual life stories and revealing an incredible amount of detail. Amongst the papers there was also an envelope containing large-format monochrome film negatives and, unable to discern what was on them, I sent them away to be converted to positives. When I opened the returned digital files, I could hardly believe my good fortune. They were family group photographs taken in 1948 when my father had returned to the sub-continent after an absence of 13 years. With help from Asif, it was again possible to identify who was in the pictures and suddenly these people, who until then had just been names, became real. There were, of course, still many unanswered questions, especially about my paternal family, and this led to frequent conversations with Asif, who was able to make invaluable contributions to the narrative.

In parallel to the documentary research, I began searching online for additional data about individual family members; the issues mentioned in the correspondence; and the wider political, social and economic context of the time, which gave me a better understanding of the world in which they were living and writing. Doing this resulted in a plethora of new contacts, including archivists, librarians, researchers, military historians, genealogists and previously unknown relatives. However, the greatest excitement came from the totally unexpected discovery of two people who had got to know my mother soon after she arrived in England, almost 80 years earlier. David Oldcorn was looked after by Karola in her job as a childminder in Buckinghamshire; and Herta Stiefel was her steadfast Jewish friend, whom she got to know after starting work in London. Being able to speak to them seemed to bring me within touching distance of my mother as a teenager.

My original intention was to spend 3–4 weeks reading the letters in the suitcase, writing up a few pages of notes and then sharing the results with my family. Only my wife knew what I was doing. I kept it a secret from everyone else, intending to surprise them with the end product. But as the weeks became months and my writing began to look more like a monograph than a few pages of notes, I decided to end the charade and sent a copy of what I had written to date to close family members and a few people who had helped me with transcription and translation.

Amongst this latter group was Gabriele Klüter, whose husband, Harald, is the brother of my erstwhile school exchange partner, Reinhold. Both brothers knew my mother and we have remained good friends for more than 50 years. Gabriele and Harald read what I sent them and, moved by the account of what had happened to my mother and her parents, wanted to do something to commemorate their lives. Unbeknown to me, in April 2019 they contacted the *Geschichtswerkstatt Offenbach*, the town's local history group, and enquired about the possibility of *Stolpersteine* (stumbling stones) being installed outside the Grünebaums' family home in Luisenstrasse.[314] Normally, the

---

[314] *Stolpersteine* (stumbling stones) are 10 cm square setts bearing a brass plaque inscribed with the name and life dates of victims of Nazi extermination or persecution. They are usually set into the pavement outside the last residential address freely chosen by the person remembered. Each stone is handmade and by late 2023 more than 100,000 had been laid in at least 23 European countries. The *Stolpersteine* project was conceived by German artist, Gunter Demnig, who has personally installed almost every stone since the first was laid in 1992, 'Stolpersteine', https://www.stolpersteine.eu/en/home/.

process is protracted, involving careful verification of the details of the person or people to be remembered before approval is given. However, with the research I had already undertaken, nothing more was needed and within three weeks Harald and Gabriele learned that the installation could go ahead. Only then did they contact me with the generous offer to sponsor the stones, if that was something my sister and I would support.

It certainly was and a few months later, on Wednesday 23 October 2019, we were in Offenbach for the ceremony. Despite all my travels in Germany, it was the first time I had returned to the town since being there with my mother 60 years earlier. By 10am about 30 people had gathered outside Luisenstrasse 69. They included family members, very long-standing German friends, representatives of *Geschichtswerkstatt Offenbach* and a few local citizens, who all came to witness the setting into the pavement of three stones, one for Friedrich, one for Sophie and one for Karola. White roses were placed around them and my sister made an emotional speech about our mother and her parents, and how much it meant to us for them to be remembered in this way.

Stolpersteine for Karola and her parents
installed outside 69 Luisenstrasse, Offenbach

Members of the local history group then accompanied us to
Bürgel and showed us where other members of the Grünebaum
family had lived, although their homes were no longer standing,
and then the Old Jewish Cemetery, a walled area on the edge
of the old settlement, which was in use until 1938. A large part
had been cleared of gravestones, reportedly for use by the military
during the Second World War, and some had been vandalised. As
a result, fewer than 100 remained upright, but many of these bore
the name Grünebaum or Reiss, including those of my mother's
maternal and paternal grandparents. Perhaps for the first time, it
brought home to the younger members of our family present that
they had deep ancestral roots in this small community.

On the same day, *Stolpersteine* for Holocaust victims were
laid in three further locations in the town and in the evening a
public meeting was held to mark the occasion, attended by about

150 people, including the town's mayor. Members of the local history group made presentations about the other families being commemorated, but I wanted to speak personally about my mother and her parents. It was the first time I had ever spoken about them at any length and it was not an easy speech to prepare or to deliver, particularly since I was keen to do it in German to avoid having translators. And whilst I knew it was important to recount the persecution and hardships they endured, and the tragic early ending of their lives, I wanted to highlight my mother's strength, her resilience, her achievements, her love for her family, and how, despite everything, she did not hate Germany or German people. And with the help of photographs illustrating her life, I tried to give the audience a sense of her as a person, not just another statistic. Judging by the response, I think I succeeded and it was a very special evening.

However, the connection with the past did not end there. By another remarkable coincidence, the co-founder of the local history group, Barbara Leissing, knew a member of the Hellwig family whose grandfather, Georg Hellwig, had been Friedrich and Sophie's landlord. He had given Friedrich some casual work and had signed Karola's emigration form in 1939. Three days later I was able to meet her and her two sisters. Understandably, they were initially apprehensive but the tension quickly dissipated once they knew that I simply wanted to learn more about my grandparents' lives. Within a few minutes, we were chatting like old friends and they generously invited me to come and meet their father, also Georg, who obviously had much more knowledge to share about his father. The family kindly gave me photographs and other mementos relating to the Luisenstrasse building. We have stayed in contact and have met again several times since then.

The events of the 23 October 2019 were covered by a variety of media representatives who conducted interviews with participants, took photographs and captured the activities on video. They included a journalist from the town's newspaper and a BBC reporter who flew out from the UK. There followed newspaper and radio reports, a television interview and online postings about the day's events. Most of the coverage was ephemeral, but an account and 30-minute film were uploaded to a website dedicated to preserving the memories of Holocaust victims.[315] And it was this that led to the most unexpected and astonishing of all the contacts made in the course of my research.

For it was this website that Bettina Mehner found when searching the internet to discover what had happened to her grandmother's childhood friend, Karola Grünebaum. Ultimately it enabled me to speak with probably the only living person who remembered my mother as a young girl. In fact, at the age of 95, Wilma Feick did not just remember, but she had a vivid and detailed recollection of the times they spent playing together, of Karola's parents, of their home and of how the Grünebaums suffered under the Nazis. Her memories were nothing short of remarkable and they hugely enriched this extraordinary story, a story that epitomises the power of love and human spirit to overcome tragedy and adversity.

---

[315] 'Gedenkplatten und Stolpersteine', Zeit- und Zweitzeugen, https://www.zeit-und-zweitzeugen.de/gedenken/gedenkplatten-und-stolpersteine/.